Jim Scancarelli

Jim Scancarelli

*Fiddler, Banjo Player
and Gasoline Alley Cartoonist*

Lewis M. Stern

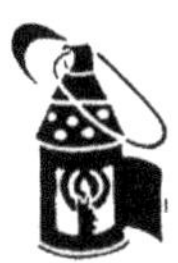

McFarland & Company, Inc., Publishers
Jefferson, North Carolina

Unless otherwise noted, all photographs are courtesy Jim Scancarelli.

LIBRARY OF CONGRESS CATALOGUING-IN-PUBLICATION DATA

Names: Stern, Lewis M., author.
Title: Jim Scancarelli : fiddler, banjo player and gasoline alley cartoonist / Lewis M. Stern.
Description: Jefferson : McFarland & Company, Inc., Publishers, 2022.
Includes bibliographical references and index.
Identifiers: LCCN 2021061066 | ISBN 9781476686004 (paperback : acid free paper) ∞
ISBN 9781476645551 (ebook)
Subjects: LCSH: Scancarelli, Jim. | Bluegrass musicians—United States—Biography. |
Mandolinists—United States—Biography. | Fiddlers—United States—Biography. |
Cartoonists—United States—Biography. | BISAC: BIOGRAPHY & AUTOBIOGRAPHY /
Artists, Architects, Photographers | MUSIC / Genres & Styles / Country & Bluegrass |
LCGFT: Biographies.
Classification: LCC ML419.S296 S74 2022 | DDC 782.421642092 [B]—dc23
LC record available at https://lccn.loc.gov/2021061066

BRITISH LIBRARY CATALOGUING DATA ARE AVAILABLE

ISBN (print) 978-1-4766-8600-4
ISBN (ebook) 978-1-4766-4555-1

On the cover: Jim and his favorite pen that has served
him well for over 20 years, 2009. Photograph by Charles Lybrand
(courtesy of Jim Scancarelli); Jim and his fiddle (courtesy of Wayne Howard);
background ©2022 Shutterstock

Printed in the United States of America

*McFarland & Company, Inc., Publishers
Box 611, Jefferson, North Carolina 28640
www.mcfarlandpub.com*

Table of Contents

Acknowledgments

My first taste of Jim Scancarelli's music came in 2017 in the middle of a writing project on Tommy Thompson of Red Clay Rambler fame. When I attempted to learn what the old-time fiddle conventions in the late 1960s and early 1970s meant to Tommy's musical life, I saw the extent to which Jim was inextricably involved in the music scene in North Carolina—bands, festivals, music making, recording. I also learned about his involvement in the production of eleven of the annual Union Grove LPs for which he did the field recordings, liner notes, and the cover art for the albums. After I finished writing the book on Tommy Thompson, I started listening to Jim's banjo playing and fiddle playing with the Mole Hill Highlanders, the Kilocycle Kowboys, and Bluegrass Sanitary Cafe. I also learned a bit about his immersion in the fiddling of Clyde Williams and Tommy Malboeuf, among others.

I spent a good part of 2017 and 2018 trying to convince Jim that he had a book in him. Jim was prepared to admit the possibility that maybe three people might buy, and then actually read, a book about him. Once we got beyond that argument, I spent 2019 and 2020 listening to his music, and reading his comic strip, *Gasoline Alley*.

COVID-19 foreclosed the possibility of travelling to North Carolina in 2020, eliminated the opportunity for face-to-face interviews, and shut down the option of doing archival work in repositories such as the Library of Congress in Washington, D.C., and the Southern Folklife Collection in Chapel Hill. However, even shuttered, these libraries and other archives managed to find ways to get digitized documents and recorded material into my hands. Musicians with whom Jim played in numerous bands, friends from a lifetime in North Carolina, and professional associates of his in the cartooning industry all did their level best to find ways to help this project in the age of remote research and "virtual" interviewing.

Jim was unfailingly polite and gentlemanly throughout this project, even when we got to the point—probably in early August 2020—when I was calling him on the phone on a daily basis. Only one or two of the 50 or so phone conversations we logged between July 2019 and early January 2021 lasted fewer than two hours. They were actually all very enjoyable conversations, increasingly valuable as time went on and his memory was jogged by my incessant questions. The tapes of those conversations, my notes from our interviews, the transcripts of those conversations are jammed with Jim's remembrances of musicians and cartoonists, friends and neighbors, banjo players and fiddlers, fiddlers' conventions, and parking lot jams. I thank him heartily for being such a good sport throughout this process. He was kind enough to dig deeply into the archeological layers of his collections, photographs, memorabilia, field recordings and correspondence for the purposes of aiding and abetting this book project.

Jim has long eschewed using—or even having—a computer. He does his art using India ink and pen. He accomplishes the task of getting the artwork duplicated and transmitted to the Tribune Content Agency in Chicago, Illinois, through the kindness of two long-reliable friends and business owners in Charlotte, North Carolina: Franklin Adams, who runs Biggs Camera Digital, and Frank Kalian, owner of Sir Speedy Printing. They undertake these tasks for Jim with good humor and marked efficiency, often telegraphing their own editorial comments regarding the *Gasoline Alley* storylines in the form of groaned reactions to Jim's occasional recycling of old jokes. Both Franklin and Frank assisted my work by keeping a steady supply of material—digitized copies of photographs, copies of articles and old comic strips, examples of artwork, reproductions of Jim's freelance work from the 1970s—headed my way. In effect, all that work qualifies Franklin and Frank as silent partners in this project.[1]

Several musicians have helped me understand aspects of the history of the old-time and bluegrass music scene in Jim's part of the country, offered their own remembrances of the fiddlers' conventions and local bands, and inspired deeper digging on my part. I acknowledge a standing debt to Bob Carlin, who was always ready to help me work my way through questions that emerged about musicians and the string band revival; to Bob Smakula, who was prepared to share his thinking that invariably reflected his deep familiarity with old-time music festivals in Virginia and West Virginia; to Linda L. Henry, whose scholarship and immersive research on square dancing, rural black string bands, and old fiddle tunings—among other topics—were reminders that nothing substitutes for relentless library work and document-focused research; and to Dan Levenson, who was willing to listen to ideas, mull over possibilities, and push back articulately in a way that righted quirky ways of looking at things, and helped smooth over the rough edges of various notions in a consistently friendly way.

Ventures such as this one required me to depend on the kindness of friends, and of strangers.

I have called on the expertise of the members of the Banjo Gathering—formerly known as the Banjo Collectors Gathering. The Gathering is an annual assembly of like-minded obsessive compulsives consumed with all aspects of banjos: banjo music, banjo history, vintage banjos, banjo art. Members sit around and talk about all aspects of banjos for three or four days, listen to learned papers about all those things, ogle exhibits of banjos and banjo esoterica, and then adjourn, return home, and start getting ready for next year's Banjo Gathering. Greg Adams, Jim Bollman, Cece Conway, Kristina Gaddy, John Huerta, Norm Peterson, Pete Ross, Hank Schwartz, Pete Szego, Tony Thomas, Stan Werbin, Lily Werbin, Bob Winans, and many, many others are always ready with a good, steadying piece of advice and guidance.

I have also, with some frequency, reached out to the old-time music community through platforms such as Banjo Hangout and Fiddle Hangout. I have always been pleasantly surprised at how gracious and accommodating the musicians who "hang out" on these virtual musical watering holes are prepared to be. Frank Weston, AKA "Jimmy Sutton" on Banjo Hangout, is a banjo and guitar player from London, England, who has consistently come to the rescue in response to "All Point Bulletins" I've posted over the last few years when I needed help finding an out-of-print liner note, an eccentric recording of a little known string band, or a photograph of some banjo player from a small band in a small town in the Appalachians. He has come through every time, generously sharing the contents of what must be a great personal library of books, recordings and other resources. The likelihood that Frank and I will ever meet is slim, but I know I can "knock on his door" on the internet with great confidence that he will be able to satisfy my odd requests for banjo-focused esoterica. I appreciate his help and the electron-fueled, internet-based friendship that derived from these interactions.

Many others who maintain a presence on these websites—including Carl Baron, Danny Bowers, Janet Burton, John Miller, Dave Schenkman—have offered sage words and useful information. Additionally, archived threads of old forum discussions provided some sturdy hints regarding where to look or what to think about. I appreciate those internet-fueled platforms, the resources they make available, the connectivity they have aided and abetted, and the concentration of talent that the membership in these platforms represents.

For me, a real dividend from diving into a writing project in a part of the country where the old-time and bluegrass scene is unfamiliar to me is the chance to meet folks who were the human infrastructure for those scenes.

Pat Ahrens shared her recollections of Union Grove Fiddlers' Convention, and her personal recollections of Jim and his music making at Union Grove.

Joc S. Cline was a member of the Kilocycle Kowboys, formed as a band in 1972. Cline logged 37 years with the Kilocycle Kowboys. He shared his deep and detailed recollections of old-time and bluegrass music in Charlotte, North Carolina, and his memories of a long friendship with Jim.

Mark Sanderford is an accomplished photographer who from time to time puts down his camera and takes up the fiddle (left-handed!) at festivals like the Galax Old Fiddlers' Convention. His Facebook page is jammed with thousands of pictures of notable musicians and just plain folks playing old-time mountain music at any number of traditional music gatherings during festival season in Virginia and North Carolina and elsewhere. He was extremely generous in sharing his photos of Jim Scancarelli, Arthur Leake Caudle, Chick Martin, Jack Reddick, and the Mole Hill Highlanders.

The musician D.M. Franklin Kane, one of Tommy Malboeuf's sons, provided copies of recorded music including jams involving Jim and Tommy, and a valuable digitized copy of an old video that Jim did featuring the fiddling of Tommy Malboeuf.

Chuck Dunlop and Mark Wingate provided their personal recollections of string band music in Charlotte during the sixties and seventies, shed light on Jim's banjo and fiddle playing in ensemble contexts during those years, and offered their meaningful memories of what it was like to play music with the Mole Hill Highlanders in those days. And what was is like? Well, imagine the earth without the benefit of the organizing force of gravity. That's what it must have seemed like for the musicians, and for the audiences, too.

Ruth Kee Wherry and Martha Kiker shared their memories of playing contra dances with Jim in the early 2000s, and Sandy Hatley and Judy Sherrill provided their recollections of Jim's music making and their long friendships with Jim.

At every point in this project, I was reminded of the continuing importance of librarians. COVID-19 did not deter Librarians of Congress from making the library's resources accessible during the quarantine. Todd Harvey, Collections Specialist, Reference, American Folklife Center, provided me with digitized copies of the documents associated with the Jim Scancarelli Duplication Project, including the very valuable eleven pages of notes on the musicians and their recordings that Jim had typed out—and illustrated. In 2016, Carl Fleischhauer retired after a 40-year-long career at the Library of Congress during which he worked as a folklife specialist in ethnographic media documentation for the Library's American Folklife Center. During my work on the book about Jim, Carl provided frank, candid and consistently thoughtful observations about the art and practice of ethnographic fieldwork, old-time festivals in the 1970s, and the old recording technology used by field recorders to capture the music at those festivals. To me, given Carl's long run with the American Folklife Center, that still counts as assistance from the Library of Congress. I am certain that I am not the only independent researcher who reached out to the Library of Congress during the quarantine and found folks willing and able to figure out how to provide access to resources, and guidance regarding other possible ways of utilizing existing archives.

I am still not sure whether it is more of a challenge to interview banjo players than it is to conduct a telephone conversation with people in the "cartooning industry." Picasso once said—or is reputed to have said, or definitely should have said— that when art critics gather, they talk about perspective, meaning, style, message. When artists gather, they talk about where they can buy cheap brushes and inexpensive turpentine. My view regarding banjo players is that they like to talk about the challenge of devising clever licks, the importance of honoring melody while exploring harmony … while banjo repair people and banjo builders care more for where one might put hands on affordable tight grained walnut, and a good supply of hardware—nuts, shoes, tone rings, tuners. I thought that in trying to focus on the history and art form of comics and cartoons I would find myself attempting to speak the language of a "subculture" fixed on the long and distinguished history of strips; the subtle evolution of characters and drawing styles; hidden meanings; cultural and social connotations. Instead, I met people inclined to talk about the dwindling number of stores that sell good quality Bristol board and India ink in industrial quantities. I found people engaged in the cartooning industry always prepared to tell a good joke, but equally inclined to dwell on the way comic strips reflect cultural and political realities, the manner in which comic strips and cartoon characters have evolved, and the nitty gritty aspects of the economics of strips, newspapers, and corporations involved in syndication. I owe a debt of gratitude to interviewees who allowed me to detain them on the telephone, people who helped me figure out where *Gasoline Alley* stood in the universe, where it was located in the world of cartoonists, and what its longevity as a strip said about the art form of cartooning—especially Marcus Hamilton, Robert Harvey, Hy Eisman, and Rick Norwood.

I cannot say enough about the depth of understanding of their areas of expertise of all the people with whom I spoke during this project—musicians and cartoonists, Jim's old high school friends, like-minded collectors. I remain impressed by their dedication to their long friendship with Jim.

* * *

My wife Mary and I had "escaped" the gravitational pull of Washington, D.C., in late 2009, finding a home in Staunton, Virginia. When our twin grandboys were born in 2016, we moved back north to Bealeton, Virginia, and situated ourselves in a home between our two sets of children. We spent several fulfilling years driving to northern Virginia to meet the challenge of changing diapers, feeding, and entertaining our two grandboys. I focused on living up to my central obligation as grandfather: to help grandchildren get into mischief in ways they had not yet imagined possible.

In Bealeton, we lived in quiet, pleasant isolation amidst deer, fox, coyotes, and cows in a simple home tucked into a corner of a patch of forest in the midst of farmland. Mary found a work-around to the fact that Bealeton, or our part of it, was a dead zone insofar as internet companies were concerned. She set to the task of learning about jetpacks and hotspots, wireless airlinks, routers, network protocols and all manner of details regarding internet access from what seemed to be the remote edge of the modern world in Fauquier County. I set up my office in the vast downstairs space with a side door that opened onto a large grassy field that I ended up sharing with deer and fox, a badger, and all manner of winged creatures (including splendid hawks). It was a great office, even though (once again) I shared the space with laundry machines, and thus (once again) ended up shouldering that household duty. I started this writing project in Bealeton, where I had great help from the librarians of the Fauquier County Public Library who demonstrated how small rural libraries can become gigantic resources fueled by the internet and the ingenuity of dedicated librarians.

In March 2020 we relocated to Reston, Virginia, a move we made to be even closer to our twin grandsons, so we could be more of a help as they entered the pre-school age. Mary made that process survivable. I finished the project in the embrace of an urban Northern Virginia and all it had to offer—but at a point the place had gone into a sort of suspended animation as the result of COVID-19.

As was the case with my previous investments of time and resources in book writing ventures, I owe Mary a debt of unfathomable proportions for the way she enabled and facilitated these ventures—especially when I'd cling to my computer screen from dawn until dusk and then, in between intensive bursts behind closed doors, sit and ruminate, jot down lengthy notes and reminders to myself about aspects of the project, get lost in my own world, and fall asleep to movies we had planned to watch together.

* * *

I alone am responsible for the contents of this book, the ideas expressed, the interpretations offered.

Introduction

Loving Old Music

Jim Scancarelli, a North Carolinian fiddler and banjo player, was born in New York in 1941. He spent his early years in New York until his family moved to Charlotte, North Carolina. The Scancarelli family moved to Washington, D.C., in 1947, where Jim attended a Catholic grade school. In 1950, the Scancarelli family purchased a home Arlington, Virginia. Jim attended Arlington County's Wakefield High School from the 7th to the 12th grade. After graduation, Jim moved to Charlotte, North Carolina, and began looking for employment with local newspapers and advertising agencies. When those job searches did not yield any opportunities, he joined the U.S. Navy, and served his four years at Naval Station Newport in Rhode Island. At the end of his time in uniform, Jim moved back to Charlotte and worked for his uncle, Bob Parati, learning the ropes in graphic art and advertising for a short period, from August 1962 to late 1963. In 1963, he secured employment with WBT, the CBS-affiliated television station in Charlotte, where he worked until 1967. Jim spent the years 1967 to 1979 as a freelance artist until he signed on as Dick Moores' apprentice cartoonist for *Gasoline Alley* in 1979. He succeeded Moores as the artist/ writer for that strip in 1986. He continued to do that work through to the year this book was published, in 2022, and showed no inclination to retire from that job.

After Jim got out of the Navy, he learned about Union Grove, which was not quite an hour drive from his home in Charlotte, so he went there, fell in love with the music and the old musicians. "I was ruined," as Jim's mother used to say.[1] He attended his first fiddlers' convention at Union Grove in 1964, having come under the spell of banjo and fiddle music by that time. He purchased his first banjo in 1964 and began sawing away at the fiddle that same year. During 1964–1969 he did some field recordings in and around Charlotte, North Carolina—recordings that found their way to the American Folklife Center's traditional musical archive. From 1967 to 1976, Jim recorded and produced the annual LP for the Union Grove fiddler's convention. He played banjo for the Mole Hill Highlanders in the 1970s, and fiddle for the Kilocycle Kowboys through to 1979. He teamed with Tommy Malboeuf in the bluegrass band Sanitary Cafe from 1989 to 1991. Jim played fiddle for a succession of short-lived bands through the early 2000s.

His involvement with the Van Hoy family and the Union Grove Fiddlers' Convention, his association with Pat Ahrens and others who have compiled what amounts to the history of that fiddlers' convention, and his own writings in *Bluegrass Unlimited* prompted me to dig deeper to try and learn about his creative trajectory in life, and to get as much of his music into my ears as I could. I was intrigued by Jim's long friendships with three fiddlers in particular—Kenny Baker, Clyde Williams and Tommy Malboeuf. I became curious about the world view of banjo and fiddle players like Jim who moved easily across the then porous borders that separated old-time music and "old" bluegrass—bluegrass that owed more to Bill Monroe than to the techniques and innovations, and diversified styles of later decades.

Since 1986, Jim has been the cartoonist responsible for writing and illustrating the comic strip *Gasoline Alley*. For over 30 years he has peppered his comic strip with references to old-time and bluegrass music. During the two years I spent on this project—in long talks with Jim, interviews with many of his musical partners, and in my own late-in-life immersion in *Gasoline Alley*—I learned how the cartooning work fit well with Jim's continuing commitment to fiddle and banjo music.

Jim continues to harbor a deep affection for the experience of playing music in the close embrace of like-minded players, friends, listeners, dancers, watchers, curious bystanders, old folks, young folks, dogs, cats and anyone (and anything) prepared to add to that moment of community.[2] He has a profound appreciation for a fine banjo, a carefully made fiddle, and enjoyed digging into the history of old instruments, exploring the way their archaic past clung to them even while they were making new music.[3] He was drawn to old string band music that was "forceful" and possessed "great drive" while retaining "tonal sensitivity." He learned to appreciate the careful playing techniques and performance exuberance of old fiddlers who showed him the way to play loud, clean lines pushed forward by clever chording. He valued tight openings and careful timing, and coordinated tune endings, executed carefully, that highlighted the orchestrated aspect of a string band performance in dramatic and memorable ways. He felt comfortable making music with the Mole Hill Highlanders, a band that sought to capture the "spirit and style" of the music that its fiddling leader first heard on the Grand Ole Opry in the 1930s played by string bands like Dr. Humphrey Bate and His Possum Hunters.[4]

The "Cartooning Industry"

Admittedly, I am not a comic book or cartoon devotee. I knew *Gasoline Alley* as a strip I'd pass over in route to *The Red Ryder* in the weekend comic section of the local newspapers, one of the few strips I read consistently until the 26-year-long run of the strip came to an end in 1964.[5] I was devoted to The Lone Ranger and had a comic book or two in those years, but I was never immersed in reading or collecting comics in my youth, and never really became committed to the cartoons that were syndicated in the newspapers that my family read when I was a kid. I read comic books during monthly visits to the barber shop that belonged to the gentleman we knew as Jack the Barber, located on Bath Avenue between Bay 34th and Bay 35th Streets in Bensonhurst, Brooklyn. Crewcuts were the style of the day, so Jack never really lingered over one customer long enough for anyone to make headway in the

Superman, Batman, and *Archie* comics that accumulated in his waiting area. I never really looked at comics as an investment I was willing to make with my weekly allowance, most of which went to the packs of thematic cards wrapped with a stick of pink bubble gum—dinosaur cards, Civil War cards, the occasional baseball cards that friends would hoard when they featured Mickey Mantle and Roger Maris. (Baseball cards bearing the images of other players ended up stuck to the rear spokes of our bicycles with a clothespin to approximate the sound a Harley Davidson might make.) So, all this was a steep learning curve for me.

Jim was not reluctant to talk to me about his music making, and his cartooning work, but he was pretty certain there was not much about him that would be worth a book. He was convinced that he did not have enough of a story to generate more than another short newspaper article, and he was of the opinion that should such a book be written, he might be the only one who'd be inclined to read it—though he was not actually prepared to commit to buying such a book. Nevertheless, he responded to my letters and my phone calls. Once we got to the point of recording interviews, we discovered that he could talk longer than the length of the tape cassettes that were still available for purchase in this digital day and age. A lover of old recording technologies, Jim was delighted that I was intimidated enough by digital recording machines to stick with an old cassette recorder, charmed by the fact that my hound Roxie had teethed on the electric chord so that I had to rely on C batteries to power the thing, and highly amused by my practice of starting an interview by establishing "levels"—meaning how far away from my iPhone I'd have to position the cassette recorder to get a decent sound.

Jim never owned a computer, and never engaged in the witchcraft of email. In fact, periodically, *Gasoline Alley* would feature a figure closely resembling Jim telling the citizens of that comic strip that computers would never catch on.[6] So, he and I wrote letters, made phone calls, and scheduled phone interviews—though at some point during the course of this project, he discovered that his flip phone had a messaging function. By December 2020, Verizon discontinued service for the artifact of old technology that his flip phone represented, and on the eve of the New Year, Jim purchased an iPhone and plunged into modern communications—with much trepidation.[7]

Jim's Narrative

Individual creative forces—people who make music, compose tunes, write poetry, books, pen lyrics; carve great wooden figures; or turn raw clay into imaginative pottery—also craft narratives that help explain the relationships between their commitments to various creative endeavors.

I have attempted to write about musicians whose creativeness took them toward teaching, and who focused on explaining the responsibilities they felt to convey the meaning and spirit of old fiddle and banjo playing to modern, diverse audiences composed of people who were enthusiastic listeners but were often not closely tied to the local traditions that gave birth to those old, traditional tunes.

I have also encountered musicians who focused on honing their own playing prowess and felt the urge to put their imprint on archaic musical traditions—perhaps to make them accessible to modern audiences, or attractive as packaged recordings in competitive markets.

And I have attempted to untangle the narratives of musicians who thought deeply about perception, art's place in modern life, the process of creativity—musicians who played music with as much energy as they wrote dramatic scripts, and musicians who sought to translate revival string band music to stage as part of modern "musicians theatre" and other unique forms of expression that sprawled across music, writing, and theatre.

This, though, is the story of a man whose creative trajectory took him through the world of string band music—including bluegrass and old-time music—old radio programming, the first years of modern television work, freelance graphic artwork, and comic strip illustration and storytelling.

His story becomes more complex when this creative trajectory is paired with his devotion to salvaging old radio acetates; building a significant collection of vintage radio show recordings; preserving the history, the imagery, the artifacts of old short-line railroads and pre-diesel locomotives; collecting original comic strip artwork; amassing parts and pieces of older recording technologies that had given way to modernity; building a museum-quality collection of radio and television "premiums"; and telling the story of early television and radio. His immersion in collecting was based in an intense interest in aspects of history and old technologies that reminded him of transformational moments in society and culture.

So, this is the story of a man who delighted in finding himself at the intersection of so many creative communities, and who lamented the fact that aspects of these art forms and their enthusiasts eventually withered away.

Each investment in art and drawing, music and lyrics, history and pointed local remembrances seemed to draw his narrative toward a quaint yearning for old ways, past times, antiquated technologies that belonged to slower, smaller, tightly knit communities of people, families and the schools and movie houses, radio stations and performance halls those communities built. A challenge that confronted Jim was balancing the celebration of old ways, simple ingenuity and social coherence that thrived in small communities in, say, the inter-war years, with a commitment to rational, planned modernization so that his narrative could make clear that he was not embracing the cotton gin but instead celebrating what moveable type meant to literacy, placing a value on development, and at the same time hoping that the old and basic values that led to thriving, coherent, just communities would somehow survive.

Jim's narrative reached back further because it has serious years on it. Jim was born—"at a very young age"—in 1941. He is five years older than the subjects of my other books about old-time musicians, and far closer to his eighth decade on this earth in a manner that makes him almost as old as some of the characters he has drawn for one of the longest running comic strips in the U.S.

He told the same core stories in a consistent vocabulary, with enthusiasm and commitment to the memories those tales evoked of earlier artists and teachers who provided him with good life guidance, writers who stimulated his way of thinking, and craftsmen whose example kindled his continuing commitment to excellence. His narrative conveyed stories about an art teacher who insisted on the wisdom of studying printing press techniques, and about comic strip artists whose line drawings were vivid and clever enough to suggest movement, life, the fluidity of motion pictures—people who set standards of excellence that inspired Jim to emulate them.

He found it hard to talk about aspects of life in the Navy—the mobilization of national resources to cope with the threat of nuclear weapons in Cuba, for example—and thus fixed his attention on the camaraderie of like-minded men in his unit, the luxury of joining up and being asked to do more of what he was doing in civilian life (making art, drawing, sketching, entertaining), and the acts of friendship and loyalty that taught him the importance of commitment to mission, unit coherence, and quality leadership.

The way he repeated core stories drove home the message that these events were formative moments for him, and the people involved were figures who played a role in defining his creative trajectory in life:

- a high school art teacher's concern for a student, and the ardent, insistent way of nudging that student toward broadened horizons and new capabilities.
- a naval officer's willingness to make decisions that bucked the choices his superiors had embraced in a way that spoke to commitment to the greater good.
- curmudgeonly old-school sketch artists, cartoonists whose professional experienced reached back to the primitive days of printing, craftsmen who made time for aspiring cartoonists, and urged attention to one's craft, the history of the art form, and the responsibilities to both entertain and teach in a way that reminded readers of foundational values and simple life lessons cartoons "back in the day" promoted.
- an old fiddler insisting on a certain sound, a specific rhythmic contribution to band work that elevated the music from being simply the sound of instruments played together to becoming the sound of musicians playing in concert with one another.

All that speaks to community. All that speaks to Jim's sense that life, to be enjoyed, needs to transpire in the embrace of friends and neighbors, in comfortable proximity, in an atmosphere where stories, cups of coffee, an occasional donut, or just a nice sunny day might be enjoyed in a town that has provided a good, loving home that engenders loving memories, and good reason to look forward.

* * *

Music and art threaded their way throughout his life, often in the company of other unique interests. From the time he shed his uniform, in August 1962, throughout the years he worked in radio and television (1964–1967), and during the 12 years he worked as a freelance artist (1967–1979), Jim pursued his interests in playing music, especially traditional old-time banjo and fiddle, as well as bluegrass, alongside of drawing and recording. His fiddling and banjoing were intermixed with his graphic art and advertising work, his years in radio and television, and his decades as the writer/artist at the helm of *Gasoline Alley*. The opportunities to rub shoulders with musicians he encountered during his years with WBT heightened his interests and sustained his attention to the task of perfecting his musicianship, building on his childhood experiences with music in a family that encouraged Jim by supplying early musical toys, and providing a sonic background to life through radio shows and recorded music. Jim continued to play old time and bluegrass music in a succession of bands during the years he worked as an apprentice to Dick Moores on the comic strip *Gasoline Alley*. When he took over the strip in 1986, he had less time for band work and fewer opportunities for old time fiddlers' conventions—though he continued to perform with a succession of short-lived bands, and played fiddle for contra dances, through the early years of the 21st century, and he worked hard to integrate musical themes and musicians into the fabric of *Gasoline Alley*.

This book is about Jim's musical life and his work in the cartooning industry.

Chapter One ("Early Life") looks at Jim's early years, his intriguing family genealogy, his youth in Washington, D.C., and Charlotte, North Carolina, his high school years in northern Virginia, and his military service in the U.S. Navy.

Chapter Two ("Radio and TV Life") talks about his start as a freelance artist for commercial advertising companies, his employment in radio and television, his days as an art director on *The Johnny Cash Show*.

Chapter Three ("Learning Music") examines his earliest musically-focused experiences, his infatuation with harmonica music as a young boy, the manner in which he gravitated to old-time string band music and his first visits to the old-time fiddlers' conventions in North Carolina in the mid–1960s. Jim attended local concerts and heard the music of Bill Monroe, Earl Scruggs, and Lester Flatt in the mid–1960s. He ended up searching for his first banjo in that timeframe. He traveled to many of the old-time music conventions in and around Charlotte. His first visit to the Union Grove festival led to a long and friendly working relationship with Pierce Van Hoy, for whom he recorded the festival, undertook production and artwork for the annual fiddlers' convention recordings, and with whom he and others worked to "modernize" the Union Grove contest rules in a manner that preserved the traditional, acoustic aspects of the music. Chapter Three will look at his dual interests in old-time music and bluegrass, and the way his playing brought together those two threads of traditional music.

Chapter Four ("Playing Music") details his spiral down the crevice in the earth that swallows up banjo and fiddle players, and propels them to a life of festival hopping, jam parties, and in some cases organized old-time music string bands that traveled circuits in Virginia and North Carolina, competing in contests, entertaining at small venues, cutting LPs for niche markets, and sustaining the good name of traditional Appalachian string band music through from 1970s to the first decade of the 21st century. This chapter will take up Jim's music making in the context of the Mole Hill Highlanders, the Kilocycle Kowboys, Sanitary Cafe, and other bands.

Chapter Five ("A Mindset to Cartoon") looks at his immersion in the underworld of the "cartooning industry," his life-long affection for the classics—*Li'l Abner, Dick Tracy, Snuffy Smith*—and his own trajectory toward full time employment as, first, an apprentice to Dick Moores, the third illustrator/writer of the *Gasoline Alley* strip, and then as the fourth artist and storyteller for *Gasoline Alley* who took the strip beyond its 100th year in print. This chapter will look at his long history with the *Gasoline Alley* strip—seven days a week since 1986, with time off for newspaper strikes, pandemics, and other earth-shaking moments that occasionally required the Chicago Tribune Syndicate to resort to "re-runs" of older *Gasoline Alley* threads. The chapter will also discuss the way he goes about the work of writing and drawing *Gasoline Alley*.

Chapter Six ("Music, and the Banjo, in *Gasoline Alley*") delves into the transitional moment in *Gasoline Alley*, when Jim took the helm of that cartoon enterprise, and the manner in which he placed his stamp on the strip. The chapter will look at how the five-string banjo—and other string band instruments including the fiddle, an occasional mandolin, a guitar or two—crept into Jim's storylines, and became in effect full time characters, citizens of *Gasoline Alley*, as much a part of the family tree as any of the more familiar characters—Walt Wallet, Skeezix, Corky, Rufus and Joel, among the more notable stars of that long running comic strip. The chapter looks at cameo appearances by all manner of old-time and bluegrass music personalities; the occasional appearances by cartoon strip facsimiles including Wayne Henderson, Willy Nelson, and Doug Kershaw and others; a special 36-week run of strips revolving around John Hartford; and the semi-regular appearances by the Briarhoppers, the Mole Hill Highlanders, and other bands of note.

The Conclusion focuses on Jim's collecting and model building interests that celebrate old radio, recording technology history, old comics and cartoons. Jim's collections in effect represent a unifying set of interests regarding community, creativity, history, and the obligation to forge ahead without forgetting old memories. Those interests run the gamut from dry cereal premiums ("Send in one box top and ten cents for a free genuine plastic replica of a Lone Ranger bullet"), old radio shows, original comic strip panels, recordings of old radio serials ("The Yellowjacket," for example), radio broadcasting equipment from the 1950s and 1960s, steam engine art and anything having to do with the Southern Railway Company. They fill a distinguished old home from basement to rafters and represent a museum Jim enjoys living in every day. Further, those collecting interests tie in closely with the monthly meetings of The Elwood P. Dowd Drum and Bugle Corps, a group of self-proclaimed "old geezers"—including Jim—who gathered in Charlotte, North Carolina, to hear featured speakers delve into wonderful stories of their own careers, hobbies, arcane interests and intellectual excursions. The concluding chapter attempts to show how Jim was animated by the spirit of old things, dedicated to the task of preserving history and honoring heroes, committed to enshrining the memory of old jokes, and serious about playing music in a way that enlivened life.

* * *

Gasoline Alley was created by Frank King in November 1918.

Bill Monroe formed the Bluegrass Boys in 1939, the first incarnation of a long-lived bluegrass band.

Jim was born in 1941, 23 years after *Gasoline Alley* debuted. *Gasoline Alley* will be

103 years old the year this book is published, making Jim one of the youngest characters associated with the strip that focused on a small, coherent, somewhat zany community of unique citizens and special families.

Jim is close enough in age to the genre of American roots music that bluegrass represents to find himself confronted each year with almost as many candles on his birthday cake as this stream of traditional music whose "birth" is still considered by many to be the singlehanded accomplishment of Bill Monroe.

This book seeks to shed light on the way music, art, and many other interests constituted important aspects of Jim's creative trajectory.

Early Life

Introduction

Pietro Scancarelli was born in Castelbuono, Sicily, in October 1898. He changed his name to Peter when he moved to the United States in the late 1930s, after falling in love with America during two visits to the U.S., one as a scoutmaster leading Boy Scouts from Italy on their first trip to America.[1] During Peter's second visit to the U.S., aboard ship from Italy to New York, he met Lella and Edward Agostini. Edward headed Agostini Brothers Construction Company in Norfolk, Virginia, in the mid–1930s. Lella's brother was Otto Parati, who was married to Mary Josephine Latta. Otto wanted his daughter, Frances Parati—who was born in June 1909 in Greensboro, North Carolina—to see Rome, Otto's birthplace. Lella and Edward escorted Frances to Italy.[2]

Peter was introduced to Frances during the return leg of his second trip to Italy. Aboard that ship bound for New York City there was a passenger,

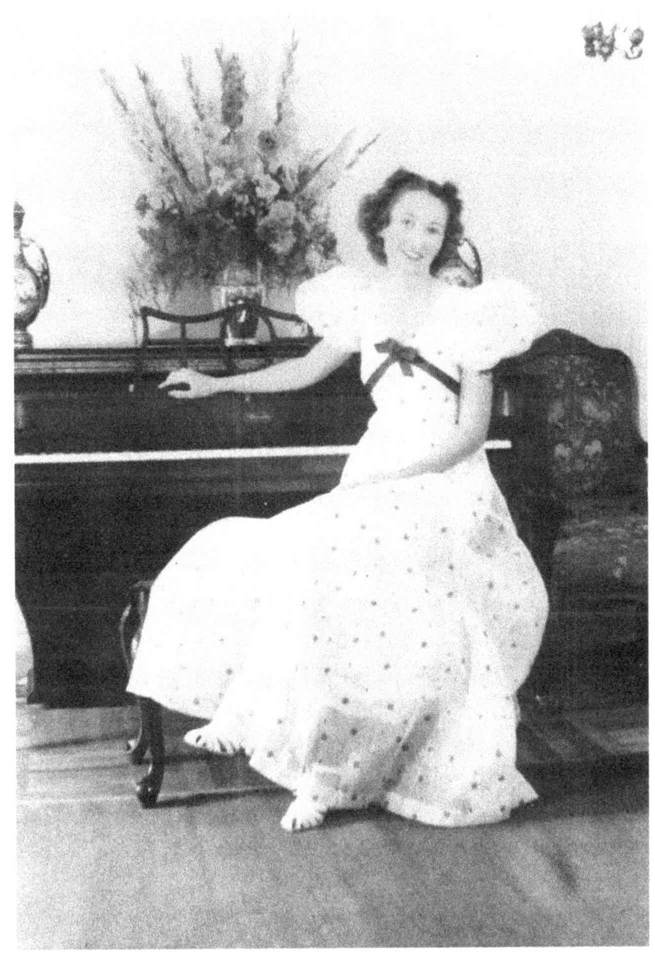

Frances Parati, Jim's mother, circa 1930s.

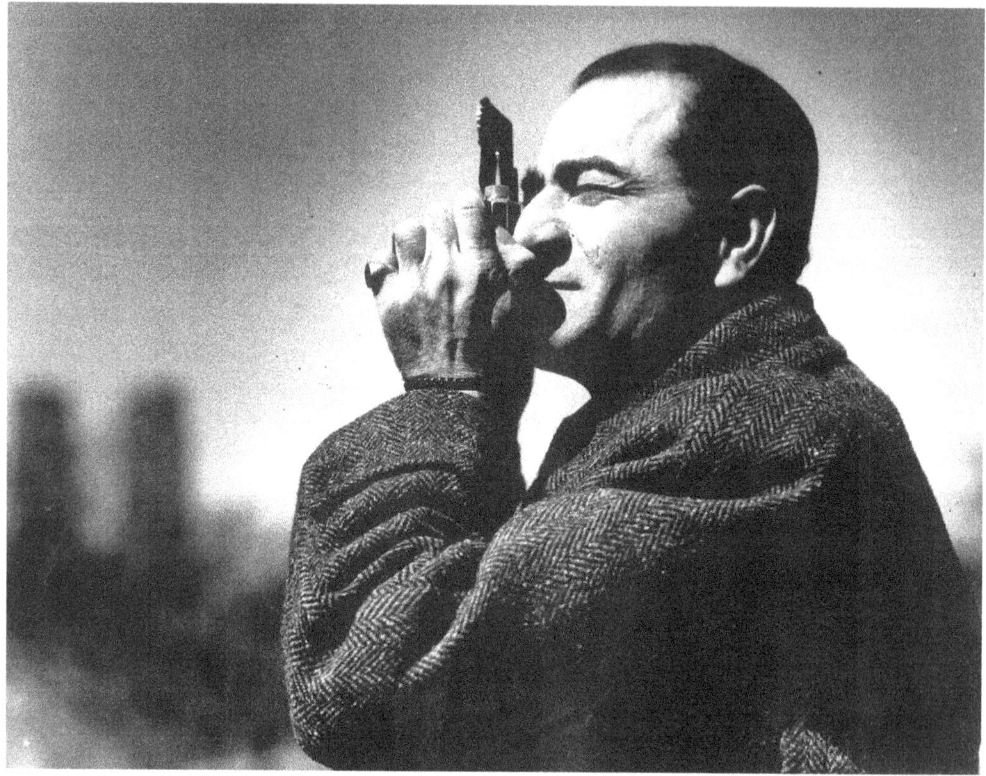

Peter Scancarelli, Jim's father, circa early 1930s.

a gentleman who claimed to hold a title of nobility as a count. As Peter's son, Jim Scancarelli, tells the story, Peter sensed that this man was a fraud and was intent on preventing him from getting too far along in his attempt to court Frances. In Jim's memory: "Momma told me the count would woo her on board the ship, take her for moonlit walks on the deck. Daddy did a good job of getting between them." A year after the ocean trip, Frances visited her Aunt Lella in her New York home for dinner. Lella wanted Frances to have some company her own age, so she called Peter and invited him to join and—in Jim's words—the romance started.

On 20 May 1939, Peter married Frances Parati.

James ("Jim") Joseph Scancarelli was born in New York on 24 August 1941. Jim recalled that his mother went two weeks beyond her expected delivery date. At some point toward the end of that two-week period, Frances and Peter strolled down to an Italian restaurant for pizza and beer. Jim remembered that his mother did not usually drink beer. Somehow, the combination of pizza and beer pushed the birth forward, at least the way Jim tells the tale.[3]

The Scancarelli Name

Jim was a little boy in the U.S. during World War II. His father worried that the family's clearly Italian name would get them into trouble, and frequently reminded his young son to never tell anyone his last name. Jim remembered going into a grocery store when he was just a kid. The butcher asked him, "Little boy, what's your name?" Jim answered: "Jimmy." "And what's your other name?" the butcher asked, intending to elicit the boy's family name. "James," Jim answered. "Oh," the butcher said, "Jimmy James." The conversation did not go any further because at that moment, a U.S. Army jeep stopped in front of the store. Jim became spellbound by the vehicle, and started talking to the soldiers, one of whom picked him up and plopped him in the driver's seat of the jeep, a moment Jim never forgot.[4]

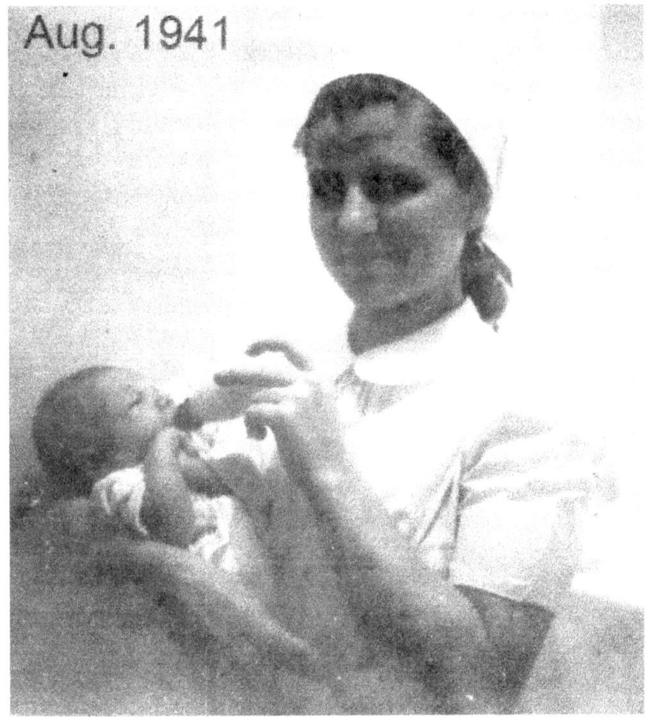

Nurse DuBay feeding Jim a day or two after he was born in Gotham Hospital in New York. August 1941.

Jim's family name is pronounced "Scan-car-elli." Jim explained:

My grandfather's real name was Scancarello. That was my father's name. But granddaddy changed it. I never knew why. I asked my daddy, and every time I asked, he would change the subject. My own inquisitive mind told me he knew something we're not supposed to know. Daddy passed away without ever clarifying things. I never knew why he changed the name. And then one day I get a call from a guy down in Florida, and his name was Samuel Scancarello. It turns out Samuel Scancarello came from the same village that daddy grew up in, Castelbuono. Daddy spoke the dialect, and he also spoke "real" Italian. Samuel Scancarello sent me a picture of himself. Guess who he looked like? My father. They could have been brothers. Samuel told me that the Scancarellos were a bunch of knife wielding, card cheating, womanizing rascals. That's why my grandfather did not want to have anything to do with them. My grandfather was a teacher and then he became postmaster in Palermo. Another Scancarello ran a scam to sell railroad stock to everyone in the village. My Godmother Lucia, my father's first cousin, invested in this. That railroad never got built. The scammer went to South America and lived high on the hog. That was probably why daddy did not want to talk about it. He did not want me to think I was from a bunch of criminals.[5]

The Cobb Family Connection

The Cobb named appeared in Scancarelli lineage in an intriguing manner. Enoch Cobb was born in North Carolina in 1786; he died in 1866. Enoch Cobb's family settled in the mid–1800s not far from Siler City, North Carolina, which was chartered in 1887. The family had a plantation near Mount Olive; they were relatively well to do. One of Enoch's sons, Benjamin Franklin Cobb (1826–1888), married and had 14 children, including a daughter, Anna, born in 1859 in Kinston, North Carolina, near Durham. Anna married Henry Clay Latta; that family traced its roots back to George Dilworth Latta who owned a plantation in Charlotte.

Henry Clay Latta and Anna Cobb had a daughter, Mary Josephine Latta, who married Otto Parati, and their marriage produced Frances, Jim's mother.[6]

Benjamin Franklin Cobb served as a surgeon in the army of the Confederate States of America during the Civil War.[7] At one point, Duke University Medical School obtained Dr. Cobb's medical kit in their collection of historical artifacts associated with local history. Jim has a copy of a photograph of the kit. He recalled that it contained hammers and saws, and that it looked more like a carpenter's toolbox than a doctor's kit.

The Cobb family included a concentration of talent—writers, poets, musicians, and entertainers. There was even a ventriloquist in the family tree. Jim often wondered whether a small bit of that genetic material had somehow rubbed off on him. Jim's mother Frances worked on an informal family genealogy that was based on information gleaned from correspondence with kinfolk.[8] From that, Jim learned that Benjamin Cobb played the fiddle; Jim has one of Cobb's old fiddle bows.[9]

The ventriloquist in the Cobb lineage was Jim's Great-Great Uncle Julius, the 11th of Benjamin Franklin Cobb's 14 children. Jim recalled hearing family tales about Uncle Julius. In one such story, Julius was a passenger on a train. There was a local politician on that very same train. Between stops, Julius would throw his voice, announcing a telegram for the politician, which meant that at the train's next stop the man would get off and head for the railway office to claim the telegram. Julius did this between every stop, and at the very next station the man would disembark, report to the railway office, request his telegram, and be informed that no such communication had been received. Finally, at the fourth or fifth station, the politician stepped off the train, went to the office, and the train departed without him. Another such story of Julius' ventriloquism involved a local country store which sat slightly elevated on pylons made of bricks or cinder blocks, leaving a crawl space under the building. One snowy day, a group of customers stood around the stove, warming themselves. From inside the store, Julius threw his voice so that the customers heard someone calling, "Help, I'm trapped under the store." The men marched outside, and several crawled under the porch, in the mud and the muck that melting snow left behind, but they failed to find anyone trapped under the building. Julius persisted, and the men marched back out, took another crack at locating the victim, but came up empty handed. Meanwhile, the town sheriff entered the store, spotted Julius, and sized up the situation. The glare on the law enforcement official's face was enough to bring the prank quietly to an end. Jim remembered the story ending with both Julius and the sheriff laughing, and Julius somehow not being marched off to jail in handcuffs.[10]

Life in Charlotte, North Carolina

Jim's grandfather Otto Parati came to the United States about 1900, when he was a young boy about 14 years old, accompanied by his father who had been assigned to a position on the staff of the Italian consulate in Norfolk, Virginia. Otto Parati took a job with the Norfolk and Western Railway shortly after he arrived, working as a "rod boy" on surveyor teams. He started working for the Southern Railway in 1902, and moved up, from working on surveyor teams to working as a civil engineer, progressing to the position of assistant civil engineer.[11] Jim suspects that he learned to love steam locomotives and railroads from his grandfather, absorbing Parati's enthusiasm for those wonders of engineering:

> When I was very, very little, he would tell me tales about working on the railroad. He was a very sensitive person. The day that they pulled the last steam locomotive, he cried. The Southern Railway was one of the first complete overhauls going to diesel engines. They didn't waste much time. World War II slowed everything down. The diesels were coming in. They called them Streamliners. Anyway, the day they pulled the last fire out of the steam engine, granddaddy called me to his side, told me about what that meant to him, and cried. And then another time, a couple of months later, he showed me some pictures in the *Ties* magazine, the Southern Railway's house organ that came out every month. He showed me pictures of them blowing up the water towers. That impressed me, and he cried again. He told me that in life, there is constant change. He helped to design the double track system from Washington, D.C., to Charlotte, North Carolina. In the early days they only had one track. You had northbound traffic and you had southbound traffic. Boy, you had to be on your toes because if you weren't, they'd have a head on collision.[12]

In the 1940s, Jim's father Peter worked for the Italian Consulate in New York City. When Italy declared war on the United States in response to Washington's

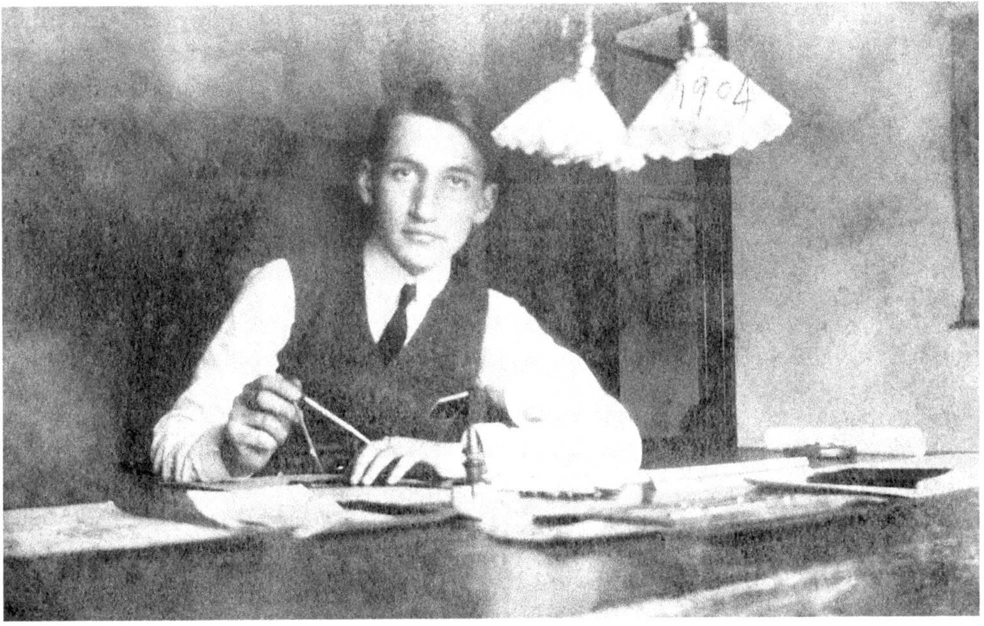

Jim's grandfather, Otto Parati, 1904.

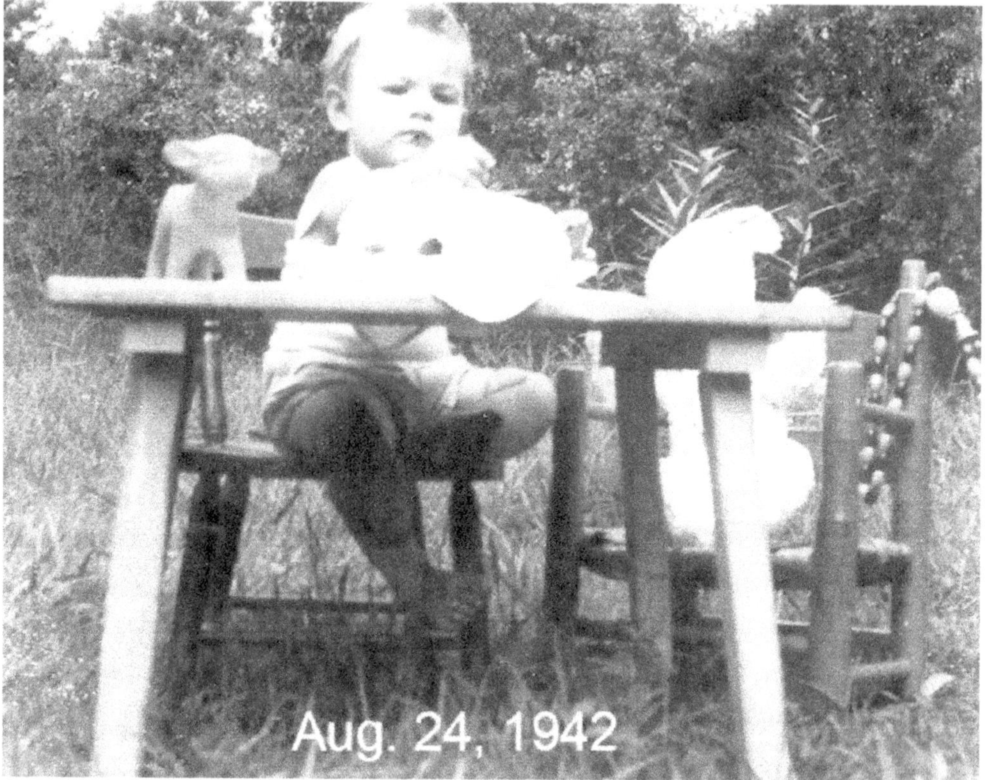

Jim's first birthday in the backyard of his home in Charlotte, North Carolina, 24 August 1942.

declaration of war following the attack on Pearl Harbor, the Italian consulate in New York closed. Peter went to work in a canning factory—Jim did not recall where that factory was located. Peter did not last long there; the machinery in the factory intimidated him and he feared for his safety. For a short time, Peter resided with his cousin Lucia in Mount Vernon, New York. Toward the end of the war he secured a position with Finchley's Men's Store in Manhattan.[13] When Jim was an infant, his family moved to his mother's home state of North Carolina. Jim remembered:

> Daddy wasn't an American citizen at the time. He had applied. But then at that crucial time the world was at war, and the processing of citizenship applications was frozen. My granddaddy worked at the Southern Railway. He was Italian, but he was an American citizen ever since he was 20 years old. Or younger. Granddaddy did not want to be accused of harboring an alien, and risk losing his job, so Daddy went up to New York and moved in with his cousin. Momma of course went with him. She was pregnant so I guess I went along too. I was born in New York, and so about six weeks later, Momma and I came back down here to North Carolina. Daddy stayed up there in New York City. So, it was a split family for a short while. I grew up down here in North Carolina. I tell everybody I lost my New York accent—but nobody laughs. At that tender age of just a few months, I didn't say anything at all, and thus never acquired an accent.[14]

Jim's father's marriage to an American eliminated the possibility of being deported back to Italy—a concern that Jim recalled was felt by family to be an ever-present risk for foreign-born residents in the United States during the war and in the immediate post-war period. Peter Scancarelli became a U.S. citizen in 1951.[15]

During the war years, young Jim joined a neighbor friend, Bobby Nowlin, collecting newspapers for the war effort. Bobby deployed his pedal-driven car in the service of patriotic attempts to collect newspapers. It was spray-painted white and had no rubber tires; just the metal parts of the tires were left after the rubber had been removed and contributed to another collection drive intended to serve the war effort. The two boys would go up and down the sidewalk, pulling the wagon, collecting newspapers from any house willing to part with their stacks of daily papers. Bobby, Jim recalled, lived on something of a farm, or what seemed to Jim to be a farm—the property had sheds where chickens, turkeys and rabbits were kept, and

that was enough to qualify it as a farm from Jim's perspective. Jim recalled one incident where he was fooling around with a latch on the gate restraining the turkey. Things went wrong, and he could not get the gate closed and secured. A turkey came flying out of his enclosure, waving its wings. Bobby and Jim were just little kids. Scared out of their minds, the two boys fled the scene, seeking refuge at Jim's grandmother's house. The Nowlins' maid, Pearl, emerged from the house, swinging a broom at that turkey until it could be coaxed back into its fenced off area. Years later, turkeys would show up periodically in prominent roles in *Gasoline Alley* after 1986, the year Jim became the comic strip's writer and illustrator.

Jim recalled wartime rationing, especially the practice of saving cooking grease in a tin can and then taking that can to the butcher where it was amassed in quantities that

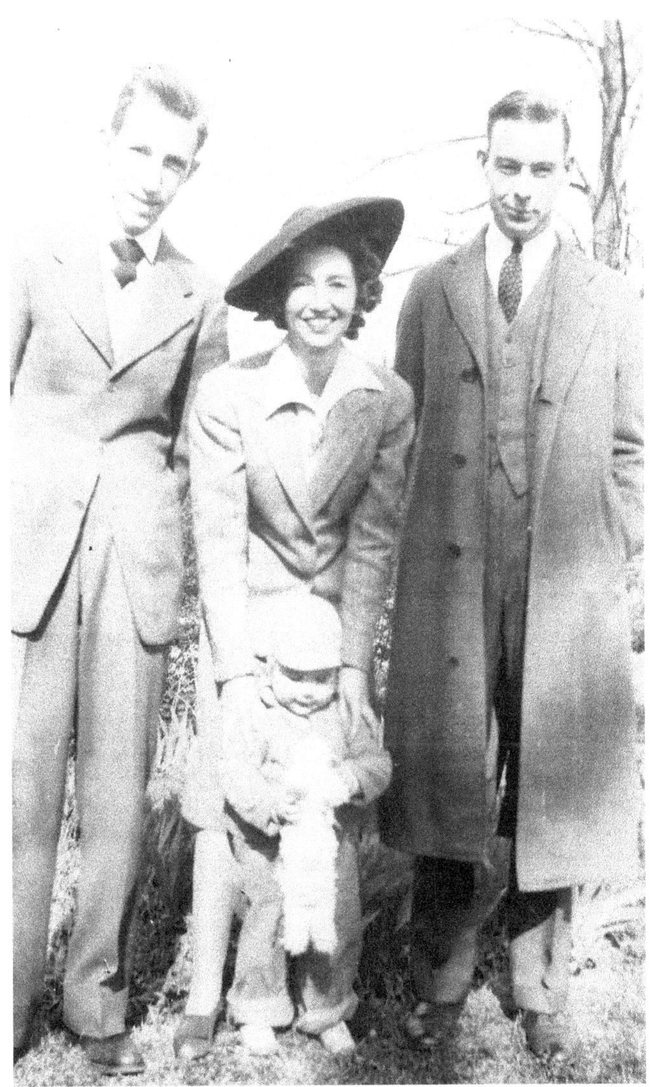

Left to right: Robert Parati (Uncle Bob), Frances Scancarelli with young Jim (and Hop Hop The Rabbit), and Julian Lee "Pete" Deal, Elizabeth Deal's husband. Photograph by Elizabeth Deal, 4 April 1943.

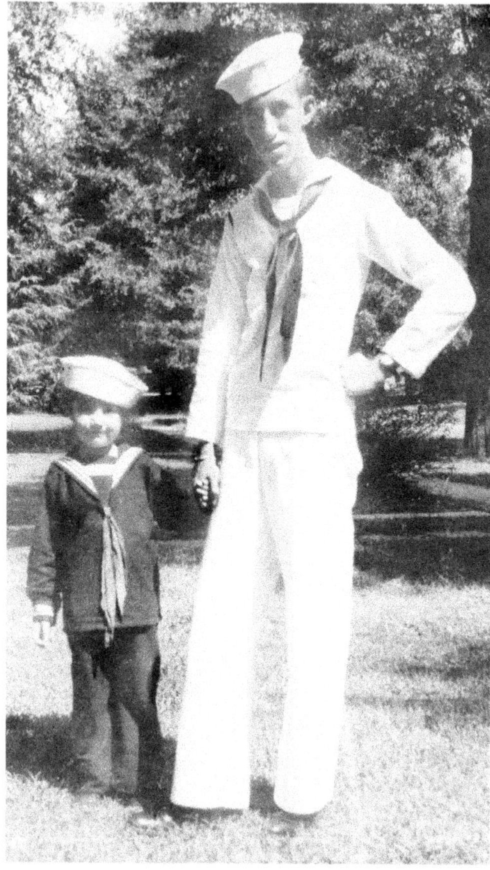

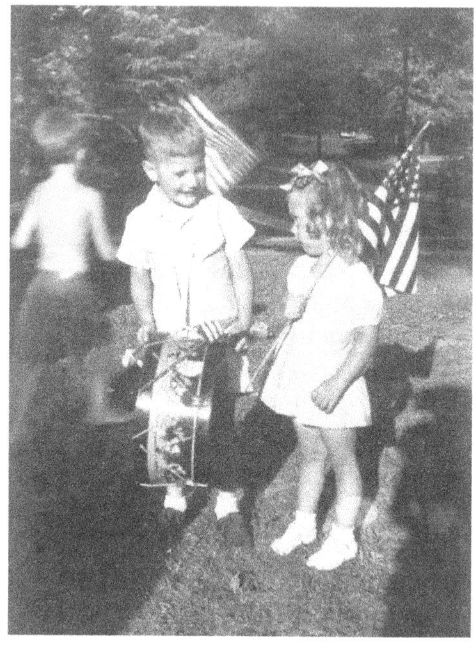

Left: Jim and his Uncle Bob Parati in 1945. Jim's uncle had just completed boot camp at the U.S. Naval Training Center in Bainbridge, Maryland. He was subsequently assigned to a troop transport that was deployed to the Philippines. Uncle Bob gifted Jim that white "Gob" sailor hat. Not too many years later, Jim would get his own Navy uniform courtesy Uncle Sam and put in his time in the U.S. Navy. *Right:* Bobby Nowlin (back to camera), Jim with drum, and cousin Linda Deal with flag on V-J Day, in Charlotte, North Carolina, 15 August 1945. Photograph by Frances Scancarelli.

would be turned over to the War Department to keep jeeps and tanks lubricated and in working order. Jim later learned that the cooking oil he and his family so assiduously saved in their kitchen was never really put to battlefield use. He also remembered gasoline rationing, and how much of a premium was placed on salvaging old, used rubber tires from automobiles. He told the story of how he and his grandfather were sitting in their front yard one day during the war, watching a pickup truck loaded with tires drive by. One of those tires fell off, and rolled downhill, made the turn into their front yard, and landed at the feet of his grandfather, who placed that tire in the pile of materials intended to support the war effort. Decades later, pieces of these stories, too, found their way into Jim's *Gasoline Alley* strips.[16]

Quite early in his life, Jim was taken with sketching. Wartime paper rationing meant that he had to husband the occasional sheets of paper that he would be given, so he'd draw on every inch of every precious piece of paper he was allowed to have. Jim recalled that his father turned out some very credible drawings when Jim was very young, art that made an impression on Jim. One Christmas, Peter Scancarelli sketched Santa Claus. Jim remembered bold and jagged lines in a drawing that showed Santa laughing. "The style he had, it stayed with me, it impressed me." In the end, though, later in Jim's life, his father was not inclined to encourage Jim in a trajectory toward life as an artist. "He did not think much of me trying to draw. 'You'll never amount to anything,' he told me, unless you become a lawyer or a doctor. And he was probably right."[17]

Jim has a memory of going to the store with his mother, a trip that involved passing a stretch of railroad tracks near their Charlotte home. Occasionally, they would see a steam engine drifting into a curve, around a bend, then coming into view. Once, Jim said, the engineer waved to him and blew the steam engine's whistle. "I was, from that point, hooked on steam engines." He was three years old. That whole love affair with steam engines continued to deepen throughout his life, at least in part owing to his grandfather's job with the Southern Railway, but also nudged forward by others. Jim's father Peter, for example, built Jim a train set out of wooden cheese boxes when Jim was two or three years old. His father took the thin wooden rectangular boxes and had a tailor friend provide a bunch of wooden spools of various sizes. From those, Jim's father made smokestacks and train wheels, fastening everything together with industrial staples. The end product was a locomotive and a box car, complete with a home-made cow catcher. Jim still laments that this toy did not survive hard use during his younger years.[18]

Jim also recalled the fear that the KKK evoked in Charlotte against minorities, immigrants, Jews and Catholics. "We were always afraid they would burn a cross in our yard." One day, Jim heard a knock at the front door. "In those days, nobody locked the doors to their homes." A man opened the front door. He was holding a roll of film that he had unfurled. He lit the film on fire and threw it into the front hall. It ignited a small hallway rug. The fire was extinguished, and the police came. Another time, he and his mother brought home a loaf of bread from a store and found that loads of pins had been baked into the bread. Jim presumed that was another way of targeting people in specific neighborhoods. He recalled wondering how whoever did this might have known that his family would buy that particular loaf.[19]

Putting Down Roots in Washington, D.C., and Arlington, Virginia

The Scancarelli family relocated to Washington, D.C., after Christmas, in 1947. Jim attended a Catholic school that was not too far from the family's apartment house at 1416 N Street. In the early 1990s, Jim went to see whether any of the landscape of his early years had survived:

> The building is gone. It was one of those old red brick buildings, and iron railings, very ornate looking—typical of the D.C. area. Visiting the area kind of made me feel nostalgic. There was an old carriage house that was behind the apartment building, and there was a cobblestone driveway that went back there to what were at one time horse stables. It was owned by the guy who owned the apartment building. He was Italian, a sculptor. And he did restoration for the White House and the capital, all this work involving Corinthian columns. I used to hang around over there and watch him work. Man, they'd be pouring these molds, these big old

things. All of the guys were Italian. Very few spoke English. I didn't speak any Italian, but it was fun to sit and watch them work.[20]

In the years since Jim lived there, the carriage house had been converted into a garage, and the cobblestone streets had been paved over with layers of asphalt. During his visit to the area in the early 1990s, Jim took his penknife, cut into the asphalt, exposing the original cobblestone. He remembered thinking to himself: "Well, that was just a shame, paving over history."[21]

Jim attended Calvert Elementary School, a Catholic school run by the Holy Cross Nuns.[22] In his words:

> It was in cahoots with—well, under the auspices of—St. Matthew's Cathedral which is right down the street from where the school was.[23] When I was on that visit in the 1990s, there was a chain link fence around it. It hadn't changed much in 60 or 70 years. They were going to tear it down, I think, and make it into a shopping area.[24]

He did not enjoy his time as a student at that school, and recalled sitting in class, fervently hoping that the school would be torn down, but decades later he grew nostalgic about the old school if only because that reminded him of the way his grandfather was inclined to shed tears in the face of change.[25]

In 1950, the family moved to a house in Arlington, Virginia. On one particularly cold and windy Good Friday in March that year, Jim and his mother were walking to church. Their route took them near a parking lot at the moment a gust of wind broke a pole bearing a neon sign. Jim and his mother were knocked to the ground by the pole. The sign caught his mother across he shoulders and broke her back. She was in the hospital, in a full body cast, for several months. The accident made the front page of *The Times Herald*, including a photograph of Jim and his mother. In one of those anecdotes that lends so much symmetry and charm to much of Jim's life story, in the 1970s Jim bumped into Bishop Curlin in a local camera store in Charlotte, North Carolina, shortly after the bishop's appointment to that position. Jim introduced himself. The bishop looked at Jim and said that he remembered him from a two-decade old newspaper story about the boy and his mother who were injured by a falling neon sign.

The Scancarelli family sued the parking lot owner, and in 1950 they won a judgment that enabled them to purchase a home in one of the first developments near Carlin Springs Road in Arlington, Virginia. Jim lived in that home through his high school years. He remembered the Old McDonald grocery store and the Reeves Dairy farm. He especially remembered playing with the cows. Jim recalled that their house was in the first little subdivision in the area, right across from Lee Highway. "There was a dairy farm across the road. Carlin Springs Road was right by the school. Behind the school was a little creek and trees, undeveloped woods, and then our development. That was in the 5th and 6th grade."[26]

In Arlington, Jim lived next door to the Rothman family whose son Ricky was six months younger than Jim, but they became good, close friends who shared pre-teen adventures. "I wanted to be Jewish, and he wanted to be Catholic," Jim recalled. "I wanted to have a Bar Mitzvah ceremony, and he wanted to celebrate Christmas." They wired up a makeshift communication system between their bedrooms, based largely on tin cans and string. Thinking back on those days nearly sixty years later, Jim was sure their conversations came across the wire clearer than the telephone service that was available in those days. Reasoning on the basis of their age difference rather than some real actuarial data, Ricky would say to Jim: "When you die, six months later I will die." And then he'd make things clear: "So let me know when you die."[27] Jim recalled that his friend Ricky was a terrific model builder. They would save up their allowance money, head to a local hobby shop, and purchase "Monogram Speedee-Bilt" wooden model kits. Jim especially remembered a Corsair fighter bomber kit.[28] They would glue the wood pieces together, following the instructions, and get all the plastic parts and gear assembled. Ricky would figure out ways to get those models airborne, which would often result in a crash and burn situation for those fixed winged models. Later, Ricky got into flying gasoline powered "cub aircraft," launched with a combination of fuel and dry cell batteries. "Not to be outdone, I made a rocket ship that I promised our neighborhood friends—in very theatrical terms—would fly to the moon." In the end, Jim reminisced, it was an absolutely clunky looking thing that resembled a V2 rocket more than a modern spacecraft. He configured some sort of runway, and with an assortment of CO_2 cartridges managed to get a burst of momentum that launched the rocket ship. Jim recalled that the thing shot up into the air, spun out, came back to earth and wildly chased all the kids and dogs around the launch area.[29]

When Jim was 14 years old, he worked for his Uncle Bob and Lee Kolbe doing menial work in their graphic art studio, all the while watching and learning the art business. Jim raked in a cool $23 for a summer of work for his uncle. "I sold my first logo design at the tender age of 14 to the Ivey Exterminators Company and got a whopping check for $14. The company still used the logo until a few years ago. Pretty good for a 14-year-old."[30]

Wakefield High School, the "Warrior" Years

In the 7th grade, Jim attended Wakefield High School, then a brand-new school. He recalled that the school was still under construction during his first year there: "I'm surprised they let that happen. A lot of electric wires on wooden stanchions, going down the hall. We were like stampeding cows, and we could have knocked them things over and got electrocuted. I was one of the first students to go from the 7th to the 12th grade in the new school."

In his memory, he was hardly motivated to do anything other than draw and sketch throughout his high school years, having decided that he would find work once he finished school in cartooning or advertising or some aspect of graphic art. Jim was not a poor student, just poorly motivated to do anything other than the scribbling and sketching that he enjoyed. However, he was not allowed to skate by. As Jim tells the story:

> When I got to Wakefield in 7th grade I had an art teacher and his name was Rupert Moure. I wanted to draw and make cartoons, so I got to work on the school newspaper and the school magazine. It sounds like it was a trade school, but it wasn't. We had a car automotive shop, a full

woodworking shop. Electric shop. Print shop and a photo lab—but the school also had an academic diploma program.

Mr. Moure singled Jim out and "in all his wisdom" said he wanted Jim to go down to the print shop:

I didn't want to go down to the print shop. I wanted to stay up there in the Art Department and work on the magazine, do drawings. He said you'll never regret it. I went, screaming and grinding my teeth. And guess what. I learned a lot down there. I took printing the rest of my time at Wakefield. I learned how to shoot pictures, run a printing press. When I went to look for a job after I graduated, I had the credentials that a lot of these guys who were artists did not have. They knew just a fragment of the whole process, but I could do it all from the pencil drawing to the finished printed product. If it wasn't for Mr. Moure, I wouldn't have made it.[31]

Jim described his learning curve:

I started off as the grunt in the print shop. They gave me a bucket, big old heavy bucket of type. It was all scattered—just a bunch of different type faces. I had to look at the type face and put it in the correct place in the California job case. Each letter had its own little case. It was a learning process. I learned how to shoot half tones, line art, negatives and develop the film. That was a wonderful hands-on experience that led to my professional calling.[32]

Beyond illustrating, Jim seemed drawn to writing and storytelling. That came easily to him, he believed, because both his mother and grandmother, and many in his family tree—especially the Cobb family—were writers and creative forces in their own right. Jim reminisced about one high school writing success of his:

When I was in school and we had English class, the teacher liked me, and I wasn't the sharpest brick in the building but when it would come to writing I kind of had the edge. To make up for poor grades, I would do extra credit. I would do little short stories, little adventure things. One time, what pushed me into getting an "A" was Chaucer. We studied his *Canterbury Tales* … and studied it and studied it. If you read the thing, there is a certain poetic device that Chaucer used. It is not a rhyme, like a song, but it had an order, a structure, and a meter. I got to where I knew how to do it. So, I invented another character and asserted him in Chaucer's *Canterbury Tales* and called it "The Pedagogues Tale." Chaucer had everybody going to St. Thomas of Beckett's shrine in Canterbury. It took them weeks to travel there, so each one of the people would tell a tale. The knight, the nuns, the priest, the blacksmith—each one had a different story to tell. So, I fabricated this thing for my English teacher. He absolutely flipped out, gave me an "A." Richard Tarravechia. He was quite a pedagogue. He ruled the class with an iron hand. He failed students who spelled things wrong on a test—but gave them credit for spelling their name right. He would walk up and down the aisles, and he carried a piece of chalk, like Humphrey Bogart did in the movie in which he walked around clicking ball bearings together. If somebody was cutting up in the back, Mr. Tarravechia would throw that chalk at them—and he'd hit them! Then he'd just go on. Strict as he was, I learned stuff. He was really a good teacher. He was a real character. I regret never seeing him after graduation to tell him how much I appreciated him.[33]

Many of the teachers at Wakefield High School were veterans of World War II, and they told frightful, harrowing war stories of their combat experiences to their students. Jim recalled them as seriously good teachers who made lasting impressions. One was James Gibson, who taught psychology. Jim had an artifact of a memory that suggested Gibson told his class about the Army recruits who had lined up to volunteer for pilot training. That was before the United States Air Force was established, and each service arm had its own air component.[34] The Army administered tests to troops who volunteered to learn to fly aircraft. Gibson told his students that the military doctors inspected the hands of volunteers, and if there were signs that they bit their nails, they were deemed too nervous and high strung for flight training—though Gibson's own interpretation was that nail biters might have actually been more relaxed and at ease than non-nail biters, having found a simple, though unsightly, release for their nervous tension. "He always made you think of the other side of the coin," Jim recalled of Gibson's teaching. He remembered his balding teacher telling his students: "Grass doesn't grow on the shady side of the street," and "Don't be psycho, be logical," a truism that continues to find its way into *Gasoline Alley* from time to time. Jim also enshrined the study of psychology in *Gasoline Alley*, prominently highlighting what Mr. Gibson referred to as "Psycho Ceramics"— the study of cracked pots.[35]

Decades later, Jim summoned up a story about a 9th grade class in which the curriculum had the students studying about the coal mining industry in Virginia and West Virginia. For his class project, Jim wrote a report on coal mining. Prior to his presentation of that report, he covertly enlisted the assistance of a classmate who he outfitted with an overcoat, and handed him a lantern, a pickax, and a safety helmet. That student hid in the hallway until Jim, at some point during his presentation, indicated that he had brought a real coal miner to class that day as a "special guest." In walked the student equipped with mining paraphernalia, a helmet and oversized coat concealing his identity, though at some point classmates recognized the student and the jig was up. "I did that kind of stuff a lot because it drove messages home"— and apparently earned him decent enough grades for those assignments. Decades later, Jim mused about whether the show-biz aspect of his high school class presentations might have portended his professional involvement in the radio and television industry.[36]

In the 11th grade at Wakefield, Jim undertook a term paper assignment in James Gibson's class on the subject of psychokinesis, the supposed ability to move objects by mental effort alone. Jim took a pair of dice, modified them so that one had all "ones" and the other had all "sixes." In his class presentation, he selected a popular girl, an eternally "giddy" classmate, as his "subject." He told his classmates that he wondered whether their classmate could summon the mind control necessary to roll "sevens" consistently. Jim handed her an unmodified pair of dice, and naturally she rolled numbers that did not add up to seven. Then Jim clandestinely substituted the modified pair, and asked that the young woman to really, really concentrate. She began turning up sevens with each roll of the dice. Eventually, Mr. Gibson casually strolled to the front of the classroom, fingered the dice, and blew the whistle on the play, but, as Jim recalled, he awarded Jim an "A" for the experiment, and for having "hoodwinked" the entire class and the teacher.[37]

He particularly remembered his time in the Wakefield High School print shop where he learned photo development methods and halftone photography, among other things. What he remembered most, though, was his penchant for finding quicker ways of accomplishing tasks. He got the same results in half the time for many of those undertakings, but eventually recognized that this was "both good and bad." "That's just how my mind works," he said, over fifty years later. "There's got to be a shortcut."[38]

Jim's Naval History

As soon as Jim finished the 12th grade, he returned to North Carolina and began looking for work in Charlotte. He interviewed at the *Charlotte Observer*, one of two newspapers in his town, the other being the *Charlotte News*, though without a car Jim would have had to walk five miles to the offices of the *News*, so he banked on landing an entry level position with the *Observer*. The *Observer* was a real old-time newspaper complete with clacking typewriters, copy boys running around, editors wearing green visors and arm bands—to keep the print from their sleeves—senior reporters yelling instructions to assistants, all of that echoing off the bare wood floors. Sixty years later Jim said that it was right out of the comic book imagery of The Daily Planet where Clark Kent, Jimmy Olsen and Lois Lane worked. Jim's job interview experience at *The Charlotte Observer* was encouraging but he did not manage to carve out a place for himself in the newspaper world in Charlotte.

He left the newspaper's offices, walked down the street, and inquired about a job with Ayre and Gillette, an advertising firm. The art director, Fred Clark, was impressed by Jim's portfolio, and summoned his staff to look at the young man's drawings. Jim remembered Clark as an accomplished artist, "an illustrator's illustrator" who built his own cameras. However, Jim gained no traction at that firm either. At Ayre and Gillette, Jim was told that though he had the right training, a respectable knowledge of printing and photography, and a clear talent for drawing, he had not yet fulfilled his military obligation, a box he would have to check before he could secure full-time employment. A week later, Jim received his draft notice in the mail. "I was not much of a camper, and I sure did not want to get shot at, so I didn't want to go into the Army. I became a draft dodger—I joined the Navy."

He applied at the local recruiting office at the age of 17. At the time, the U.S. Navy (USN) had an arrangement, the "High School Graduate Program," that became known as the "Kiddie Cruise." The program offered young men the opportunity to sign up as soon as they were 17 years of age and serve a three-year enlistment instead of the usual four years.[39] Jim reported to the U.S. Naval Training Station at Bainbridge, Maryland, where he completed a battery of proficiency tests, and scored decently enough, though the test revealed that he lacked proficiency in things like mechanics and Morse code, so he was instructed to take the test again. That resulted in Jim duplicating his first test score. By that time, he had reached his 18th birthday and was no longer eligible for the U.S. Navy's High School Graduate Program, meaning he had to do the full four-year enlistment. He recalled the scene at the swearing in ceremony in Washington, D.C., as "a terrible good-bye." His mother could not bear to attend, so his father accompanied Jim. The enlistees were ushered politely upstairs, and naval officers mingled with parents until the actual swearing in ceremony, after which the parents departed. Suddenly, the language and demeanor of the officers changed. The "boys" became "sailors," were instructed to stand at attention in orderly lines and make their way to the "ladders"—the Navy term for staircases. To Jim, that signaled life had changed. "I knew right then that I had made a mistake."[40]

Basic training took place at Naval Station Great Lakes located on the shores of Lake Michigan, 35 miles north of Chicago, in the far northeastern corner of Illinois, 16 miles north of the Wisconsin state line. What Jim remembered most of all was that it was near Waukegan, where Jack Benny had grown up. The first week of training took place in sunny weather, but by the second week rain, cold temperatures and snow closed in, and the recruits found themselves training outdoors in freezing temperatures. One of the first tests the recruits had to endure was the swimming test. Recruits had to jump off a ten-foot tower into an indoor pool and propel themselves 50 yards away from the point of entry, the theory being that the undertow of a sinking ship would take a sailor down under the water, so this basic swimming capability was a critical skill.

Jim could not swim. He recalled plummeting into the pool, hitting the bottom, and rocketing back up to the surface. Sixty years later he said that he quickly summoned to mind the lessons Bobby Nowlin's father, a doctor, had taught him when Jim visited his boyhood friend during the summer months at their cabin on a river near Charlotte. "Dr. Nowlin taught me how to float." That came back to Jim, and in the midst of the havoc that the Navy instructors were purposely causing on the side of the pool—yelling, throwing stuff, trying to create the confusion of a "battle situation"—Jim composed himself long enough to float the 50 yards to the other end of the pool, amidst other recruits who were themselves crying, panicking, getting pushed back into the pool by trainers. "I tried peacefully to remember I was back on the river. I amazingly got out of boot camp, went home for Christmas, and on Christmas day prepared to leave for Rhode Island."[41]

Jim was initially assigned to the USS *Arcadia* while waiting for a desk force assignment on a destroyer.[42] He eventually found his way to a print shop, and—in his memory—was personally quite relieved to have avoided destroyer service. Later, he qualified as a photographer, and during the years from 1959 to 1962 he was assigned to COMDESLANT—Commander, Destroyer Force, Atlantic. Jim was eventually assigned to the staff of the Rear Admiral on the USS *Yosemite* (AD-19), the DesLant flagship. In April 1962, the cruiser and destroyer commands that had their origins in the 1940s were merged, and COMDESLANT became COMCRUDESLANT—with the USS *Yosemite* as its flagship.[43]

At first, Jim was assigned to the print shop on the USS *Arcadia* (AD-23), a reconstituted freighter.[44] He recounted:

> It didn't look like other USN vessels. It was a repair vessel that worked on destroyers and smaller ships. So, I was on the deck force, chipping paint. I didn't enjoy that. We started at one end of the ship, chipping our way all the way around, and then we'd start painting and by the time we got all the way around it was time to start chipping again. Drove me crazy.

He was transferred to the USS *Yosemite* where he held the position of Art Director in the Public Information Office and did both photography and art-related work. Jim found reprieve from those deckhand tasks, in a manner that could have been lifted straight out of a script from the 1960s television show *McHale's Navy*. In Jim's words:

So, there was a chief petty officer, and he was an Italian. Looked sort of like Ernest Borgnine. He stood up on the small deck above us and he'd watch us chipping paint. He was the overseer. One day he called me. He had a thick Italian accent. "Scancarelli, get up here." I got up, and I said, "Yes, Sir." He replied: "You don't need to call me sir." He asked where I was from and I told him. He wanted to know if Scancarelli was an Italian name. I told him yes, and he told me a joke. I laughed. And he said, "OK, go back to work." And then the next day, same thing. He called me back up and told me another joke. I laughed. And he said "OK, go back to work." This went on for a while, and one day he called me up there and he didn't tell me a joke. He wanted to know what I wanted to do in the Navy, and I said, "well, no disrespect, I'd rather get transferred to the print shop or photo lab so I could do what I was more comfortable with." "OK, he said, go back to work." And two days later I was in the print shop. How about that. What's the lesson learned? Know when to laugh at a joke.[45]

Reassigned to an admiral's staff aboard the USS *Yosemite* AD-19, Jim worked in the print shop that was located in a warren of offices in the Pier Building—technically, that was considered sea, not shore, duty, Jim recalled. Because he was just a Seaman, he was still in the lineup for mess duty in a rotation that had him getting up early and finishing a long day of work in the galley late at night every three months or so. Since the print shop only had one or two other Seamen, Jim's rotation started coming up quickly, so he talked his way out of the print shop and into the photo lab. He took the test for Third Class Photographer, passed the test, but at the time there were no Third Class billets aboard the *Arcadia*. However, that was less important to Jim than the fact that duty aboard the *Arcadia* meant he would not get assigned to a destroyer. "The low water lines on those destroyers, that was not to my liking." Since he managed to get seasick on the *Arcadia*, Jim reasoned that on a destroyer, life would be far worse for him.[46]

He worked the Public Information Office under an admiral in the company of sailors who were photographers, journalists, and artists in their civilian lives. This was in October 1962, in time for the 13-day confrontation between the U.S. and the Soviet Union over Moscow's deployment of ballistic missiles in Cuba. Jim remembered:

When I was on the Admiral's staff the closest thing to war that we got into was the Cuban crisis. We knew that the next day we would be at war. The old-timers with 20 years or more in the Navy, man, they were scared. I was scared, too. We got to do slide art for the Admiral's briefing. I don't know whether the President saw our briefings but all the big Navy brass, they got to see what we were doing. One of the cool things I got to do was develop film that the aerial people took over Cuba. [...] You could see farmhouses. You could see silos. You could see carts with donkeys, people walking around the roads. I didn't have any idea whether there were missiles in those silos. I had Secret clearance, but they said I needed to have Top Secret (TS). So, I had to fill out all this paperwork. I was the only one there who could do the photography work, so they said: "Hocus Pocus, you've got TS clearance."[47]

At some point, Jim bumped into an old high school friend, Ned Stern, who was three years ahead of Jim at Wakefield High School. Ned had been assigned to Naval Station Newport (NAVSTA Newport) at the same time that Jim received his assignment to the base. After high school, Ned was called to active duty from the Naval Reserves and became a sonar man, though he was not enjoying life aboard a destroyer. With a bit of finagling, Jim managed to get the admiral to support transferring Ned to the Public Information Office where his notable artistic talents could be put to good use. A combination of (1) Jim's charm—that worked wonders with the old southern gentleman who was his immediate commander—and (2) the reality that the shop could use the talent of a capable artist to head up the art department showed Jim the relevance of old southern manners as one tool necessary to convince bureaucracies to act in their own best interests.[48]

Jim's time in uniform gave him a chance to work on unique photographic equipment, state of the art developing systems, and Polaroid innovations. His time in the print shop honed his capabilities in the area of building presentations, slides, and projection work. He learned discipline, U.S. Navy style, and came to understand the importance of leadership and the order that results from a sturdy and dependable chain of command. He got his fair share of watch duty, shore patrol responsibilities, and learned to weather being chewed out by the best officers in the Navy. He also learned the informal "economy" that evolved between offices on the admiral's staff where a twenty-pound tin of coffee could buy access to the hot showers reserved for officers, to 16 millimeter prints of popular new movies that were sent to the U.S. Navy by movie companies for shipboard entertainment before they were released in theatres, and to opportunities to build a stock of salami, cheese, and ice cream through clever and often complex bartering between duty stations.[49]

Jim found an outlet for his model building interests in a model railroad club in Newport run out of the home of a Yeoman First Class. They would meet several times a month, lay track, build railway car models, all the while in civilian clothes, a pleasant change for them.[50] He learned a bit about jazz music in Rhode Island, at some of the many clubs in the area that featured the likes of Dizzy Gillespie.[51] There was another musical story connected to Jim's time in uniform. President John F. Kennedy came to Newport to watch the America's Cup yacht race from the destroyer named after his father, Joseph P. Kennedy. Jim wanted to get a chance to see the President. He knew many of the musicians in the Navy Band that was scheduled to march down the hill from the band drill hall, past the Art Department which was located in the Pier Headquarters Building. Jim arranged the opportunity to stand in the doorway in his dress uniform, holding his Professional model chromatic harmonica. The band came by playing a rousing marching tune. Jim slipped into the formation, got in step, and started playing his harmonica, which miraculously was in perfect pitch with the band. Jim recalled:

> We formed up in a semi-circle at the gangway, and suddenly the President's limo drove up. The band began playing "Hail to the Chief," and I could have reached out and touched the President! Unbeknownst to me, Secret Service men were stationed on the roof, the various decks on the destroyers that were tied up alongside the pier, and in other positions up and down the pier. Not one of the President's protection people saw me sneak into the band— or so I thought.[52]

Jim's tour of duty was scheduled to end in September 1962. His uncle, Bob Parati, who needed help in his advertising agency in Charlotte, appealed to the Navy to consider releasing Jim short of tour. Jim mustered out in August 1962 and returned to Charlotte to begin life as a civilian. One day, a year after he left the Navy, his mother called him from her home in Arlington, Virginia:

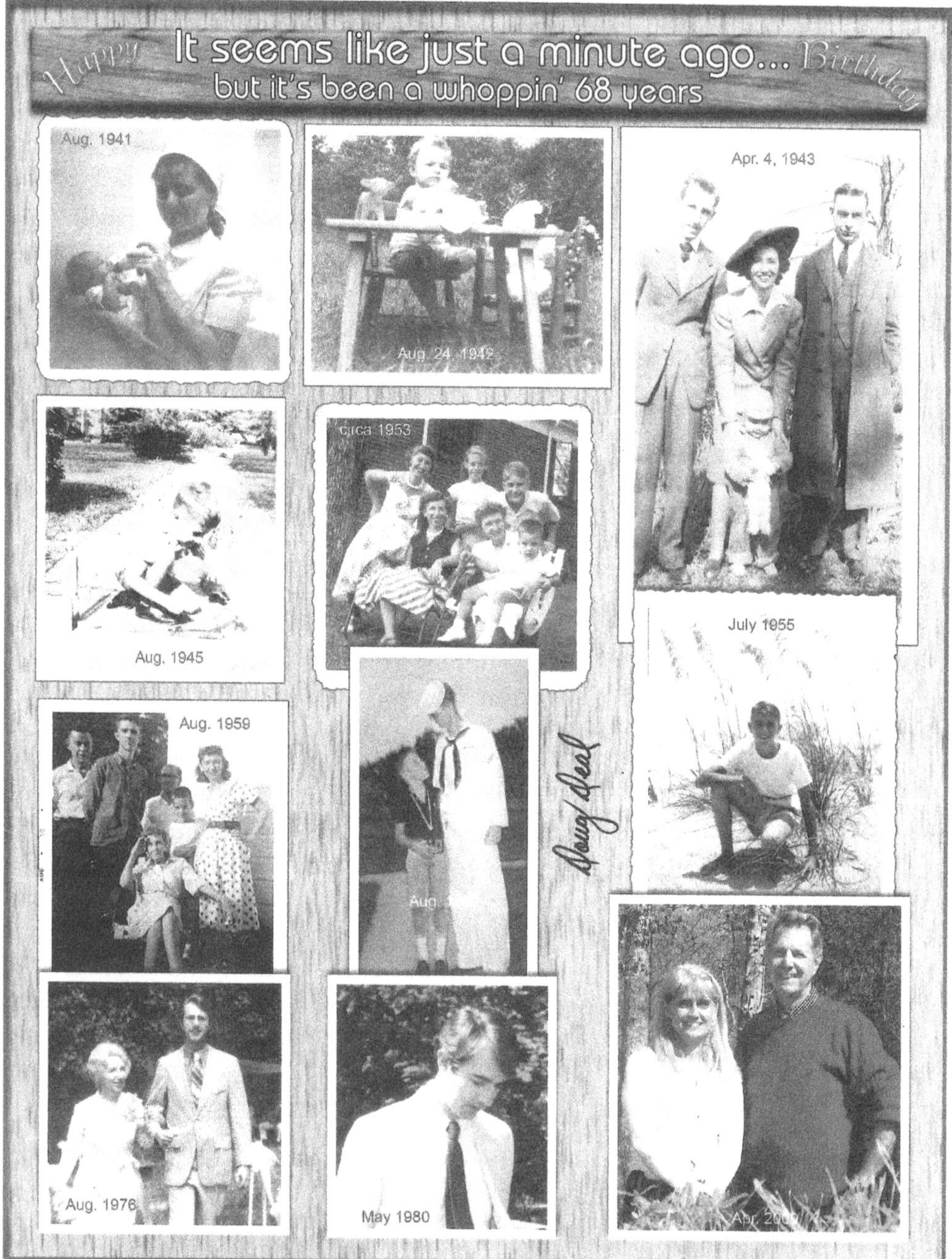

A montage of family photos assembled for Jim's 68th birthday by his cousin Doug Deal.

She said: "You got a letter from the Navy Department." I asked her to read it. It said that I was cleared for TS—top secret—over a year after the application had been submitted. There's your government for you. I don't see how we got anything accomplished.[53]

Thinking back on his time in uniform after 57 years, Jim mused:

It was a good experience. I'm glad I did it. I don't think, though, that I'd want to do it again....[54]

Two

Radio and TV Life

Introduction

In August 1962, at the end of his hitch in the Navy, Jim returned to Charlotte, North Carolina, and went to work for his uncle, Bob Parati, a talented graphic artist and good-natured man who taught Jim all about "the art business." Parati's small company, focused on local advertisement artwork, got even smaller when Parati decided to work out of the basement in his home in Charlotte. His uncle's biggest account was with *The Yellow Pages*. Jim earned $2.50 for each drawing he did for that account, "but there were hundreds of them." He recalled that he could earn $150 a week "if I put my nose to the grindstone … or my pen to the paper." Eventually, as new technologies emerged that made generating small ads easier and quicker, Jim and his uncle saw *The Yellow Pages* account dry up. Probably by late 1963, his uncle advised Jim to look for another job.[1]

WBT–Charlotte, North Carolina

Jim applied for employment at WBT, the CBS-affiliated television station in Charlotte, North Carolina. He remembered driving to the interview and being rear ended while he sat in his car, stopped at a red light. He was so afraid that he would miss the appointment. When he got out of his car to size up the situation, he learned that the fellow in the car behind him who had done the damage was in fact an insurance agent. "Imagine that," Jim said, reflecting on precisely the kind of a situation that might still find its way into a *Gasoline Alley* thread one day.[2]

At WBT Jim was interviewed by an art director from New York, who he remembered as nice enough, though without a memorable sense of humor. When the gentleman observed that Jim did not seem to know much about television, Jim replied that this was certainly the case, but that he would be willing to read up on it and would be more than happy to immerse himself in learning. "He remembered that," Jim commented, suggesting that his answer impressed the interviewer—and when Jim went for a second interview at WBT, he was brought on board with a weekly salary of $50.00.[3]

Jim started working in January 1964 creating scenery for WBT shows, preparing cue cards, and working for the station's graphics department drawing cartoons on maps for the WBT noon weather report.[4] Jim loved the job. At WBT, he met Marcus

27

Hamilton who joined the company in 1965. They became fast friends. Hamilton went on to become the cartoonist for the daily *Dennis the Menace* cartoon strip. Jim remembered that even then, Hamilton was a terrific illustrator: "I was his supervisor, but he should have supervised me."[5]

WBT's history as a radio station dated back to the 1920s. In those days, the station broadcast a lot of southern string band music, and was the home base for the Briarhoppers, a band that became prominent in Charlotte. In the 1960s, Clyde McLean hosted a weeknight program, Monday through Friday, called "Project 60," that featured classical music, dramas, and documentaries—and an occasional narrated satire such as the 1964 April Fool's show about the Glick Family's long history in recorded music. Henry Boggan's show, "Hello, Henry," ran for 16 years from 1979 to 1996.[6] Over time, Jim had the chance to assist with several of those long-running WBT programs.

The Johnny Cash Show: Jim worked as Johnny Cash's art director for four or five shows in January 1965.[7] Jefferson Productions, a WBT subsidiary, had the account to do *The Johnny Cash Show* as a half-hour program shot in black and white. Color television was a brand-new technology at the time.[8] WBT had a color camera; Jim remembers it being about the size of his bed. Jim was responsible for creating slides and camera cards for Cash's television show: "In those days it was pretty primitive. I was the teleprompter, with 16 by 20 cards and magic markers. I would sit underneath

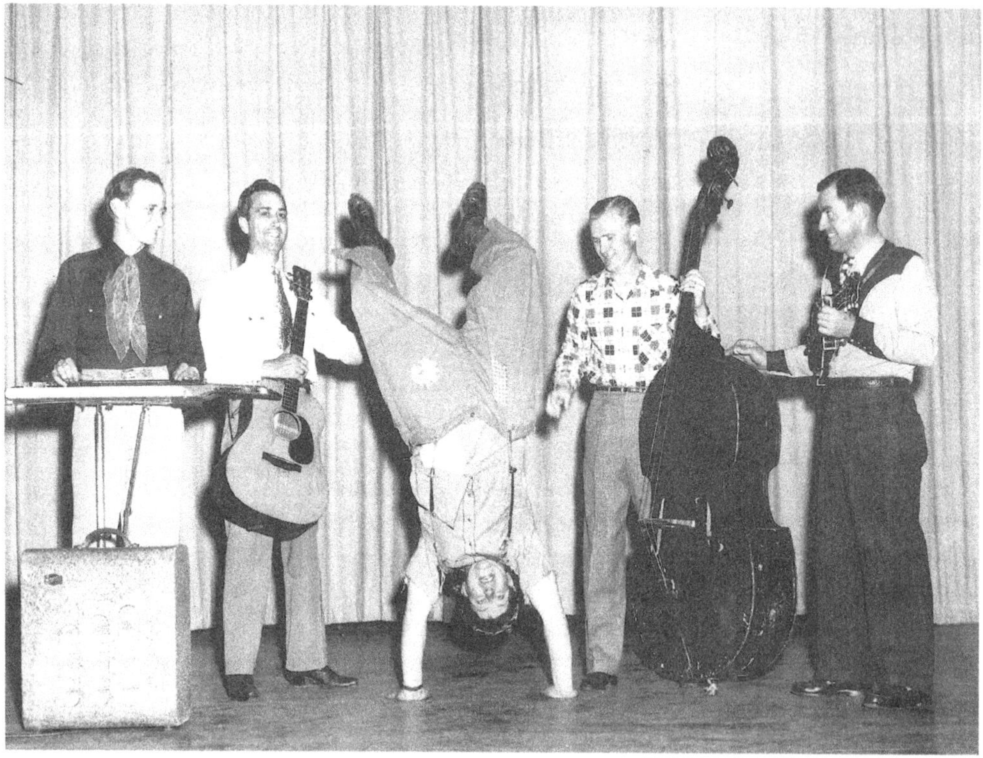

The Briar Hoppers. Left to right: Nat Richardson, Claude Casey, Hank Warren (upside down), Roy Grant, and Arval Hogan. That was the band's basic lineup from the late 1930s to the late 1940s.

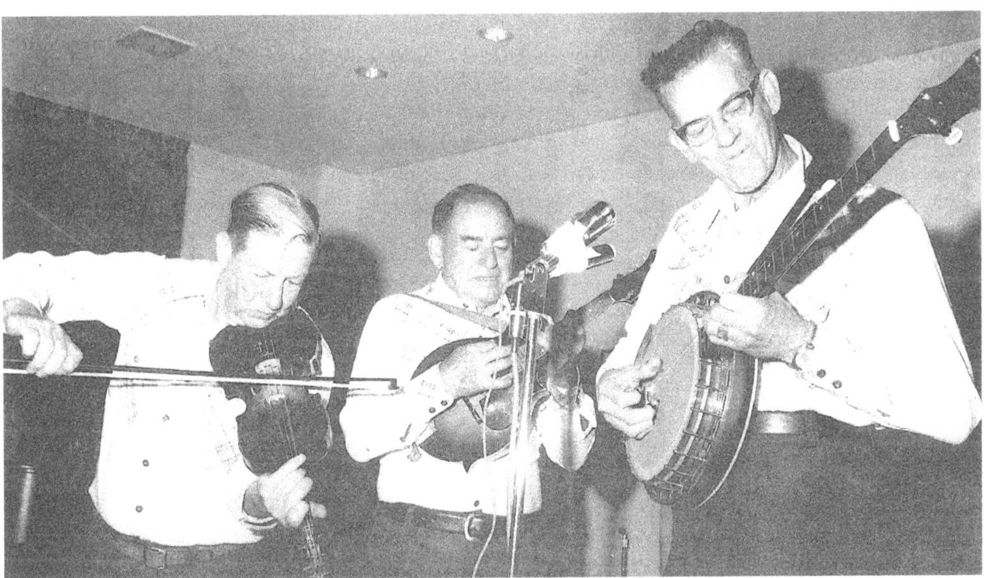

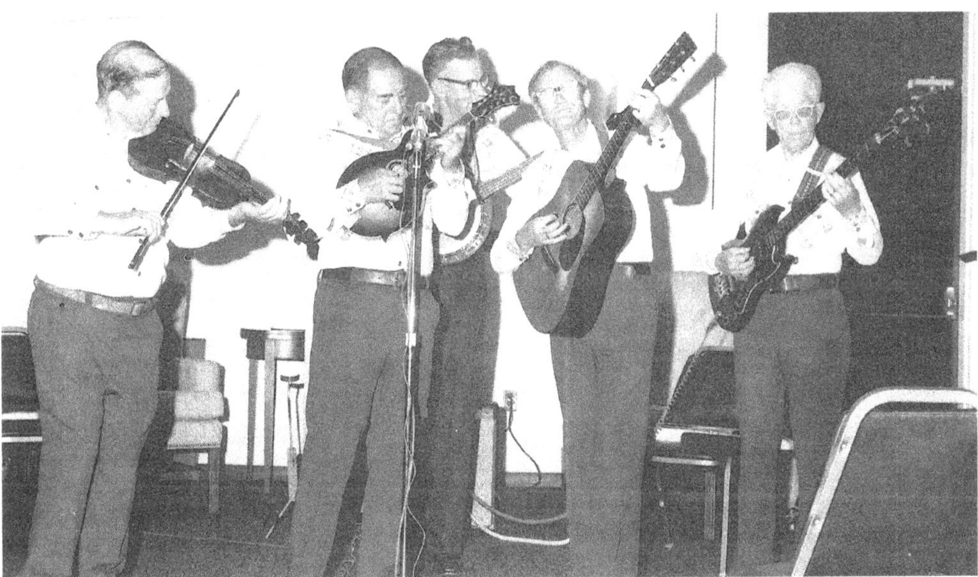

Top: The Briarhoppers. *Left to right:* Fiddlin' Hank Warren, Arval Hogan, Shannon Grayson at a retirement center in Charlotte, North Carolina, mid–1980s. Photograph by Jim Scancarelli. *Bottom:* The Briarhoppers. Left to right: Fiddlin' Hank Warren, Shannon Grayson, Roy "Whitey" Grant, and Don White at a retirement center in Charlotte, North Carolina, mid–1980s. Photograph by Jim Scancarelli.

the lens of the camera so that I wasn't on screen." Jim recalled that the talented Norman Prevatte, who had directed the Arthur Smith show, was the director for Johnny Cash's program. June Carter appeared from time to time as a guest on the show. In Jim's words:

They would start the program on video tape. The tape was two inches wide. I had to letter the words to the song or whatever Johnny was going to say. In those days there was really no digital editing. It was all physical splice. And, boy, when you made a splice on a video tape, it would jump. And you could see it. So, in taping the show, if a mistake was made anywhere in the course of the recording, they'd have to back the tape up and start all over again. I was working a lot of overtime. You'd get almost through the whole show and someone would screw up. They'd have to go back and re-record everything. So, Norman came up with this idea. They would start, finish the first song, fade to black, and then fade back up. That ended many long hours of re-dos. Nashville had just gotten color taping equipment, so "The Man in Black" left black and white TV behind for the colorful studios in Nashville.[9]

Whispering Bill Anderson: Jim was around when WBT had a show in its lineup that featured the country singer and songwriter Whispering Bill Anderson ("They called him Whispering Bill because he talked so low"). Grandpa Jones and his wife Ramona were regulars on that show. Jim built a set for Grandpa Jones, a storefront of an old gas station, and managed to capture that in some of his own photographs. He remembered:

> I had to do drawings of different country singers for that show. I did get credit for the Whispering Bill Anderson thing. It was on a crawl. My father never thought much about me doing artwork. He wanted me to be a doctor or lawyer. Daddy saw my name on that credit and, oh man, he told Momma how proud he was. Then he told neighbors. Then he told strangers at the grocery store. I wish he'd told me.[10]

Arthur "Guitar Boogie" Smith's Radio Show: The station broadcast Arthur Smith's "Corner Store" from the late 1940s to the early 1950s. The show featured Arthur and his brothers, Sonny and Ralph, and Roy Leer. They were later joined by Tommy Faile and Don Reno. In the early 1950s, Arthur Smith had a thirty-minute radio show on Saturday nights, called "Carolina Hayride." Arthur Smith and his band, "The Crackerjacks," appeared on a 60-minute WBT radio show, "Carolina Capers," that ran in the 1950–1951 period, and starred Grady Cole, Betty Johnson, and Smith's band. Arthur Smith was well-known for his 1945 recording, "Guitar Boogie." Tommy Faile recorded "Brown Mountain Lights" and "Phantom 309" in roughly the same timeframe. Smith's fiddling, and Faile's notable baritone, were constants on WBT's music programs.[11] Jim designed brochures and advertisements for programs and learned how to run a TK60 camera while working for Smith. Jim said:

> Arthur Smith was quite a character. I got to cut up with him, play harmonica. Play the banjo. The Arthur Smith show was one of those that was cut in Charlotte. The show was carried by the Southeastern Network and was broadcast up and down the Eastern Seaboard and into other subscribing states. Arthur Smith, he was a good singer, and a good musician. Arthur played the fiddle, mandolin, and guitar—real well. He didn't have the bow arm like most of the real terrific fiddle players, but he knew what he was doing.[12]

Don Reno was a fixture on that radio program, and on one of the shows he debuted his tune "Charlotte Breakdown." Jim told this story about an early encounter with Don Reno:

> I was 12 years old and I would hang around the Wilder Building downtown, where the radio and the TV station were located. Norman Prevatte was the Producer-Director at WBT Television in Charlotte. Prevatte's wife, Fuzzy, who was my cousin Linda's cousin, gave us permission to hang around. That's all I wanted, boy. My cousin Linda and I, we caught the bus going downtown. My grandma was in charge of us, and she let us do it—which was a real surprise. We got to hang around the TV part, the radio part. They were doing the TV studio and the radio

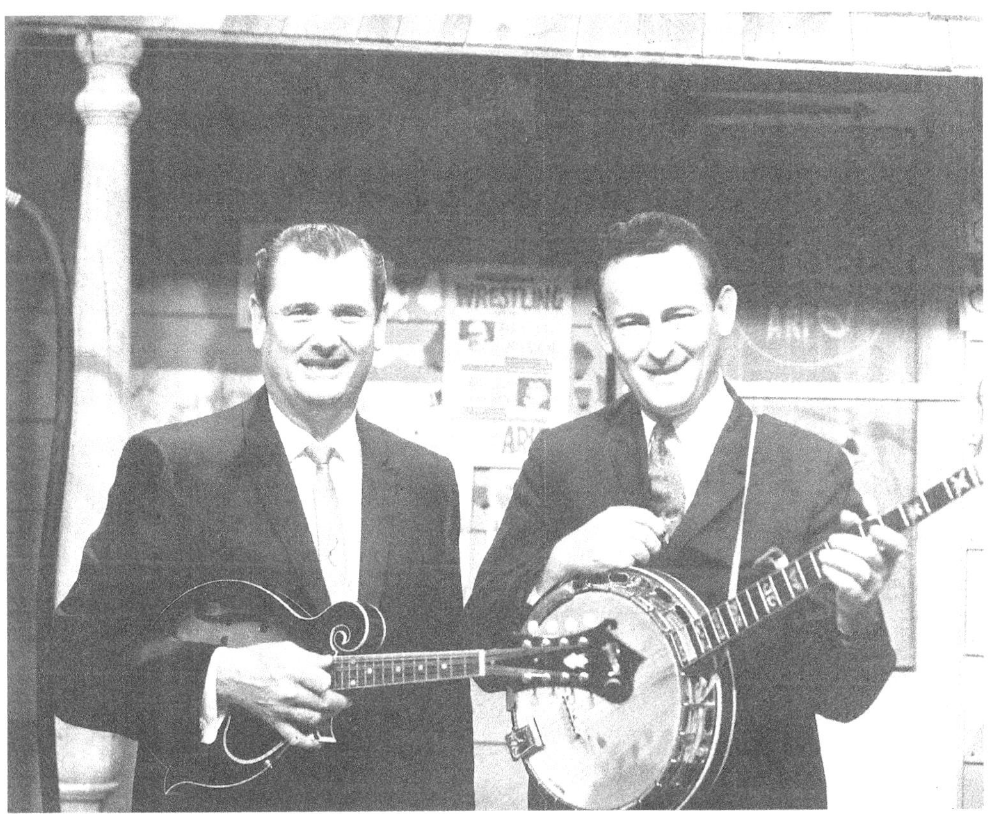

Arthur Smith and Don Reno played "Feudin' Banjos" on Arthur's syndicated show on WBTV Charlotte, North Carolina, on 17 January 1966. Smith and Reno used the set Jim had designed for Grandpa Jones' appearance on WBTV. Photograph by Fiddlin' Hank Warren.

> studios. Don Reno was there. I was this precocious youngster, and on one visit I was standing in the studio. It was such a small studio. They had a post, a stanchion, that was holding up the ceiling, and they only had two cameras so they would have to sling the camera from one part of the studio to the other without hitting that stanchion. Well, in my inimitable way, I had some Mortimer Snerd false teeth. Mortimer Snerd was a ventriloquist dummy, Charlie McCarthy's bumpkin pal. I put those on, and Don Reno looked at me, cracked up, and in that instant got hit by the moving camera.

When Jim got to be Arthur Smith's art director years later, right after he came out of the Navy, he reminded Arthur about that episode. Arthur said he remembered that moment, though Jim was not convinced of that.[13] Arthur Smith's brother Ralph and Tommy Faile did a stand-up comedy routine for the show.[14] Ralph was Brother Ralph. Tommy Faile was Cousin Fud. Don Reno was called Chicken Hot Rod.[15]

Hello, Henry: Henry Boggan had a multi-hour radio show at night on WBT after Jim left the station. The signal from this 50,000-watt radio station went up and down the east coast. The station advertised that its programs were broadcast from Canada to Cuba, but after the relationship with Cuba soured, the station revised that, and began saying in promotional material that its signal went from Canada to the Caribbean. Boggan's was a call-in talk show with a wide-ranging mandate; as Jim said, "he'd talk about any and everything." From time to time, Boggan would have Jim as a guest to talk about old radio. Jim remembered Boggan as a wonderful person, and a skilled interviewer with a relaxed demeanor and an open way of conducting discussions. During one show Boggan announced, "We've got Jim Scancarelli here. We're going to be talking about old-time radio. Call and ask your questions, he's the authority." Jim said:

> Well, I'm not an authority in any way, shape, or form. Anyway, some lady called. Boggan says, "You want to talk to Jim?" And she says, "Who?" She told Boggan: "I just wanted to tell you I bought some stuff on discount at Harris Teeter," and Boggan was overjoyed that she had gotten such a discount. Then he asked, "Well, do you want to talk about old-time radio?" and she says, "no."[16]

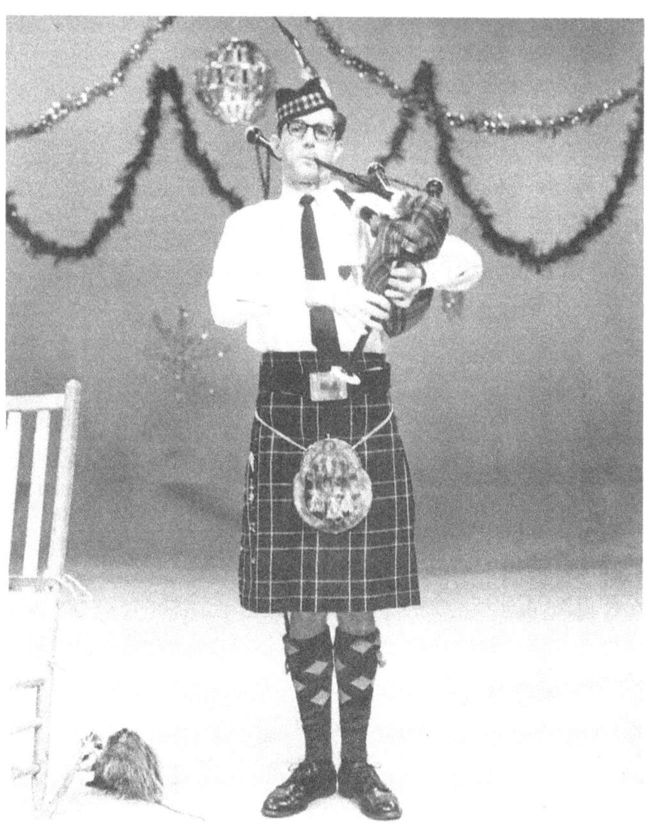

Jim Scancarelli playing the part of the piper in "The Twelve Days of Christmas" on the Arthur Smith WBTV Christmas Show in 1966.

Jim relished that memory, and told that story with an eye to capturing the sense that every "instant expert" dreads: the moment the reputation for expertise is punctured, or the point in time when an experience like this telegraphs the message that one's subject matter expertise won't get you a seat on a bus, "or a five dollar cup of coffee."[17] Jim inserted Henry Boggan into the *Gasoline Alley* comic strip in a thread that ran from 28 December 1986 to 3 January 1987:

> I called him Arnold Bicep. Henry was large—a very big man. He dwarfed a chair. So, I stuck him in the comic strip as a character who had an exercise class that was broadcast on radio. We pictured him being like Arnold Schwarzenegger. Arnold Bicep was this big, seedy looking guy. And Slim in the comic strip was listening to Arnold's radio show while lying down in a recliner, with his hand on his stomach. His wife Clovia would say, you can't do exercises just by saying one two, one two. You've got to get out there and work. That was one of my early *Gasoline Alley* stories.[18]

The Yellowjacket: In 1967, WBT started a show, "The Yellowjacket," a broadcast that was never more than five minutes in length. It was developed around the time *Batman* was on TV. "BT Memories," a project on the history of WBT and WBTV, described the show this way:

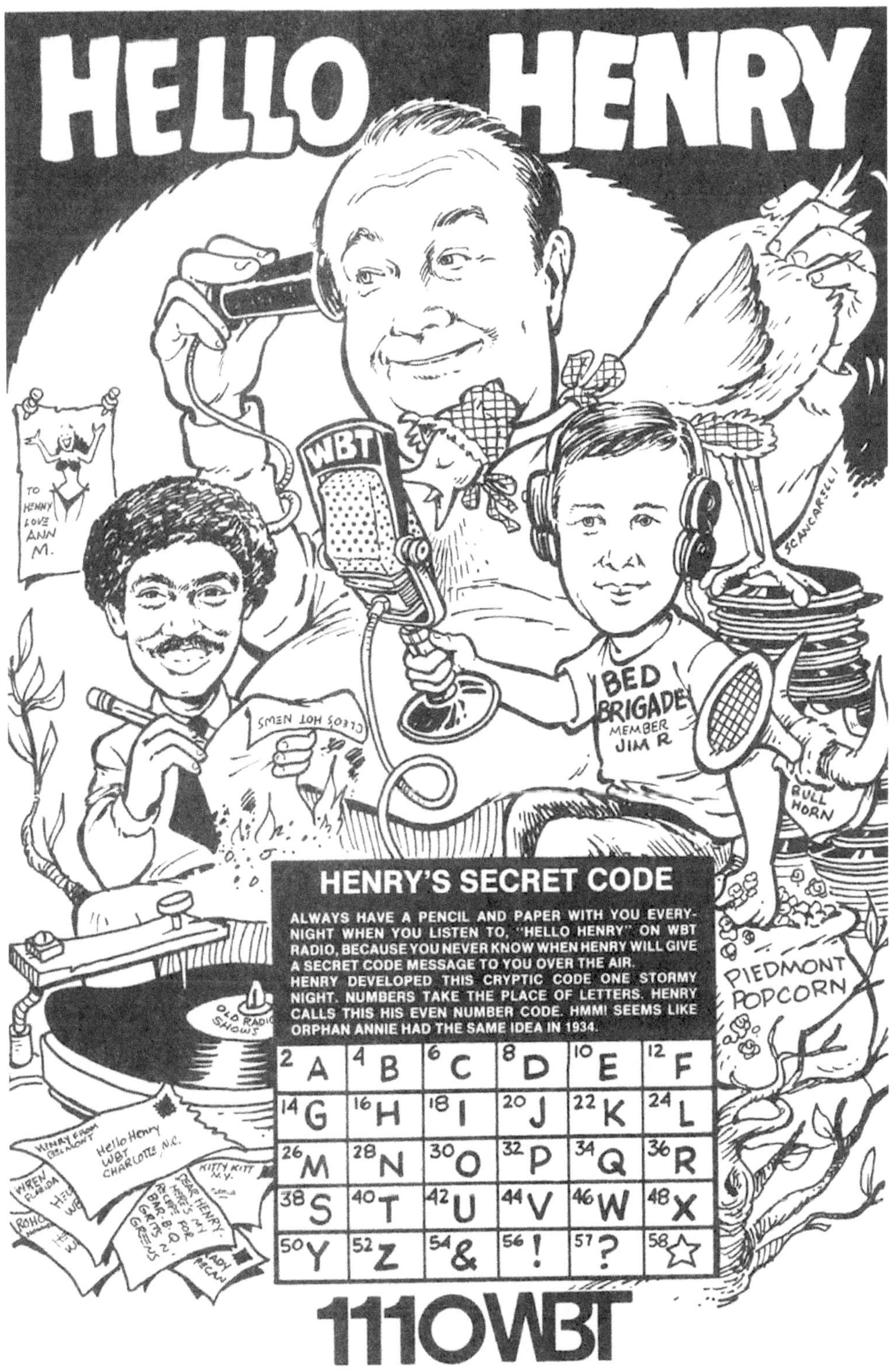

WBTV advertisement for the "Hello Henry" show, drawn by Jim Scancarelli.

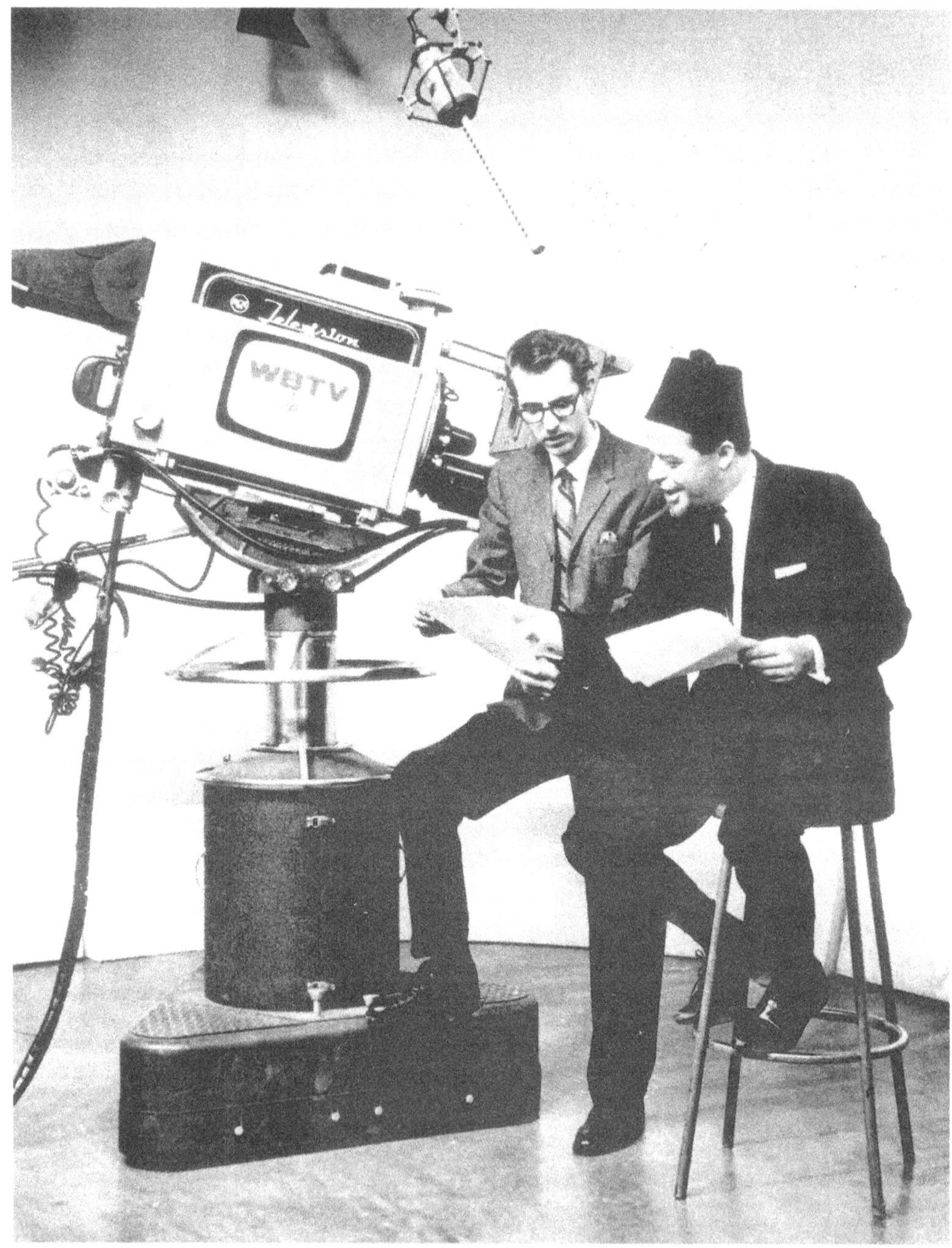

Jim Scancarelli playing the part of "the Director" of Phil Morris' WBTV Friday night horror movie show, "Dr. Evil's Horror Theatre," 1966. Photograph by Hank Warren.

The Yellowjacket was a twice-weekly five-minute feature on WBT's afternoon drive time with Bill Curry, sponsored by Zenith. About 1967, after the demise of the Belmont Tunnel series, several of us around the shop had withdrawal pains and came up with something closely akin to—but more outrageous than—ABC-TV's *Batman* (then the current rage), and heavily influenced by *The Green Hornet*, Stan Freiberg, *Peyton Place*, Bob and Ray, and *National Lampoon*.[19]

The originator of that show, Reno Bailey, had taken on more directing and producing responsibilities at the station, and as a result Jim ended up writing the scripts for "The Yellowjacket." Jim recalled the challenge as an experience that was continuously fun:

> I would put all kinds of crazy things in there. Cannons going off. Horses galloping along. Whatever fit with the story. Then I came up with this idea. The show was sponsored by Zenith. Zenith would say, how about pushing some record player or entertainment center? I'd write this story for "The Yellowjacket" and his partner Calvin. For example, they would be running away from some bad guys or being chased by dogs. They would stop in front of the Zenith store. The crooks, the heroes, the dogs—they would all stop in front of the store, look in the show window, and say, "Hey, look at this, there's the Zenith RB 200" or whatever it was—and there, ladies and gentlemen, was the commercial. Then, all of a sudden, they're back running down the street chasing one another. It went over big![20]

From time to time, Jim would take the voice role of characters such as "Sandy Claysoil," an "ace reporter" on the fictitious newspaper *The Daily Clarion*. Jim made the case that Reno Bailey's "Yellowjacket" series was probably one of the last vestiges of really old-time radio broadcasting:

> The "Yellowjacket" show aired around the same time as the network's "The Chicken Man" was broadcast. "The Chicken Man" was a network thing. "Chicken Man" was not nearly as good as "The Yellowjacket." […] It just sort of fell flat.[21] We did everything like they used to do it in old radio. The microphones we had were the old ones. We wanted to boost things up with sound effects. We knew we had about five minutes to play with, and I knew if it ran over, who cares. The funny thing, the President of the company, Charles Crutchfield, heard it, and he thought it was a network thing from CBS. He thought it was a real professional thing. It was us clowning around in the basement! The key sponsor, Zenith, liked what we were doing because we ran Zenith commercials every show. However, the salesmen at WBT failed to take a renewal contract to Zenith, and so "Yellowjacket" died on the vine. We did not get a bunch of money for it. I think I got 20 or 25 dollars, but I wasn't doing it for the money, I was doing it for the love and excitement of doing old radio. It was absolute, deliriously fun. Everything from TV to radio was just pure exciting. I wanted to stay there and enjoy the excitement. I never wanted to go home.[22]

* * *

By 1967, Jim had been promoted to a supervisory position, and was earning $120.00 a week. However, the company had begun hiring personnel from out of the state, and the "family atmosphere" at the station began to erode. Additionally, Jim stated, WBT promoted sales personnel in supervisory capacities, displacing staff with production experience. In 1967, Jim left WBT in what he described as a "You can't fire me, I quit!" moment.[23]

Freelance Work

From 1967 to 1979 Jim put his drawing skills and printing experience to use as a freelance artist, at one point opening his own studio where he did slide art and specialized in "realistic" drawings for catalogues and magazines.[24] In those days, companies were recruiting artists to help dress up their slide presentations, to add a bit of humor and color to their formal pitches. Jim recalled doing a few illustrations for

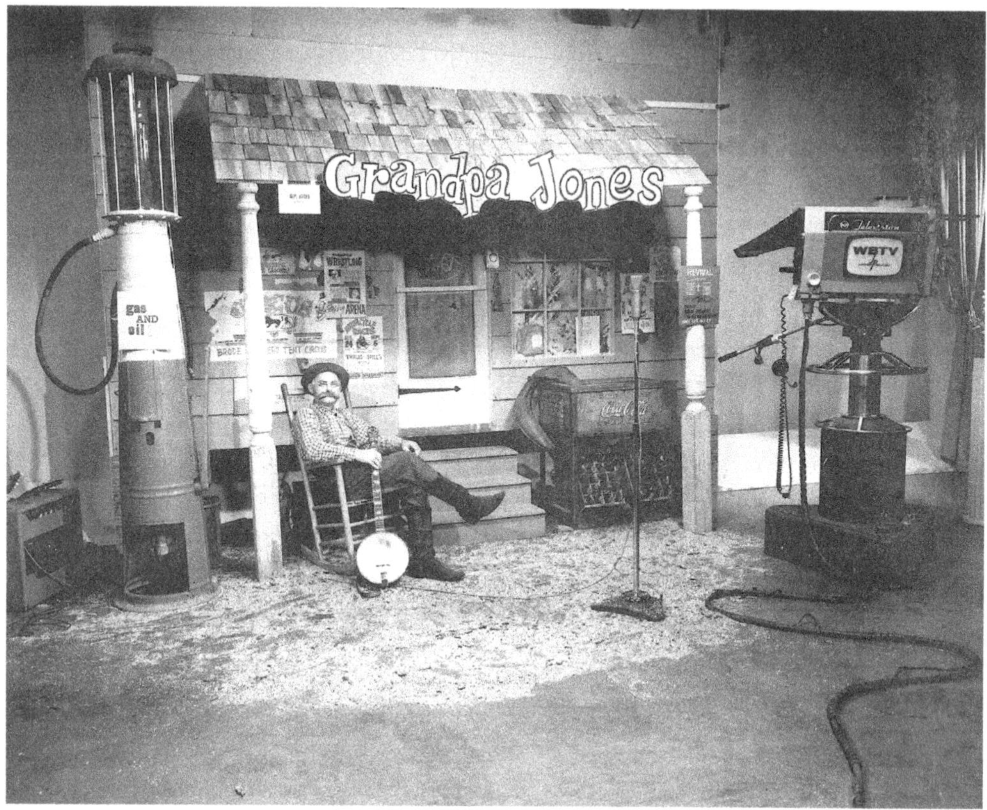

Grandpa Jones on a set that Jim designed for his appearance on Bill Anderson's WBTV syndicated show (Jefferson Productions), 1965. Photograph by Hank Warren.

the magazine of the National Automotive Parts Association, NAPA Auto Parts, an American retailers' cooperative established in 1925. The magazine featured advertisements and stories focused on automotive replacement parts. NAPA was looking to add something lighter to their sales pitch scripts. Jim remembered that a fellow who worked for NAPA wrote a slide show during the late 1970s, in the midst of the energy crisis, when gas prices spiked and supplies dwindled. That slide show featured a character who sold chariot parts during the days of the Roman Empire. The author of that slide show wrote about how chariot drivers were facing a drought, meaning that water for their camels was scarce and supplies unpredictable, forcing the Roman Empire to institute rationing schemes where one hump camels could water on Mondays and Wednesdays, and two hump camels would gain access to drinking troughs on Tuesdays and Thursdays. It was "hilarious stuff," Jim recalled, material that added a measure of humor to otherwise ponderous business narratives and sales pitches. Such presentations went a long way toward educating sales departments on the wisdom of including humor and original cartoon characters in their work.[25]

Jim did illustration work for publications that came under the umbrella of the Saturday Evening Post Company, located in Indianapolis at the time. Marcus Hamilton, who had also left WBT-WBTV in the late 1960s, tapped into the jobs available for illustrators working for large publishing companies.[26] Jim sent some sample

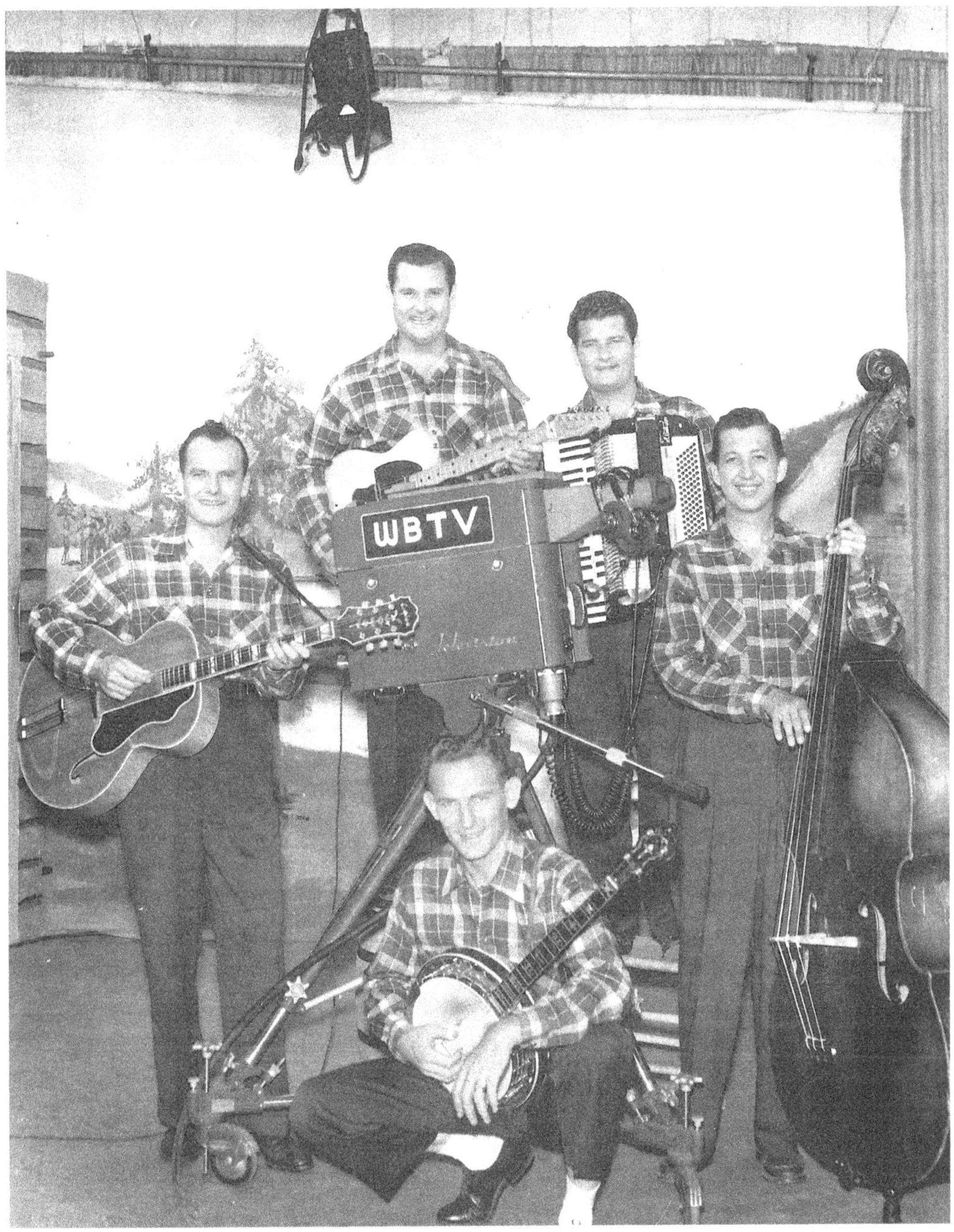

Left to right: Sonny Smith (guitar), Arthur Smith (electric guitar), Ralph Smith (accordion), Tommy Faile (bass), and Don Reno (banjo), January 1952 at the WBTV studios in the Old Wilder Building, Charlotte, North Carolina. Photograph by Hank Warren.

drawings to the Saturday Evening Post Company and was brought on as a freelance illustrator. The jobs did not pay much, he recalled, and the company owned all the rights to the art. His clients were mostly magazines for children that, by the early 1970s, had begun to focus their publications on child health issues. For a 1981 issue of *Humpty Dumpty*, Jim found himself doing the artwork for a story in which

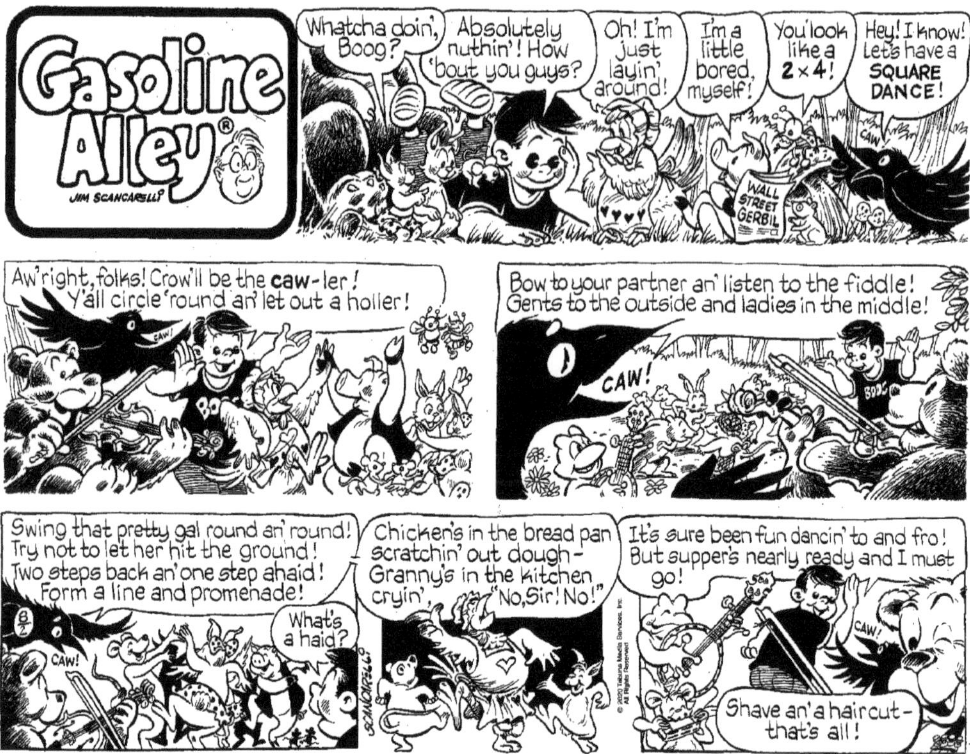

Gasoline Alley, 2 August 2020, a copy made from original production art files in Jim's personal archive for that strip, reprinted courtesy the Tribune Content Agency, LLC, and Jim Scancarelli. Jim listened to Fred Waring's radio show in the 1940s, and was captivated by the Little Orley stories created and narrated by Hugh "Uncle Lumpy" Brannum—who, in 1955, joined the Captain Kangaroo show as Mr. Green Jeans. When he was a little boy, Jim would sit in his backyard and watch the insects and critters with the same intensity as Boog.

Humpty's sister Peggy was scolding her brother for his messy room and unkempt appearance. "Clean up your room, and yourself," she said, in the story that Jim illustrated. "Don't be a rotten egg."[27] He also illustrated for *Medical Detective* and *Turtle*, magazines intended for pre-school children. For *Turtle*, he invented a character, Cousin Cooter—cooter being a reference to the North American river turtle, and a term that is used as a generic reference to turtles in the south. In one strip, the character Cooter was talking to a bird that was eating a sandwich while standing on one leg. The bird explained to Cousin Cooter than he was trying to achieve a more balanced diet. The story ended with the admonition: "You won't be a bird brain if you eat well."[28] Between 1976 and 1978, Jim did cover illustrations for *Child Life Magazine*, *Children's Better Health*, and for *Jack and Jill*. He found himself in the company of other notable cartoonists including Jared Lee. By the late 1970s, the artwork for these kinds of freelance jobs could be performed by computers, and jobs for illustrators in that area began to dry up. Jim began looking for other opportunities, setting his sights on breaking into the cartoon industry.[29]

Three

Learning Music

Music Early On

Jim had a record player when he was in the first or second grade. His first records included pressings that featured Arthur Godfrey comedy songs. The records he played on that little machine, and the radio programs that he looked forward to with great anticipation every day, "molded" his life, as he put it. He listened to Fred Waring's radio show in the 1940s and heard the Little Orley stories created and narrated by Hugh "Uncle Lumpy" Brannum—who, in 1955, joined the Captain Kangaroo show as Mr. Green Jeans. Jim was so taken by the Little Orley character that his Uncle Bob drew him his own comic strip commemorating the original stories. Jim was especially fond of his Uncle Bob's sketches of a Big Band composed of bugs that used leaves and twigs to make music. Charmingly, that bug band tried to break into radio. That home-made strip might still exist in Jim's holdings, a vast personal archive of memories, but he has not seen it in years.

Jim's grandfather, Otto Parati, had an Edison wind-up phonograph the size of a large, hefty piece of furniture. The hand crank would wind up the spring to get the thing rolling. Jim remembered hearing Christmas music on that phonograph, and he heard some folk tunes—possibly including "Floyd Collins," a tune that stuck with him because of the lyrical reference to a "lonely sandstone cave."[1] Parati listened to the news, to WSM's Grand Ole Opry broadcasts, and to Jack Benny, Amos and Andy, and the "hillbilly bands." Jim's father was partial to WARL in Arlington, Virginia, and had a special fondness for a show that featured Don Owens and Connie B. Gay who broadcast bluegrass music in the Washington, D.C., area during the "formative" years of that music scene.[2]

When he was five years old, Jim's mother gave him a little plastic Magnus harmonica. He took to that musical instrument. Jim's Uncle Bob showed his nephew a thing or two on the harmonica.[3] Jim recalled:

> I picked it up and I started playing it. I could play "Oh, Susanna" and stuff like that. I don't think I was five years old if I was a minute. As time went on my grandma brought me a real chromatic harmonica. It was five dollars, and it was a Hohner Professional model. I still have it. I just couldn't believe anybody would spend five dollars on a harmonica, or five dollars on anything; nobody had five dollars. Anyway, I learned how to play by ear. I would listen to Larry Adler, and to Jerry Murad's Harmonicats.[4] I got where I could play, and I thought, hey, I'm a showman. In 1993 I went to a harmonica festival and got around some of the pros and I realized that I stunk. They were so good, and I was so bad, and that ended my harmonica career.[5]

Jim's mother's second cousin was Pitts Cobb, who at one point was the night manager of the Franklin Park Hotel in Washington, D.C. The hotel was known in the family for its reputation as a wild flophouse; Jim heard stories of drunk sailors and knife throwing incidents on the premises. Once, Pitts Cobb met sailors from the U.S. Navy band at the hotel. One band member, Richard Bain, played the harmonica, and Cobb told Bain about his little nephew Jimmy who loved listening to harmonica. Bain gave Cobb a little four-hole harmonica for Jim, who was 8 or 10 years old at the time. Years later, during Jim's time in the Navy, he met Bain who was still in the Navy, and still a member of the Navy Band. Jim told Bain the story of his uncle, the Franklin Park Hotel night manager, but somehow that story was not enough to earn him an invitation to play the mouth organ on stage with Bain and the Navy band.[6]

During his high school years, Jim was not nearly as enamored of rock and roll as friends and classmates. He remembered going on vacation with his family to Myrtle Beach, South Carolina, and staying at accommodations where aspiring local rock bands performed in the evenings. Bill Haley and the Comets played there. None of that music moved him, and he was not much of a dancer. Instead, he immersed himself in the harmonica playing of Larry Adler, Johnny Puleo and the Harmonica Gang, and the Harmonica Rascals. He liked the stage "shtick" of some of these acts as much as the music, especially the antics of the Harmonica Gang.[7]

Learning Bluegrass

Jim got his first taste of bluegrass music while serving in uniform at Naval Station Newport (NAVSTA Newport). He was wandering the streets of Newport one evening on Shore Patrol duty and paused outside a club: "From within wafted this great, wild fiddle music that set me on fire. I think it was Scotty Stoneman playing. He was a wild man on the fiddle."[8] Jim lingered by the door of the club until it was time for him to continue his patrol duties, but the wild music continued to haunt him.[9]

After Jim went to work for his uncle in late 1962, illustrating advertisements for *The Yellow Pages*, his uncle, Bob Parati, began borrowing albums from the local library that he and Jim would play in his uncle's basement office while they worked. They listened to all kinds of eclectic music. Jim remembered being enamored of the traditional music he heard on those recordings. In 1963 Jim saw Lester Flatt and Earl Scruggs perform the theme song for "The Beverley Hillbillies" television show, and came away saying to himself, "I gotta have a banjo." As Amy Worthington Hauslohner noted in a 1989 article, "the budding musician" ordered one out of the Sears catalogue.[10] In Jim's words:

I first saw Earl Scruggs playing and thought "Boy that's incredible." At that time, right when I got out of the Navy, at that time all of this hootenanny and folk craze came along. You couldn't find any banjos in a pawn shop. Everybody had bought them. I ordered a banjo from Sears. For 75 dollars. And it turned out it was a long neck banjo like Pete Seeger's banjo, and the strings were so high it was like a dobro. Holy cow, it hurt your fingers. Well, I sort of went up there to Union Grove and nosed around and watched what they were doing, trying to see what was what.[11]

As Jim tells the story, the main influence that drew him to bluegrass and old-time music was one of those albums: Mike Seeger's 1961 Folkways album "The 37th Old Time Fiddlers' Convention at Union Grove, North Carolina" (FA 2434). "I listened to that Union Grove recording and I said 'Wow.' I kind of always liked string band fiddling but I didn't know much about it, so I said, Union Grove, that's near here, and I went in 1964 and met Pierce Van Hoy." Pierce was the oldest son of Henry Price "H.P." Van Hoy (1887–1976), who founded the Old Time Fiddlers' Convention in 1925. Pierce became the organizer and promoter of the annual event.

Jim has vivid memories of jams that he attended at places like Union Grove, often with musicians who he categorized as being among the "Big Biggies" in the business. They were musicians of consequence who were prepared to help newcomers. That impressed him, and he remained eternally grateful to those people. One musician who fit that description was Vassar Clements, who made brief cameo appearances throughout Jim's musical life—and who consistently served as a role model for Jim, an example of a professional musician and a creative force. Jim jammed alongside Clements in 1970 or so at Wolf Trap in the Washington, D.C., area, and met John Hartford through Clements. Jim frequently recalled the thrill having Vassar play harmony to his fiddle lead. It seemed to amaze him for several reasons—first, for the shear spectacle of someone as talented as Vassar taking the role as second fiddle to a self-taught musician, and second, as an example of generosity of spirit that Vassar exemplified, helping out younger, less experienced fiddlers to boost their confidence and nudge them to make progress on the fiddle.[12]

Figuring Out Banjo and Fiddle

Jim learned to play the banjo before he tackled fiddle. He played the Sears long neck banjo that he purchased when he got out of the Navy from 1964 until 1965, by which point he was working at WBTV, the CBS affiliated television station in Charlotte, North Carolina. In Jim's words:

> Arthur Smith was the big country musician—Guitar Boogie Arthur Smith not fiddling Arthur Smith—but he could play the fiddle. Anyway, during the years Smith had a show on WBT, the Fender instrument company outfitted his band with its instruments, and they were getting free plugs on his show. The show went into a lot of different markets and areas. So, I thought, hey, I'd like to get a good banjo. Neither Arthur nor his brother could play five string. They played plectrum. So, I went to Fred Nance, who ran a music store in Charlotte. Fred played and taught classical guitar. I ordered the cheap Fender model. I think it was called the Allegro banjo, and they sent me a gold-plated Concertone. I didn't know what to do because I couldn't afford that thing. It was 1,000 dollars and I didn't have that kind of money. So, Fred Nance said take the banjo, take it home, and pay me when you can. And he said he would let me have the banjo for his cost. And this was 500 dollars, so I got the top-of-the-line gold plated Fender for 500 bucks. That banjo made all the difference in the world.[13]

That Fender Concertone served Jim well on stage, in recording situations, in jams at fiddlers' conventions for over 50 years. Jim never felt he needed another five string. In his memory, Fender made only about 90 of those; Jim's was number 21.[14]

Jim tried three-finger up picking, Scruggs style, but "I couldn't get the roll

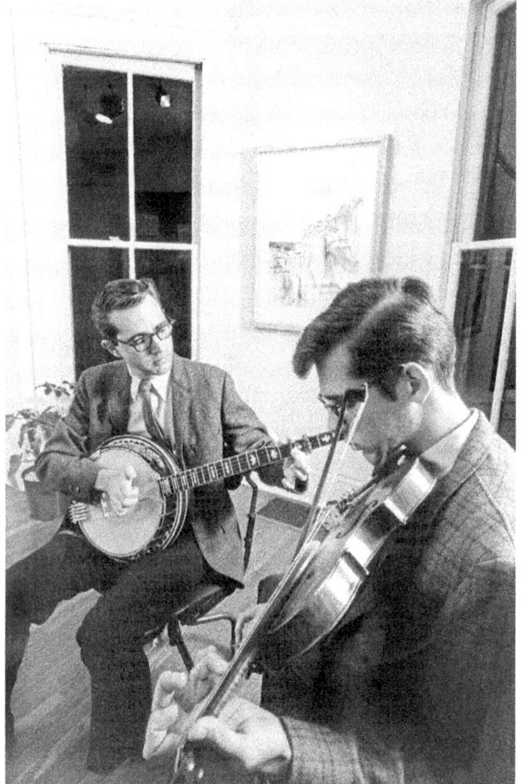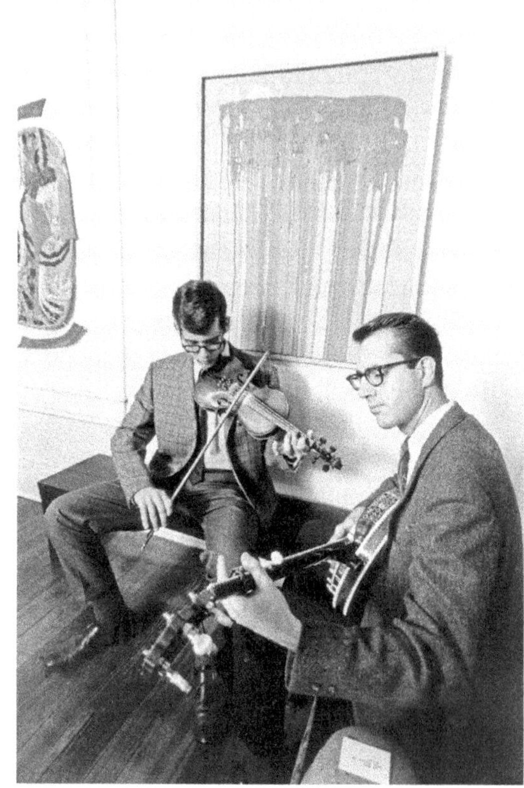

Left and right: Mark Wingate on fiddle, Jim on his Fender 5 string, at an art gallery opening in Charlotte, North Carolina. No date.

down." He took a crack at playing clawhammer, but he never could bring his thumb over to get that percussive clawhammer down-picking pattern. He had his own kind of a "plunky plunky sound," as he put it. He recalled:

> Well, I went up there to Union Grove, armed with the Sears long-necked banjo, and nosed around and watched what they were doing. And then one day I bumped into Kyle Creed, and he said: "Cock your thumb over a little and you got it." That was pretty good advice.[15]

Jim learned the basics of fiddling by listening to fiddlers and by picking up the fiddle and just sawing away at it. He probably started in earnest in the mid–1960s. At one point, well into the time Jim was trying to get up to speed playing the fiddle and building his repertoire, he cobbled together a "sound system" that involved a turntable, a power unit—which he included to boost a weak signal up to a line-level signal—a cassette player, a CD player, and a tape recorder. He rigged all of that together into a system that enabled him to make copies of recorded material and allowed him to easily put the jury-rigged system into a "repeat" mode. He used that system to help he learn Kenny Baker's fiddling. Eventually, not long into the 21st century, the system gave up the ghost. Worn out, it just quit working.[16]

Jim felt that because of the way he taught himself to play fiddle, he really did not have the basic fiddling skills down in correct and proper ways:

I didn't know it how to do it myself. I had to pick all this stuff up on my own. At the time I would listen to records, LPs, but I kind of advanced when I got out to these fiddlers' conventions and got around real people. They could play. My timing got better. I still didn't know what I was doing. One day I was at a fiddlers' convention and an old-timer, a good fiddle player, came up and said, you'd be real good if you'd use your little finger more.[17]

Jim learned a good deal by just being in jams with musicians at Union Grove. He discerned his own goals for fiddle playing in that context, in part by watching and listening, and in part by developing the relationships with accomplished performing musicians whose fiddling he hoped to emulate. After his first trips to Union Grove in the late 1960s, he formulated a first goal: "In my head I wanted to fiddle with the power, creativity and the wildness of Scotty Stoneman." At one of his first Union Grove festivals, he saw five-year-old Jimmy Edmonds playing fiddle: "His little fingers were flying all over the fingerboard. He wiggled his hand, just like a classical violinist, to get a vibrato-like sound. He just extracted such clear notes."

Joining festival contests established the sorts of relationships that would eventually lead to participation in bands and gave Jim a measure of fearlessness—or relative fearlessness—about performing on a stage. Learning who to listen to, whose LPs to buy, was critical, too. Jim found himself most comfortable with what he called "The Galax Sound," a term he used to refer to a music that bridged the gap between old-time and bluegrass, the sort of music that Jim felt was typified by the work of The Mountain Ramblers, and by the fiddler Otis Burris ("You talk about power…").

At some point, early in his fiddling, Jim took the advice of C.E. Ward and shifted his attention to figuring out "long bow" fiddling. "Long bow, that changed my fiddling. As C.E. Ward said, you slide 'from frog to the tip and back again.' Just getting coordinated took some doing." He found his way to fiddlers such as Clyde Williams and Tommy Malboeuf, who helped define the role a fiddle ought to play in the midst of a band trying for a certain approach to making music. Jim quickly learned that fiddling alongside "elders" led to a symbiotic relationship where fiddling partners in effect contributed to the process of improving one another's bowing, timing, and "attack."[18] Jim came to appreciate the fiddling of Bobby Hicks, the complicated way he played, the way Hicks "threw everything into a fiddle break, including the kitchen sink." Jim admired, and attempted to emulate, Kenny Baker who, as Jim put it, played simple, straightforward stuff with such clarity and power.[19]

Reflecting on his fiddling learning curve fifty years later, Jim mused that there are three things to keep in mind when tackling the fiddle. The first came to him from listening to Kenny Baker: go for cleanliness of notes. That is what distinguished Baker's fiddle playing.[20] If the fiddler does not play his notes cleanly, the whole thing sounds "like Hogan's goat."[21]

The second probably derived from the advice Jim received at a fiddlers' convention from an old-time fiddler: use the little finger on the fiddle fingerboard to reach for notes. The Mole Hill Highlander fiddler, Clyde Williams, did not do so, but in Jim's view Williams did a lot of unorthodox things in his fiddling.[22] Trying to get clear notes and using the pinky on the left hand makes a real difference, in Jim's view. Jim was, interestingly, surrounded by fiddlers like Mark Wingate, who fiddled alongside Clyde Williams in the Mole Hill Highlanders. Jim remembered that Wingate had significantly

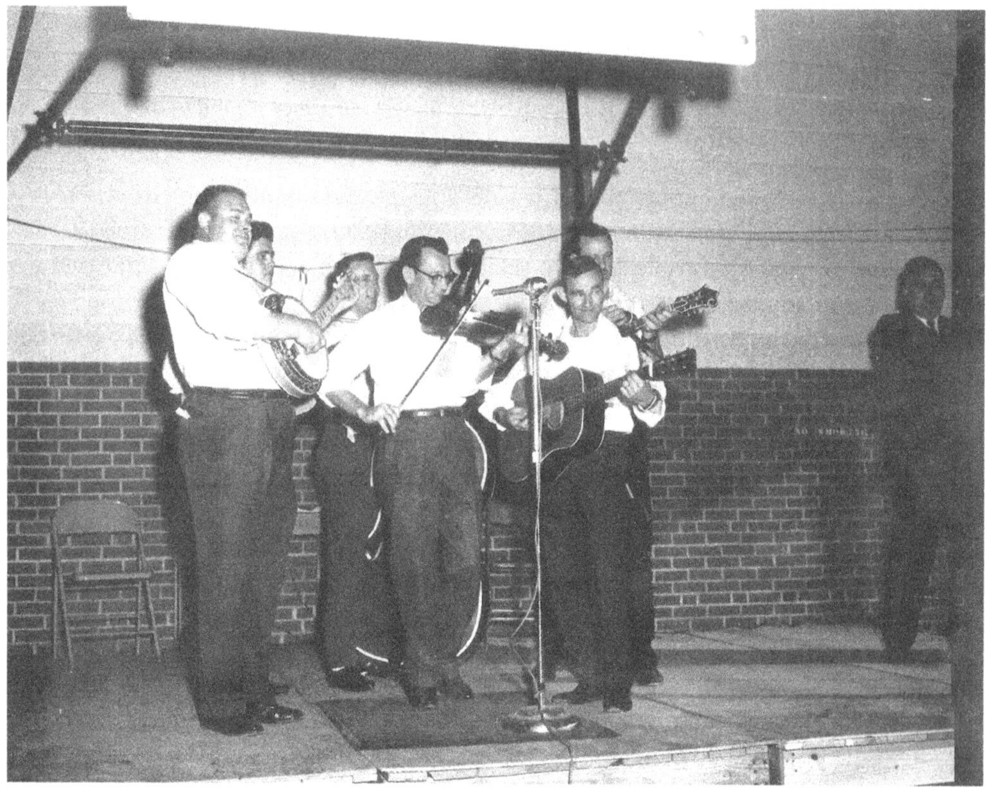

The Mountain Ramblers from Galax, Virginia making music at Union Grove in 1965. Left to right, front row: Charlie Hawkins (banjo), Otis Burris (fiddle), and Eldridge Montgomery (guitar). Back row, left to right: unidentified guitar player (behind Hawkins), Thurmon Pugh (bass), and James Lindsey (mandolin, and band leader). Pierce Van Hoy, Union Grove Master of Ceremonies, stands off to the right side of the stage. Photograph by Jim Scancarelli.

large hands and an impressive wingspan between fingers that allowed plenty of reach on the fingerboard. Wingate, like Williams, used his index finger to reach notes on the high string, and then moved his left hand back quickly on the fingerboard to the first position, thus sacrificing only a fraction of a second by this method.

The third was a result of his own learning curve on the fiddle. "I started too late. Gotta learn fiddling when you are a kid." Mark Wingate was a teenager when he started, Jim recalled. That was an important head start.[23]

Jim echoed the advice and guidance of many a jam-hardened old-time musician: the best thing to do is learn some basics, and then throw oneself into jams at festivals, on the margins of stage performances, at local old-time music gatherings. Being in the midst of seasoned, capable fiddlers is the best way to get up to speed quickly, learn tunes, develop technique, pick up basic licks and tricks. The fellowship of total immersion worked for Jim and many of his colleagues, and he remained convinced that it was the best course of action for a newcomer to fiddling. It was also a good way to get introductions in the community of musicians and settle into the camaraderie that is, from Jim's perspective, an important part of the experience of learning and playing old-time music.[24]

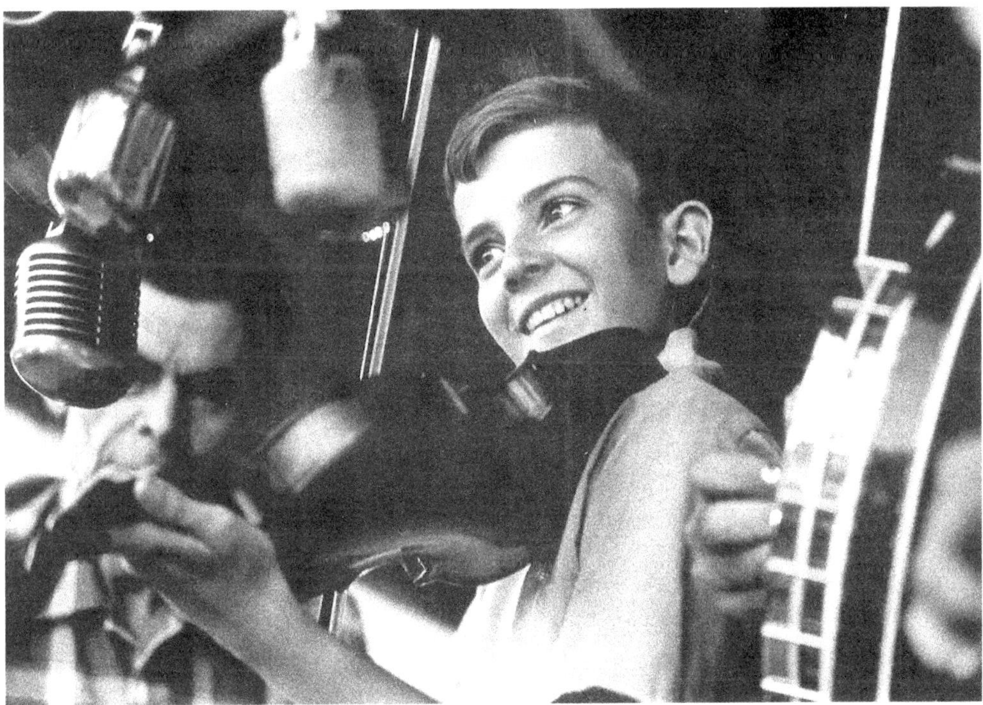

Jimmy Edmonds on fiddle at Galax, Virginia, with Jack Reddick (guitar) and Lanny Reddick (banjo), date unknown.

Perhaps most importantly, as the result of this immersion in fiddling, Jim figured out his place in the musical universe: "When I played in a bluegrass jam, bluegrass musicians would say was playing old-time fiddle style. And when I played in an old-time jam, old-time musicians would say I was too much bluegrass." Jim grew content with occupying what he called "the sloppy middle" between archaic mountain style fiddling, and the emerging contemporary bluegrass increasingly characterized by hot licks, astounding speed, and death-defying breaks.[25]

Jim's Fiddles

Playing with Clyde Williams in the Mole Hill Highlanders in the early 1970s gave Jim a chance to see and hear a great fiddler pull textured, nuanced, complicated sounds out of the instrument. Around that time, Jim began looking for a fiddle that would serve him well. A friend, Terry Black, offered up his father's fiddle as a loaner—if Jim would get the set-up work done to make it playable. Jim played it for a few years until his friend's father decided he wanted it back. So, Jim went to a junk store and picked up a fiddle for about forty dollars. He took it to C.E. Ward and got that fiddle fixed and playable. Meanwhile, Jim's Uncle Bob had grown frustrated over his son's disinterest in learning the fiddle. So, Uncle Bob placed his son's fiddle in a trash can. Jim just happened by his uncle's house before the refuse pickup people got there and found a perfectly good fiddle in the garbage. It turned out to be a big-name fiddle, or more accurately a copy of a copy of a big-name fiddle. C.E. Ward took it apart, pronounced it a junker, but managed to set it up so that it was quite serviceable.

Jim played that for a while, until he happened on a musical instrument dealer at Galax one year who offered him a fiddle that was just so easy to play. Jim junked the junker and played the fiddle he got from the dealer. Not too long afterwards, a friend gave Jim a fiddle he found in a music store in Georgia. Jim recalled that one as a pretty decent instrument that had a distinctive look. It was an extensively inlaid Stainer fiddle, sold by Montgomery Ward.[26]

In the meantime, Darrell McCumbers, a West Virginian musical instrument dealer who at the time was living in Woolwine, Virginia, called Jim and offered him a "head fiddle," a nice fiddle that was a German made copy with a "wonderfully carved figure of a bearded man's head resting on top of the peg box—instead of a scroll."[27] At the same time, another dealer called Jim with a Gaspard Duiffopruggard copy from a French violin maker. Jim opted for the more expensive fiddle, the French maker's copy, with the words of a friend ringing in his ears: "You get what you pay for." Jim took the fiddle to George Chestnut, Kenny Baker's fiddle repairman in Nashville, Tennessee, and had a new fingerboard made for the fiddle. C.E. Ward carved a new bridge—one like Scotty Stoneman's preferred bridge, flatter on top. A sound

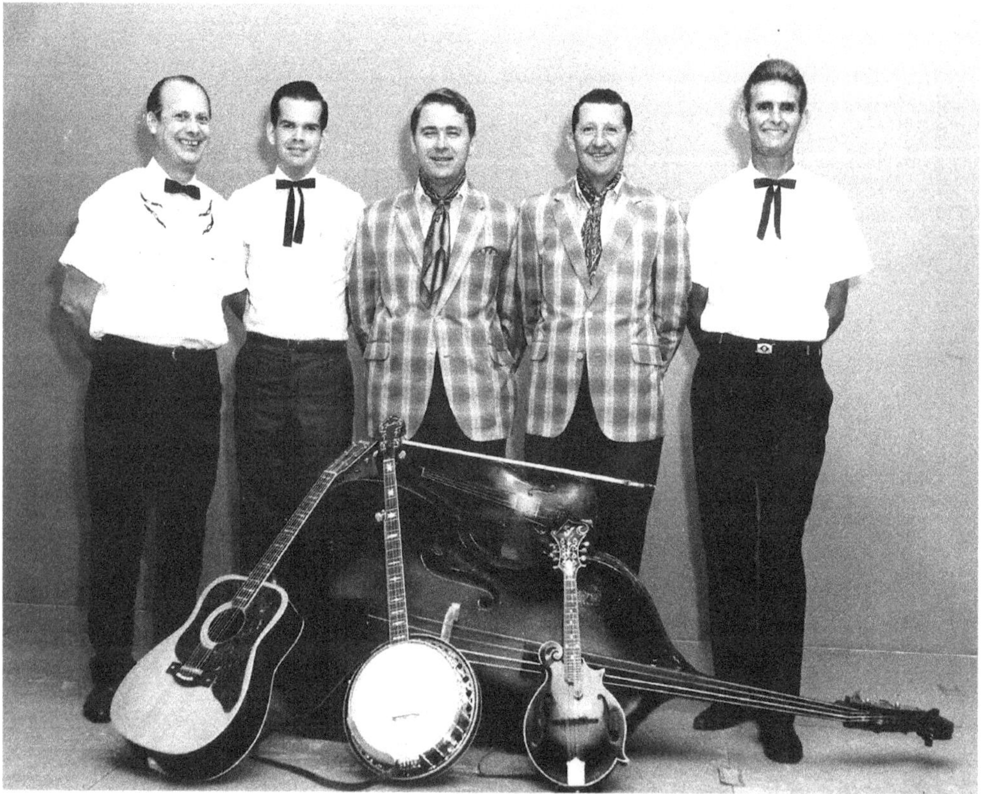

Left to right: David Johnson, Ronnie Prevette, C.E. Ward, Joe Smith, and Bill Cooper. The band went by the name "C.E. Ward and Joe Smith and the Bluegrass Review." 16 August 1970. Photograph by Hank Warren.

post replacement was all it took to get Kenny Baker to call that instrument a "honker" of a fiddle that played clean and loud. "I had more fun with that fiddle. Kenny Baker 'smoked it over'"—played it hard and put his fingerprints all over it. Around that time, a local college in Monroe, North Carolina, was selling off some musical instruments, and Jim got his hands on a fancy viola bow. It weighed more, and since that "head" fiddle had the dimensions of a ¾-sized viola anyway, Jim purchased the viola bow. "The weight of the bow was a perfect match for the fiddle," he recalled. Jim played that fiddle through the first decade or so of the 2000s when a lifetime of fiddling and drawing cartoons with a death grip on the India ink pen caught up with him in the form of right thumb joint pain, diminished cartilage between the finger bones and other osteo challenges. He pulled the fiddle out in 2018 or 2019 when Chuck Dunlop paid him a visit along with a bluegrass banjo player friend, Randy Debruhl, but Jim recognized that his capacity to bow the fiddle had diminished, and that he would not be getting back the "creative stuff" again. "I never did have the fortune of being able to practice eight or twelve hours a day," he said, acknowledging that this clearly made a difference in his ability to reach back and find his way around the fiddle again, and reclaim the tunes he played years ago.[28]

A Bagpiping Interlude

The account of how Jim came to learn bagpipes is one of those wonderful stories that loops through so many aspects of Jim's life, keeps tracing the origins of the tale back further and further, and ends up linking so many aspects of his life into a single piece.

Fred Clark was the art director at Ayre and Gillette, where Jim had interviewed for a job after he got out of the Navy. Fred knew Jim's Uncle Bob; they went to the same church. Jim knew Fred as a wonderful illustrator and got to know him after Jim got out of the Navy. Myers Park Pharmacy was around the corner from Jim's home in Charlotte.

> Dr. Lawrence ran the place. He filled prescriptions, developed film, worked the soda fountain. When I was a little boy, my grandmother would leave me in the pharmacy while she went shopping at the local supermarket. I'd read the comics, dribble ice cream all over them; that attracted Dr. Lawrence's attention.

Jim recalled that when they were young, he and his friend Bobby Nowlin would head to the drug store for ice cream and soda, and occasionally Fred Clark would come in and "hold court." Jim remembers boisterous arguments over politics and other matters, loud disagreements over issues of the day "that Fred and other curmudgeons were eager to voice." One time, Fred introduced Jim to Jim Culp, "a brilliant designer" with whom Jim became fast friends for over 60 years.

At some point, Jim met Henry Graham at the drug store. Graham was a pharmacist. And he played bagpipes. Jim said:

> I appreciated the antiquity of it, and I joined a bagpipe band, the Caledonian Pipe Band. That was in 1964. They say it takes seven years to make a piper. Well, I can't read music, and we had a real Scottish Pipe Major who lived in Winston-Salem who came to Charlotte once every week

or so to teach bagpipes. Henry Graham started out teaching me on a practice chanter. I'd pick the tunes up by ear, and eventually I became the Pipe Corporal—the bagpipe hierarchy had a real military aspect to it. One day, the Pipe Major set some sheet music in front of me. I knew the tune and tried to play it—by ear—but what I was playing was not what was on the sheet of music. I was found out.[29]

Jim ceased his bagpipe phase in 1970. It's not clear what became of his uniform, which included a kilt.

A Brief Ride with the Briarhoppers

WBT's history as a radio station dates back to the 1930s. In those days the station carried a lot of southern string band music. WBT was the home base for the Briar-hoppers, a band that became prominent in Charlotte. The WBT website tells the story of the band's origins this way:

In 1934, a potential advertiser called WBT's Charles Crutchfield to ask if the station had a hill-billy band to help advertise its products. Telling a fib, Crutch said "Yes," which led to the birth of the Briarhoppers. The name comes from WBT announcer Bill Bivens who, during a hunting trip with Crutch, was startled by a rabbit jumping out of a thicket, and Bill yelled, "Look at that briarhopper!" At that moment, Crutch found the name for his hillbilly band. The original band members were Johnny McAllister, Big Bill Davis, Don White, Thorpe Westerfield, Clarence Etters, and Jane Bartlett. The last original 1934 Briarhopper, Don White, died in 2003. [...] The band kept going through the years by adding new musicians to replace those who left the station or who died.[30]

Hank Warren joined that band as their fiddler in 1938. His first band (probably in the 1930s) was Warren's Four Aces. He played in the Swingbillies, Doug Poole's band—Doug was Charlie Poole's son. Warren also fiddled for the Tennessee Ramblers.[31] In the late 1930s, Warren was cast in several Gene Autry movies.[32] In fact, many of the Briarhoppers found their way into movies, often in scenes that had them playing the guitar, and sometimes acting in multiple roles—in one film, Warren portrayed a cavalryman, and later in the same movie a Native American. The Briarhoppers continued through the first decades of the 21st century in several different configurations. Jim inserted the Briarhoppers band in *Gasoline Alley* as the Thorn Jumpers in three daily strips in October 1986.[33] Hank Warren was WBT/WBTV's photographer when Jim met him at WBT:

I knew Hank really well. He was the fiddle player for the Briarhoppers, and a pioneer in photography.[34] Hank was in his late 70s, early 80s when I got to really know him. He was always playing around with new photographic technology. He'd come down and say, "I've got this new lens and it's a 20mm." [...] He always was doing things like product shots. He had to shoot a picture of a car for a commercial. So, he decides to drive the car into the studio, and to knock the background out he took an open flash, exposed the front and blurred out the background by firing the flash, repeatedly. It was beautiful. He was experimenting around doing stuff like that. And he was a real good fiddle player. He knew classical music. I've got a picture of him in a tuxedo as a "violinist," but then he knew the real deal as far as fiddle tunes were concerned. He once said that the Briarhoppers might not be the top bunch of musicians, but they were the top-notch entertainers, and he was 100 percent right. I mean, they were good musicians, they could cut it as far as singing and playing, but as far as entertainers, they were tight and were right.[35]

Jim filled in for Warren on the fiddle from time to time in the mid–1970s:

> Once, I had to sub for him on the fiddle because he was not available. I rode with the band. We never had a practice. We drove up into the mountains and had to ride a sky lift to the concert hall which was in a little western town. It was kind of nerve wracking because you are sitting on this tin seat, on a metal rod, riding up vertically in the air. I don't do well with heights. We loaded our instruments into a pickup truck, and they drove up into the mountains. I would have done better in the truck. We hit the stage. There was very little audience there. The first tune was in the key of F. I didn't know the key of F from the key of B flat, and the next tune was in B flat. I didn't take many breaks, I was just doing little fills, but I was in the right key. If it wasn't for that I would have fallen flat. But they were kind enough to ask me what tune I wanted to play. Do a hoedown, I said. And then they had a clogging team that came out. In the end, I was an honorary Briarhopper. They called Hank "Fiddlin' Hank," and when I went onstage with them, they called me "Fiddlin' Scank."[36]

Local Fiddlers' Conventions

Jim remembered the many small fiddle contests scattered throughout the Piedmont region during the 1960s and 1970s, sometimes hosted as fundraisers for local schools. These were off the beaten track events that were opportunities to listen to the polished, accomplished acts of touring bands and professional musicians who still played schoolhouse concerts and included such modest, local festivals in their schedule of gigs. Ralph Stanley, Jim and Jesse McReynolds, Bill Monroe, among others, traveled a circuit that brought them to some of these smaller festivals, where they would find a receptive audience of musicians and dedicated fans who could be counted on to listen to their music with enthusiasm.

Fiddlers' conventions and old-time music festivals in North Carolina in the 1960s and 1970s were important opportunities for musicians to shape their repertoire by learning tunes that old masters who attended such gatherings played, and taught, to devoted fans who gathered around such seasoned old fiddlers at these events. Those annual summertime fiddlers' conventions gave younger musicians the chance to negotiate the kind of relationships that would enable continuous contact, field recording opportunities, and in-depth discussions with those Appalachian master musicians. The fiddlers' conventions galvanized musicians to work up tunes, and to form bands at the conventions for the purpose of entering contests. Aspiring banjo and fiddle players looked to these events as laboratories where the archaic tunes and old styles could be studied closely.

Jim was familiar with the fiddlers' conventions that took place around Charlotte in the late 1960s and early 1970s, though Charlotte itself, as Jim put it, "never did subscribe to the better things in life," and consequently did not host a fiddle festival in those days.[37] In the 1970s, February was the month the Mole Hill Highlanders took to the stage at the Ball's Creek festival in in Newton, North Carolina. After that, there was a short-lived festival outside of Charlotte in an old schoolhouse in Denver, North Carolina—"the Denver of the South," as it was called. The school's auditorium was furnished with removable seats and could quickly be turned into a venue for old-time music. The Mole Hill Highlanders played there, too. In the beginning of March, there was a festival in Star, North Carolina, outside of Asheboro:

> We'd drive to Albemarle, stop there, and go to the Whispering Pines Restaurant for barbeque. Boy, was that good, and I say that as someone devoted to southern barbeque. It was the best. Number one. The number two barbeque was at Troutman's over in Concord.[38]

North Moore, in High Falls, North Carolina, hosted a fiddle festival, "an old-time gathering with 'a real nice old-time flavor,'" way out "in the sticks." There was another one near Mt. Airy, in Francisco, close to the Virginia state line.[39] The Mole Hill Highlanders often played at a festival in Mooresville, outside of Charlotte. Statesville, outside of Charlotte, also had an annual old-time music gathering, and so did Mt. Pleasant and Cool Springs, where Jim recalled hearing the fantastic banjo playing of Clermon Edmond "C.E." Ward. Jim also remembered a gathering in Elkin, and one in Ashe County at the same time as the Galax festival.[40] Those fiddlers' conventions were where he met at least some of the elder fiddlers and old-timey banjo players he captured on reel-to-reel recordings in the late 1960s and early 1970s.

Jim's Field Recordings

Beginning in the mid–1960s, Jim recorded old-time banjo and fiddle music at the homes of elder musicians he met at old-time festivals and elsewhere. He also made occasional field recordings at fiddlers' conventions. Jim gifted his field recordings to the Library of Congress in 1970. The Jim Scancarelli Duplication Project at the Library of Congress was added to the collection when the repository was still known as the Archive of Folk Song (AFS). The AFS was part of the Music Division of the Library of Congress. In 1978, the AFS became part of the American Folklife Center (AFC), housed in the American Folklife Collection at the Library. The Jim Scancarelli Duplication Project consisted of seven reels of tape containing the music of seven people recorded by Jim between 1964 and 1969: Uncle Frank Rayborn (1964), Bascom Lamar Lunsford (1966), Norman Edmonds (1969), Chick Martin (1969), Uncle Wade Ward (1969), Arthur Leake Caudle (1969), and Wilson Douglas. Jim wrote 11 pages worth of narrative about the circumstances in which the recordings were made, and listed the tunes captured on his tapes.[41]

Jim's notes describe the circumstances of his encounters with the musicians. Jim saw Frank Rayborn, a one armed banjo player, sitting on South Tryon Street in Charlotte, North Carolina, in a chair that a friend built for Rayborn to facilitate his banjo playing—Jim sketched the chair that was equipped with a pole fitted into the front left hand corner of the chair, topped with a piece of bone, against which Rayborn would position his banjo neck so as to fret barre chords across the strings.[42] Jim ran to WBT, the radio/television station where he worked, and borrowed a "portable" cassette recorder. He recalled the machine as a big, heavy device powered by a battery; it was "portable" compared to prior recording technology that were the size of armored cars. He returned to the place where he had spotted Rayborn, who was still sitting there on the sidewalk, playing the banjo.[43]

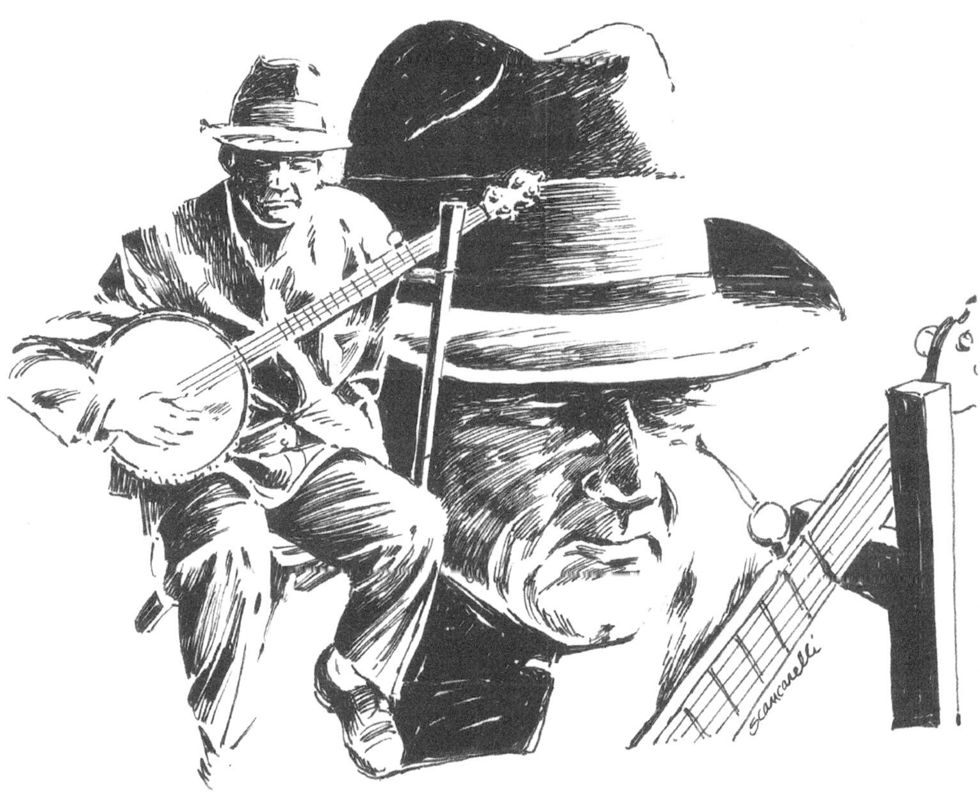

Uncle Frank Rayborn, a one-armed banjo player recorded by Jim in Charlotte, North Carolina, in the summer of 1964. The tapes are among the field recordings in "Jim Scancarelli Recordings of Fiddle and Banjo Music (AFC 1970/017)," Library of Congress. Sometime in the 1950s, Charles D. Webb took several photographs of Uncle Frank. The quality of those photographed diminished with time, so Jim sketched Frank based on the four remaining grainy, washed out shots that he had saved in his files. 13 September 2020.

Jim visited the home of Bascom Lamar Lunsford in South Turkey Creek, North Carolina, twice. He visited Lunsford for the first time a few days after the musician had written "Living in the Kingdom," a song Lunsford wrote around them time Winston Churchill died—Churchill passed away in January 1965. Jim was the first to hear it performed in Lunsford's home. On his second visit, in February 1966, Jim was accompanied by Stan Seiler. They recorded 14 tunes, including "Living in the Kingdom." Jim wrote:

> I first met Bascom at Union Grove with his wife Frieda. Their music knocked me out. Stan and I drove to Bascom's home in December or January. It was cold. I was equipped with a Rayvox tape recording machine and a good quality microphone. They sang, and Bascom played at least one tune that he had written, but it started snowing, and we had to cut things short. He was a southern gentleman from the word go, always dressed in a suit, vest, and tie. I remember him encountering a woman with an operatic voice who was singing the lyrics to "Cripple Creek." After listening, he told her: "That's not the way it goes."[44]

Norman Edmonds performed 20 tunes for Jim on 14 June 1969 on the front porch of the musician's home in Woodlawn, Virginia. Jim captured four additional tunes on that same porch in a subsequent visit to Edmonds' home on 10 August 1979, at which time Edmonds was joined by four musicians who added banjo, guitar and mandolin to the mix. Jim got to know Norman through his father, Nelson Edmonds, who everyone called Harry. Harry was a truck driver who pulled loads up and down the east coast. Once, when Harry Edmonds was driving through Boston, he stopped in music store and purchased a silver clawhammer pick for Jim, who recalled the pick as the prettiest, shiniest pick he ever saw. Harry played the guitar, often with banjo player Rufus Quesinberry. Norman Edmonds' grandson, Jimmy Edmonds, was probably about five years old when Jim did the recording in Woodlawn, Virginia, but even that young he had the gift of being able to sing notes out clear and clean. Norman, Jim said, was a true old-time musician's musician. At one point Norman had a weekly show in Galax, Virginia. He told Jim about the circumstances in which he lost his hearing, or most of it. As Jim recalled, Norman was home fiddling when a storm came up. A bolt of "ball lightning" rolled into his house, across the floor, and blew up his radio, and that was it for Norman's hearing.[45]

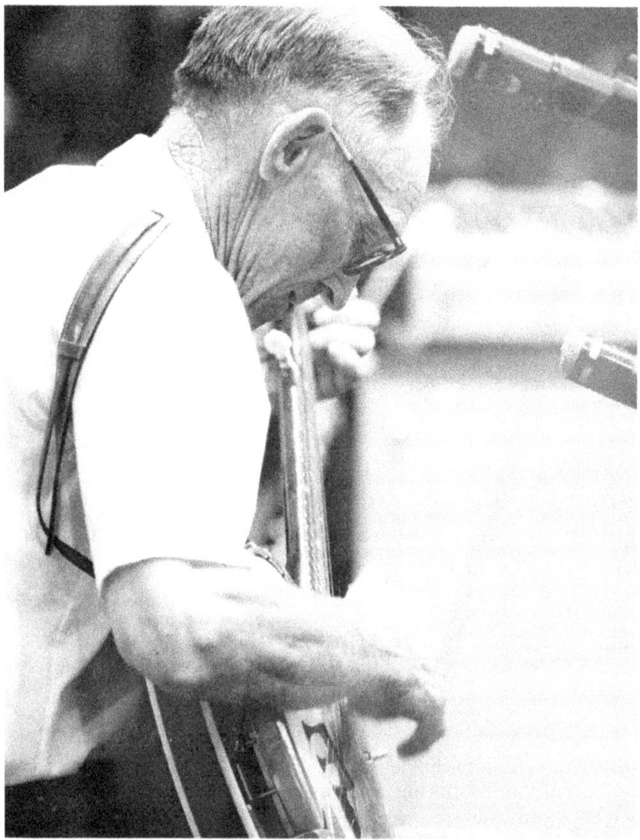

Jim's field recordings of James "Chick" Martin (1969) are among the seven reels of tape in the Library of Congress' Jim Scancarelli Duplication Project. Jim Scancarelli snapped this photograph around 1973 at Mars Hill College in North Carolina.

Jim taped 15 tunes played on the banjo by his good friend James "Chick" Martin on 16 August 1969, and recorded two stories, including one narrative in which Martin related the tale of an old man, crippled, who when he stumbled over a piece of a fiddle tune he was trying to play, not quite finding what he was looking for, would say: "It's in there—but gettin' it out...." That was a phrase that Jim called upon in his own life to describe how he would have an awful time getting to a tune, digging deep in the memory, only to come up with nothing much at all.

Chick Martin lived and farmed in Siler City, on what Jim remembered as a nice old farm located on a road called Rabbits Crossing.[46] Jim was not certain that the name was official; it might have just been a sign that Martin made and posted himself, motivated by the many rabbit tracks that appeared on the road every morning. The Martin farm was where Jim had his first—and probably last—experience milking a cow. The cow "didn't go along with the program," and so Jim did not have milk that day.[47] Martin and his wife equipped their kitchen with a wood burning stove, and at some point Martin purchased a new electric stove for his wife and installed it, but it was not too long before his wife insisted that the wood stove be brought back in. The electric stove was unplugged but remained in place as storage for pots and pans. Jim recalled that Martin was an avid festival attendee, and by late 1969, at the time Jim did his field recordings at Rabbit's Crossing, Martin had travelled 43,277 miles to and from 269 fiddlers' conventions. Martin would often report his mileage records on festival stages in the midst of a performance. Chick Martin played banjo with what Jim described as an index and thumb-driven clawhammer style that was powered by an "odd up and down thrashing action" of his right arm. Martin, Jim said, learned banjo tunes in the old wagon yards, where farmers would bring their produce to sell. The yard would be filled with horses and wagons, and some farmers would spend the night there waiting for the market to open. Martin told Jim he learned some tunes from African American farmers who hauled their produce to the market. Some also hauled banjos with them; Martin remembered learning tunes from a man named Branch at that market.[48]

In May 1969, Jim recorded 26 tunes played by the fiddler Arthur Leake Caudle from East Bend, North Carolina, near Winston-Salem. The recording work was done at the home of Mack Samples in Lancaster, South Carolina, after Caudle had secured his first-place win at the Andy Jackson "Old Hickory" Fiddlers' Convention. Samples played fiddle and guitar, and Danny Cockerham, also from East Bend, played mandolin alongside of Caudle on Jim's tape.[49] Caudle had a cowboy look to him, Jim recalled, a real "old West" appearance, with hair down to his

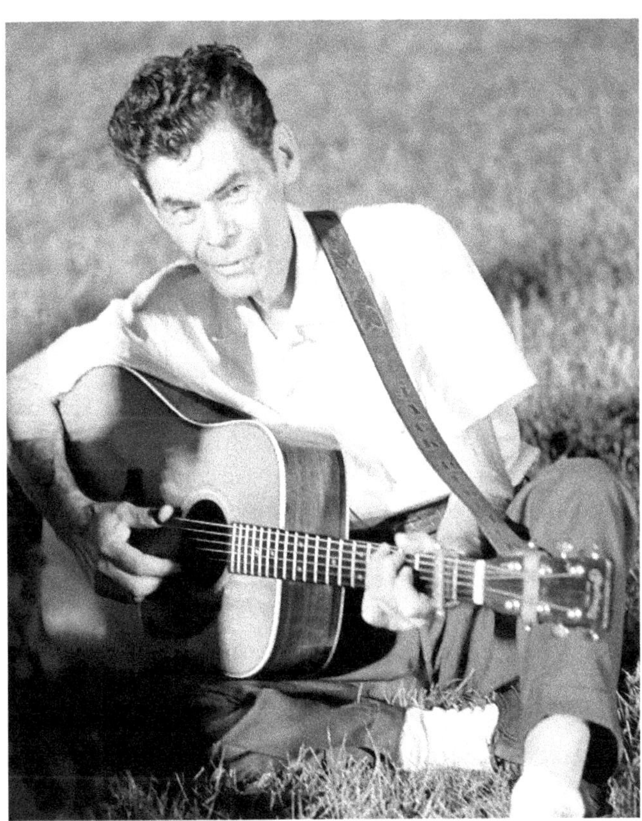

Jack Reddick. No date. Courtesy the photographer, Mark V. Sanderford.

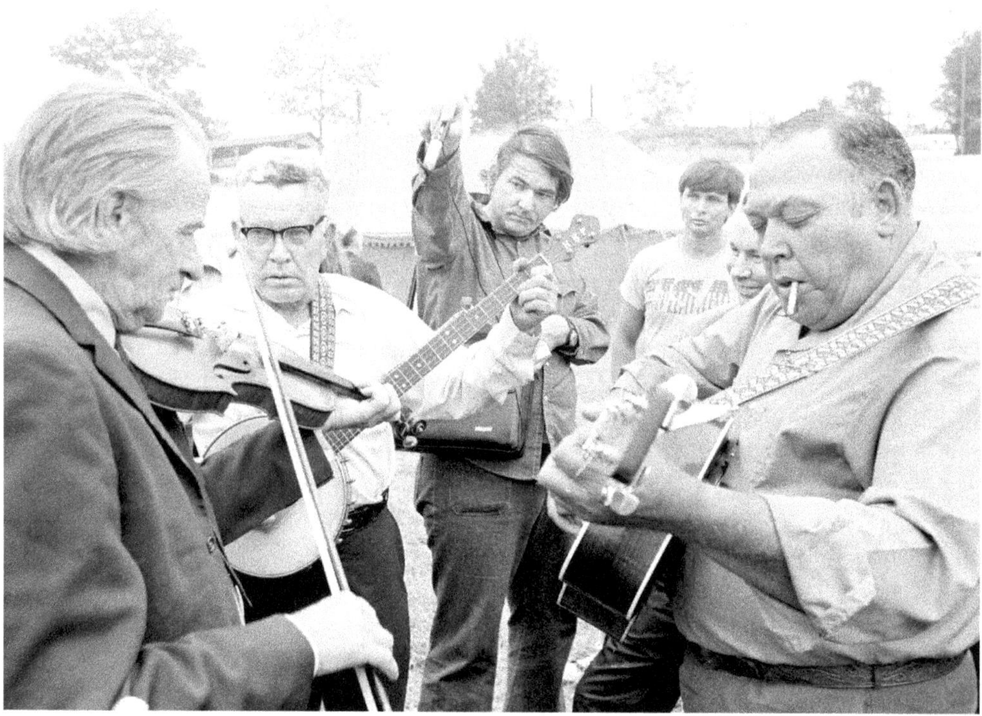

Arthur Leake Caudle, right—with fiddle. No date. Courtesy the photographer, Mark V. Sanderford.

shoulders. He was, Jim made clear, a real good fiddle player. Caudle came from eastern North Carolina. Jim would see him from time to time at Union Grove and Galax. "He was just a wonderful old-time guy who could play circles around most people."[50]

Wade Ward recorded 13 tunes for Jim at Ward's home in Independence, Virginia, on 25 May 1969. Jim met Wade Ward for the first time at Union Grove in 1964, but he had earlier listened closely to his music on a Folkways record that Jim's Uncle Bob borrowed from a library in Charlotte. "That started the ball rolling." When Jim first saw Ward at Union Grove in the mid–1960s, Ward was seated on the steps outside an entrance to the Union Grove schoolhouse and was surrounded by a bunch of banjo-bearing young clawhammer aspirants who were hanging on his every word. Jim saw him in that same kind of situation the next year, too, and at another fiddlers' gathering. They got to talking at Galax a year or so later, and Ward invited Jim to visit him. Jim made that first visit in 1969, armed with a portable Roberts tape recorder. Ward lived on Peachbottom Creek Road, off Route 21, not far from Independence, Virginia, near a courthouse that dated back to about 1905. He was a mile up a hill, not too far from a little abandoned church. His home overlooked a valley that was a tableau of pastureland, rolling hills, old farm fencing, and herds of cattle. Jim visited Ward several times, and he would always stop the car on his way up the hill to drink in the beauty of the landscape. In those days, Ward's home had no plumbing. Two granddaughters, who lived with Ward in the late 1960s, had to go down to a nearby creek to draw water for the household. Jim was invited to eat supper and recalled a

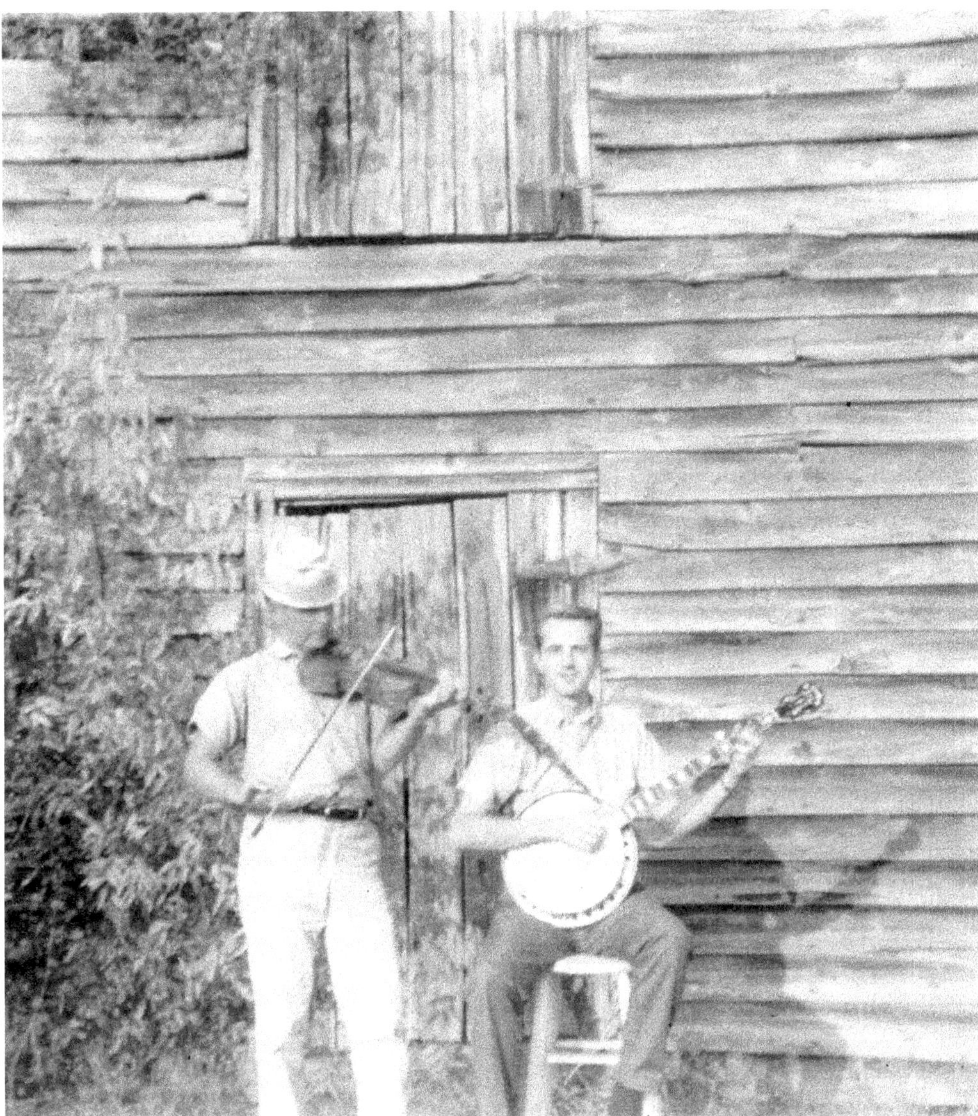

Jim Scancarelli and Mack Samples at Samples' home in Lancaster, South Carolina. No date.

great meal of biscuits and hot gravy. They talked and traded tunes, and Jim recorded Ward's music, but he recalled that Ward was most impressed by the fact that Jim played bagpipes. "I had them in my car, brought them in and played them. What a racket. His granddaughters were easily entertained."[51]

In those days, Ward played some local "show dates" with Jimmy Edmonds. Jim got invited to play with them on one visit in the late 1960s. As Jim recalled, the Parsons Auction Company would hold land sales, and Ward and Edmonds would be invited. The auctioneer would climb up onto the back of a pickup truck and begin touting the quality of the lots of land and other auctions items on the block that day. Then he would start the bidding. When the auction began to lose momentum and looked as though it was headed toward a deadlock on the price tag for the item in question, the auctioneer would turn to Ward and say, "strike up the band." Ward and Jimmy would play a few numbers, and when it looked as though the bidding was going to pick up again, the auctioneer would signal Ward to stop the music, and commerce would once again become the center of attraction.[52]

Jim also captured four tunes played by Wilson Douglas at the West Virginia State Folk Festival in Glenville, West Virginia, on 21 June 1969.[53] Jim remembered Douglas as a real good fiddler who could play all kinds of tunes that Jim just had never heard before. He could chord a fiddle and played a very sophisticated music.[54]

Sometime in the early 1970s, perhaps after the Library of Congress Duplication Project was completed, Jim also made recordings of Hubert Caldwell. Jim visited Caldwell's home in Austinville, just outside of Galax, Virginia, in the company of the photographer Mark Sanderford, who had photographed Caldwell at the Galax convention in the late 1960s.[55] Caldwell, a classically trained musician who could read music, was quite short in stature. He had built a home for himself outside of Galax, Virginia, that was sized to his proportions. Jim remembered having to bend to get through the front door. He also remembered that the tapes he recorded captured the hilarity of the visit. In the 1970s, at various fiddlers' conventions, Caldwell would spot Janet Kerr in the crowd. Kerr, from England, collaborated on several commercial recording projects that featured traditional music recorded at festivals, including the 1970 "Blue Ridge Mountain Field Trip" released in 1970 on the label Leader Sound. In those days, Kerr had very long hair, and Caldwell would wonder out loud to his audience whether anyone had ever heard a fiddle played with a bow made out of human hair, implying that his own bow might just include such hair.[56] During Jim's recording session with Caldwell, a work crew was fixing the telephone lines outside the fiddler's home. He'd be playing, Jim would be taping the tune, and the phone would ring. Hubert would stop playing, get up, pick up the phone, and there would be no one on the line. He became increasingly annoyed at the interruptions as the day went on, and his polite phone voice began to shift in tone. This went on throughout the whole session, during tunes, between tunes, as he'd be talking about where he learned the tune. Jim caught all that on a 10.5-inch reel using his Revox, a semi-professional recorder with top-of-the-line specs.[57] Caldwell played hornpipes, schottisches, and reels; he did not play much of the traditional southern mountain music repertoire. He set up his music stand, flipped through his sheets until something caught his fancy, and demonstrated a gift at fiddling.[58] Caldwell, Jim remembered, would place a penknife under his fiddle's bridge. He said it made the sound "keener," though Jim recalled it merely added a buzz to the fiddle's sound.

* * *

Jim's field recordings were sometimes informal, often accomplished on a machine that turned out 5- or 7-inch reels. The tapes frequently captured much in the way of background noise and other signs of life transpiring while the recording session proceeded. Jim had a good appreciation of field recording techniques and was attentive to what he had to do with the technologies of the day to achieve decent sound quality—but it seemed he was always more intent on staying in the moment with the elder fiddler or the distinguished old banjo player than waiting for the noise to cease. Beginning in the mid–1960s, Jim became adept at working his way into the middle of a jam with a directional microphone at fiddlers' conventions such as Union Grove.

Jim looked at the field recordings he made in the late 1960s and early 1970s as both a resource that could help him learn more tunes and a way to pick up hints about how his elders worked their way through particular tunes, but also as his own modest attempt to preserve something of the old music by fiddlers who had learned their music way before he did. "I knew I wanted to preserve the music. Everything was passing, dissolving. Everything I was interested in was going away." The work of Alan Jabbour, and the Folkways albums that Jim and his Uncle Bob had borrowed from the local library—and worn grooves in while listening to them over and over again— were a catalyst for Jim's own attempts to capture the fiddling and banjo playing of Appalachian Masters he had met over the years at Union Grove, Galax, and else- where. Jim recognized that his field recording efforts were a modest gesture toward preserving the old music, and that there was more music lost to history than there were tunes preserved by field recorders. That added an air of mystery, a special qual- ity, to the tunes that field recorders failed to capture in their recording work. In the last quarter of 2020 Jim remembered that Clyde Williams played a tune called "Going Uptown" in a completely unique way. "He had a bow hop that I just could not get." Clyde's version of that tune was just never captured on recordings of Williams' music made by fellow musicians. In one video of Williams that Ruth Wherry made, Wil- liams played the tune but not the way he used to play it, not the special way that Jim remembered. Jim recalled that lot of people around Charlotte played a second part of the tune "Going Uptown" that sounded a little like a portion of the tune "Ragtime Annie," but Williams' own recipe for fiddling the tune was never captured on tape.[59]

Union Grove, Jim's Learning Platform

The Union Grove Fiddlers' Convention started out in 1929 as a way of raising money for the local school. The fiddlers' convention was, in effect, a melting pot for younger, aspiring old-time musicians where they could be immersed in a mixture of early bluegrass and traditional mountain music.[60] From at least 1958 to 1970, the Annual Old Time Fiddlers' Convention did not include a "single performer" com- petition. Bands were divided into two "classes"—Old-Time and Modern. Bands or musicians who used "any electric instrument" were automatically placed in the "Modern Band" category, even if they intended to play old-time tunes in the com- petition. Band leaders were "instructed to feature fiddle, banjo, and guitar players as bands perform," and judges were expected to select the best three bands in the two categories—"Old-Time and Modern"—and to determine the best three individual fiddle, banjo and guitar players across the entire population of competitors.

Beginning in 1958, the Union Grove festival ran two competitions, one in the Gymnasium and one in the Auditorium, awarding prizes in the Old Time Band and the Modern Band categories, and honoring winners for "violin and banjo" in each of these two competitions. In 1961, the festival began referring to the Gymnasium competition as the "Afternoon Session," and the Auditorium competition as the "Night Session." In 1968, the fiddlers' convention "Instructions to Judges" excluded "Rock and Roll" bands from the competition and eliminated brass and drums from the list of permitted instruments. In 1970, the Union Grove contests were organized into World Championship competitions in five categories: "Old-Time Bands," "Bluegrass Bands," "Modern Bands," "Instrumentalists"—fiddle, banjo, guitar, mandolin—and "Single Performers."

Jim described how the decision was made in the early 1970s to level the playing field at the Union Grove festival so that the old-time category of musicians would stand a chance against the flashy, louder, and more modern bluegrass banjo players. He recalled having the distinct sense that by the early 1970s, a Scruggs-style banjo player would almost always win against an old-time clawhammer banjo player whose banjo playing just sounded "clunky" against the three finger up-picking style. Through the early 1970s, Union Grove provided for a "Modern" and "Old-Time" category in the competitions, but those like Jim who remembered the festival from the early 1960s came to think that by allowing pianos and electric instruments and rockabilly bands to compete, the festival had taken a turn toward being more "like an amateur show" than a fiddlers' convention.

By the early 1970s, some old-time festivals had begun to differentiate between groups competing in the old-time clawhammer style and three-finger Scruggs style. Fiddling contests were not really bifurcated in this same way, and sometimes the two styles—old-time and bluegrass—met in the context of a fiddle contest. Musicians who attended Union Grove and competed in festival contests in those days recalled that the master fiddler of the late 1960s at Union Grove was Clark Kessinger from Charleston, West Virginia. Kessinger often used Gene Meade, a Scruggs-style banjo player, to back up his fiddling, and a strong guitar player, Wayne Hauser, who played bluegrass style runs between the chord changes in the tune.

The 46th Annual Union Grove (1970) was the first at Pierce Van Hoy's farm. Spark Gap Wonder Boys won first prize. The Constitutional Wiretappers—John Burke on fiddle, Jim Watson on guitar—won second prize. The Fuzzy Mountain String Band took fourth place. Roger Sprung won for banjo. Tom Edwards won for guitar. Joe Drye won for fiddle. The New Deal String Band competed that year, though available information did not reveal whether they placed. By 1971, Jim recalled, musicians from Virginia, North Carolina, South Carolina, and Tennessee who were involved in managing and sustaining the convention made the decision to reorganize the contest into two categories of competition: bluegrass and old-time, and to eliminate the long-standing proviso that bands could deploy electric instruments, but that those bands would automatically be classed as "Modern" bands even if they played old-time music.[61]

Pierce Van Hoy called a meeting in 1971 to discuss a change of rules for the contests at Union Grove. Van Hoy was joined by James Mathis—the principal at Union Grove School who later moved to another school in Granite Quarry, North Carolina; Pat Ahrens; Olin Gardner; and Jim.[62] The gathering at Van Hoy's home was a "relaxed event." The four friends may have shared a meal together. They batted ideas around. Pat Ahrens may have taken notes. Jim's position was the old-time banjo pickers simply could not compete with Scruggs style players. Clawhammer was a "whole different idiom," and should not be judged against standards by which musicians playing three fingered picking were evaluated. The judges, Jim observed, were—at least initially—mostly high school music teachers who did not necessarily have a good grasp of the music, or a sense of the two different styles. Van Hoy decided to get rid of the "modern" category. Bluegrass became a separate category.[63] Shortly after the Union Grove rule change, other local contests adopted the same altered rules. Jim said:

> The judges in those times were the band teachers in the school. They didn't know bluegrass from beans or apple butter. Most of it was if the musician was dressed nice, they won, or how loud the audience applauded. Still, that was wrong because the poor old-time musicians got out there and played their hearts out and never got anything. And Galax got on the bandwagon, cut out electric instruments, too.[64]

The new set of rules for the "World's Championship Winners" competition, and new contests divisions that eliminated the "Modern Band" category, were deployed for the first time at the 47th annual Union Grove Old Time Fiddlers' Convention in 1971. That year the contests were organized into two "Divisions." The individual winner in the "Old-Time Division" was awarded a World's Champion ribbon. First, second, and third prizes were awarded to old-time bands. In the "Bluegrass Division," there was also an individual World's Champion ribbon. First, second, and third prizes were given to bluegrass bands. The "Single Performer Division" recognized a "World Champion" and awarded three additional ribbons to performers for first, second, and third prize in that "Division." The Best Instrumentalists Division awarded prizes in the "Bluegrass Category" and the "Old-Time Category." In the Bluegrass Category, the awards went to "World Champions" in fiddle, banjo, guitar, and mandolin. In the Old-Time Category, the awards went to "World Champions" in fiddle and banjo.[65] Clark Kessinger won the title "world champion fiddler" at the 1971 Union Grove contest. The first runner-up was Clyde Williams of the Mole Hill Highlanders. In 1971, the contest took place at the old Union Grove School. The decision to split the contest into "Old-Time" and "Bluegrass" categories meant that if a musician played in the bluegrass band competition, that person could not enter the old-time band competition.[66] There was no separate banjo contest. Musicians who played as a band were rated individually by the judges and scored according to their prowess on their instruments.[67]

Jim recalled that his band, the Mole Hill Highlanders—Clyde Williams and Mark Wingate, who played twin fiddlers; Chuck Dunlop on guitar; Jim Whitley on bass,[68] and Jim Scancarelli on banjo—won second runner up in the 1970 Union Grove band competition, playing "The Possum Hunter's Step Dance," captured on the Union Grove Talking Machine Records album SS-4, "Union Grove: Hub of the Universe."[69] The Mole Hill Highlanders competed in the 1971 contest at Union Grove and were on the 1971 Union Grove album playing "Chinese Breakdown."[70] In 1971, at Union Grove, Jim earned a ribbon in the contests.[71] As he put it:

> I actually got second place and I thought the second prize [was] for the banjo but it said on the ribbon "Special Performance" and I don't know why they did that unless they wanted to give me something because I was putting the record out. I got every banjo prize except first at Galax,

not because I was any good but they used to have it set up so that you had to play twice and the
banjo competition on Friday ran so late that the old-time guys like Kyle Creed, Wade Ward
and all those fellows went to sleep so they got disqualified. That's how I ended up getting my
prizes—by default.[72]

The Union Grove Talking Machine Records

Jim recorded the Union Grove band contests for the Van Hoy family beginning
in 1967, captured some of the parking lot jam music, and some interviews with performers.[73] Charlie Faurot, who did a lot of work for Dave Freeman's County Sales,
undertook a good deal of recording at Union Grove up to about 1967, the first
year that Jim put out a record of the festival music under the Union Grove Talking
Machine Records label. Fiddlers' convention attendees recall that in the course of
doing his audio work for Union Grove, Jim developed the habit of hanging around
with a very fancy portable tape recorder that he used to produce the official festival album. By then, Jim was himself a fixture at Union Grove and other festivals, and
from time to time competed as a clawhammer banjo player and fiddler in bands that
took the stage at these festivals.[74] Jim recalled:

[Charlie Faurot] happened to be there at Union Grove the first time in the 1960s that I put out
a record. I think it was like 1967. [...] I got the tapes and things from him. I think we had to
buy them. We put out the record from those. I had rented a Nagra, a professional monoaural
tape recorder. Movie companies used that kind of recorder because it was portable, and battery
powered; it was a very high-quality machine at the time. I would wander around out in the field
with the Senheiser shotgun microphone hooked up to the Nagra and I could record a band at a
moment's notice. I would go from stage recordings to field recordings.[75]

Terry Black shot the photos for the first Union Grove album (SS-1, the 43rd
Annual Old Time Fiddlers' Convention, 1967). The second album (SS-2, the 44th
Annual Old Time Fiddlers' Convention, 1968) featured Uncle Henry Van Hoy on the
fiddle on the album's front cover. Jim did the sketch of Wade Ward that appears on
the third album (SS-3, the 45th Annual Old Time Fiddlers' Convention, 1969). Jim's
sketch on the fourth album (SS-4, the 46th Annual Old Time Fiddlers' Convention,
1970) depicted three musicians: Chick Martin armed with a banjo, a "generic" old
fiddler, and Johnny Hilt, with fiddle in hand, who was 90 years old when Jim knew
him. Mark Sanderford shot the photo of Clark Kessinger on the front of the fifth
Union Grove album (SS-5, the 47th Annual Old Time Fiddlers' Convention, 1970),
as well as the photo on the back cover of the album of Wade Ward's final resting
place with his hat perched on the grave marker, and his banjo in the background.
The sixth and the seventh albums (SS-6, 1971 and SS-7, 1972)—highlighting music
from the 48th and 49th Annual Old Time Fiddlers' Convention—used design graphics and type styles that boasted bold colors with the goal of improving album sales.
A photograph of L.W. Lambert's band graces the front of the eighth Union Grove
album issued in honor of the 50th anniversary of the festival (SS-8, 1973). That anniversary album was assembled from tapes in a cardboard box found by Pierce Van
Hoy's wife in their home.[76] Jim selected reels that captured the music at the 1955 festival, edited the taped music, cleaned up the sound by re-recording the tapes through

a frequency balance control equalizer, adjusting the treble or bass as necessary. In doing the re-recording work, Jim compensated for mistakes made in the field recording process when the recorder was started or stopped in a way that cut into tunes in progress. To fill out the anniversary album, Jim selected tunes played on recordings he made at the 1962, 1965 and 1971 Union Grove conventions, from the "Union Grove archives."[77] The ninth Union Grove album (SS-9, 1974), recorded at the 50th annual Old Time Fiddlers' Convention, is an "artsy" depiction of a fiddler. Joe Abernathy—not a fiddler—was selected as the subject, probably because his good looks, rangy appearance, suitably casual haircut and moustache. With a fiddle drawn into the portrait, Abernathy looked like the archetype of a string band revival fiddler. The front of the 10th Union Grove album (SS-10, the 51st Annual Old Time Fiddlers' Convention, 1975) has a drawing of a "cartoon fiddler" by Jim. The back of the album cover sports a drawing of a "cartoon banjo player" that was also done by Jim. The front cover of the 11th Union Grove album, the last in the series of Union Grove LPs that Jim produced, is a picture taken at the festival by *The Charlotte Observer* photographer Don Sturkey. The back cover is a photograph taken on the stage, looking toward the audience in the festival's big circus tent, that showed two musicians from behind: George Pegram and his banjo on the left, and on the right Red Parham, playing guitar, both of the men leaning into a single microphone. They performed "Home Sweet Home," the 3rd cut on the 11th album (SS-11, the 52nd Annual Old Time Fiddlers' Convention, 1976).[78]

Jim served as the go-between in the relationship involving Pierce Van Hoy and the Wakefield Recording Company that was initially engaged to do the work of pressing the Union Grove records. Jim and Chuck Dunlop compiled festival stage recordings, contest music, and jam music, and constructed the master tape. At some point, perhaps in the early 1970s, when Union Grove became too frenetic and crowded for Jim's taste, he asked his cousin Doug Deal to do some of the recording work. Jim remembered Doug telling him that he was out in the field recording and someone came up to him and tried to sell him drugs. Jim had no desire to be around any of that. At some point, the crew that filmed at Woodstock was engaged to do some of the work on an annual audio project for the Union Grove festival. The last Union Grove convention that Jim attended was in 1976.

Conclusion

Wade Hargrove, a Union Grove contest judge in 1971, recalled that he and his wife Sandy, and their friend and fellow contest judge Wade Smith, were walking around the schoolhouse area at the Union Grove convention when they heard a loudspeaker announcement that the convention organizers needed a lawyer, and if any were in the area, would they kindly come to the schoolhouse area. Hargrove recounted that both he and Smith laughed in amazement, never having imagined that they would witness one of those famed "Is There a Lawyer in the House" pleas for assistance.

As it happened, the local sheriff's department had begun policing up young convention attendees for infractions of the laws pertaining to the consumption of alcohol and, as the two lawyers recalled, drug use. The sheriff's department had begun processing those who were arrested on a school bus on the convention grounds. The law enforcement officials had informed convention organizers that the arrested Union Grove attendees needed lawyers so Smith, a criminal lawyer, and Hargrove, a media lawyer, responded by lending their legal skills on behalf of the Union Grove convention.[79]

Jim's recollection was that by that point, Union Grove became a bit of a rough and rowdy scene, increasingly fueled by drugs, drink, amplified by the presence of motorcycle gangs. The festival was trending toward a scene that was definitely not what Jim appreciated about the traditional music gatherings.[80] Decades later, musicians recalled that the Union Grove in the early 1970s was a mad house, with crowds often approaching 50,000 people. One story suggested that the reason for this was that the local authorities had banned rock and roll festivals, so thousands of young people looking for a good time showed up at Union Grove, and the convention became a combination of old-time music and bluegrass jamming into the small hours, along with the acid rock emanating from car radios. By 1972, according to what might be apocryphal stories by musicians who were at Union Grove for that year's fiddlers' convention, the number of festival attendees had doubled, and the event began to present significant challenges to the local community in terms of traffic control issues and transgressions against law and order by convention attendees, so the authorities stepped in and banned it. By then, from Jim's perspective, Union Grove was no longer the springtime gathering that offered a few days of refuge from work and obligations, and a chance for nonstop music in the embrace of like-minded old-time and bluegrass music enthusiasts.[81]

Four

Making Music

Introduction

Jim Whitley graduated from high school in 1966. He won a full scholarship to Wake Forest University to study Latin. At some point in 1967, Whitley posted a notice at Wake Forest looking for musicians, and that led him to Thom Case.

Mark Wingate spent the summer of 1968 in Winston Salem, hooked up with Whitley and Case, and played tunes at a coffee house in the area.[1] Wingate met Jim Scancarelli at The Festival in the Park in Charlotte in 1966, after Wingate graduated from high school.

Chuck Dunlop moved to the Charlotte area in late 1969 and posted a note on several university bulletin boards seeking bluegrass musicians.[2] Not long after that, Wingate knocked on Dunlop's office door in response to that note.[3]

Around that time, Wingate had heard that there was a fiddle player who lived nearby named Clyde Williams. Wingate reached out to Williams and asked if he could visit with some musician friends.[4] At the time, Williams was not playing with anybody, so Wingate, Jim Scancarelli, Jim Whitley and Darrell Gray very quickly formed a band around Clyde Williams. By 1970, that band had crystallized into the Mole Hill Highlanders.[5] Chuck Dunlop came later on and became the band's guitar picker. By then, Darrell Gray had bowed out of the band.

Clyde Williams and the Origins of the Mole Hill Highlanders

Williams was in his late forties when he started trading tunes with the twenty-year-old musicians who formed the Mole Hill Highlanders. To those young musicians, he seemed to be a real old fiddler. Williams had learned many of his tunes listening to the Grand Ole Opry on his living room radio, and he favored the music of the Gully Jumpers, the Skillet Lickers, and Humphrey Bate and His Possum Hunters. He paid close attention to the Grand Ole Opry fiddle tunes; when a song came on the air, he would turn down the volume and practice the tune he had just heard.[6]

Jim explained the origins of the band's name:

The reason we called the band the Mole Hill Highlanders was, well, Clyde lived in this part of town called Mole Hill. I think it changed names over time. He lived on the Old Plank Road. The reason it was called a plank road was back in the 1800s they laid boards instead of having a paved highway, and I think it went up to Winston-Salem; it was an old wagon road. The

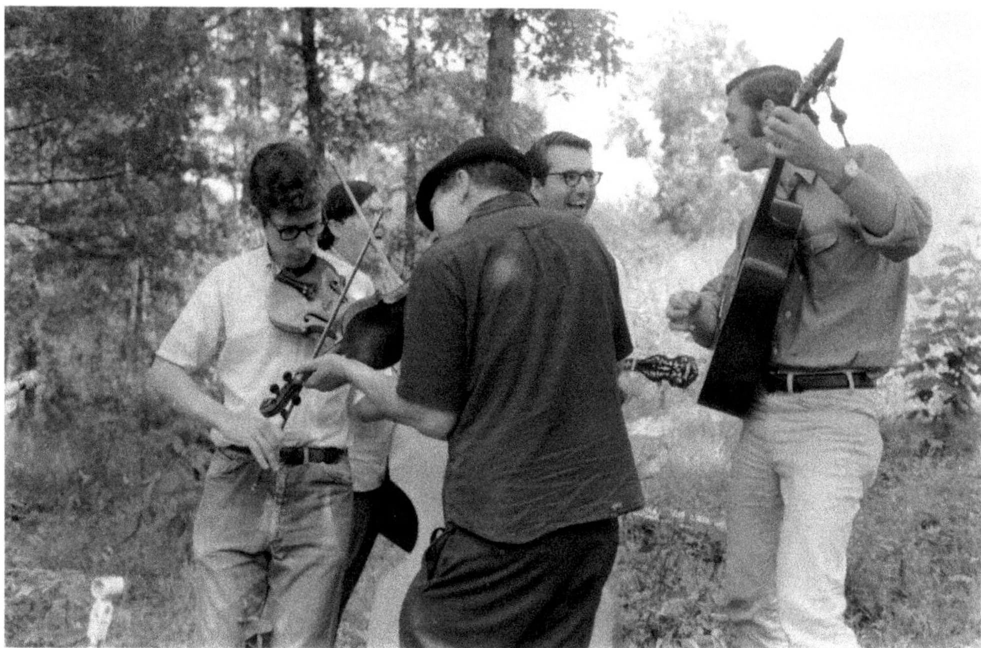

The Mole Hill Highlanders, circa 1969, in Huntersville, North Carolina. Left to right: Mark Wingate (fiddle), Jim Whitley (bass), Clyde Williams (fiddle), Jim Scancarelli (banjo), Chuck Dunlop (guitar). Courtesy of Jim Scancarelli.

band used to get into these horrendous arguments about, oh, "this is the way a tune should be" and "no, it doesn't sound right that way" … and those would go on and on and on. We'd make mountains out of molehills, and there it was, the right name for that band. One time we got a booking, and I didn't know what to tell them when they asked for the band's name, so I said we're the Mole Hill Highlanders, because we made mountains out of mole hills, and we played Scottish music—that's the Highlanders part. So, the name stuck.[7]

Beyond being captivated by the old fiddling he heard on the Grand Ole Opry, Chuck Dunlop recalled that Williams had long been taken with the sound of the Grand Ole Opry "horn" that George D. Hay, the "Solemn Old Judge," blew at the beginning of each show back in the 1940s.[8] Williams made several attempts to build himself a similar horn that could replicate that sound he heard on the Opry broadcasts. Sometime in the early 1970s the band was driving to Virginia, to the Beulah School fiddlers' convention. As Jim told the story, the band got lost and ended up driving in the dusk hours over rolling hills on the Virginia side of the border. At a high point on that road, Charlotte was visible in the distance. When they reached that point, Williams shouted to stop the car. He got out of the vehicle, reached into his luggage and pulled out one of those horns. By then, the other band members had disembarked from the car and followed Williams to the edge of the road. There, Williams blew that horn, getting an echo that pleased him. The band piled back into the car, and they drove on.[9]

Chuck Dunlop noted that Williams attempted to reproduce that horn several times without ever feeling that he had gotten it quite right.[10] At some point, perhaps in the early–mid–1970s, Dunlop received a thickly-wrapped package in the mail containing a handmade wooden object, about 18 inches long, with a slot on the top and a mouthpiece at one end. The back of that wooden object, finished with a mustard-colored stain, bore the inscription: "Built by Clyde L. Williams for Chuck Dunlop." A short time later, Dunlop began hosting a two-hour long bluegrass radio show on the local NPR station, WFBE, in Flint, Michigan. Dunlop was given a free hand to play tracks from his vinyl record collection and provide whatever commentary came to mind. During one show Dunlop deployed Williams' device, giving it a good, long blow on the air, and invited listeners to guess what it was. Some callers identified it as a Coke bottle, and others as a jug. Dunlop recalled that just as the show was coming to an end, a woman called the radio station and in a distinctive Southern drawl she confidently proclaimed, "I do believe that's the horn that the Solemn Old Judge used to blow on the Grand Ole Opry." That phone call eliminated any doubt about whether Clyde Williams had managed to replicate the sound he recalled hearing on the radio during the Grand Ole Opry shows.[11]

Whitley played a conventional bass fiddle in the band, but he also played a three-string bass that Clyde Williams built out of plywood. Chuck Dunlop remembered that Williams had a 55-gallon oil drum in his backyard, in which he lit a fire and concocted an apparatus to heat wood for bending into shape as the sides of the fiddle—the upper, middle and lower bouts. As for the strings, Clyde's view was that only three were truly necessary for the music the Mole Hill Highlanders played, so why bother with a fourth? Dunlop stated that Williams had not finished the homemade bass when the band first started playing with him, so Jim Whitley would have used a conventional model at first, which of course would have had four strings.[12] Jim Scancarelli recalled the "oversized doghouse bass" that Williams built as being about the size of a doghouse. It was larger, taller, wider than a conventional bass fiddle, and was essentially in the shape of a bass—though Williams did not manage to duplicate the traditional curvatures of the bass in the manner he rigged together to bend heated wood for the sides of the bass. The neck, Jim recalled, was immense, and thick, and it was only because Jim Whitley had pretty big hands that he was able to play the instrument. Williams took some liberties with the traditions of neck carving. For example, he fashioned the scroll out of a series of disks of wood of graduated sizes that he glued together. Some of those disks might have given up the ghost and

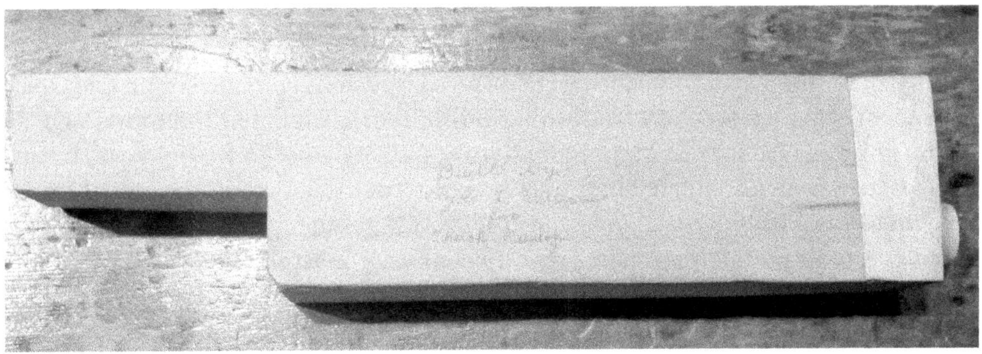

Clyde Williams' "Opry horn," no date. Photograph courtesy Chuck Dunlop.

fallen away by the time the bass was deployed in the Mole Hill Highlander stage performances. Jim's memory was that Williams painted the bass red and yellow, and that he did indeed make the bass a three string instrument largely because of his sense that the fourth string was rarely used, did not add anything to the music, and would thus not be missed.[13] Mark Wingate concurred with that recollection, noting that it reflected the two aspects of Clyde Williams' approach to the music: the tendency to make things up as he went along, and a real practical streak that often led him to do things "Clyde's way." Jim Scancarelli recalled that Jim Whitley got a strong, robust bass sound out of the three-string bass fiddle. He played coherent, complete runs on it, and he managed to hit the last note of a musical phrase in a way that conveyed the tune to the next part. "Whitley extracted music from that homemade bass," at least in part because his big hands managed to wrap around that neck and pull music from it in a way that more average sized mitts would have found too difficult.[14]

* * *

The Mole Hill Highlander band members shared an interest in local musical elders. Mark Wingate recalled that Jim Whitley made contact with some local musicians, one of whom was a guitar player named Rex Hodges. "He was almost blind if not legally blind. He played the guitar and idolized the Stanley Brothers."[15] Hodges had played with some of the older musicians in town, including Harold Haymore, so he introduced Whitley to Haymore. Through that network of musicians, Wingate met Johnny Ham. Wingate recalled:

> It is significant to me that these guys—Red Haymore and Johnny Ham—who were pre-bluegrass fiddlers, landed in the tradition in much different ways. Harold Haymore was born in the 1890s; he was a young man when the depression hit. He made his living at a time when country music was getting recorded on 78s but before the modern era of communications and technology, a time when different dynamics, different forces shaped regional and community music.

Haymore and Ham, Wingate observed, had different starting points:

> Haymore learned tunes from his mother, who may have even played the banjo. He really only played one tune that I remember he learned from his mother, a hymn tune or ballad. The point being, he was learning from his mother, his family—presumably his mother had learned from the family, so there is this sort of romantic notion of people handing music down from generation to generation and certainly that has occurred. But Haymore was probably the only person I have known that was really in that stream.[16]

Johnny Ham, and Clyde Williams, were inspired by listening to the Grand Ole Opry. Haymore's starting point in traditional fiddle music predated the Opry, and 78 records. He was from Pilot Mountain in Surry County close to Round Peak, meaning that he was firmly situated in the geographic space that defined a regional sound recognized as "Round Peak" music, a tradition that encompasses the region that includes Mt. Airy, Pilot Mountain, and the Galax area of Virginia. Wingate observed:

> Harold Haymore was not a professional musician but when this new world came—the new world that radio stations with hillbilly bands brought into being—Harold Haymore got with some of the other musicians and eventually had a radio show of his own in Winston Salem. He and his contemporaries probably had some sort of unbroken tradition, playing music for

community dances. It wasn't about getting on a stage and putting on a performance for paying customers. That became the pattern after the recordings came into being.

Haymore was a plasterer. He learned the trade and must have been good at it because he told Wingate stories about big plastering jobs he undertook in West Virginia. "He would hire a crew to work with him—and he would make sure if possible that they were musicians. They'd play music together when they would go on these jobs." By the time Wingate and his friends met him in the 1960s, Haymore "already had this family experience of getting started in music and valuing music as part of his actual family and cultural heritage." Wingate continued:

> Haymore had embraced radio and avidly listened to musical broadcasts. In the 1940s, he and his band would go down to a furniture store and cut records. They'd get the band together, warm up, record, and listen to themselves on record. So, he embraced that and by the time we met him he had already discovered Tommy Jackson recordings and was learning tunes off Tommy Jackson records, tunes that he would play in his own style. Plus, he would play the pop tunes like "You Gotta See Momma Every Night or She Won't Be Home When You Come," "Twelfth Street Rag," "Blues in My Mind." He would change things as he learned them. One of my favorites was a tune that we called "Something's Gonna Jump Out of the Bushes and Grab You" because it had a particular note that sounded like it was blues. Haymore didn't have a name for it, so we referred to it as "Somebody's Gonna…" because it had that odd part where it lingered on the flatted seventh note.[17]

At some point during those years, the fiddler Tommy Magness passed through town and went to one of those sessions where Haymore and his fellow musicians were making records at a furniture store. Wingate said: "One of the records I have is Tommy Magness playing 'Lost Indian,' but the band improvised a skit where Haymore introduces the tune, and it is Magness playing the fiddle, though on the recording it appears to be Haymore. It's just a humorous skit that took advantage of the characteristics of the recording—you could kind of create special effects if you want to call it that. You couldn't do that in a live performance. That always stuck out as kind of interesting." To Wingate, that skit underscored the fact that people conceived of music differently in days before recording technologies:

> Music then was something that actually existed in our brains. Like the difference between spackling from a plastic cup and mixing plaster of Paris the old way. There's been a loss of faith that we can connect to something beyond ourselves. We have to learn from something that is already out there. I think that goes to the point of where fiddle players entered the story and navigated the stream. Whether they entered the stream before technologies made communications and transportation instantaneous or entered the stream after 78s came into being. When we met Haymore, he was happy someone was interested in his music. He had a little notebook in which he kept a list of the tunes he played. His daughter must have helped put that together. I never had a copy of that. A few traditional tunes he learned from just growing up around them—maybe a dozen.[18] The rest of his repertoire was popular music, Tommy Jackson tunes and bluegrass. He was indiscriminate. He just learned anything that appealed to him.[19]

Haymore mentioned two musicians to Wingate and his musical friends that he felt the young men should meet. One was named Frank Freeman, an eccentric but evidently a skilled five-string banjo player. Johnny Ham was the other.[20]

Johnny Ham came to music in a different context, at a point in the "stream" after Haymore found his way to fiddling in local string bands. A shy and reclusive man whose father was a successful businessman, Ham lived just outside of Winston Salem in the midst of a rural farming community. Wingate said:

> Johnny listened to the Grand Ole Opry. He became a devotee of Fiddling Arthur Smith. Like Clyde Williams, he was obsessed with the Gully Jumpers, the Fruit Jar Drinkers, the Possum Hunters—Tennessee square dance music. Smith was the Earl Scruggs of the fiddle. He was saying, in his radio shows, in his performances, that fiddling can be about virtuosity, creativity—tunes could be made up. Fans wrote in to name original tunes he created—that was a process. And he was using radio in a unique way. Because Smith had extraordinary fiddling skills, he was able to incorporate jazz and pop influences, and black influences. However, at the same time, he was a great traditional fiddler.[21]

Ham learned all the tunes Smith had played, and many tunes from other Opry fiddlers. So, for Ham—and for Clyde Williams, too—the Grand Ole Opry was their major source of tunes.[22]

Clyde Williams' Point in the "Stream"

Roy Acuff joined the Grand Ole Opry in 1938, a point that represented the beginning of the ascendency of singer-based band formats. For Clyde Williams, that was the end of an era, the beginning of a trend toward singer-focused Opry entertainment that squeezed out the fiddle tunes–focused string bands. In Mark Wingate's words:

> To Clyde, this was a sea change and an insult, a bad step in a bad direction. He considered Roy Acuff and singers as being in category with Sinatra and Crosby—a step into popular music, and away from the traditional music that he cherished and which he thought was a heritage that should not be turned away from, that should instead be embraced and encouraged.[23]

Williams, Wingate observed, was a man of "fierce intelligence" who thought and spoke about traditional fiddling in a manner that captured both the abstractions and specific conceptual meaning of archaic fiddling traditions—without necessarily having the precise vocabulary that could propel those notions forward. Williams, Wingate explained, "perceived a complexity and depth in this music that resonated with his intellect, his artistic vision, and I think he just knew in a flash that there was something in this music of intrinsic value."[24] Wingate continued:

> He wasn't equipped culturally to use his mental horsepower, but it would spill out anyway. To a certain extent I think the value that he placed on the fiddle music came from his personal position in life. He was from a real lower working-class family, cotton mill workers who never had much money at all, no access to education. I think he perceived a disparity in his place in society. He felt different from his family and marginalized from the rest of society—he thought that he was looked down on and considered a hillbilly.[25]

Williams probably thought of the Anglo-Saxon origins of this music as a central testimony to the value of that heritage. He "embraced" that identity—possibly in a manner that shunted aside the relevance for his life of his partly Native American origin and imputed an idealized importance to life in the "mountains," which he saw as the native home of this music. He was in the U.S. Army during the Korean War years and may have been posted to an assignment in the United Kingdom. He came back to the U.S. at the end of that assignment with recordings of Irish fiddle music, and a deepened affinity for that music.

Williams' fiddling was unique, and his way of organizing a band sound around his fiddling placed a primacy on sharply delineated roles for band members manning banjo and bass and guitar. Wingate remembered Williams' penchant for orchestrating traditional tunes around a "leap beat," a term that the Mole Hill Highlanders band members learned from Williams. Sometimes Williams referred to this as adding an "extra chord" to the mix. Wingate explained that the "leap beat" involved playing a chord that was not necessarily integral to the tune in a manner that anticipated the downbeat. Williams' practice of having the band hit that "extra" chord early introduced a bit more syncopation into the equation. Clyde heard this technique used by the Possum Hunters and was clearly enamored by that band sound.[26]

What is clear is that Clyde Williams had a particular recipe in mind for string band music that shaped the Mole Hill Highlander sound. He appeared to have had a model in mind, based on how he recalled the music of the band called Humphrey Bate and His Possum Hunters—and possibly (though secondarily) what he remembered of the playing of the Gully Jumpers and the Skillet Lickers. He wanted strong rhythmic guitar playing focused on straight chords for the Mole Hill Highlanders band; as Chuck Dunlop recalled, "Clyde made it clear that he did not want to hear any runs played on the guitar!"[27] Williams wanted Jim Scancarelli to play the banjo with a pick; to Williams, that yielded a close approximation of what Humphry Bate's banjo player got out of his five-string. Jim recalled that Humphrey Bate's band had a tenor banjo player in the lineup. The band also had one fiddler, one guitar player, a bowed bass player. That band's sound was what Williams wanted in his own band, a sound with a heavy beat; how Williams remembered that band's sound shaped Williams' thinking about the way the banjo player should contribute to the sound of the Mole Hill Highlanders.[28]

Basically, Williams wanted Jim to play banjo in a way that was more percussive than it was melodic.[29] To Jim, his job on the banjo was to avoid stepping on the melody played by the fiddler. Jim was playing the banjo clawhammer style, trying to play in that down-picking method more sparsely than melodically. Jim's banjo playing provided the rhythmic basis for a good deal of the Mole Hill Highlander's approach to string band music. Whether he stayed on the melody or directed his attention to counter melody to complement what Clyde Williams was doing on the fiddle, Jim's timing contributed to the band's drive.[30] Jim showed himself to be perfectly capable of playing melody in the numerous banjo contests he entered over the decades of his music making at festivals such as Galax and Union Grove. In the Mole Hill Highlanders, though, his usual approach was to leave the melody to the lead fiddler. Dunlop stressed that for Williams, it was an article of faith that the melody was essential and needed to be carried by the fiddle. In the end, according to Dunlop, "even though Jim was not usually playing recognizable melodies in our band, his banjo was a prominent instrument—much easier to hear than the guitar. And his timing was perfect, exactly on the beat. That's what prompted me to think of his banjo as a 'rhythm instrument' in the Mole Hill Highlanders."[31]

Wingate recalled conversations between Williams and Jim Scancarelli that aimed at trying to figure out how to get to that particular band sound. To Wingate, though, the notion that Williams had of the Possum Hunters might have been something that existed in Williams' mind and memory in an "idealized form." Williams may not have been remembering what the Possum Hunters played but was instead hearing what Williams would have played to get to that particular sound:

> Clyde is remembering his experience of hearing the Possum Hunters on the radio, not on a phonograph that you could repeat, so it was a fleeting impression. It is a different experience to hear something that is not going to be repeated. Can't just put the needle back to repeat it so your frame of mind will be different. Clyde remembered the deliciousness of hearing this over the airwaves on his radio and he wanted to recreate that with his band. He wanted to be able to create a sound that would enable him as the fiddle player to experience that moment again.[32]

This, Wingate averred, is a kind of idealized music, and Williams did not have the musical vocabulary necessary to formulate his views in ways that might have represented those ideas musically. At the same time, Jim Scancarelli—and the rest of the Mole Hill Highlanders—probably did not have the musical vocabulary necessary to integrate those notions that animated what Williams remembered of the music of the Possum Hunters into their band sound, even if Williams had succeeded in transmitting his ideas about Bate's band sound. As Jim Scancarelli saw things, Williams was not playing what he thought he heard. He was playing what he remembered, but he was also playing what he wanted to play. As Jim put it: "The Mole Hill Highlanders did not play what we heard; we played what we had in our hearts."[33] Williams' memory of the string bands of yesteryear that he admired might not have actually matched the music played by bands such as the Possum Hunters, but the "memory" of that music that stuck with Williams led to a Mole Hill Highlander sound that had a lot of "color" to it, as Dunlop put it. Wingate described the Mole Hill Highlander music in terms that suggest at least a vague similarity to what Walt Koken has characterized as "trance music."[34]

> If Clyde reached a certain ecstatic point, then he would not end the tune. He was in charge of ending the tune, and he would not end it. It's like low temperature electrons. If you bring things close enough to absolute zero, it is like a frictionless system. Like perpetual motion. Clyde would achieve this ecstatic state, the band would lock into a groove, and Clyde would lock into something in his brain where he felt weightless, frictionless. We would play a tune for ten minutes … ten minutes! That's the way we remember it.[35]

Wingate suggested that his recollections of playing with Williams were probably just as subjective as Williams' recollections of listening to the Opry, adding that he was probably too involved in the music they were playing in the 1970s to recall the experience now, decades later, in "objective" terms:

> My experience of trying to play fiddle with Clyde is also kind of a mysterious unknown space to me because I was both trying to learn the tunes and play something complementary to him at the same time, without stepping on the tune. I either wanted to play in unison with him which I could not always do because he was in a sense improvising and not playing it exactly the same way every time—he was exploring. But I also tried to harmonize at times. That's a tricky thing to do. Without changing the music into something different than where you started. You want to make people glad that you're playing harmony, you don't want people saying, "I wish that second fiddle would stop playing so we could hear Clyde." That was always a judgment call on my part, but I wasn't completely aware of it because I was "building the airplane while it's in the

air." That was my experience of playing with Clyde. Because the only time you could play with Clyde was when you were playing with Clyde. We could have taped the tunes and gone back and studied, to be prepared for the next session, do our homework—that kind of thing—which is definitely a paradigm that I was oriented towards BUT that is not the way I approached playing with the Mole Hill Highlanders. It's something that I know is possible, and I am doing it more now than I did at several points of my life when I really wanted to analyze what was happening and learn something note for note. It was much more of a gestalt that happened when we were playing with Clyde. With the Mole Hill Highlanders, I didn't want to be in an analytical space. I wanted to be in the space Clyde was in, which I didn't understand but which I definitely respected. For me to go into the left-brain way of approaching playing with Clyde would have been the opposite of the experience that I really wanted at the time. So, none of us knew what was happening, but Clyde was driving the bus. The whole idea was to just go with Clyde. It was a "Whole Clyde Experience" that none of us were really prepared for in the sense that it was something different than our family experience, our school experience, our musical experiences or any other kind of leadership experience. He was our leader into this unknown world.[36]

Wingate suggested that Scotty Stoneman's music may have been on the same order of magnitude in terms of its power and originality, uniqueness and inventiveness, and Jim shared that view of the furious, driving energy that he felt characterized Stoneman's fiddling.[37] In the end, Clyde Williams was Wingate's introduction to fiddle tunes, to "pre-bluegrass" music. All that got Wingate—as well as Jim Scancarelli— interested in the deeper history of the music beyond bluegrass and the commercial offshoots of country music.[38]

A Taste of Mole Hill Highlander Performing Art

Mark Wingate observed that the Mole Hill Highlanders "stole stuff from other bands and put our own spin on it. The Country Gentlemen had a slow-motion 'Cripple Creek' bit that we did our own thing to. That was the main one you could trace directly back to the source. Then there was our Old-Time Radio skit. That was heavily inspired by Arthur Smith's 'Carolina Calling' TV show, especially the Counselors of the Airwaves segment featuring Ralph Smith and Tommy Faile dressed in cap and gown, reading letters seeking Ann Landers–style advice for their hilarious problems. Brilliant stuff."[39]

In the middle of all the chaos of old-time music festivals, the Mole Hill Highlanders often found themselves trying to make good music in parking lot jams. Jim recalled that Wingate worked out a "devilish little system" for the Mole Hill Highlanders during their festival-going days.[40] Dunlop said that it was aimed at "throwing off would-be jammers who wanted to join in with us when we were playing off-stage. The abrupt key changes threw them off and discouraged their participation."[41] Mark Wingate described that system—and thought of it as more of a smart-aleck device than a "devilish little system":

I've waited many years to explain this to someone! I have never had an audience that was
even remotely receptive. Here's how it worked: We would all be set up to play in D or A. Not
ideal for banjo players who wanted C versus G tuning for those keys; that was a trade-off, but
totally worth it. We would choose a D tune we would start with and agree which A tune would
be next. We would launch into the D tune and play until the designated high-signer—me, in

this case—would decide we should change tunes. Here is the trick: When we got back to the beginning of the tune we were playing, I would start playing a different D tune. That was a signal that communicated two things, in a way. First, that after we played this new tune once, we would abruptly start playing the A tune. Second, that when we eventually changed back to D, the "new" tune I used as the signal would be the tune we would go to. So, we had to pay attention and keep some information in "memory" to be used later. It was an algorithm, I guess you could say. It maximized variety and surprise and minimized verbal communication. Example: We would agree to start with, say, "Soldier's Joy" and "Bill Cheatham." The session would go like this: "Soldier's Joy" (X number of times until the spirit moved me), then "Mississippi Sawyer" (1 time). Nobody knew what was coming but me, but everybody adapted on the fly, hopefully catching on before the first chord change. "Mississippi Sawyer" was followed by "Bill Cheatham" (X number of times), then "June Apple" (1 time), then "Mississippi Sawyer" (X number of times), followed by "Goin' Across the Sea" (1 time), followed by "June Apple" (X number of times), then some other A tune (1 time), et cetera, ad nauseum. It could, theoretically, go on forever and probably seemed to, to onlookers. The payoff for us was the enjoyment of the illusion of mental telepathy when the band would suddenly change keys with no nod, yip, look, or other observable signal.[42]

Each time the band would go through this musical sequence on stage, the energy would ratchet up a notch. Wingate remembered pulling this somewhat elaborate stunt one time at Galax. He thought of it as a device that would allow the band to let the energy build instead of stopping between tunes to discuss what to play next. Additionally, Wingate recalled that Clyde Williams was not a part of this routine; this "would have been Mole Hill Highlanders and Friends, minus Clyde." It is not clear whether that "system" was ever captured on a recording of a Mole Hill Highlander session.

Chuck Dunlop remembered one other "trick" that the Mole Hill Highlanders sometimes used while playing the tune "Mississippi Sawyer," a D-tune with a second part that goes to A at several points. Dunlop recalled: "Sometimes, instead of going to A, we would choose some other key, such as C, or—in some instances—we would stop playing altogether and make chicken-cackling sounds for the duration of the A-chord, then resume the tune with our instruments when the tune returned to D." Dunlop credited Jim Whitley as the inspiration behind this Mole Hill Highlander version of the tune "Mississippi Sawyer." He added: "I can remember Whitley shouting out 'Go to C' just before the crucial moment on at least one occasion."[43]

The Mole Hill Highlanders music was a combination of respectable musicianship and frenetic showmanship—"shtick," as Jim called it.

The Radio Stations and Mole Hill Music

Radio stations figured prominently in Jim Scancarelli's life in a way that engrained their identities—their call signs and their signal strength—in his memory. The story of some of those relationships shows the interconnectedness of radio work, local music stores, aspiring local musicians, and record companies—and underscores the way they were central to the lives of performing and recording bands through the 1980s.

WFMX in Statesville, North Carolina, broadcast primarily country music.[44]

Mark Wingate and Jim would visit the station to root around in their holdings of old country bluegrass records, either 78s or 45s that WFMX basically dumped after utilizing them on the air. Jim remembered:

> We hit the treasure trove over there. They had an outbuilding just filled with old rare records. Blue Ridge Recordings, one shot deals, and so we gobbled up as many as we could.[45]

Odell Wood worked at the Statesville radio station. He was the brother of banjo picker A.L. Wood whose band, the Smokey Ridge Boys, occasionally opened for Bill Monroe and the Bluegrass Boys. Tommy Malboeuf—who Jim had met in the mid–1960s and later partnered with in the Sanitary Cafe band—was the fiddle player with A.L. Wood. At some point, perhaps when they became familiar enough with the radio station personalities—after scarfing up old records from the LP graveyard at the radio station—Mark and Jim took a tape recording of the Mole Hill Highlanders to Odell Wood and asked him whether the band could get a half hour of airtime on the station. As Jim recounted the story:

> Odell Wood kind of jumped on it because he said he would get paid whether or not he talked or played records or did nothing. So, we put together a professional tape. We couldn't all get there to the radio station at the same time to do the show live, so we took these tapes that we recorded over in Chuck Dunlop's home to WFMX. I think we did about a dozen shows for WFMX. Finally, the station manager caught on and he said we would have to pay for the time or get knocked off the air. He even gave us a preacher's discount. But we didn't have sufficient funds to do that.[46]

One of the avid listeners for Odell's radio show was J.E. Mainer. When Mainer was on the radio in the 1930s and 1940s, he got hundreds and hundreds of letters in response for station-hosted offers—"send us a letter and get a copy of a photo of Mainer and his band."[47] In Jim's words:

> So, when the Mole Hill Highlanders were on WFMX, the signal did go pretty far. Gus Meade in Washington, D.C., heard us, and that's pretty far. Could have been a freak skip of the radio waves. We had a lot of the Union Grove records that I had recorded and put together. We would offer a copy of the record to the first letter we'd receive at the radio station. But we gave everybody a record because we had a lot of them. Well, we got 40 or 50 letters and I noticed they were all on the same typewriter. They were from J.E.! He was trying to recreate his experience of getting a lot of mail from fans listening to the band's music on the radio. We went to visit J.E. one time. It was Chuck Dunlop and Mark Wingate and Jim Whitley and me—Clyde didn't go. So, we went over to J.E.'s house and he wasn't there. We kind of hung around. Well, J.E. was in the woods, behind his house. We started picking in his yard, and after a while he came up and said he thought we were really good musicians. That said it all. We had his approval.[48]

In the early 1970s, the Mole Hill Highlanders music was broadcast on 13 separate WFMX radio shows between 1 May 1970 and 21 July 1980 before the station manager decided the band ought to pay for its airtime.[49] "The band broadcast a variety of stuff," Jim explained:

> Early bluegrass, old fiddle tunes, we would talk a little bit about the musicians, where they were from, who they were. We did some bluegrass, and the older form. We had the audience. People loved it, but we didn't have the money to keep it going on the air. So, it went the way of the wild goose.[50]

Kilocycle Kowboys

Later, after the Mole Hill Highlanders band ran its course, Jim and some of the members of the Highlanders became the Kilocycle Kowboys, a band name that Jim noted, unabashedly, was stolen from a radio band in the 1930s. They played at fiddlers' conventions in Charleston, South Carolina, and Durham, North Carolina, and from time to time entered band contests. "We fooled the judges," Jim remembered, "and won."[51] Joe Cline remembered meeting Jim in April 1970. Cline had just finished his service in the Coast Guard and had taken a job working for a textile company in Stanley, North Carolina. About that time, Cline purchased his first Martin guitar. One day, he ventured over to a jam in Charlotte and saw Jim Whitley playing banjo alongside Jim Scancarelli, who was playing fiddle, so Cline asked whether they needed a guitar player.[52] Cline did not have specific memories of how the trio morphed into a band. He suspected that the Kilocycle Kowboys were cobbled together as a band for one job, that someone in the audience heard them, and that their second job materialized from that first gig—thus making them a band.

The band, Cline said, started out "more or less" as an old-time band and evolved into a bluegrass band, and then added swing to its repertoire. The Kowboys always played some bluegrass because both Cline and Jim Whitley were bluegrass musicians.[53] Cline suggested that the band could probably be called a "Galax-style band" built around old-time fiddling and bluegrass banjo playing. Whitley was well known to Cline; they had sung duets together beginning in the mid–1960s. Their voices, combined with Jim Scancarelli's occasional stab at the bass part of a song, drove the Kowboys' vocal work.[54]

The Kilocycle Kowboys did not do much in the way of formally working up repertoire: "When we played a new song, one of us would learn it, and we'd put it in our tune list toward the end of a gig and leave it at the back end of the set list until we had all learned it." The band had a dismal record insofar as practice sessions were concerned. There were only two rehearsals in the memory of band members, one in 1979, during which a fiddler—not Jim Scancarelli—got into an argument with the bass player, who recommended that they both take the argument outside and settle their differences "like men." The next rehearsal in 2000, Cline remembered, "went a lot better." So, in place of practice sessions, "we made it up as we went along."[55]

Cline provided the guitar work for the band, backing up the fiddler and banjo player. At some point, he remembered, he pushed the idea of finding a bass player. "The guitar player works hard, providing the bass line and the melody, so I'd be working all night." The Kilocycle Kowboys brought Darrell Gray on as their bass player; he had played with the band, from time to time, on an informal basis when the musicians first came together, so he was familiar with their repertoire and band style. The Kowboys played tunes like "Mississippi Sawyer," "Liberty," and "Soldier's Joy," as well as tunes from Earl Scruggs repertoire including "Ground Speed," "Foggy Mountain Breakdown," and "Foggy Mountain Special." Cline remembered Whitley as a fine banjo player. He recalled that the Kowboys tended to take traditional tunes, such as "Mississippi Sawyer," and put "odd chords," and quirky twist to the tunes to "dress it

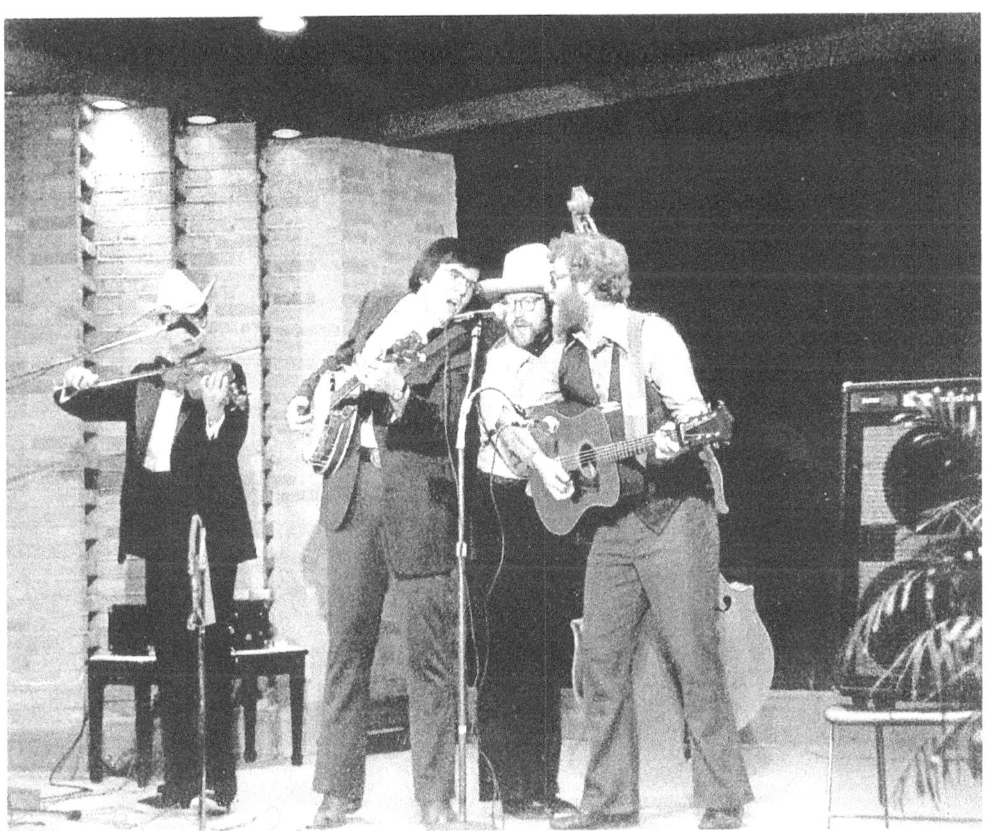

The Kilocycle Cowboys at Spirit Square, Charlotte, North Carolina, February 1978. Left to right: Jim Scancarelli (fiddle), Jim Whitley (banjo), Darrell Gray (bass), Joe Cline (guitar). Jim said: "I had rented a tuxedo for another gig the day before, so I thought it would be stunning to wear it at the Spirit Square show. If you look closely you can see I had on tennis shoes with the monkey suit." Photograph by Ron McCain.

up" a bit. For their first six or so years, in Cline's words, they were not a "performing band." Instead, they were a "strolling band." "We would just roam around, and play music," wherever music was being played. They carried a sound system with them, Cline noted, but more often than not they did not require one. Most of the band members had experience in radio or television, or theatre work, and were quite capable of projecting their voices and their music without much in the way of electrification. "We could be heard...."[56]

In effect, the Kilocycle Kowboys was a "non-band band." Joe Cline or Jim Scancarelli would book a job and string together as many musicians were needed or were available, which meant that the band membership shifted over time, often from one gig to the next. The band structure evolved toward what the Briarhoppers eventually achieved: two distinct ensembles, a stage band and a road band. That enabled the Kilocycle Kowboys to avoid turning down any jobs that came their way. At least one advertisement the band used to attract gigs boasted that they would play parties, bar mitzvahs, and goat ropings. Various members took a hand in booking gigs and managing the dollars and cents aspect of profit-sharing from those performances.

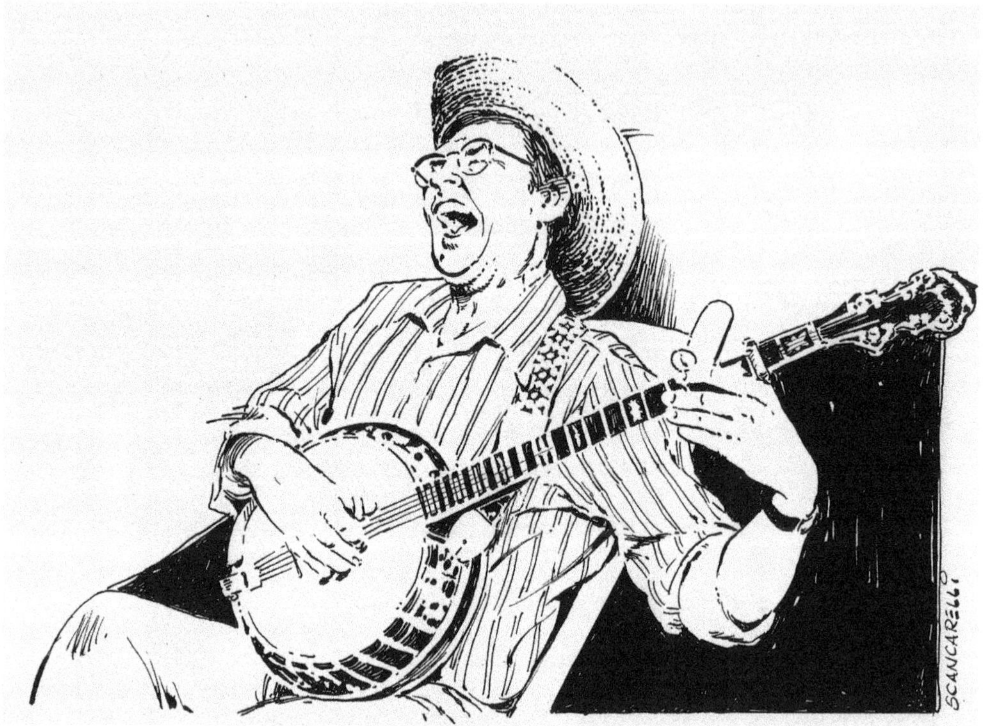

Drawing of Jim Whitley on the banjo by Jim Scancarelli. No date.

Between that and the band's fraught record with practice sessions, sometimes tempers flared in a manner that cut into the band's longevity.

During their most active playing days as a band, Jim was self-employed as a freelance artist. By the time he started working for Dick Moores on the *Gasoline Alley* strip in 1979, Jim recognized the need to detach himself from commitments to playing music so he could focus closely on the cartooning work. Jim probably logged about seven years as the Kilocycle Kowboy fiddler.[57] Eventually, toward 1979, he spent less time fiddling and more time drawing. After he took over the comic strip in 1986, as Jim put it, "I did not venture away from the drawing board for about a year!"[58] He played at Galax with Tommy Malboeuf, and he played on stage at Galax in band contests a few times, but his attendance of these events dropped off as his *Gasoline Alley*–related responsibilities increased. One thing Jim remembered clearly was the premium the Kilocycle Kowboy band members placed on stage antics, and how quickly anything funny became incorporated into their act—as well as how often Jim himself failed to remember punchlines, which itself became part of their stage shtick over time.[59]

"Old Oblivion," Jim's Recording Label

In the 1970s, Jim did the artwork, and engineer and design work, for seven LPs recorded on a label named "Old Oblivion," "headquartered" at 1320 South Church Street in Charlotte, North Carolina.

The first LP, "Chicken Hot Rod," recorded in 1971 and released in 1973 (OO-1), captured the music and humor of the bluegrass band Chicken Hot Rod. Jim did the engineering and design, and artwork, for this first and only album by that band.[60]

Old Oblivion's second recording, "The Mole Hill Highlanders: Old Time String Band Music" (Old Oblivion OO-2), was recorded by Sam Rowe, and produced and designed by Jim; the cassette was digitally re-mastered at Audioworks in Charlotte, North Carolina, by Mike Robinson, and released as a home-made CD in 1993. The recording featured Clyde Williams on fiddle, Mark Wingate on harmony fiddle, Chuck Dunlop on guitar, Jim Whitley on bass—and playing Jew's harp on the cut of "Molly Hare"—and Jim Scancarelli on banjo. That recording was made in Chuck Dunlop's backyard in Huntersville, North Carolina.[61]

The third recording released as a cassette on the Old Oblivion label was "The Mole Hill Highlanders: Old Time String Band Music, Volume 2" (Old Oblivion OO-3), with music by the same lineup. Jim wrote in the liner notes that in the spring of 1970, the band stopped in Statesville, North Carolina, at radio station WFMX where Odell Wood, the brother of banjo player A.L. Wood, broadcast a daily radio show of country and bluegrass music. When the analog tapes of those broadcasts were re-mastered to digital form for the CD released in 1993, Jim pointed out that the band "discovered things on them that were previously inaudible years ago. The thought struck that if we put the tapes back on the shelf another 20 years, with the inevitable future technological electronic advances, perhaps we would discover things that were never on them to begin with."

The fourth release under the "Old Oblivion" label was "Carl Joyner: Hot Tarheel Fiddlin'," recorded at a session in June 1974. Jim did the production and recording work, and the cassette design. Two of the musicians who played with Carl Joyner on the recording—Jim Whitley and Darrell Gray—had just gotten off the college circuit playing with the band Chicken Hot Rod. Jim Scancarelli wrote in the liner notes: "I set up my recording equipment outside in Mother Nature's own studio on Jack Reddick's farm and you can hear roosters crowing and bird chirping in the background. Thank goodness the cows were out on the south 40 that day." Jack Reddick played guitar on the "Hot Tarheel Fiddlin'" recording. He passed away several years after that cassette was made.

Number five released on the "Old Oblivion" label was "Bluegrass Sanitary Cafe," featuring Jim and Tommy Malboeuf. Don Wright played banjo on the recording, and Steve Kilby played guitar, mandolin, and mandola. Bill Williams played bass, and Pat Cocklin provided vocals. Tony Anaya played guitar and Angelica Anya played cabasa on one cut. The sound effects were recorded at the Philadelphia Deli in Charlotte, North Carolina, and prepared as cassette tapes from those original recordings in December 1991 by Mike Robinson at Audioworks, in Charlotte, North Carolina.

The sixth "Old Oblivion" product number (OO-6) was assigned to a project originated by the musician Thom Case, but the recording work was never completed. Case's goal may have been to record his original compositions and songs in order to be able to send them to agencies and radio stations, but that effort never resulted in an Old Oblivion product.[62]

The seventh recording, "Twin Fiddles" (OO-7)—released as a CD—featured the music of Jim Scancarelli (lead fiddle), Tommy Malboeuf (harmony fiddle), and Jim Greene (guitar).[63] The three met at Greene's home in Charlotte for a jam session in June 1996. "After a couple of tunes," Jim Scancarelli wrote in the brief liner notes for that recording, "Jim Greene reached over and turned the cassette player on and recorded the music for our enjoyment later. All tunes were done in one take and whatever clinkers and imperfections were left in as we kept the tape rolling. Tip, Tommy's dog, can be heard banging his tail against the microphone stand."

The Sanitary Cafe Band

In the late 1980s, Jim Scancarelli started a little band called Sanitary Cafe centered around Tommy Malboeuf playing harmony fiddle to Jim's lead fiddle work. Jim and Tommy had the habit of working on a passage in a tune over and over and over again until they got it just the way they wanted to hear it.[64] Don Wright played banjo, Steve Kilby played guitar, and Bill Williams played bass in the Sanitary Cafe band. Tony and Angelica Anaya brought guitar, Guiro, Claves and Cabasa on the song "El Manisero." Early on, Pat Cocklin signed on as a singer, and worked with the band at several gigs including one at Carowinds, an amusement park in Charlotte, North Carolina, that stuck in Jim's mind.[65] The band stayed together from 1989 to 1991 and cut an album sometime around 1991. Then Cocklin had a baby and left the band. Kenny Baker admired Cocklin's voice and said he was going to try and fix her up to go to Nashville, but she decided to stay home and raise a family.

Jim said that Tommy Malboeuf came up with the name for the band. In his mind, naming the band this way honored those old, simple restaurants that were often called "Sanitary Cafes," eateries that the band frequented on their trips through North and South Carolina. The cafes were usually equipped with a well-worn jukebox loaded with bluegrass music.[66] The simple country restaurants after which the band was named "went the way of the wild goose," Jim observed. However, the Sanitary Cafe band continued on, at least in name: Jim continued to register the band name for the competitions at Galax through at least 2019, though when they did play together at the Galax contest, they would often have to recruit different people to fill out the band's ranks.[67]

"Tommy was such a good bluegrass fiddler," Jim remembered, but he still loved playing old-time fiddle tunes, too. Malboeuf played with the Border Mountain Boys and recorded the LP "Bluegrass on the Mountain" with them in 1969 (Homestead Records, 101).[68] He appeared in the documentary that captured Carlton Haney's Labor Day Weekend Festival in Camp Springs, North Carolina, in 1971.[69] In 1972, Malboeuf played with the Blue River Boys, reorganized that year by banjo player L.W. Lambert to include Herb Lambert (mandolin), Ray Cline (lead guitar), Joe Greene (bass), and Elbert Buck Arrington (guitar).[70] Malboeuf's take on "Orange Blossom Special" was immortalized in the 1973 album commemorating the Union Grove Old Time Fiddlers' 49th Convention (Union Grove Talking Machine Records, SS-7).[71] In 1998, Malboeuf fiddled on three tracks for Big Country Bluegrass—on tracks 2, 3, and 13, "Coal Mining Man," "Long Grave on the Hill," and "I'm Going Back to

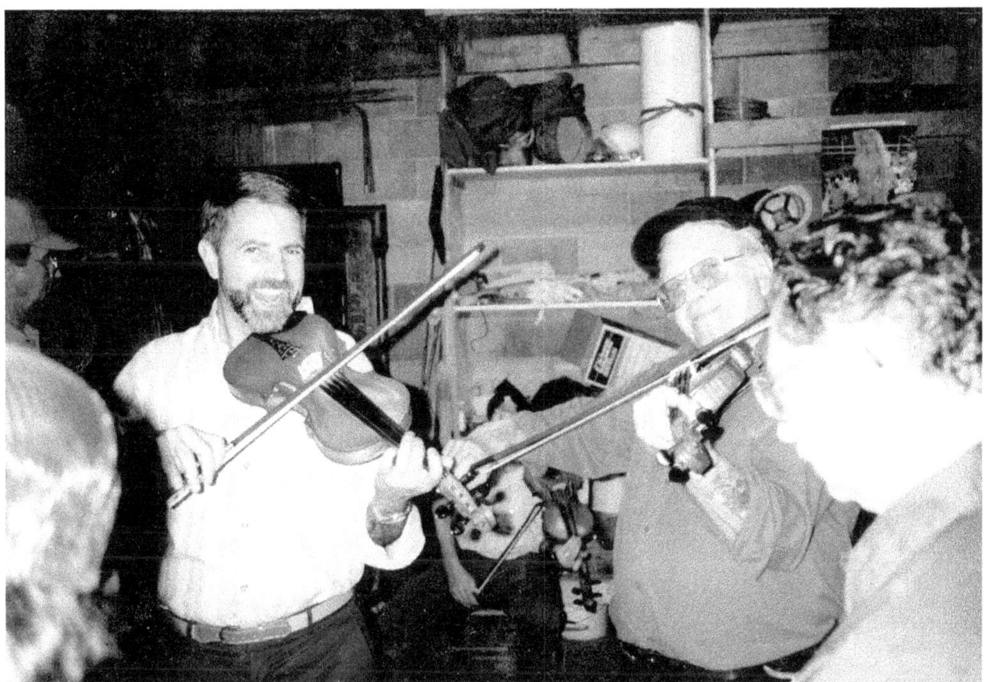

Jim Scancarelli and Tommy Malboeuf. No date.

Carolina"—on the band's album "Up in the High Country" (Hay Holler Records, HH-CD 1340).[72]

Malboeuf was a showman. Jim remembered that in 1964, at Union Grove, banjo picker A.L. Wood led a band, the Smokey Ridge Boys, that used to open for Bill Monroe and the Bluegrass Boys. That band was on stage at the first Union Grove festival that Jim attended, with Tommy Malboeuf as their fiddle player:

> They're on the stage. They played Bill Monroe's tune, "Uncle Pen." Tommy takes a break on the fiddle ... and it was like turning a bull loose. He finished the break, tucked the fiddle under his arm just as A.L. is getting ready to take a break on the banjo. Tommy walks off the stage and starts chatting with people in the audience, shaking hands. He's having a good time. All of a sudden, he runs up on the stage, slides into the microphone, hoists the fiddle up under his chin, and without missing a beat takes his break. The crowd went wild.

Malboeuf was always doing things like that to catch the attention of the audience. He would jam a lit cigarette into the peghead of the fiddle and play his part in a tune, or just hold the lit stub of his cigarette in his bow hand and fiddle away. Malboeuf was also inclined to take a drink or two, or more, and was from, time to time, consumed by his drinking. Kenny Baker once told Jim that Bill Monroe would have hired Tommy Malboeuf, and Tommy would have gone on to be Kenny Baker, instead of Kenny Baker.[73] The drinking flattened Malboeuf's chances of that kind of success.

Malboeuf lived right outside of Statesville, North Carolina, with his mother in a house on a lake in an extremely picturesque setting. Malboeuf never forgave his mother for selling that place. Eventually, he moved into a rented apartment in Troutman, North Carolina.[74] For a time in the 1970s and 1980s, Jim would drive to Malboeuf's home once a week, making what he described as a "pilgrimage," to hang around, talk, play music, eat country food, and pick more music.[75] Jim remains devoted to Malboeuf's memory, to his reputation as a terrific fiddler, and a good friend. "He was just so creative. He said I helped him learn more about playing harmony on fiddling. I couldn't believe that, so I asked how on earth was it possible for me to teach him anything, and Tommy said because I was playing the lead so consistently that he could figure out harmony easily."[76] Malboeuf was insistent on the value of using the "little finger" to fret the strings on the fiddle's fingerboard. He felt it was a good exercise and added a capacity to reach up to notes. He held his bow in an "unorthodox" way, copying Kenny Baker's habit of putting his thumb on the bottom of the frog, meaning that he would grip the bow down low, holding it at the very end in what amounted to a clutched fist. Jim was having trouble with his wrist and thumb holding the bow in a more conventional manner, but when he changed to Malboeuf's way, "the Kenny Baker way," he managed to get a better grip on the bow, and the hand pain diminished. Both Jim and Malboeuf preferred to tuck the fiddle under the neck, reasoning that old-time fiddlers who held the instrument low on their chests ended up constraining their ability to run the length of the fingerboard with their left hand.[77]

Jim and Tommy Malboeuf were both partial to good old fiddle tunes—old-time southern mountain numbers, Appalachian fiddle tunes and festival favorites, waltzes and music with a Celtic flavor, as well as worn out oldies such as "Golden Slippers," tunes that fell into several categories and sprawled across various rural and urban traditions. However, they were not shy about venturing beyond the comfort zone defined by the conventional old-time and bluegrass fiddling repertoire. Jim and Tommy shared a taste for films with a nautical flavor, especially if the movie's storyline was firmly anchored to naval

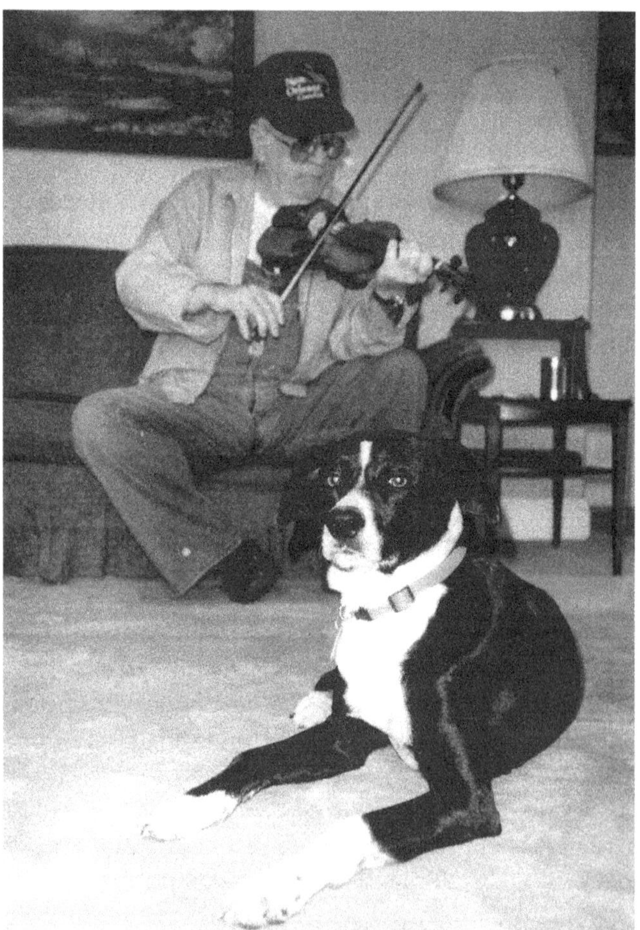

Tommy Malboeuf and Tip, circa late 1980s.

history. *Billy Budd*, a 1962 film starring Terence Stamp, was one of Jim's favorites, but so was Russell Crowe's 2003 maritime action movie, *Master and Commander*. Jim and Tommy, both U.S. Navy veterans, watched those films often, essentially memorizing the lines of the central characters—which they would integrate into their everyday discussions. Both men were taken with the fiddle tunes in *Master and Commander*, including "O'Sullivan's March," a tune that first appeared in print in *Lynch's Melodies of Ireland* in the mid–1800s.

One tune they tried to work up from *Master and Commander* suggested their willingness to venture into uncharted musical territory for traditional fiddlers. Both Jim and Tommy were captivated by "Musica Notturna Delle Strade di Madrid," ("The Nocturnal Music of the Streets of Madrid"), Opus 30 No. 6, a quintettino for stringed instruments by Luigi Boccherini, an Italian composer in service to the Spanish Court from 1761 to 1805. Tommy captured a recording on a video camera of his, and Jim taped the composition as it was played in *Master and Commander*—he may have also located an orchestral version of "Musica Noctturna." They each tried to work out the tune on their fiddles separately and sought to figure out a twin fiddle version. Jim remembered:

> We never got very far with the tune. I heard it one way and Tommy heard it another. I couldn't get the hang of the extra measure and it sounded more like a train wreck than a sea chanty. We never inflicted it on anyone, but it was fun trying. It's still a fine piece of music that sends shivers up my timbers.[78]

To Jim, the Sanitary Cafe band experience was an intensive chance to work out tunes and achieve real musical goals. "That was mainly Tommy Malboeuf's doing," Jim noted, suggesting that the unique musical achievements of the vocalists and the instrumentalists in that band owed much to Malboeuf's way of setting goals and keeping an ensemble locked in on the same mission. The "experience" also spoke to the decision to keep things informal, loosely organized, without a clear band hierarchy: "Nobody was in charge," Jim observed. What that meant, in practical terms, was that while the business end of the band's work—recording work, bookings, hiring studio time—was in fact organized and undertaken in a coherent fashion, the musicians were not hemmed in by strict guidance on what to do onstage: "I did not tell the guys what to do or how to do it," Jim made clear. However, what the band hoped to achieve, if it had any articulated goals at all, was to come to a music that might make people wonder how they got the sound they did. Some of that, Jim acknowledged, was achieved through technological means. On some tunes, Jim played double stops on his fiddle, and Tommy played double stops, and then they recorded two more over those. The depth of the singing could be enhanced by capturing the harmony and melody of the song, then running a third part on top of that through clever recording work. Pat Cocklin nailed the singing in one take and had the engineer back up the tape so she could add the harmony vocals to the mix. Then she'd have Robinson back it up once more and add another layer of harmony. "She was One Take Pat," Jim said.

Jim and Tommy could not quite nail it in one take. The band embraced the options afforded by high tech interventions that allowed them to add nuances to instrumentation, though on some tunes—such as "F-eneezer," "Ebeneezer," in the key of F—the band refrained from technological manipulation to get where they wanted to go.[79] Given Jim's desire to provide as little guidance to the musicians as possible, a lot of the distinctive touches captured on that recording derived from what started out as "monkeying around" in the recording session on tunes such as "F-eneezer" and "Daydreams." "I didn't tell anyone what to do," Jim emphasized. They had to feel their way along, play what worked for them, and what fit with what the band could do, or would be prepared to do, experimentally—especially in "El Manisero," the first number on the second side of the original cassette, which translates as "peanut vendor," and was an old tune sung throughout Latin America in those days. On that tune, Jim played all the fiddle parts. At one point on that cut, Tommy Malboeuf can be heard in the background, imitating Bill Monroe's voice, saying "Just doesn't have the bluegrass sound."[80]

Grade B Cowboy Movies and Grade A Cowboy Music

Sometime in the early 2000s the Western Film Fair hired the Sanitary Cafe band to play at that event. Tommy Malboeuf played harmony fiddle, Jim played lead fiddle, and Ronnie Miller did the duty as a singer and a guitar player. Don Wright played banjo. Briarhopper band member Don White played bass.[81]

Jim recalled that one of the celebrities at the film fair was Shelby Fredrick "Sheb" Wooley (1921–2003), an American actor and singer best known for his 1958 novelty song "The Purple People Eater." Wooley played in popular Western films from the 1950s to the 1990s, including *High Noon* and *The Outlaw Josie Wales*, and appeared in several television series including *Rawhide*, *The Lone Ranger*, *My Friend Flicka*, and *The Life and Legend of Wyatt Earp*.[82]

The "star" of that local event was Tommy Sands. Sands started working in show business in 1949 and skyrocketed to fame as an "instant teen idol" after appearing on the Kraft Television Theatre in January 1957. He made a career recording and performing and acting in movies in the fifties and sixties. He appeared on television (*Combat, Bonanza, Hawaii-Five-O*) through the mid–1970s. He married Nancy Sinatra in 1960; the couple divorced five years later, after which his career went into a tailspin, triggering rumors—later denied by both Sands and Sinatra—that Nancy's father had Sands "blacklisted."[83]

To Jim, events such as the Western Film Fair were intriguing because they represented the points at which various kinds of music intersected. Such local events pushed old bluegrass bands together with up-and-coming country stars and newer repertoire in a way that worked to emulsify the music. Old fiddlers raised to play the archaic tunes found space in bands that played newer country sounds. The intersection of celebrities and local talent, commercially successful bands and local musical ensembles, and—in the instance of the Western Film Fair—an assembly of B grade actors, rhinestone bespangled singers and ten-gallon hats produced a cultural event with a kaleidoscopic dimension to it. Jim remembered a particular aspect of this culture clash:

Tommy Faile, "Guitar Boogie" Arthur Smith's guitarist, was the emcee of the festival. I had worked as Arthur Smith's art director. Arthur and I enlisted Tommy Faile to help us out in the rhythm department that evening. We were in the rehearsal room. There are a couple of ways you can hit a G chord on a guitar. I don't know my way around a guitar, but one old-timey country way is to catch the fat string with your thumb. I don't know where the other fingers go. Anyhow, Sheb Wooley comes over and says to Tommy Faile, "What in the world are you doing? You're doing that wrong." And Tommy said, "What do you mean?" So Sheb Wooley grabs a hold of Tommy Faile's fingers and says: "This is the way you make a G chord." And plunks his fingers down. That made Tommy mad. He curtly said he was going to play it the way he grew up doing it, the way he knew how. So, already, the brick wall was going up.

Jim remembered that the tune "The Orange Blossom Special" was one that Sheb Wooley intended to play:

Tommy Malboeuf could really show off his fiddling on that tune. I was kind of acting as the "music director," I guess, since there wasn't anybody else coordinating the thing. I knew most of the people there. So, I said, "well, Tommy Malboeuf can pick a whale of a break on 'Orange Blossom Special.'" And Sheb says, no, we're not going to do that. He was thinking that we were going to take the shine off of him. I can understand that, I guess. So, anyway, Tommy Faile played the G chord the way he knew how; I know that made Sheb mad. But good old Tommy Sands, every time we played something, and he sang, he would wave his arm over to the band and give us all the credit. "Let's hear it for the band." Most of the "stars" did not do that.

Songwriter and guitarist Ronnie Miller, who joined Jim and Tommy Malboeuf at the Western Film Fair, was from Statesville, North Carolina. Miller sang a song called "Montana Cowboy" at the fair: "We're gonna sing you a song called 'Montana Cowboy,'" Tommy Faile announced. Jim remembered: "As soon as he said that, we went into the song. Oh, man, we were tight, tight, tight. There's a tape recording of that somewhere. We were on top of the game at that time. So, anyway, I think we each got paid 50 dollars for that one—a good payday in those days."[84]

Some Short-Lived Bands

Jim recalled playing with a succession of short-lived bands from the early 1970s to the early 2000s that were, as he has explained, short-lived "largely because of me."

With Gus Meade: In the early 1970s, Alan Jabbour served as the head of the Archive of Folk Song (later, the Archive of Folk Culture) at the Library of Congress, and in 1976 he became the director of the Library's American Folklife Center. In either the early or mid–1970s, Jabbour introduced Jim to Gus Meade, and the two became close friends.[85] Meade began working at the Folk Music Archives of the Library of Congress in 1965. He later took a position at the National Archives where he worked on archival automation. Jim visited Meade at least once at the National Archives and was treated to occasional opportunities to see the old treasures, especially radio program transcription disks—a special interest of Jim's. Jim remembered "miles" of metal shelving loaded with stacks of Armed Forces Radio transcription disks, giant 16-inch records shelved upright, shelves that included all his favorite radio shows—the Lone Ranger, Amos and Andy, Little Orphan Annie. Jim picked banjo and played fiddle with Meade during frequent visits to the Washington, D.C., area to visit his parents. Meade once told him that he came down often enough and sat in on Meade's band practices with more frequency than some of the band members, so he should therefore just consider himself a part of Meade's "regular band." Jim particularly recalled playing banjo and fiddle behind Gus at an Irish pub in Washington, yet one more memory that made him say that he was so thankful he got to meet all these people in his lifetime, share good music, trade life stories, and keep good memories.

Mallard Creek String Band: Tom Walsh formed the Mallard Creek String Band in the early 1970s, possibly on the basis of relationships kindled at the fiddlers' conventions.[86] In 1974, the band's cut of "Whiskey Before Breakfast" was captured on an album, "Fiddler's Grove Old Time Fiddler's and Bluegrass Festival, 1975" (Volume 5), released under the label Galaxie III Studios.[87] The Mallard Creek String Band was the first band in which Joe Cline and Jim played together. Chuck Dunlop was also in this short-lived band.[88]

Gene Meade's Band: Jim also played in a small, short-lived band with Gene Meade—no relation to Gus Meade. Gene was from Eden, a place just outside of Danville, Virginia. In Jim's assessment, Gene Meade was a fantastic guitar player who had backed Clark Kessinger in a string band that Kessinger formed in Galax, Virginia, in the mid–1970s along with banjo player Wayne Hauser.[89] The band in which Jim played, at least briefly, may have been christened The Gene Meade Band; Jim did not know that group by any other name. The band included the banjo player Keith Merrill. Jim had some reel-to-reel recordings of the trio playing together in the 1980s. He

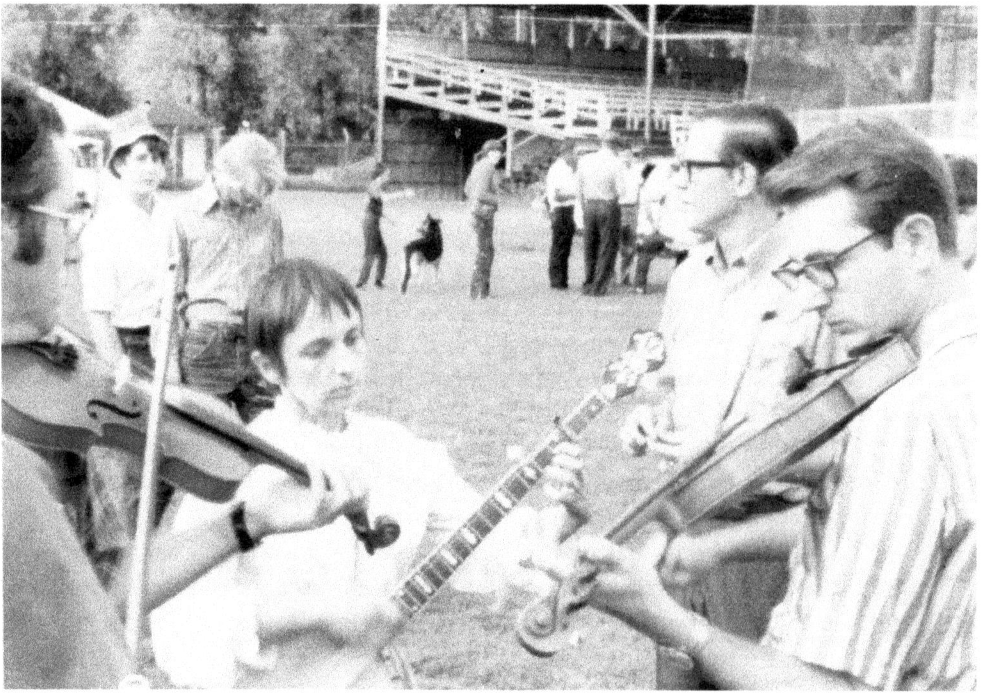

Tom and Bambi Walsh and Jim Scancarelli, the Mallard Creek String Band, Elkin, North Carolina, no date.

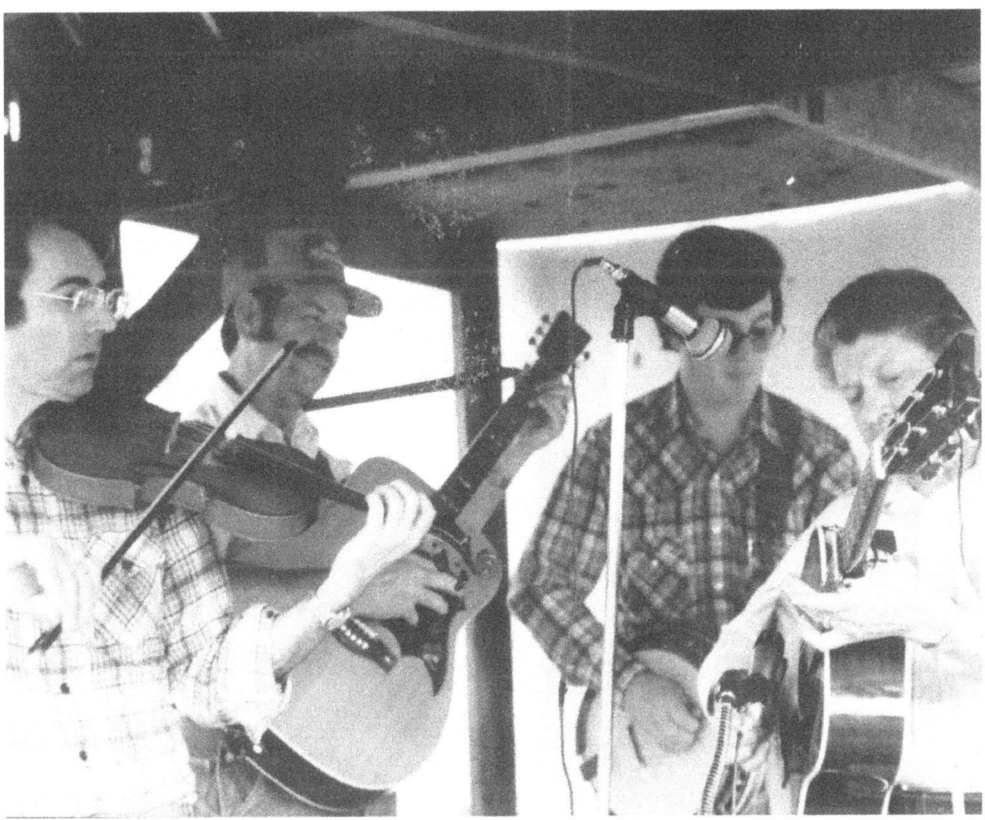

The "Gene Meade Band." Left to right: Jim Scancarelli (fiddle), George Underwood (guitar), Keith Merrill (banjo), and Gene Meade (guitar). The musicians were playing at a small festival in North Carolina. No date.

recalled playing a bluegrass festival with the band in Burlington, North Carolina, and being a little more than clueless at the time about how to fiddle a good deal of their bluegrass repertoire.[90] Jim thought that Gene had a deep and endless "stock bunch of different twangs," unique licks and stylings that distinguished his guitar playing.[91]

Dirt Creek Band: In the late 1970s and early 1980s, Jim played fiddle with the Dirt Creek Band, formed by the mandolin player Leonard McPherson. The Dirt Creek Band, which used the same agent as the Kilocycle Kowboys, played gigs in South Carolina and around Charlotte. The band, Jim explained, was not bluegrass, old-time, or country; at times it just seemed to be a gaggle of musicians playing instruments.[92] In 1976, the band lineup was: Leonard McPherson (mandolin), Jim Scancarelli (fiddle), John Whitley (bass), Susan Jackson (guitar), and Pat Wingo (banjo).

Pine Ridge Something or Other: Sometime in the 1980s, Jim did a short run with a band whose name he could not recall—though it might have had the geographic place name "Pine Ridge" somewhere in the band's handle; they may have later adopted the name Bluegrass Fever.[93] He remembered that Tommy Joy was the banjo player.[94] They played in bars and night clubs, and offered as their repertoire what Jim called "ricky ticky music," his own term of art for music that was contemporary,

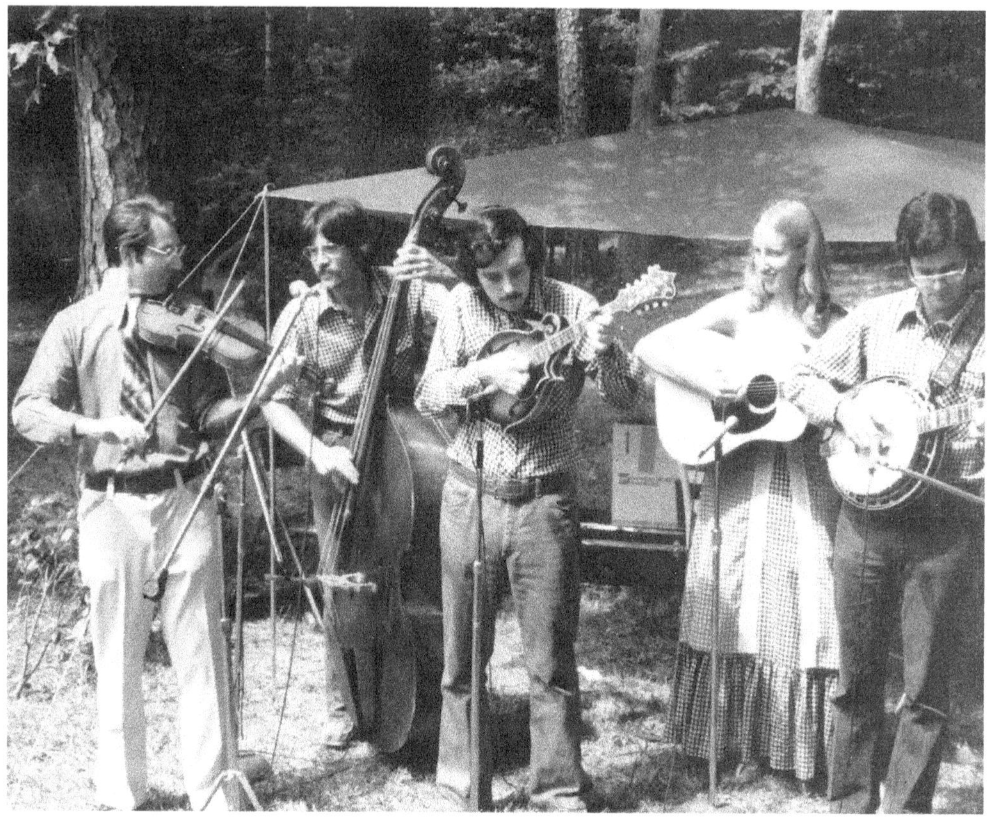

The Dirt Creek Band at Lake Wylie, 1980. The band played at the wedding of Doug Deal, Jim's cousin. Left to right: Jim Scancarelli (fiddle), John (Last Name Unknown) (bass), Leonard McPherson (mandolin), guitar player, and Pat Wingo (banjo).

popular, commercial, and faded quickly into the background in venues of the sort in which these four or five musicians played. Jim was more inclined to fiddle tunes. He admired the repertoire of the Mountain Ramblers from Galax, Virginia, and might have hoped that this band would have been a good platform for developing ensemble versions of their tunes.[95] He did remember getting booked into a beer joint on the outskirts of Charlotte one time. He arrived at the venue a little late, entered the bar, and was enveloped in darkness punctuated by thick, blue cigarette smoke. He made his way to the stage, tuned up, and looked out at the audience. The place was loaded with topless ladies, and both the audience and the band seemed to be soaking up the atmosphere. Somehow, the wives of his fellow band members blamed Jim for booking the gig, even though he had nothing to do with that decision.[96]

Maiden Dixie: In 1988, Jim played fiddle in an all-female band called Maiden Dixie—all-female band except, of course, for Jim. Adael Perkins played bass, Jill Helms played guitar, and Jill Jones played banjo. Jim recalled a story about an "all gal band" that had a male fiddle player: "He would come out on stage in a dress, smoking a cigar, his hairy legs a stark contrast with the other band members. The crowd would go wild." Jill Helms and the other Maidens wanted Jim to do get dolled up in a frock, but Jim refused. "Me wear a dress? Absurd. A kilt, maybe...."[97]

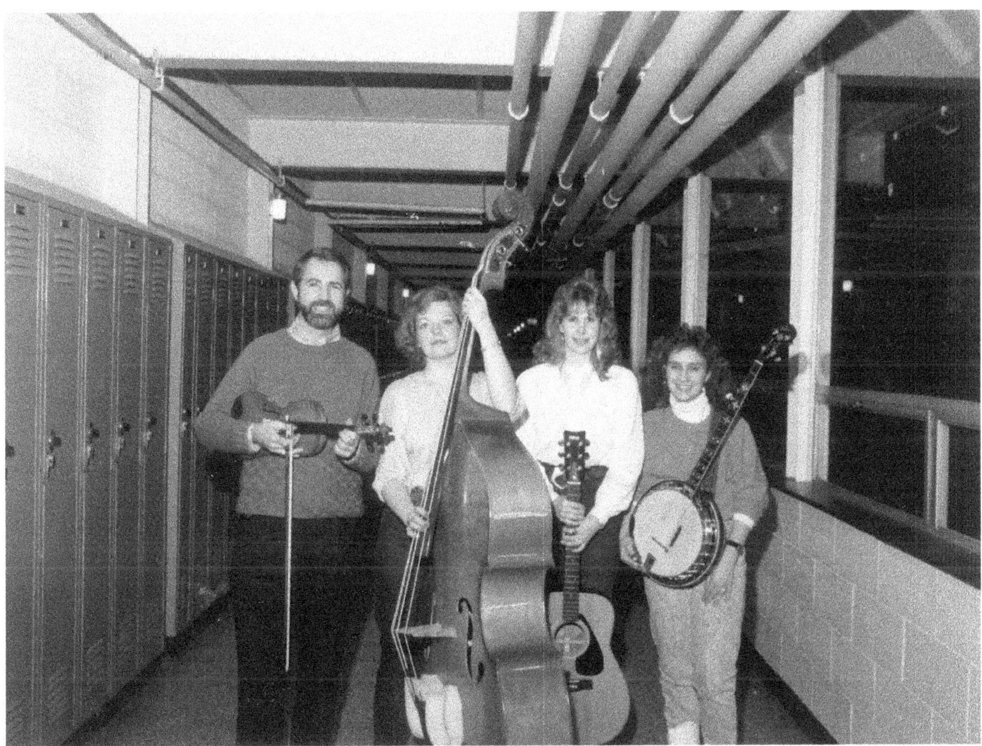

In 1988, Jim played fiddle in an all-female band called Maiden Dixie—all-female band except, of course, for Jim. Adael Perkins played bass, Jill Helms played guitar, and Jill Jones played banjo.

Steve Kilby Band: Jim played fiddle on an album that Steve Kilby recorded for Heritage Records in 1988. The name of the album was, simply, "11–26–54" (Heritage HRC-074), Kilby's birthday. Clarence Greene played mandolin on that recording. Jim recalled that Greene's father was a recording artist in the 20s and 30s; his name was on a lot of 78s. Clarence shared Jim's enthusiasm for trains, and Jim felt that this shared interest provided the basis for a good relationship.[98] Additionally, Jim played fiddle with Steve Kilby (guitar), Jeff Michael (mandolin), Debbie Gates Larsen (bass), and Jill Brown (banjo) in 1989 at the 54th Annual Old Fiddlers' Convention at Galax, Virginia.[99] They put that band together for the Galax contest right at the convention, and took 15th place in the band competition.[100]

Clearwater: In the late 1980s, Jim played fiddle with Johnny and Jeannette Williams in a band billed as Clearwater. Jeannette went on to have a significant career as a singer and songwriter. Jim remembered Johnny as a terrific singer himself, with a rough, unpolished voice that gave a lot of feeling to a song. Jim was the band's first fiddler.[101]

Twisted Laurel: Jim played in a band called "Twisted Laurel" in the 1990s. He joined that band late in its lifespan, and played alongside of Ruth Wherry (bass), Martha Kiker (banjo), and Jim Greene (guitar) at contra dances.[102] The band played at least two year's-worth of contra dance gigs at an old, abandoned Catholic school in Charlotte that had been converted to a dance hall.[103] Ruth's father, John D. Kee, played

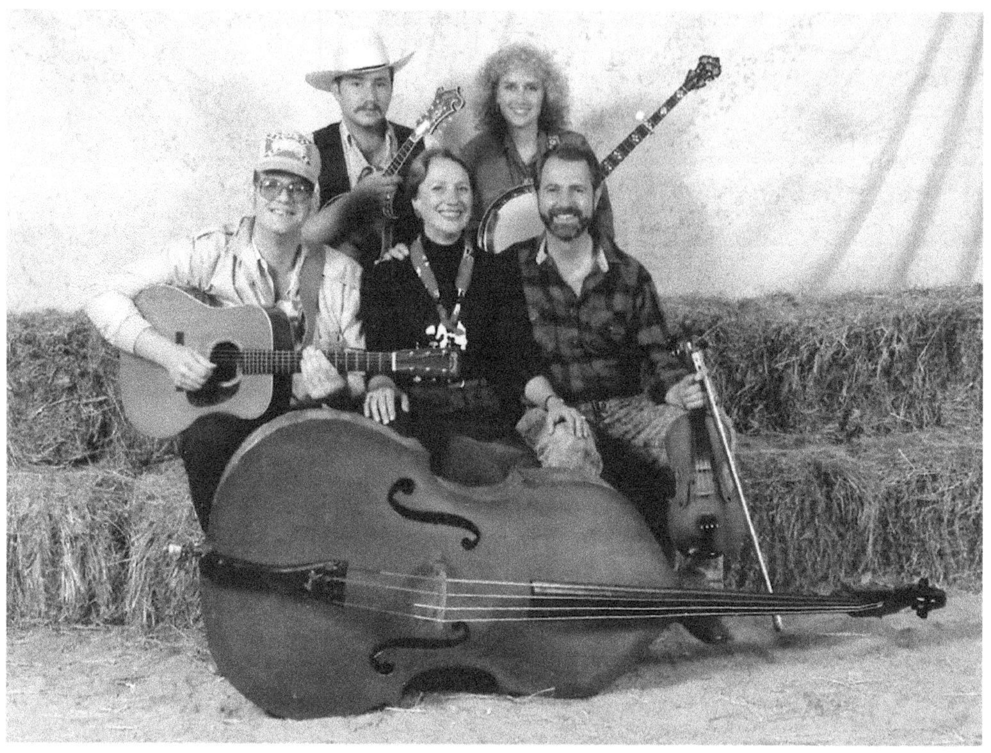

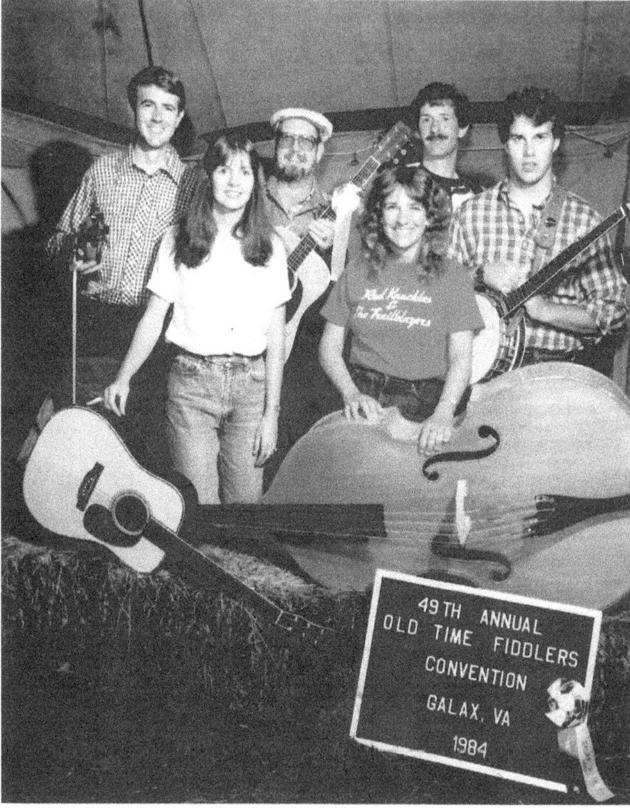

Steve Kilby band, a pickup band that won 15th place at the 54th Fiddlers Convention at Galax, Virginia, in 1989. Seated, left to right: Steve Kilby (guitar), Debbie Larson (bass), Jim Scancarelli (fiddle). Standing, left to right: Jeff Michael (mandolin), Jill Brown (banjo).

with J.E. Mainer and His Rambling Mountaineers and The Tar Heel Cornshuckers in the forties and fifties. Ruth played bass for

Back row, left to right: Jim Scancarelli (fiddle), Jim Greene (guitar), a mustachioed Chuck Dunlop, and Don Wright (banjo). Front row, left to right: Pat Cocklin (guitar), bass player (name unknown). 49th Annual Old Time Fiddlers Convention, Galax, Virginia, 1984.

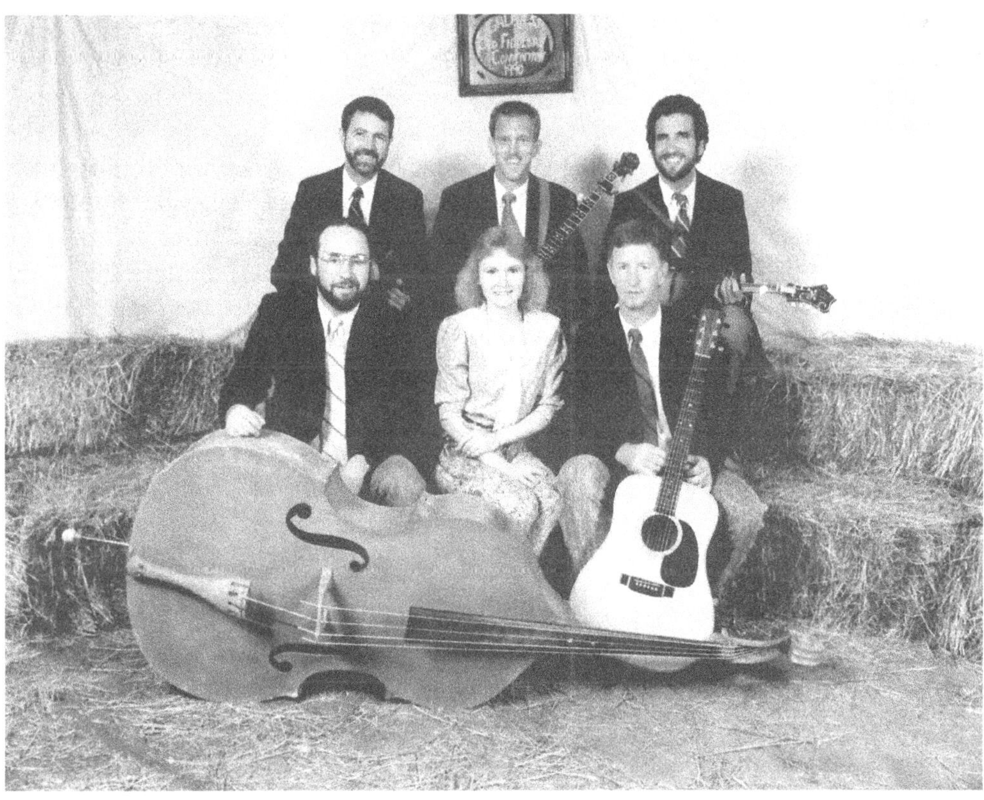

Johnny and Jeanette Williams and Clearwater at Galax in 1990. Back row, left to right: Jim (fiddle), Greg Radford (banjo), and Arnie Solomon (mandolin). Front row, left to right: Tim Jefferson (bass), Jeanette, and Johnny Williams (guitar). Jeanette remembered that Jim liked to play the tune "Ebeneezer."

the Flat Possum Hoppers, which gigged around Charlotte, North Carolina. The band was Jim's first crack at playing contra dances, and he found it to be awfully hard on the fiddler. The band played a couple of tunes Jim enjoyed in the keys of F and Bb. Taking the steps necessary to capo up the banjo, get the banjo and fiddle musically aligned, retune other instruments, and figure out chords was a major muscle movement, so Martha Kiker, the banjo player, said she'd just learn to chord in F and Bb when and where she could—on the five string or the autoharp—and when she could not get to a note or a chord that made sense, she would just leave it out and the band sound would drive things forward until she could join up again. Ruth, Jim recalled, was a good bass player—a slight woman who had to stand on a wooden box to play the upright bass. At some point, Tommy Malboeuf and Clyde Williams, separately, tried to help Ruth learn some fiddling so she could play on the instrument her father played.[104] In the first months of 2016, Ruth told Wayne Erbsen that she was still trying to learn to play the fiddle that she inherited from her father.[105]

Poultry in Motion: From time to time, Jim played at a weekly Monday evening contradance held in Charlotte, North Carolina, in 2010. Two videos on YouTube, both posted in March 2010, are attributed to a band named "Poultry in Motion" that included Jim on fiddle along with Jon Singleton (fiddle), Phil Lesser (banjo), Joe

Cline (guitar), and Ruth Kee Wherry (bass). One video captured the band playing "Jack of Diamonds" at a contradance that featured Dean Snipes as the caller.[106] The second video featured the band playing two fiddle tunes: "Crockett's Honeymoon" and "Dixie Hoedown."[107] Jim did not recall being associated with a band by that name and thought it might have just a gaggle of musicians who got together to play these contradance events, and found themselves operating under the handle "Poultry in Motion," perhaps after those gigs. Jim also remembered that, at the time, he knew the tune "Crockett's Honeymoon," as well as "Dixie Hoedown," but thought that "Jack of Diamonds" was one he probably did not know—though he made clear that not knowing how to fiddle a tune never stopped him from figuring out the basic chord structure and providing some sort of contribution to the ensemble work.[108]

The "Galax Sound"

Jim tended to seek out musicians immersed in what he termed "pre-bluegrass" music, which he defined as a music somewhere in between the old-time style fiddling and the "hot licks bluegrass fiddle styles" of the late 1980s.[109] He looked at what he called the "Galax sound" as the niche fiddle style he learned at festivals such as Union Grove and Galax in the late 1960s and early 1970s. He saw the music of Otis Burris as a good example of that fiddling style.[110] The fiddling of Clyde Williams, Johnny Ham, and Chick Martin's banjo playing fit into that category of "old bluegrass," referring to the early beginnings of bluegrass dating to the first recordings of Bill Monroe and his Bluegrass Boys recorded in the mid–1940s by Columbia Records. In a November 1988 letter to *Bluegrass Unlimited*, in which Jim sought to answer a question about his fiddling and the "classic bluegrass" genre, he pointed to two albums on which he could be heard fiddling: (1) the 1988 Flyin' Cloud release (FC 0007) on which he played "Leather Britches," "Ouk Pic Waltz," and "8th of January," and (2) Steve Kilby's album, "11/26/54" (Heritage HRC 074) on which Jim fiddles alongside Steve Kilby (guitar), Eric Ellis (banjo), Clarence Greene (mandolin), Butch Barker (bass), and Helen White (old-time banjo, mandolin).[111] Jim did not necessarily imply in the 1988 letter that his fiddling in these two recordings still had that "pre-bluegrass" sound, but he did suggest in 2020 that his fiddling in the period during which he was playing contradance music was essentially characterized by the "Galax sound" that he learned in the late 1960s and early 1970s, and refined during years of playing alongside Clyde Williams and Tommy Malboeuf.[112]

Jim viewed the "Galax Sound" as resulting, at least in part, from fiddlers, such as Burris, who were "of the first generation of mountain fiddlers influenced by radio and phonograph." He looked at the music of Mike Seeger and the New Lost City Ramblers as having been derived from close study of early commercial recordings but took the position that when the Ramblers played what they had learned from old recordings, "it became their own thing." In some ways, that suggested music learned at festivals, tunes derived from close listening to old records, were the stuff from which musical styles could be developed in a manner that was as legitimate as learning at the feet of elder fiddlers. That is, Jim's philosophy was that a musician could make music

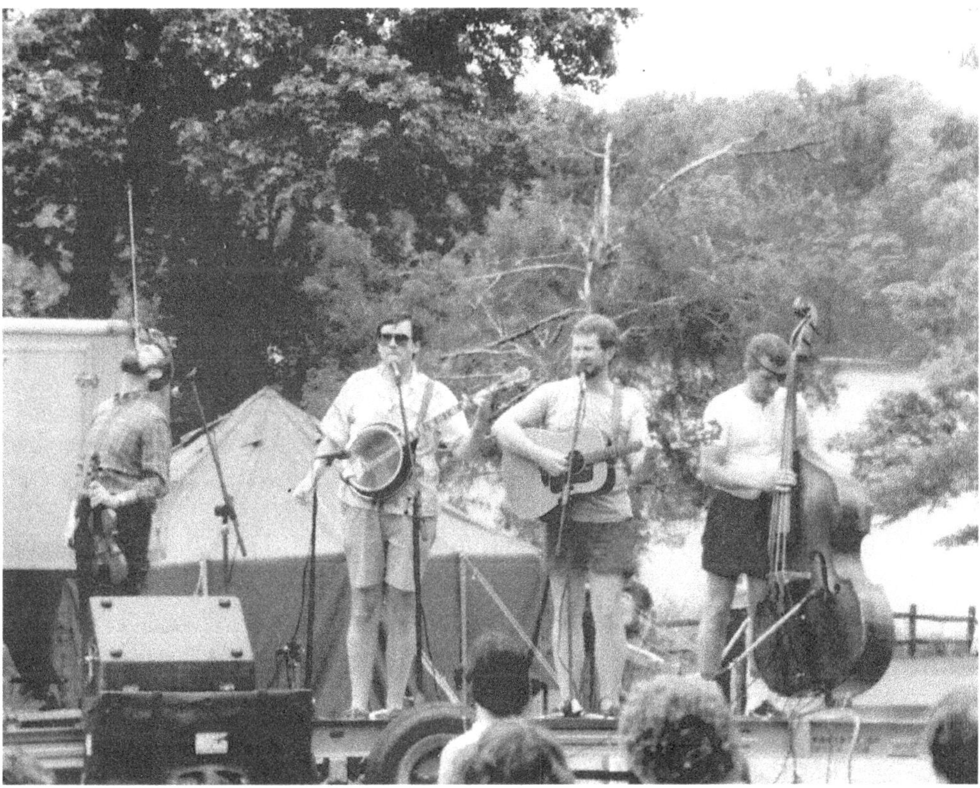

Jim Scancarelli (balancing fiddle bow on his nose), Jim Whitley (banjo), Joe Cline (guitar), and Jim Brown (bass), at the Latta Plantation Festival, Huntersville, North Carolina, 1987. Photograph by Barbara Pinner.

that sounded old—and was essentially true to authentic archaic fiddle tunes—without copying a particular musician or a rendition of a tune note for note. He made the case that it was good to preserve the old music, but it is "nicer" if you can get that old music to have traction in the context of your own way of fiddling. He thought fellow band member Mark Wingate had a way of hearing a tune, playing it back, and then making it his own music.[113]

Jim thought that younger musicians, like himself and his guitarist friend Jim Greene, were afforded particularly unique opportunities to learn from elders in that group of musicians they met at Union Grove and Galax, and other festivals in North Carolina and Virginia, beginning in the late 1960s and early 1970s. Musicians such as Jack Reddick gave young, up and coming fiddlers a lot of guidance, pushed them to play fiddle in a driving way, and encouraged them in a manner that promoted fiddling with "range and drive and dynamics."[114]

John Hartford

Jim and John Hartford had a relationship that went back to the 1970s, fueled by occasional interactions, periodic phone calls, and enduring common interests.

Jim remembered meeting John for the first time at Wolf Trap, outside of Washington, D.C., in Vienna, Virginia. Pierce Van Hoy had gathered up a bunch of musicians from the Union Grove area including Jim and Tommy Malboeuf, and supposedly booked them to play a folk festival at Wolf Trap. Jim noted: "We got out there and they didn't know who in the world we were or why we were there. Pierce was a pretty good talker and he persuaded them to put us on the bill."

Jim may have been referencing the National Folk Festival when it was staged at Wolf Trap. Beginning in 1971, the National Folk Festival, organized by the National Folk Festival Association, held the daytime concerts and workshops on multiple stages throughout the Wolf Trap Park grounds, and the evening events at the 3,500-seat indoor/outdoor amphitheater in the Filene Center. Notably, the August 1971 National Folk Festival, to which John Hartford was invited as a "featured artist," began including artists who were "interpreters."[115] There was a big jam session in one of the fields at Wolf Trap, Jim remembered. "When we got on the stage, we didn't know what to pick. Time was running out. I knew 'Mississippi Sawyer' pretty good. I should have been more polite, but I called out let's do 'Mississippi Sawyer.' And Vassar was playing harmony to me! It was an incredible time. I wish I had a tape of it."

After that brief chance to rub elbows with John Hartford, a series of serendipitous circumstances led to a more continuous interaction between the two musicians. Jim continued:

> Jim Reyland, buddy of mine at WBT radio, moved to Nashville. He was a copywriter and worked at a talent agency in Music City. He put out some flyers for a show that John Hartford did on the Julia Belle Swain or the General Jackson riverboat. They did a live broadcast. It was a Christmas show. After the show was over, Hartford sat next to Jim Reyland. They got to talking and Jim Reyland mentioned my name. John said, well, I know him. John autographed a picture. Sent it to me. I sent a "thank you" to John and we ended up corresponding. John wanted to be a cartoonist and an illustrator, and I wanted to be a musician.

That was the beginning of what Jim described, tongue in cheek, as a mutual admiration society. They had episodic contact over the years, including some musical moments shared during phone conversations:

> The funny thing was, John would call me on the phone and he'd say, listen to this. He'd put the phone on the floor to have both hands free, and then he'd play something, and ask, "What do you think of that?" And I would tell him. He had a series of index cards, 4-by-5 cards, on which he wrote lyrics that were left over from previous song writing efforts. Once, he threw them down on the floor and shuffled them all up, picked them up in the order in which they landed, and he was reading them to me. They didn't make any sense! He'd ask my opinion. I gave it to him. I'd say, hey, that's pretty sharp, or something and I got my name on an album credit from John. But that was a thrill, having him call to bounce ideas off of me.[116]

Jim recalled the story—told again in the Greg Reish's foreword to the *Mammoth Collection of Fiddle Tunes*—of Hartford and his index card collection of "leftover lyrics," parts and pieces of songwriting efforts that did not make it into tunes he wrote. John would shuffle the deck, throw the cards onto the floor, and try to make a song out of what emerged from that card toss. One day, he called Jim with a song that consisted of all "special effects" sounds—"cars driving, trucks crashing, horns beeping, tires squealing." Jim recalled saying what he often said when confronted with the patch-work quilt of lyrics that emerged from those exercises: "That's pretty good."

Jim integrated Hartford as a character into a string of thirty-six panels for his comic strip *Gasoline Alley* in 1991 that constituted a narrative about the "PVT Jaxon," a paddlewheel type riverboat that finds itself in the same circumstance as the steamer *Virginia* that was run aground in January 1910 in a cornfield on the Ohio River, recounted in John Hartford's book, *Steamboat in a Cornfield*.[117] Jim remembered:

> That decision to feature John Hartford in a long string of *Gasoline Alley* strips was not generally well received by management. They didn't know much about traditional music or old-time and bluegrass musicians, and they didn't know who John Hartford was. I told him John was famous worldwide, and in the end they weren't against it, but they weren't for it either.[118]

Jim wanted to take photographs of John, to serve as the basis for the drawings he planned to do for the "Gasoline Alley" thread that he envisioned. John Hartford invited him to come on out to Nashville. In Jim's recollection:

> I took a ton of photos at John's house. The story was, he was on the river boat, and there was a big rain—remember he put out a book, *Steamboat in a Cornfield*. That was the impetus for this whole storyline [in *Gasoline Alley*]. The riverboat landed in *Gasoline Alley* on the pitcher's mound in a ballfield. The water receded, and the boat is stuck, and they couldn't get it off the mound. I wanted some action pictures on an actual river boat. John had to go play some-where, he didn't have time, so we couldn't take photos on the riverboat. He took a garden hose and pretended to be on a boat in a storm. His house was right on the river. The third story of the house was just like the bridge on a riverboat. You just look out the window and for the most part it was like you were looking out the window of a riverboat bridge. I shot some pictures of him playing like he was on the deck of a river boat. We got down to the river and, by golly, here comes the General Jackson under steam. And, so, it was coming by and every time they would see John they would blow the whistle. Well, I shot pictures of it approaching and I have pictures of John waving at the boat. I thought that was pretty good luck and a rare opportunity.

Jim took hundreds of photographs of John Hartford over the course of several days in preparation for that long thread of a *Gasoline Alley* story. He gave them to Hartford at some point, and Hartford used some of them on CD covers. Jim recalled: "He was nice enough to write a blurb on our Sanitary Cafe album."[119]

Rufus and Joel, characters who were fixtures in the *Gasoline Alley* strip, figured prominently in the storyline that featured John Hartford. Rufus and his little cat were heading to his friend Joel's shack when their little town was flooded. Joel and his ever-present cat were rescued by Hartford and Captain Dinghy. For the dura-tion of the run of those thirty-six strips, the steamship remained poised precari-ously on a mound of earth just above Joel's shack. As the captain and his crew, with the assistance of Rufus and Joel, tried to figure out ways to nudge the craft back to the river, John Hartford appeared, banjo in hand, strumming and plucking music. He is seen lending a hand to the effort by providing a beat to which Rufus and Joel could nail the scaffolding intended to refloat the steamship; lingering in the com-pany of the ship's captain during attempts to hawk "Mama Dinghy's dynamic, mul-tipurpose, dual flavored, anise scented reptilian lubricant"—supposedly a powerful "natural" anti-depressant; attempting to tap a keg of beer and float the steamboat on the resulting suds as a way off the hill on which the ship is grounded; playing for the local crowds who attend the town's 4th of July pageant hosted aboard the grounded steamer; and finding inspiration for "Gentle on my Mind" in something Walt Wallet is heard whistling. In the 15th strip, Hartford is told to quit tapping his toe so vigorously because the ruckus threatened to scuttle the stranded steamship.

Probably the most relevant banjo-focused line placed in the mouth of the comic strip Hartford character is a retort in the 11th strip spoken when the steamship captain admonishes Hartford for playing his banjo in the middle of efforts to assess the ship's situation. Hartford pushes back, telling the captain that "a banjo will get you through times of no money—but money won't get you through times of no banjo."[120]

Jim's Repertoire

The first tune that Jim enjoyed playing on both banjo and fiddle was "Mississippi Sawyer," which he learned at a fiddlers' convention, though he could not recall where and when he first tried to pick it up. "I just plunked along," he said, referring to how he got to the basic melody line in his early days on fiddle and banjo. Later, Jim went to the Folkways recording of Wade Ward playing "Mississippi Sawyer" to fine-tune things (Folkways Records FA 2380 released 1973).[121]

Jim deliberately avoided playing tunes on his fiddle exactly the way he learned them from the musicians who taught him tunes. "Play what you are feeling," was the rule of thumb he used, a practice he learned from both Clyde Williams and Tommy Malboeuf, who urged Jim to stick to the parameters of the tune in question, adhere to the melody, but take the tune where his fiddle led him.[122] Jim felt that the example of playing a tune "straight" on the first run through, and taking things "into outer space" on the second pass, was a particularly Dixieland way of playing music. Tommy Malboeuf and Jim played the tune "High Country." That was their "big one." Kenny Baker played a "jazzed up" version of the tune. Baker and Joe Greene played that tune as the second cut on their double fiddle recording, "High Country" (County Records, released January 2011). Jim said that version of the tune "lit us up." Jim and Tommy Malboeuf gave their version of "High Country" pride of place on the first cut on their recording "Bluegrass Sanitary Cafe" (Old Oblivion 00–5). They played it straight the first time and jazzed it up the second time through the tune, the way they learned to do things from Baker and others.[123]

Jim had a real "affinity" for "Sally Ann," a tune he felt was raw and just lent itself to being played in all manner of ways by different musicians. "Sally Ann" was one of the several tunes to which Jim added a third, low fiddle part beyond the traditional A and B parts. "I'd go in low on the fiddle. I had to stretch it out—especially at dances. 'Sally Ann' was not a crooked tune," not a difficult tune for dancers to follow, but even so, a third part contributed to making it more symmetrical, more danceable. Clyde Williams fiddled "Sally Ann" in A. Jim liked doing it in D. "Billy in the Low Ground" was another two-part tune with a third part that was seldom played. Jim learned the tune from two or three different fiddlers, and from banjo player Jack Reddick who knew the tune's third part that Jim felt evened out the tune for dancers. "Ragtime

Annie" was yet a third tune for which Jim liked to add a third part that dropped from the key of D to G, and—in his view—added a kick to the tune.

Jim knew the tune "Walking in My Sleep," and started putting in the extra slides and chords that Kenny Baker brought to the tune to spice things up, but Jim found that those added touches made it too slick for an old-time music crowd. Jim preferred to play the tune "Ebenezer" in the key of F. His friend Debbie Larson, with whom he played in a pickup band at a 1989 Galax contest, played the tune in G, and they took to calling it "G-Benezer" to distinguish it from "F-enezer," played in the key of F.[124] He picked up the tune "The 8th of January" from listening to Scotty Stoneman's version, though Jim recalled that Stoneman would go wild with his variations of the tune.

Clyde Williams played a tune called "Feather Beddin.'" Jim recorded it and transferred what he regarded as a low-quality reel-to-reel recording to a cassette that remains in his personal archive. "I was playing counter melody and, boy, it didn't sound bad." He made clear to Williams that he thought the tune sounded great. Clyde just shrugged in response, Jim recalled, but Jim never heard anyone else play that tune, and it remained for Jim one of those special musical memories, a distinctive moment of fiddling to which Jim returned now and then when remembering his days with the Highlanders.[125] Jim learned some of the contradance tunes that he played from the recordings of Canadian fiddlers, tunes such as "Petronella." He learned "Hollow Poplar" and "Bluegrass in the Backwoods" from listening to Kenny Baker, but when Jim started fiddling alongside Tommy Malboeuf, he began learning more intricate stuff because "Tommy would get bored playing repetitious tunes." Malboeuf would take Kenny Baker tunes and jazz them up.

Kenny Baker's fiddling had a profound influence on Jim's way of learning and playing tunes. Jim remembered the point in time when Baker had just left Bill Monroe's band, probably in 1983. Baker teamed up with Jimmy Martin at a stage performance outside King's Mountain, North Carolina. Martin was playing a 1948 D-18 Martin guitar that he had borrowed from Jim Greene at a time when the D-28 model was far more popular. "Martin tuned that guitar, and Kenny Baker and Martin started playing a tune. Martin, he'd just drag the music out of you," and every tune they played struck Jim as just so special. Jim remembered when he would attempt to test drive a tune in front of Baker, or ask Baker how to do a lick, Baker would say: "Come on, Jim, it's simple!" Jim had a very different sense of the degree of difficulty involved in drawing a bow across four strings: "Trying to do the thing, that was simple, but getting it down, that was simply confusing."[126]

Jim's contradance musician partners tried to put more of an "Irish" spin to tunes for such dances. Jim would learn a tune, like "Daley's Reel" in B flat from Jim Greene, and then hear that tune played by Kenny Baker in a distinctly different way. Jim would try to roll them into one version. He learned how to play harmony fiddle at a fiddlers' convention in Liberty, North Carolina, from Carl Joyner, who taught Jim how to find his way to the harmony part for the tune "Liberty." "That harmony stayed with me," Jim said, fifty years later. By the early 2000s, Jim was playing West Virginia tunes, and other music—reels, for example—by feeling his way around the music of his fellow band members, "playing around" on various tunes, identifying holes he could fill or harmony he could play to complement the melody, without necessarily having immersed himself in each tune that came up during these dances. He was, in effect, making it up as he went along.

"Red Wing" and "Buffalo Gals" were tunes that Jim just loved playing. There was something to those tunes that just ignited the desire to dance in listeners. He tried not to play those tunes in a "conventional way." Jim recalled the time that he was joined by Martha Kiker and Ruth Wherry at an old folks' home. "We played, they just sat there," but when they got to the tune "Buffalo Gals," the small crowd of aged folks suddenly turned lively. "A guy in a wheelchair started taping his foot. An old lady jumped up and started dancing. Jim figured they just heard music that used to make them dance and were glad to hear tunes that brought them back to long ago times. Jim's rule for those kinds of gigs: 'You don't play rock music at an old age home.'"[127]

Time in the Contradance Fiddling Trenches

In the early 2000s, Jim played fiddle at contradances with Jim Greene (guitar), Martha Kiker (banjo), and Ruth Wherry (upright bass). Jim felt that he never got to the point where he could match a tune with the dance. He often had the sense that he was out of sync with the caller for much of his contradance fiddle playing time. Jim Greene, he felt, had a closer appreciation of which old fiddle tunes fit what dances, but between the shouting of the caller and the stomping of the dancers, Jim often was hard pressed to hear where the rest of the band was in a tune, much less hear his own fiddling.

Sometime during those contradance playing years, Jim wrote out a list of tunes in the keys of G, A, B flat, C, D, E, and F. A second list, typed by a friend of Jim's, listed G, D, A and C tunes, and showed the tunes that he and his contradance musician friends tended to play together—such as "Whiskey Before Breakfast" and "Fisher's Hornpipe," and "Goin' Uptown" and "Soldier's Joy." The lists did not represent the band's complete contradance repertoire. There was a clear overlap between the tunes they played in the early 2000s and the tunes Jim played with Clyde Williams and Tommy Malboeuf. Those two lists are the only surviving indication of his contradance repertoire.

Jim had a "play it and forget it" attitude toward thinking systematically about the number of tunes in his quiver, the total list of tunes he could reach for in a jam or during a performance without having to tax his memory. However, he did have good memories of learning and playing particular tunes.

Martha Kiker played banjo tunes such as "Goodbye Liza" and "Sweet Sixteen," a tune that was called "Too Young to Marry" in North Carolina.[128] Martha knew the tune "Rock the Cradle, Joe" on banjo—Jim thought she might have learned that tune in West Virginia. She taught it to Jim who "transposed" it from her banjo version to a fiddle version that he devised. He was fairly certain he did not play it "correctly," but that he managed to render it with enough power to muddle through the tune in the band context in a way that served the purposes of the dancers. Martha and Ruth Wherry were good at figuring out how to present the melody of a tune in a manner that would suggest to Jim what he might play on the fiddle to provide harmony. Jim tended to refrain from trying to match the banjo player note for note, preferring to stay "in the ballpark" when it came to melody. When he was playing banjo to Clyde William's fiddle, there was less in the way of trying to get the two instruments into sync; Jim would play something other than whatever Williams was playing on the fiddle, finding a counter melody that would work with Williams' fiddle. In Jim's view, there was some aspect of that approach to the banjo-fiddle pairing that approximated what pipe bands did, with half the band playing melody, the other half finding harmony; the result, in Jim's opinion, was something "really extremely wonderful."

The amplification used at such dances, so the band could be heard over the din of stamping feet, did not do much to keep the band's instruments in balance. Jim remembered that by 2008 or 2009, after Jim Greene had passed away, Joe Cline had taken up the chair as guitarist, and Phil Lessor stepped in on banjo, replacing Martha Kiker. About that time, during one gig, Jim's ring finger on his left hand cramped up. John Singleton, a fiddler friend in the audience, jumped onstage to fill in for Jim. "That was the end of me," he said, thinking back on what the last time he played fiddle or banjo for a dance.[129]

Conclusion

Jim remembers when the distinctions between old-time music and bluegrass were not drawn so cleanly, and when those distinctions were not invested with what seemed to have become ideological meaning, much less specific prescriptive guidelines for differentiating the two kinds of string band music.[130] He also remembers going to jams and clearing different rooms. He would enter one room, join in on a jam tune, and the musicians would quietly exit, looking for another corner in which to play, saying that Jim was too intensely bluegrassy. In another room, he'd shut down a jam for being too "old-timey."

Jim played with bands that straddled old-time and bluegrass music. He tended to speak of "old" bluegrass, to distinguish that brand of bluegrass from the more experimentally inclined, less strictly traditional ensemble music that came to include electric guitars and other instruments (keyboard, drums)—later characterized as "Newgrass." Jim seemed to pinpoint the juncture at which the separation between these two styles started to become institutionalized, suggesting that the watershed was around the time fiddlers' convention contest rules were rewritten in the early 1970s to draw clearer distinctions between "old-time music" and "bluegrass." The old-time music/bluegrass divide seemed to be most forcefully articulated in tune choices. The elder fiddlers did not shrink from songs with racially sensitive themes that characterized some traditional fiddle tunes that harked back to the mid–1800s. Younger musicians in the old-time music orbit seemed acutely aware that this was treading a path that was potentially consequential, but lived with the repertoire choices because at the time it seemed that only the song titles were offensive, and the music itself was representative of the realities of the days when the tunes were first fiddled, and thus was in effect a historic artifact deserving of preservation in some manner. Bluegrass musicians, it seemed, were inclined to make different repertoire choices, and to play modern, popular tunes as well as some rock-and-roll numbers and bluesy tunes arranged specifically for bluegrass-appropriate instruments. For Jim, untangling all that in the years from the mid–1980s to the first years of the 2000s became increasingly complex, and sticking to his preference for older fiddle tunes did not necessarily meet the requirements for contradance music.

The last jam Jim played was at Galax in 2010. He probably did not play the banjo much after that, but he did fiddle from time to time through at least 2013. As he put it, he could no longer get his fingers to go where he wanted them to on the fiddle or the banjo. Holding the bow for a long time became a chore. The fiddle, he said, just started sounding better in the case. He recalled having a dream in which Kenny Baker was playing on stage. After Jim's break, he turned the spotlight over to Malboeuf, who tried to outdo Baker—which Jim made clear was an impossibility for anyone—and then Baker would throw it over to Jim. Jim remembered that in this dream, "as soon as I would get up to the microphone, the bow hair turned to linguini. I couldn't get any sound out of the fiddle. That was really scary...."[131]

Jim had a broad and deep network of old banjo friends going back to the 1960s. He knew a bunch of people in the northern Virginia area who were, by his measure, wonderful pickers, including Tom Knowles. He met Tommy Thompson and his Red Clay Ramblers and recalled that band's creative energy: "Their music, it wasn't old-time and it wasn't bluegrass. It was just music." He made the acquaintance of Kyle Creed who first advised Jim to bend his thumb on his right hand, a simple suggestion that made it easier for Jim to figure out clawhammer banjo.[132] Jim knew the innovative musicians, the mainstays of bluegrass and old-time who straddled several musical worlds and sought to be both creative and to honor the old music and music makers. He got to know Bobby Patterson from Heritage Records, and Jack Reddick. He knew Jimmy Edmonds and Norman Edmonds and his band called the Old Timers. Norman, Jim said, fiddled the definitive version of "Breaking Up Christmas." He met Talmadge Smith and Otis Burris, members of the Mountain Ramblers. Jim met and recorded a bunch of elder musicians and valued his relationships with those elders who brought unique twists to the traditional music Jim thrived on. He had a deep affection for the experience of playing music in the close embrace of like-minded players, friends, listeners, dancers, watchers, curious bystanders, old folks, young folks, dogs, cats and anyone (and anything) prepared to add to that moment of community.[133]

Five

A Mindset to Cartoon

Introduction

From the mid–1960s to the 1970s, Jim was building a career as an artist, largely in graphic arts and advertising, though by the late 1970s he had turned his attention to securing a position in the cartooning industry. His interests in comic strip art, and cartoons, dated back to his youth in a family that encouraged his interests in drawing, and his earliest efforts at creating cartoon characters.

In the Catholic school he attended as a young boy, Jim recalled being asked every year about his life and career goals. "The first time I was asked, 'What do you want to be when you grow up?' I said a garbage man. I thought riding on the back of a truck would be fun." He was sent to the principal's office to think about his life choices. The next time he was asked the same question, Jim answered "a cowboy." He was directed to return to the principal's office for another opportunity to evaluate his life choices. When he was a little older, perhaps in 7th grade, he answered the query by saying he wanted to be an archeologist. From the 7th to the 12th grade at Wakefield High School in Arlington, Virginia, Jim and his friend Wiley C. Grant III fantasized about going to Africa on safari, working their way up to Egypt, wearing pith helmets and jodhpurs. None of that, of course, came true in his lifetime, though Jim did memorialize the spirit of that high school ambition in a *Gasoline Alley* story that had Uncle Walt spinning a yarn for a local reporter about the time he travelled from Africa to Egypt in search of the fountain of youth.[1]

When he did turn his attention to life goals, and the business of making a living, Jim had the sense that coming from an "artistic musical family," he just knew that he wanted to be a cartoonist for at least two reasons: first, because he took to that part of drawing more than fine art painting, and second, because his enthusiasm for cartoons and comic strips was matched only by his love for simple, vigorous, southern mountain string band music. To Jim, then, the energy he derived from reading and drawing cartoons ran parallel to—or dripped over onto—the way he embraced old-time music and old-style bluegrass. The creative energy he devoted to archaic fiddle tunes, and to cartooning, seemed to be channeled in a manner that converged, allowing him to echo his views in art and music about life, community, and friendships. Together, music and art enabled him to stick to rules that spoke to earnest, simple, straightforward ways of navigating hardships, enjoying family, and being thankful on a daily basis for just waking up.

Cartooning Came First

The affection for fiddling and banjo playing came after the urge to draw cartoons took hold of Jim. Jim observed:

> The cartooning thing came first. The only entertainment we had growing up—and this was wartime—was radio, movies, comic books and newspaper comics. These were my friends. Newspaper comics—oh, boy. Daddy would bring home at least three different newspapers from work at the Embassy of Italy when we lived in Washington, D.C. and it was just wonderful to read the comics.

In Charlotte, North Carolina, the family read two papers, *The Charlotte Observer* and the *Charlotte News*. The *Charlotte News* carried *Gasoline Alley*. Jim's grandfather would put young Jim in his lap and read the comics to him:

> Granddaddy had this wonderful way, wonderful sense of analyzing a painting or a drawing. Or the comic strips. He'd point out all the little details in a drawing. Even a fine art painting. There was one painting that he showed me of a bunch of colonial era men with the three-cornered hats and 18th century garments, the ladies in long, flowing dresses, and they were all going to church. The sun was filtering down through the trees. And Granddaddy would point out little details. "Look at that little dog over in the corner." Or a deer behind those trees. It made me aware that there were things other than what was in the foreground. He did that with the comics. He would explain things.

Any sort of visual stimulation would prompt Jim, as a young boy, to draw things:

> When I would go to a movie and I would see *Pinocchio* or *Snow White* or any of those great Disney features, I'd go home and try to draw them. I would make little synopses of the stories. I couldn't draw, I was only 2 or 3, and you couldn't tell what it was that I'd drawn. Once I drew a car. I had great big wheels on it. I colored the hubcap yellow, and I left the wheels white. My granddaddy looked at it and said, "Ummm. That's a good picture of two fried eggs." Boy, did I get insulted. But he was right.[2]

Donald Duck and Mickey Mouse were the key figures in the first comic books he read:

> I really loved Donald. I loved it when he and Uncle Scrooge would get together. This was the Carl Barks era. They would go out on these terrific adventures. The whole comic book would be about these adventures of Donald, Scrooge and the nephews who really had more sense than Donald did. That just influenced me a lot.[3]

Jim's mother tried her own hand at cartoon work, thirteen years before Jim came along. In 1928, Frances Parati devised a single panel comic called "Ramblin' Rose Says…" about a country girl named Rose who offered her observations about what was going on in the big city. Jim recalled her drawings as being impressive. Only a couple of the originals have survived:

> Momma went to the syndicates in New York and they all turned her down because she was a woman. They said she didn't have the business acumen to keep the thing going. She could have fooled them. She was good.[4]

In 1928 Frances had another chance to work in a small part of the cartoon industry. At some point, the Chicago Tribute Syndicate began farming out the engraving work on their comic strips to the Charlotte Engraving Company where Jim's mother worked. One of her assignments was to color some of the funnies. Jim said:

One of them was *Orphan Annie*. She would get the original art and she would color it with either colored pencil or watercolor. Orphan Annie had a red dress, so that was the standard. She would make up the colors for all the rest of the characters and the printer would try to match what Momma had done.

Jim thought that none of the artwork for *Orphan Annie*—especially the hand-colored Sunday strips from the years during which his mother did the coloring work—survived, probably because those drawings were not fine art, just production art.[5]

Jim's mother also wrote and illustrated a book for children that she called *Bunky the Big Book Brownie*. It was a Christmas story, Jim explained, that was not published, and was probably intended just for Jim when he was a little boy:

> Santa's elf named Bunky kept the book on all the good and the bad kids. Momma illustrated the book with large, beautiful 11-inch-by-14-inch watercolor paintings. Those drawings stayed here at the house in Charlotte for years and years and years. Momma was living up in Arlington, Virginia, and one day she said she'd like to take those home with her to northern Virginia. So, I packed them up and gave them to her, she put them down in the basement, and later the basement flooded. Two feet of water, and those watercolors were ruined. That was it for them. So, in my daily comic strips for *Gasoline Alley* at Christmas time, Bunky the Elf makes an occasional appearance as a little tribute to Momma.[6]

Decades later, Jim remembered looking at his mother's

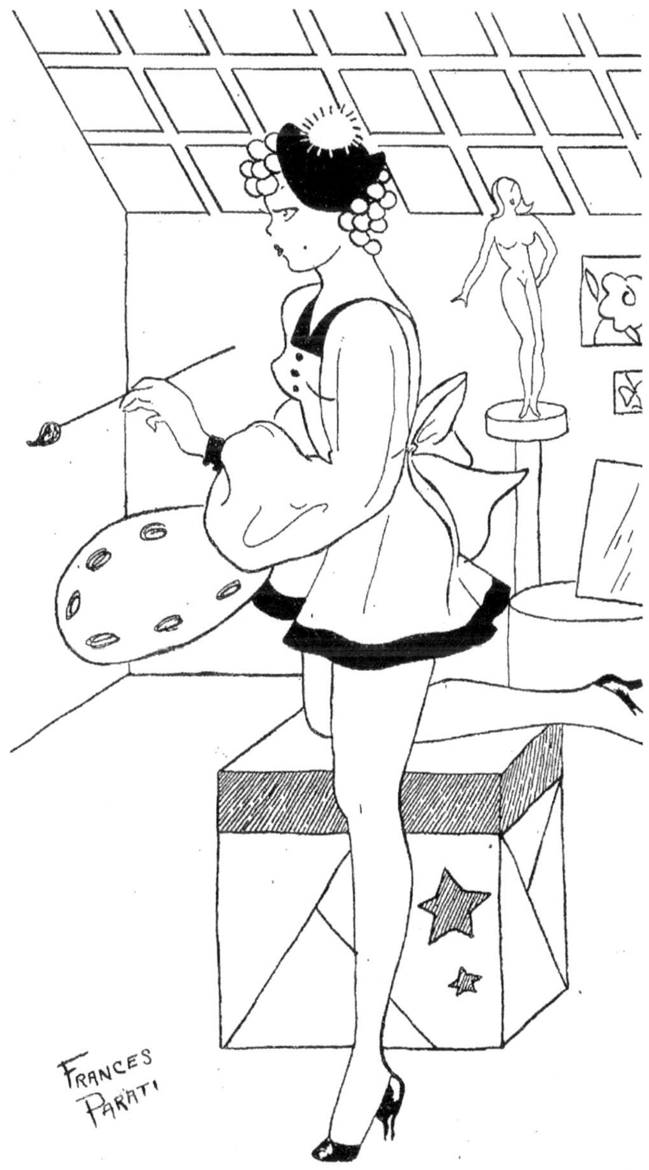

In 1928, Jim's mother Frances devised a single panel comic called "Rambling Rose Says" that was about a country girl named Rose who left her small town, landed in a significant metropolis, and offered sage observations about life in the big city.

drawings when he was a kid and asking his mother, "How can you do this?" He wondered how does an artist know what to draw, where to put each color, where to press hard with a pen, what to do with a pencil? Jim's mother told her son that eventually, he would know what to keep, and what to leave out, so that with one little flick of a paint brush or a pen, the artist can tell a story. "Let your mind fill in the blank spots," she told Jim.[7] Jim came to understand that sometimes, those blank spots stay blank. Years later, he recalled, his mother had started a painting before she suffered a stroke, laying out a base coat canvas of white and orange, probably for a floral scene. Much later, she decided to return to the painting but never could muster the strength to finish it. Gertie Rose, Jim's mother's caretaker, wondered why Frances would spend an hour or so staring at the canvas. Jim remembered: "I told Gertie not to worry. Momma was probably completing the painting in her mind."[8]

For Jim, the comic strips in the newspapers were far and away a first source of influence and inspiration before the comic books. The newspapers were far more affordable during those post-war years.[9] On Sundays, after the family returned from church, they were just in time to tune in a radio show called "The Comic Weekly Man." The host would read the funnies, using different voices for the various characters. The "Comic Reader Man" would instruct his listeners to spread the newspaper out on the floor, and then he would say, "OK, boys and girls, turn to *Flash Gordon*. He'd have a little jingle that would be the intro to the comic, and then he'd read the funny. That impressed me."[10] Fifty years later, Jim recalled reading *Flash Gordon, Blondie, Li'l Abner* in the newspapers his father brought him.[11] He loved *Wash Tubbs*, a popular adventure comic strip. "It was well drawn and super well written. It would hold up today."[12] When Jim was in first or second grade, he had what he recalled as rheumatic fever that, over time, led to other complications including a kidney infection—nephritis. He was confined to his bed for a long stretch of time. During those months he immersed himself in drawing, reading comics, and listening to the radio. The cartoon characters, especially as they were personified in radio programs, became his "friends." He could count on their company. He relied on the humor in those strips and their radio versions as a salve.[13]

In the mid–1950s, as a high school student in northern Virginia, Jim wrote and illustrated a comic strip for the Wakefield High School newspaper, *The Signal*. He christened that strip "Gus Todian," in honor of the school buildings and grounds maintenance man, Mr. Walthal. Jim would draw "little vignettes" that featured the custodian, "a good old guy," and captured aspects of the school's "culture." He remembered that at lunchtime, some students would tear the end from the wrapper that contained drinking straws. The application of a burst of air from young lungs would propel the wrapper off the straw and into space. A breath of air that was sufficiently forceful would send the wrapper toward the ceiling, and with luck (or what was considered luck in the minds of some of the students) end up embedding the paper in the ceiling tile, which was a porous, presumably sound absorbing material that just allowed the wrappers to hang there, dangling down from the ceiling tile, like so many stalactites. Jim featured that aspect of Wakefield High School life in one of his cartoons. Another cartoon in the *Gus Todian* series drew attention to a large glass terrarium that existed in a certain classroom. In "real life" at Wakefield High School in

GUS TODIAN

Jim   Scancarelli

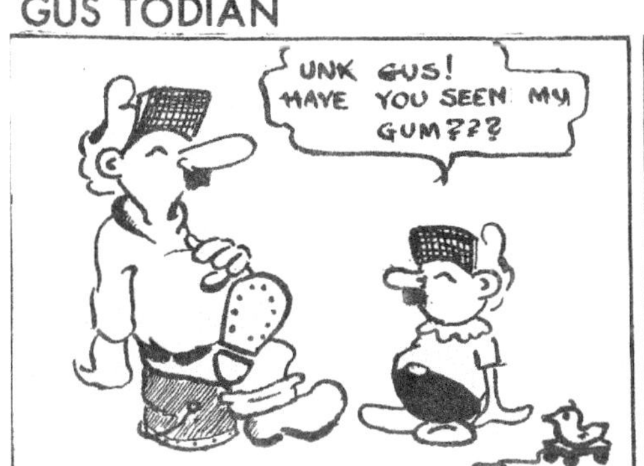

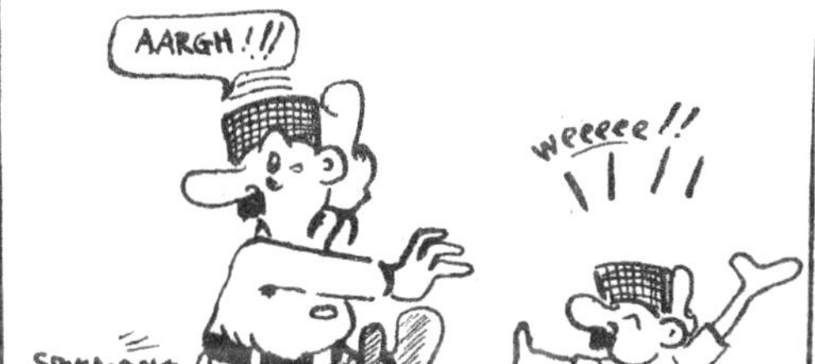

Gus Todian, **a cartoon strip that Jim illustrated and wrote during his years at Wakefield High School in Arlington, Virginia.**

Jim's day, the terrarium housed a Praying Mantis. One day, the back room erupted in ear piercing screams and the girls in the classroom began abandoning their desks, petrified because an onslaught of little baby mantises had been spawned and managed to breach the glass walls, exiting the terrarium via the screen that sat on top of what proved to be their temporary home. Jim recalled that the teacher called a recess, and summoned the custodian, who solved the problem by discarding the terrarium, and deploying his broom to end the great suffering caused by those little insects.[14] Jim memorialized that episode in his Wakefield High School comic strip.

Jim won second place at a cartoon competition in 1958, at the age of 17. He drew a *Pogo*-inspired cartoon, submitted it to the *Washington Evening Star*, and walked away with the $35.00 prize. "I drew a cartoon of Pogo playing a gourd banjo." It was an intricate drawing. One of the staffers at the newspaper told Jim he should have nailed down the first prize, but his sketch was too finely detailed to translate well into print.[15]

Mad Magazine

Jim thought that the "adventure" comics—comics such as *Dick Tracy*—were drawn in a way that was artistically spectacular. When he was a schoolboy in Washington, D.C., every day his mother would prepare breakfast before Jim struck out for a day of reading, writing, and arithmetic. In that interval before he had to make his way to school, he got to look at the funny pages in *The Times Herald*.[16] The humor, the characters, and the way they continuously developed over time—all that defined for him the hallmarks of a well-wrought cartoon.[17]

As he got older, Jim became more discerning about which strips were really his favorites. He began to recognize the variance between the skill levels of different illustrators and writers. Thinking back on how that shaped his own sense of excellence in drawing technique and competence in story line formulation, Jim stated:

Cartoonists who really blew me away, really influenced me—I don't want to say stylistically, but it sure was a big influence—were Jack Davis and Bill Elder and Wally Wood. *Mad Comics* and *Mad Magazine*. Boy, those guys were just incredible. I could not see how any human being could draw like that. So, I tried to emulate it, but I'm not Jack Davis or Wally Wood. Momma and Daddy did not approve too much of me looking at the *Mad* stuff because—oh, boy—those guys could draw girls like you'd never believe. When I was growing up in Arlington, Virginia, there was a little old country store near us. McDonald's Country Store. It looked just as you'd think such a place would look in your wildest imagination. Barrels of pickles. Caskets hanging from the ceiling of the place. Old great big hand-hewn planks of wood for flooring that was always covered with sawdust. It was within walking distance of our house. I'd always go up there and that's where I started seeing *Mad Comics*—which became *Mad Magazine*. I would try to imitate Jack Davis' style. I was always amazed at how he could animate something, distort features, and yet you'd know exactly what he was drawing.[18]

In early November 2019 Jim was honored by the Southeast Chapter of the National Cartoonist Society with the Jack Davis Award. The award underscored the way that *Mad Magazine*, and Jack Davis, informed Jim's sense of good comic strip work.[19] Jim owns a full-page drawing by Jack Davis depicting two boxers in a ring in the midst of a serious brawl:

Thousands of people in the audience. And you can recognize some of them. There's Joe Louis. Jack Dempsey. Remember, there was a TV show called *The Medic*. Richard Boone was in it. There he is, in the audience dressed as a doctor. Alfred E. Newman's image is visible in the audience just above the boxing glove of the fighter on the left side of the drawing. That was one of the first actual appearances of Alfred E. Newman. At that point, they didn't call him Alfred E. Newman. They called him the "What, Me Worry?" Kid.[20]

The "What, Me Worry?" Kid character, Jim recalled, was a reference to a post card drawing for patented medicines that dated to the 1800s featuring a kid with the space between his teeth, and one eye cocked.[21]

Early on, Jim had the sense that the skill involved in writing novels and short stories, for example, was not necessarily something that could be transferred to the task of writing comic strips. Comic strips required a focus on continuity of story line, and brevity—the memory of past strips needs to lead the reader back to the newspaper looking for the next panel in a story arc. The meaning of a comic story emerges from a commitment to following that strip with consistency—a strip needs to be read every day in order to deliver "meaning." Books, and short stories, deliver their messages in the fullness of time, messages that stand and can be revisited to derive the experience of having that meaning repeated. Comic strips are a lot like the old radio shows—they impart their humor quickly, the story moves on, and one needs to stick with the arc as it moves forward to derive any pleasure from the strip, especially since the daily newspapers in which the comics are printed are often tossed in the trash bin at the end of the day. Even comic book writers were bewildered by the experience of working on daily story strips and often were not able to introduce characters in the "gag-a-day" format, or transition to a format that placed a premium on brevity, imagery, and the memory of the immediate past of the strip. Comic strips, Jim said, outlive their cartoonists, and need to transition over time. "Nobody can be their own predecessor," Jim noted, so the priority focus for strip work ends up shifting to the task of keeping the characters in character and sustaining the focus on brevity as a way of achieving what is, in the end, the primary goal: selling tomorrow's newspapers so readers come back continuously for one more day of the story.[22]

The Road to Gasoline Alley

In the 1970s, Jim was confident that his high school time in the print shop, his time on the job in the photo and the print shop during his years in the U.S. Navy, his experience as a graphic artist, and his work in radio and television gave him a firm enough grounding in technique, production art, and writing to get a job as a cartoonist. He was also convinced that those capabilities combined with his own long term love affair with comic humor equipped him with the instincts to turn an idea into a sketch, then a drawing, and a story.

Jim was not without good, solid connections and friendships in the cartooning world that owed to his time on the job at WBT. One friend, George Breisacher, who worked for the *Charlotte Observer*, introduced Jim to Dick Moores, the writer and illustrator for the strip *Gasoline Alley*. That proved to be a critical step in landing the position as Moores' assistant. Breisacher, Jim said, was a great talent[23]:

> He was a real terrific cartoonist, good humorist. And he could draw—his style was way ahead of conventional art. His work was modern looking, and he was a good designer. He picked up on the computers right in their infancy. George made the computer do stuff that I don't think they designed them to do. I don't know how he knew how to fool with it, but he did, and he turned out some terrific stuff. He tried to get many comic strips syndicated but they all turned him down.[24]

Breisacher called Jim one Friday in 1977 and asked whether Jim would care to join him on a trip to visit Dick Moores. Jim, an avid reader of *Gasoline Alley* from his very young years, was familiar with Moores' work. In fact, forty years later Jim recalled that he had a slight acquaintance with Moores' daughter, Sara, in the 1960s. Sara was friends with a certain young lady named Sally who Jim was dating at the time. On one occasion, Sara visited Sally's house and Jim met her. He remembered asking Sara how to go about being a cartoonist and getting to work for her daddy. That strategy did not work very well. He never got an answer to his question and thus failed

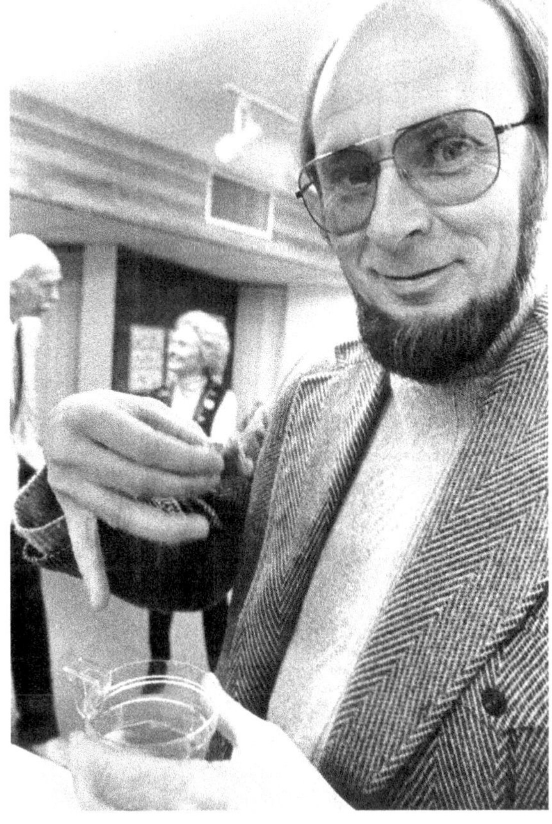

George Breisacher at Dick Moores' art exhibit, Asheville, North Carolina, 1984. Dick Moores is visible on the left side of the photo, engaged in conversation. Photograph by Jim Scancarelli.

to achieve the traction that would have catapulted him into the world of drawing cartoons.

Jim seized on the chance to ride with Breisacher to visit Moores. He recalled a wonderful drive through the mountains of North Carolina, and a very pleasant visit. "Dick was a great host. He and I hit it off. It was fun to talk comics." Two years later, the Syndicate that owned *Gasoline Alley* wanted Moores to have an assistant, and since the Syndicate owned the strip, they were in a position to get what they wanted from their artist. When the Chicago Tribune–New York Daily News Syndicate started out, back in 1918, cartoonists had a little bit more power over their strips. Eventually, syndicates started buying shares in the ownership, and worked their way toward 50–50 splits between a syndicate and the comic strip illustrators/writers. In the case of *Gasoline Alley*, from the beginning, Frank King, the strip's originator, owned 50 percent of the strip. When he died, the Syndicate sought to purchase total ownership of the strip, but King had given Dick Moores 25 percent—at least according to the story that Moores told Jim. Before he became ill, sometime in 1982 or 1983, Moores sold his 25 percent back to the Tribune Syndicate. By the time Jim hitched a ride with Breisacher to Moores' home, the Syndicate was in a position to issue instructions, like the one aimed at prodding Moores to find himself an assistant.

As Jim tells the story, what Moores discovered in conducting interviews for the position of assistant was that many of the applicants did not read the strip, and consequently were not familiar with the characters. Jim, though, knew the strip characters and the long arc of *Gasoline Alley* dating back to Frank King's time at the helm. At some point during the process of interviewing applicants, Moores privately asked George Breisacher if Jim was truly interested in the job. Breisacher called Jim and put that question to him. Jim stated his interest with enthusiasm, and that fact made its way back to Moores.

Dick Moores required all the applicants for the assistantship to draw some of the *Gasoline Alley* regulars. "Trying to draw something that you are not used to is a little difficult," Jim remembered. In 2020, he ran across one of the drawings he had done at the request of Moores during the interview process. "Oh, boy, was it bad." Now, at that point, one of the leading applicants for the job pushed his luck and apparently tried to talk Moores into making a quick decision to hire that applicant straight away. Moores did not like the fact that the applicant attempted to exert leverage by suggesting that he was in a position to get any job he wanted and had several other potentially lucrative options in front of him. Moores wished him luck. The next call Moores made was to Jim:

> Dick called me and said I'm going to send you a tryout. He sent me an original. I copied it and you couldn't tell it from the original. I sent it back to him. He said, "OK. I'll start sending you stuff on a trial basis. You ink everything except the faces." So, he sent me a week of penciled dailies. And I would fill in all the bodies, hands, background, black area. Dick would ink the faces for if they didn't look like who they were supposed to look like, the readers would certainly have objected.[25]

At that point Jim still did not really have the job, at least "officially." Moores just kept sending Jim assignments to ink, and Jim kept drawing them. Every time Moores sent a batch of sketches for Jim to do the final ink work, Jim would get a check. After several years, Jim concluded that he had in fact been hired.

Cartoon Boot Camp

The way an aspiring cartoonist learned the business in Jim's day was basically through arrangements that facilitated an intensive old-style apprenticeship—arrangements that perhaps had some aspects of indentured servitude imbedded in the relationship. Many of the younger assistants to cartoonists moved in with their bosses. For example, Fred Lasswell lived and worked with Billy DeBeck before he took over *Snuffy Smith* from DeBeck, the original cartoonist.[26] Frank King had eight assistants over time. Jim knew Bill Perry (1905–1995), and Jack Fox, who went on to assist Ed Dodd on the strip *Mark Trail*. Jim also knew Bob Zschiesche who replaced Perry when the latter retired in 1975.[27] Moores hired Zschiesche to help on the Sunday strips. Zschiesche had just retired after 12 years doing editorial cartoons for the *Greensboro Daily News* in North Carolina and was working on plans to do an editorial cartoon when he took the assistant's position with Moore. By April 1979, Zschiesche and Moores had parted company, and Moores resumed doing the work on all seven days of *Gasoline Alley*. Not long after that, he hired Jim to assist on dailies.[28]

Jim had contact—mostly phone conversations—with John Chase (1905–1986) and Albert Tolf (1911–1996), "graduates" of the Frank King comic strip boot camp.[29] Chase attended the Chicago Academy of Fine Arts and worked for King before returning to New Orleans in 1927, where he became an editorial cartoonist for *The New Orleans Item*, a position he held until 1964. Tolf, an artist known for paintings and cartoons featuring the history of San Francisco, worked for King in the 1930s, and later took a job as a scenic painter at Disneyland before that theme park opened its doors. Tolf also worked for a railroad sleeping car manufacturing concern before moving to San Francisco in 1949, at which point he turned to fine art.

The relationships and the common experiences of aspiring cartoonists who cut their teeth working as assistants for Frank King, and later Dick Moores, created the atmosphere of a small, tight,

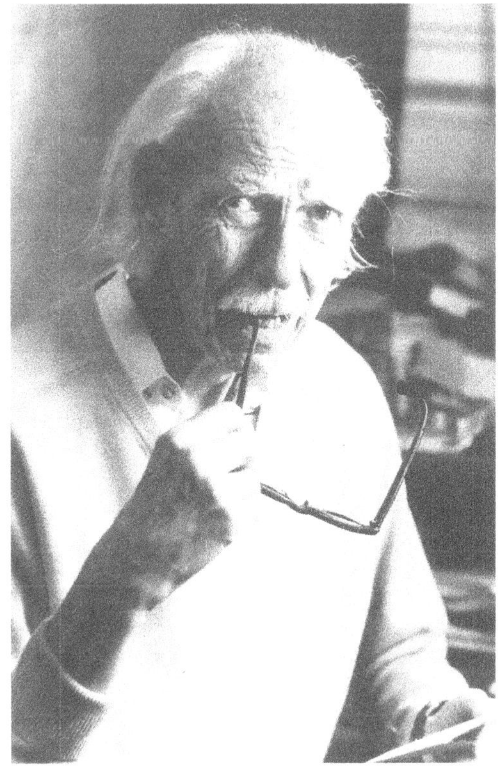

Dick Moores. Photograph by Jim Scancarelli, 1984.

rather jovial and good-natured fraternity. The apprentices served their employers by taking on jobs that relieved their bosses of some of the more mundane tasks involved in the production of the strip—inking, outlining, coloring. They also took on responsibilities that lapped over into doing personal chores for the principal artist.

Jim made the case that the practice of having assistants live with the principal cartoonist made sense largely because the complexity of the artwork and writing required that kind of on-the-ground collaborative work as deadlines approached. A good assistant needed that kind of proximity to be able to absorb the "mind set" of the principal artist/writer. In time, a good assistant would be able to assimilate an understanding of the personalities of the key cartoon characters so that the assistant could begin to figure out how those characters would act, how storylines would evolve, what characters would be likely to do in the face of challenges and predicaments.[30]

Jim referred to his apprenticeship with Moores as "The School of Mooresian Cartooning."[31] When he took the job, Jim understood that to perform effectively, he would have to figure out a way to discern how Moores' approached the stories, how he primed the characters to act out the actions required by story plots. Jim thought about how he would have to find a way to match the sketches with the words the characters spoke and the actions they were undertaking in each frame.[32] To be an effective assistant, he had to try to discern the style and technique that informed Moores' artwork, so Jim could make his work look as though Moore had done the illustrations. Thirty-five years after he assumed responsibility for the comic strip, Jim suggested that the test of his success was that readers never complained that aspects of the *Gasoline Alley* characters had changed in recognizable ways during the years Jim worked for Moores. Jim managed to learn the intricacies of Moores' style to the point that he could replicate that approach consistently.[33]

During Jim's assistantship, Moores wanted to "indoctrinate" Jim into the dimension of the cartoonist apprenticeship that had the assistant living with the cartoonist, integrated into the cartoonist's daily life, immersed in his thinking, and capable of sketching and telling stories in a manner that reflected the cartoonist's way of thinking about his comic strip characters, envisioning the way they thought and acted in different circumstances.[34] While Jim did not take up residence in Dick Moores' home, the cartoonist had Jim spend a week every month with him—except during the winter months because of just how treacherous driving in winter weather was on the roads from Charlotte to Fairview, North Carolina, outside of Asheville. Moores owned 75 acres, and he had a pond near his house. He lived with four Doberman Pinschers.[35] Jim would travel to Moores' home and stay in the guest house, and Moore would "lend" Jim one of his dogs to keep him company.[36] Jim remembered that he always had a significant pile of work to do. Moore would critique Jim's product: "He'd say, 'I think you need to white this out. You've gone too far this way.' And he was a stickler for doing it his way. I have respect for that." Thinking back on those days over forty years later, Jim said:

> The interesting thing: one of the Dobermans would crawl onto my lap as I was inking and he would be looking at what I was doing. I'm inking away. The dog is drooling all over the artwork! I loved that old critter. Dick Moores used to drool over the artwork, too. He had a pipe and he'd drool great big volumes of stuff over the strips, leaving tobacco stains on it. He had a guest

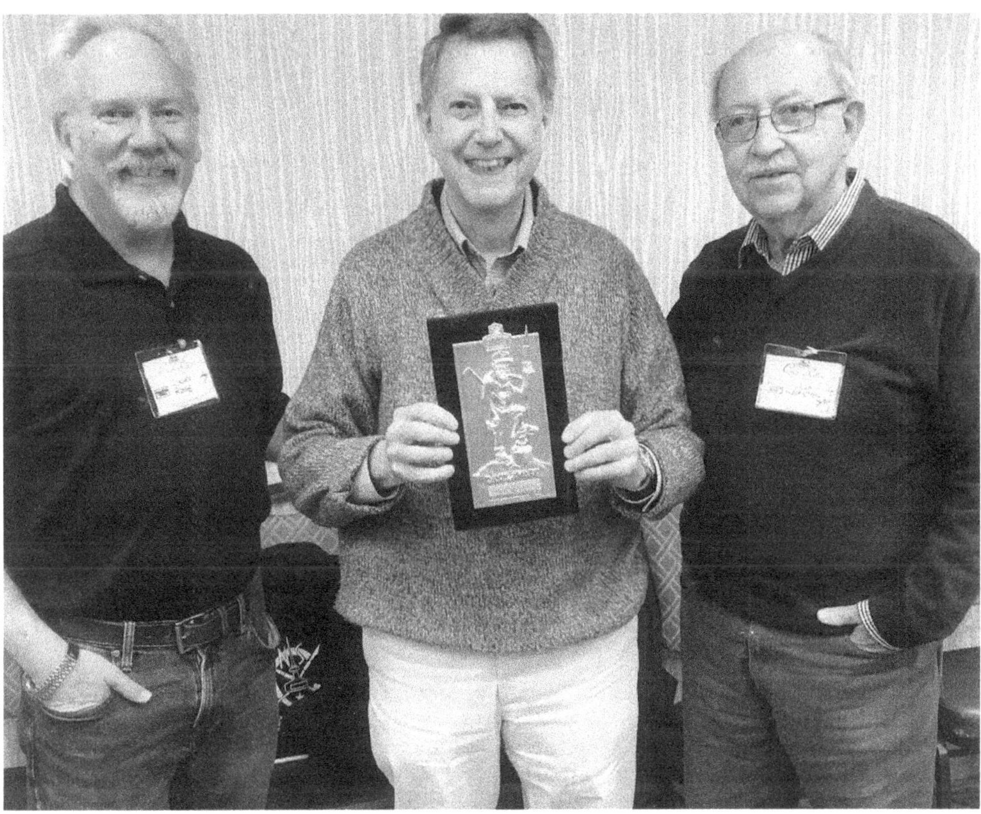

Left to right: John Rose, Jim Scancarelli, and Marcus Hamilton in Braselton, Georgia, for the 2019 meeting of the Southeast Chapter of the National Cartoonists Society at which Jim was awarded the Jack Davis Award honoring him as the Cartoonist of the Year.

house and I got the run of that house. He would tell me stories. Indoctrinate me in inking techniques. Lettering. Every aspect of the comic. Then we'd have think tank sessions where he'd say he was up against a wall and couldn't think of anything. I'd say something, but most of the time he didn't like my ideas.[37]

Jim's sense was that Moores prided himself on that independence of mind and personal capacity to undertake the job on the strength of his own imagination and artistry. While Moores accepted some of the suggestions Jim pushed forward, more often than not he responded to such offerings with the remark, "well, that's your idea." Jim recalled: "I did use a lot of that stuff after he'd passed away, because I'd thought of those stories, and I had them in reserve." Jim stated:

Dick would always say, "Try to draw this better than I'm drawing it. Don't try to imitate it line by line. Put yourself into it. Try to take this away from me."[38]

Occasionally, while walking Moores' hounds around the lake in back of Moores' house, Moores and Jim would kick ideas around. Sometimes Moores would acknowledge a recommendation by Jim. Other times, he would tactfully but unequivocally reject Jim's ideas. Forty years later, Jim thought that this way of managing the give and take between the cartoonist and his apprentice had less to do with Moores' pride

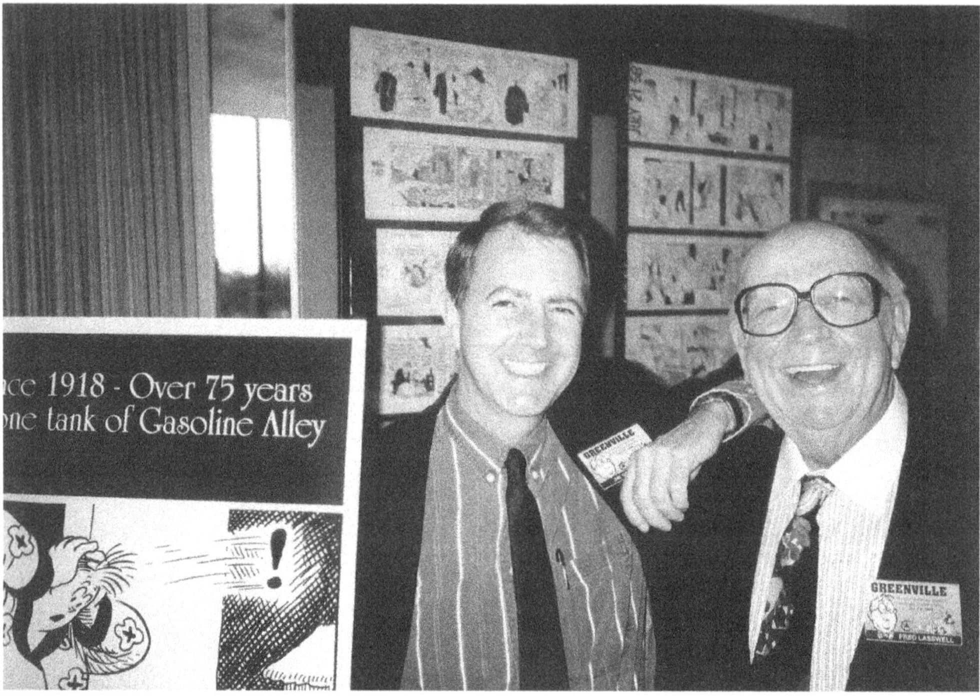

Jim Scancarelli and Fred Lasswell at an exhibit in honor of *Gasoline Alley* and *Snuffy Smith* in Greenville, South Carolina, in 1998. Following the 1942 death of Billy DeBeck, who originated *Barney Google* in 1919, "Uncle Fred" took over the strip. Lasswell, who introduced the character Snuffy Smith to the strip in 1943, drew that cartoon for nearly 59 years.

of authorship, or his desire to keep his own sense of where a story should go than with what Jim has long felt was a cartoonist's need to put ideas for a strip through his own mental filter—what Jim's cousin Doug called "The Jimmy Filter." That is, in order for a piece of character dialogue, a story arc, the trajectory of a thread to make sense it had to fit with the manner in which the cartoonist would think about a particular idea, and how he would envision the characters he drew reacting in a particular situation. That seemed to be Jim's view of the way a cartoonist would lend authenticity to the behavior and words of a cartoon character in a particular situation. Here, Jim's idea was that the "Jimmy Filter" acted as a mechanism that would keep the words Jim would put in the mouths of the *Gasoline Alley* citizens true to the "personality" of cartoon character. Jim believed that a cartoon lurches off course once a cartoonist begins to "self-promote," to feature his own artistry in drawing and his cleverness in writing more than merely keeping to what would strike the reader as authentic and reasonable in the context of the strip's history, and credible given the nature of the characters they had grown used to.[39]

"Modernizing" Gasoline Alley

Marcus Hamilton, the illustrator for the "Dennis the Menace" daily strips, looked at the impact of taking over a comic strip enterprise from its originator in the same way Jim thought about having joined the line of writers and artists responsible for *Gasoline Alley*. Time imposes the requirement to "modernize" aspects of the strip. Writers and illustrators need to look at how current social and cultural circumstances mandate alterations in the characters, the kinds of situations the characters encounter, how the characters speak and interact, and how they are depicted—what physical characteristics no longer work in drawing the characters. That invariably leads devotees of the strips to picking apart minuscule deviations in the artwork and offering their critical assessments of character "behavior" in the numerous online platforms that carry the strips—and afford avid comic strip readers the chance to make their comments known. Hamilton recalled *Dennis the Menace* being a bit more brash in the years before he began working on the strip. He recalled abandoning the ubiquitous sling shot in Dennis' rear pocket—once that "toy" became "weaponized," it no longer had any comic resonance.[40]

Jim also recognized the need to "modernize," to have current life situations, challenges, social realities reflected in *Gasoline Alley*. At the same time, both Jim and Hamilton were committed to staying as close to the original ideas and spirit of their mentors—Dick Moores and Hank Ketcham, respectively—who shaped the strips for which Jim and Marcus Hamilton assumed responsibility.[41]

So, between 1979—when Jim began working for Moores as his assistant—and 1986—when he began working the daily and weekend strips on his own—what showed up in Jim's work on *Gasoline Alley* was his consistently unerring ability to complete the inking of the strips that Moores had penciled in a manner that captured his mentor's artistry. However, during that stretch of years there were some things about Jim's drawings that readers, and other cartoonists, picked up on. Russ Myers, who created *Broom Hilda*, mentioned to Moores sometime in 1979 that the thickness of line in some of the strips had become inconsistent. At that time, in 1979, Jim was using a Rapidograph pen that required him to hit the pencil outline with ink from the pen several times before he could get it to the desired thickness. Both Moores and his friend Myers noticed this. Moores did not quite like the effect of that inflexible steel point pen for drafting. After Jim's second week on the job in 1979, Moores telephoned. "Stuff looks good," Jim recalled him saying, adding that Moores recommended the Joseph Gillott Pointed Dip Pen Nib 290 as an alternative to Jim's choice of pens because that Nib 290 was more elastic, and produced both wide and thin lines on Bristol board or smooth surface paper.[42] In a subsequent phone call, after Jim had switched tools, Moores told Jim, "You got it."

* * *

There was a brief period during which Jim worked on both *Gasoline Alley* with Dick Moores, and *Mutt and Jeff* with George Breisacher.

Breisacher had tried for a long time to get a comic strip of his own. He assembled what Jim recalled Breiscacher describing as an impressive array of rejection slips that he could have easily used as wallpaper. A lot of the cartoonists sang the same song. In 1980, one of the comic syndicates asked Breisacher if he wanted to do *Mutt and Jeff*. He jumped at the opportunity. Jim stated:

Al Smith was doing *Mutt and Jeff* at that time. He was up in his 80s. That doesn't sound so advanced now, as I approach that age. Anyway, George got the account. He started writing the gags, and he was drawing them in his style, and his style was very different. At the time he didn't know who was the tall one and who was the short character. Mutt was the tall one. Jeff was the little one. He had them looking too modern and too animated, and complaints started coming in. At that time, *Mutt and Jeff* was in about 40 papers in America and Europe.

Breisacher asked Jim if he would be interested in drawing the strip and splitting the paycheck 50–50. Jim recalled: "I think each of us got 150 bucks, and at that time that was a lot of money. I had just started working on *Gasoline Alley*, and I asked Dick Moores if that would conflict with my responsibilities to that strip, and he said, no, it would probably help." Jim continued:

> Well, it sure did because I did a lot of inking. I had some old books that contained some reprints of the comic and old stories, and I liked the way the cartoonist Billy Liverpool did *Mutt and Jeff* better than the artist who started the strip, Bud Fischer. Liverpool was also an assistant to the cartoonist who did *Crazy Cat*. His style was loose, compared to the stiffer, thinner lines used by the originator of *Mutt and Jeff*, whose drawings had a cardboard aspect to them. So, I emulated Liverpool's work. One of the first ones that I did was 18 January 1982. It was pretty crude, but as we got into it, things became easier. The last strip was published on 25 June 1983. So, the Thursday before the comic came to an end, I wrote and drew it and I was proud of that one.[43]

In 1983, *Mutt and Jeff* went into re-runs using strips from the years during which Al Smith was drawing the cartoon. "They wanted to know if we wanted to keep it going. George figured that they had cut back and we wouldn't be making what we had been making. It was not worth the time for the money."[44] *Mutt and Jeff* remained in syndication until 1983. After that, the two characters would make periodic guest appearances in *Gasoline Alley* beginning in the mid–1980s. Jim explained:

> Mutt was the emcee for the 100th anniversary celebration at the Retirement Home of Old Comics. It was just fun to do. I had no idea where the story would go. It just kind of ambled along. I made a six-month long story out of it, which was probably longer than it should have gone, but it was fun. It ended up with a pie throwing melee. Snuffy Smith came in, and they were going to have their 100th anniversary in a few months, so he wanted recognition. He got mad. They started throwing pies at each other. It was like the scenes in old silent movies with a great deal of mess, but it was fun.[45]

The Baton Is Passed

The last Sunday page Moores completed was on 24 August 1980.[46] Jim assumed responsibilities for the Sunday pages and the dailies at that point. In the first third of 1986, Jim inked the last *Gasoline Alley* strips that Moores sketched in pencil. Moores died in Asheville, North Carolina, in April 1986.

That month, Moores was scheduled to receive the National Cartoonists Society Story Strip Award for 1985. Jim traveled to the Society's annual dinner in Washington, D.C., to accept the honor for Moores, who had been hospitalized by then. At that point, Jim and Dick Moores were about four months ahead in terms of having inked *Gasoline Alley* strips for future runs, but Jim did not have any sense of the direction in which Moore intended to take the story in the thread on which Moores had been working before he took ill.

Jim returned to North Carolina after the National Cartoonists Society meeting and visited Moores in the hospital in Asheville on 21 April 1986. Jim brought the award, a plaque, with him. He recalled that there was a crucifix over Moores' hospital bed. Moores asked Jim to take the figure of Jesus off the wall and replace it with the National Cartoonist Society Award. "Man, that's nice," Moores said, admiring the plaque. After a while, Jim recalled, Moores told him that he had "better put Jesus back so he can look over me." Thirty-four years later, Jim recalled that Moores, a Christian Scientist, had moved toward Agnosticism in the last years of his life, after he had been urged by a doctor to set aside the Christian Science life rules regarding medical care that could have had implications for his longevity. Toward the end of his visit, Jim inquired about the story line of the unfinished *Gasoline Alley* arc on which Moores had been working before he was hospitalized. "Oh, I don't know," Moores told Jim. "We can talk about it later. I've got a lot of stories to tell. We'll get on it." Jim continued:

> I had no idea what to do about the unfinished strip, but I knew it was time to leave, to let Moore sleep. I got into my car and just started to cry. I got home, went to bed, and by the morning [23 April], Dick's son-in-law called to tell me that Moores had died during the night.[47]

Jim called the Syndicate to report that Moores had passed away. Jim had met Bob Reed who had been named president and CEO of the Tribune Company's syndication arm, Tribune Media Services, in 1974—a position Reed held until his retirement in 1993. However, the Syndicate did not know Jim well. "They didn't know me from Adam's house cat," as Jim put it. The Syndicate had Jim agree to a schedule of keeping two weeks ahead of publication dates for each strip, and he fell into a routine of writing the stories, inking the strips, and dispatching the products to Chicago via an overnight delivery service. He kept up that pace for over a year. The pace and scope of the work was overwhelming for a single person. Before he became ill, Moores had been writing the stories. For Jim, the writing work was an immense addition of responsibility, especially since Moores had made the Sunday page a continuation of the daily strip.

That arrangement for the Sunday page did not work for Jim, and he gradually discontinued the practice of kicking off a story line in the Sunday strip and unspooling the details in the dailies. That was a practice that Moore had adopted following Chester Gould's way of managing the *Dick Tracy* comic.[48] In late 1986, Jim began to shift away from that practice. On Jim's watch, the dailies were reserved for the story lines, and the Sunday strips became stand-alone frames heralding major holidays (Thanksgiving, Christmas), or an opportunity for Jim to spool out a special poignant story or a self-contained gag or focus on a continuing comedic routine that was self-contained and not related to the dailies. One such recurring Sunday strip featured a format that had Rufus reading questions from supposed readers who wrote in hoping for a response from Joel who answered these imaginary "inquiries" from readers in ways that frequently spun out into a *non sequitur* that misconstrued the original query, thus allowing Jim to have Joel's response launch on a trajectory toward the gag humor stratosphere. The last Sunday *Gasoline Alley* that continued a story from the daily strips was on 19 October 1986.[49] After Moores died, for a while the Syndicate kept running *Gasoline Alley* in newspapers with Moores' byline, even though Jim was drawing the strips, writing the stories, and signing them. Jim's stewardship over Gasoline Alley began in earnest on 13 October 1986.

There were several strips that ran into story threads of various lengths which Jim regarded as "transitional" from Moores tenure to his time at the helm. One featured a nephew of Skeezix's who took over the farm run by the parents of Skeezix's wife, Nina. Nina's maiden name was Clock—as in Nina Clock … nine o'clock. The reference is a verbal pun—a "groaner" of the sort that Jim always enjoyed, especially when those puns spawned other similar plays on words that led to a cascade of groans. Nina's name was also a reference to Frank King's hobby of repairing clocks. In a tsunami of such puns, it turns out that Nina's aunt is named Ada—Ada Clock … eight o'clock. Adam, Corky Wallet's son, takes over the farm after Grandfather Clock passes away. Adam married a Pacific Islander, Teeka Tok.[50] Another strip that Jim considered transitional referenced O. Winston Link (1914–2001), an American photographer known for his black-and-white pictures—and sound recordings—of steam locomotives on the Norfolk and Western lines in the 1950s. Link was a pioneer of night photography methods featured in two books, *Night Trick* (1983) and *Steam, Steel and Stars* (1998).[51] That thread was an idea that Jim had proposed to Moores who gently suggested to Jim that he save it for the future.

Jim's "maiden voyage" as the writer/illustrator for *Gasoline Alley* on 13 October 1986 involved a story that began with Rufus and Joel uncovering an old U.S. Army radio transmitter buried in a junkyard. They load the transmitter onto their cart, take it home, and hatch a plan to start their own radio station, WJUNK. The pair of them build a radio signal tower out of scrap wood, and when Rufus climbs up on a nearby power pole to try and jump start transmissions, he gets zapped by the current. Sparks flew off of him, his arms stiffened. Jim drew the bursts of electricity emanating from an electrified Rufus in the forms of stars, and had Joel declare that Rufus had truly become a star.[52]

The next set of dailies released during the week of 27 October 1986 featured the "Thorn Jumpers," a band meant to reference WBT's Briarhoppers. The storyline started with three days of action in Joel and Rufus' junk yard. A pickup truck full of musicians—including a fiddler meant to resemble Hank Warren—shows up at the junkyard. With the new radio tower cobbled together from old wooden planks looming large in the background, the banjo player for the Thorn Jumpers approaches Rufus and Joel seeking an audition for WJUNK.[53] The next few days have Joel and Rufus coping with a surprise visit from several officials from the FCC who make clear that the *Gasoline Alley* duo are transmitting on radio frequencies without a license.[54]

Not long after that, on 16 November, Jim ran a *Gasoline Alley* Sunday page that featured a musician who looked uncannily like Willy Nelson. The character shows up at Corky's Diner for a meal, a little bit disheveled, to the point that one of the cook staff suggests that this guy looks as though he could use a free meal. The character is dubbed "Willy Wilson," and he proceeds to show that he can pay for his order, handing over a twenty dollar bill, telling the staff to keep the change—at which point a young girl rushes in, recognizes the musician, fishes around where Willy had just eaten, and announces "Oh, I've got his napkin!," signaling that Willy had some traction in a fan base in or around the fictitious town depicted in *Gasoline Alley*.[55]

Jim clearly knew the citizens of *Gasoline Alley*. As a consequence, it was easy for him to reflect those personalities in the strip and remain consistent with the long history of the comic. He had developed the capacity to discern the rhythm of a character's speech, and to understand how the characters would each react to a particular challenge, to any situation.[56] However, he did have to endure the formalities of an interview for the job. The initial interview for the job of writing and illustrating the *Gasoline Alley* strip after Dick Moores passed away was conducted at The City Club in Chicago. At one point, one of the interviewers from the Tribune Syndicate asked Jim whether he liked to play golf. Jim said, "It's been so many years since I played, I wouldn't know which end of the racket to hold." That joke might not have been a resounding success, though the job did go to Jim.[57]

Jim was scrupulously committed to the broad guidelines for managing the art and storylines for *Gasoline Alley* that he learned from Moores. He also knew the long history of the strip that created fealty among readers to the basic narratives, the core running jokes, and to the strip's characters whose personalities were reliably consistent over 100 years. That was the strength of *Gasoline Alley*, in Jim's view, and the reason why it continued to survive. He was not about to trifle with that equation for success. At the same time, during his apprenticeship Jim had received Moores' messages regarding the responsibility Jim had to learn how to put his imprint on the strip. Moores telegraphed the notion that Jim had to figure out the way he could improve on the way things had been done. Jim had to make the artwork his own, and concoct his own story lines, in ways that improved the strip while sticking to whatever it was that caused the strip to remain popular for so long. Moores urged Jim to dig deeply into his own stock of stories, the "well" in which his own life experiences were warehoused in memories, and reminded Jim of his obligation to figure out ways to go beyond duplicating how Moores drew the characters, how he captured their action, and the way he figured out situations that would be the basis for storylines.

Bristol Board, Pen and Ink—Jim's Tools and Approach to the Work

During his brief stints with graphic art departments working for advertising firms, his time with WBT radio and television, and his experience as the art director for various television shows, Jim developed a deep appreciation for the contemporary techniques and technologies, and an abiding curiosity about what came before in terms of preferred approaches and reigning techniques in the earliest days of cartooning. Decades later, reflecting on the main tool of the cartoonist's trade, he said:

> The pen was the way you used to do the finished art. You could sketch the thing in pencil to get the action form. But then when you want to ink it you had to use India ink. The pen points, nowadays, are endangered species. The India ink, you get a quart of Dr. Martin's Black Star Matt wonderful India ink, for 180 or more dollars. I called the company a bunch of years ago,

and I don't think you can order direct from them anymore. You have to go through an art store. I called years ago to get a quart. They said oh, we don't sell it by the quart. We've got it in 32 ounces ....

Jim remembered that in the earlier days of cartoon illustration work, an artist would use a paper that was three to four-ply in thickness. There were two kinds, one with a smooth finish and one with a pebble finish. The cartoonists would sketch lightly, and then ink over that pencil work. After that step, the cartoonist or his assistant would erase the pencil. Following that, the production people would shoot the pictures and make a negative at the engraving plant, and then burn a plate. "If you had too much dark pencil after working on the strip with black ink you'd still see the pencil lines. You don't want that. So, some of them would use non-photo blue pencil. Walt Kelly, who drew *Pogo*, used a blue pencil. He was a great artist."[58] Jim continued to prefer some of those classic approaches to drawing, with the pencil and India Ink as the main tools of the trade. In his life, he never had a computer as part of his home office equipment; he only came to the point of being able to utilize his phone to telegraph text messages in 2010 or so—though, astoundingly, he was thrust into the 21st century in January 2021 when his flip phone died, and friends urged him to surrender to modernity and purchase an iPhone. Though he would clearly adapt to the manner in which current technologies shaped the nature of cartooning work, he preferred to approach his basic responsibilities as illustrator and writer using the tried-and-true tools, pencil and pen.

His approach to the overall task—thinking up a story line, shaping the idea into panels, writing the dialogue, working the illustrations—has remained very consistent across more than four decades of work on *Gasoline Alley*. Jim begins by thinking up a story line. If he starts doing that on a Monday, he can usually have "a germ of an idea" regarding the structure of the story by Tuesday, but he would generally keep kicking that idea around until he could shape it into something with which he was comfortable. In his words:

> I get the spark of an idea. I write the thing out. And I'll write it on an old piece of paper. You can't call it typewriter paper because nobody's using typewriters anymore. It's an 8.5-by-11-inch sheet of paper. I'll write Monday through Saturday. I'll get a little bit of an idea. The characters, I know them well enough that I know what their feelings would be, how they would act in a certain situation, and as I used to say, I throw them into the ring and they go about what they are supposed to do.[59]

If, on Monday, or by the latest, Tuesday—in this notional work week cycle—Jim had not yet come up with an idea around which he could build a weekday story, he would switch his attention to doing a Sunday *Gasoline Alley* because those were basically one gag jobs and were thus somewhat easier to manage from start to finish. Working on a Sunday one-gag *Gasoline Alley* strip gave him a moment to collect his thoughts, breaking up the manner in which a story line running in the dailies would build to a crescendo.

Jim learned from Dick Moores that the closer the illustrator/writer is to deadline, the more pressing it becomes to develop the ability to let the product go, to get it into the system on its way to preparation for printing. Moores made clear that strips leaving the hands of the cartoonist are never perfect, though the further ahead a writer/illustrator gets in building up a stock of stories, the more chance there is of having the "luxury" of making changes, editing and re-drawing, before the strip leaves the cartoonist's hand.

From time to time, Jim observed, all comic illustrators and writers confront the "blank page" that just does not seem to want to turn itself into a story frame. In such moments, Jim has sought ideas from some people close to him. He recalled: "When I had a blank spell, I used to talk to my Uncle Bob and my cousin Doug. Now I'll bounce things off of a friend who has a good sense of humor and he'll come up with something. Either I'll like it or I won't."[60] He credited his good friend Ben Barry, for example, with the idea that motivated a long story in September and October 2020 that involved Joe Pye's estranged wife, Shari Pye. A brief reunion of the separated couple gave Joe Pye and his sons the chance to enter his ex-wife's church and search for things (such as stringed instruments) that they could

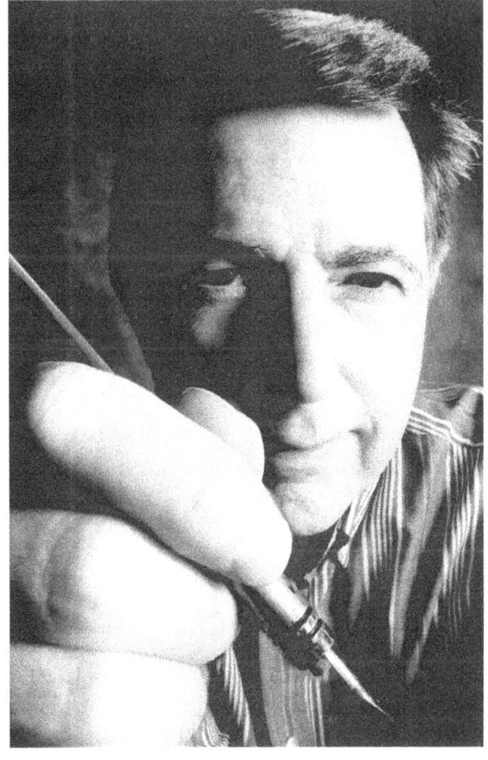

Jim Scancarelli and his favorite pen that has served him well for over 20 years, 2009. Photograph by Charles Lybrand.

steal and sell. They were ultimately scared off by a rubber snake they stumbled upon in a basement closet of the church. Jim's friend Barry recommended a real snake, and Jim changed that to a toy snake, thinking that this would soften the threat a real snake might have posed to life and limb—an example of the "Jimmy Filter" at work.[61]

Jim never took on an apprentice of his own and the Syndicate never urged him to engage an assistant. The Syndicate did press the case for an apprentice with Dick Moores, but they did not pursue that argument with Jim. However, for many years Linda Hager was a behind-the-scenes contributor to the industry necessary to get *Gasoline Alley* into print. Linda helped with aspects of the work on *Gasoline Alley* strips, doing some of the inking and undertaking the tasks necessary to keep Jim's work on schedule. Jim continues to consider Linda his "all-around studio gal" who has also stepped in at critical moments with a good idea for the strip. For example, Jim noted that Linda provided the closing gag for the 15 November 2020 Sunday story, which revolved around a visit to Clovia's father's old farm, a brief greeting with Clovia's nephew Adam busily working the land on his tractor, and a reference to Adam's wife Teeka who with Adam sought to devise some money-making schemes to bring in additional income. Teeka, Adam explained, had taught their "naughty hens" to lay "deviled eggs." That was Linda's contribution to the 15 November 2020 Sunday strip in which Adam and Teeka explained that they thought those deviled eggs would bring in some money, along with Teeka's new recipe for chicken soup, a money making scheme that failed when Adam's wife could not get the chickens to eat the soup.[62] The 22 November 2020 Sunday strip for Thanksgiving—conveying the wish "Happy Thanksgiving, All Pilgrims and Pets"—depicted a table laden with the makings of a great Thanksgiving meal, with the central characters of *Gasoline Alley* seated together. Walt is leading a prayer and an array of multi-generational *Gasoline Alley* citizens are posed with hands folded in front of them, eyes closed, deep in thought— except for Slim who is clearly licking his lips in anticipation of a feast. Rufus and Joel are standing slightly to the right of the Thanksgiving Day table, hats in their hands, eyes closed in prayerful contemplation. On the top of this single panel are the words: "Bless the food before us—the family beside us and the love between us!" The strip looks forward to a good future in the embrace of family, with youth represented by Boog and his sister.[63] Jim said: "Linda came up with the prayer. I had the basic gist of the idea, but I floundered around for what it should say. Right away Linda came up with the right words."[64]

Walk-On Roles in Gasoline Alley

During his time at the helm, Jim inserted characters into the *Gasoline Alley* strip with clear references to real life friends and relatives, acquaintances, radio and television stars, friends from the world of bluegrass and traditional music.[65] For example, a character in Jim's comic strip who resonated with Jim's friends and relatives was the Physician Assistant with the condition Synesthesia, Dr. Peter Glabella, to whom Jim ascribed the phrase Jim's father used, memorably, to drive home a key life lesson early in Jim's life: "Una Faccia, Una Razza" ("One face, one race"). Jim gave the character a clearly Italian name, to strengthen the association with his father. He was not sure, years later, that readers picked up on the meaning of the phrase in Italian, though he recounted that his editor thought it was a good idea, and that it needed to be said.[66] Jim also stuck his uncle, Bob Parati, in the strip from time to time:

> When they were in the garage, Slim and Clovia get a call from a Mr. Parati asking if his car is ready, and that got to be a running theme. It never was ready. I actually drew Bob. He had a white beard later in his life, and he wore one of these fisherman's cap—like Pete Seeger. He looked like Pete Seeger—who I had met once, and who looked like he could have been Bob Parati's brother.[67]

Wayne Henderson, a guitar builder and an accomplished guitar player from Rugby, Virginia, who worked as a mailman, appeared in the strip as himself on 30 July 2006.[68] Dolly Parton had a walk-on role as Dolly Pawton in a strip that had her conversing with Chef Meowrice on 29 May 2008.[69] In a 29 July 2012 strip, the character Slim is quoted as saying: "Well, as the late guitar picker and philosopher, Jim Greene, once said … a cat may have nine lives, but a bullfrog croaks every night!"[70] The "Ragin' Cajun"—Douglas James "Doug" Kershaw, a fiddle player, singer and songwriter from Louisiana—had a lead role in a *Gasoline Alley* thread that ran from 11 June to 12 August 2003. The storyline had Kershaw and his band seeking assistance from Joel and Rufus when the band's bus broke down on the way to a performance at the Octane Theatre. Slim traded the repair work needed to get the bus going again for several Doug Kershaw CDs and a signed publicity poster, which he placed on his wall right next to a poster autographed by Dale Earnhardt.[71] The actor in the movie "Support Your Local Gunfighter," Jack Elam, had a "bit part" in a *Gasoline Alley* story in September 2017.[72] Elam had a squint that Jim added to the image he created of a scruffy character with a beard that Jim integrated into a story. Jim called the character Elam Jackson in the strip, which was about a poor family Rufus was trying to help. Rufus liked the kids and tried to do a belated Christmas for them.[73]

Jim's formula was simple: look at life, then twist and turn it until the absurd, or the humorous, drips out. When Dick Moores died, the Tribune Syndicate that owned the strip said they wanted *Gasoline Alley* to have more humor in it. Gag-a-day comics had begun to edge out the story strips to the point that there were very few story strips left. Jim put his mind to having both humor and story.

On Language

Dick Moores had two *Gasoline Alley* citizens, Rufus and Joel, speak in what he thought was Appalachian mountain talk. Jim's view was that Moores had them saying things that people who lived in Appalachia just would not say:

> I grew up here and I've heard this all my life. I know how to speak English and I also understand the vernacular, the rurality of the mountain folks. I had Rufus and Joel speak more of what I thought was authentic mountain talk. The readers I know from the city don't appreciate that kind of humor and they certainly don't like the language because they say it's hard to read. I sort of refined the lingo, but I found out over the years, if you go to Danville, Virginia, they have a different kind of twang. They don't sound like they do around here in Charlotte, North Carolina, or in the western part of the state. They start saying "aboot" instead of "about." If you keep going east you get toward the coast, and they are speaking what linguists say is a remnant of Elizabethan English. They are speaking in what is in effect a different dialect, and their formation of sentences is different than the way we put words together. Here's an example. Regarding the old buildings and other structures in North Carolina and Virginia, talking to a farmer out on the eastern shore, a documentary film maker heard locals talking about a "fade barn." He did not know what that meant. So, he'd ask different people about this, and finally came to someone who simply said, "Well, a fade barn is where you keep your fade for the cattle." Fade. Feed.[74]

Jim remained fascinated with language and sought to reflect some of the unique ways of putting things in the comic strip. He has, over the years, found it challenging to reflect those differences in the language that some of the citizens of *Gasoline Alley* use in their daily life. From time to time, Jim has written script for the comic that editors just did not get, and that might just confuse readership:

> They don't know what I'm saying because they don't talk that way. Giving somebody "Down in the Country." Know what that means? If you get mad at them and fuss at them, you're giving them "down in the country." I had *Gasoline Alley* characters saying that, and I had to change the copy. Reno Bailey, he came up with a glossary of terms in Cliffside, a Carolina mill town, that captured a lot of southernisms. Every one of them I heard as a kid. "Beans from apple butter." Readers and editors don't seem to understand that.[75]

Gasoline Alley, *Politics, and Other Straying Themes*

Throughout his days at the helm of *Gasoline Alley*, Jim has stuck to a set of his own rules. He would not draw characters in a way that would insult them. He would not stoop to humor that was tinged with politically or racially sensitive themes or overtones. He was guided throughout his long and continuing cartoon career by what he looked at as the personalities and capabilities of the characters, and he would not push beyond words and actions that fit closely with what he felt the characters were prepared to do or say. There were guardrails for his drawings.

Jim "drew the line" at sketching and writing about politics. From his perspective, that was a completely different end of the cartooning business. He personally professed to have little use for politicians from any party. However, broadly defined, some "political humor" did sneak into his strips especially during the first two decades of the 2000s. For example, he ran a thread once that lampooned a fictitious local elected official who wanted to buy Corky's diner, a bit of a sleazy sort as it turned out. And he did have Slim and Clovia supporting different candidates in a local election, and consequently becoming involved in a "war" of signs supporting their preferred candidate—each one's sign growing larger than the others until Clovia threatened to cease cooking for Slim. That thread was "inspired" by political differences between a friend, a guitarist, and that musician's wife. For many years, Jim has played on a relationship between the mayor of *Gasoline Alley* and Rufus, a romance that gains a minor head of steam, but in the end is thwarted by something or other. Some of those storylines had punchlines that revolved around aspects of the lives of people holding elected offices. He did have a strip in which Rufus supposed that the then newly elected President Obama was Irish—O'Bama. And Jim did have "The Donald" appear at least once, before 2016, in a brief walk-on role in a scene. Jim lampooned George Bush and Al Gore, depicting them as Woody Shrub and Pierce Gouge.[76]

In the first quarter of 2020, Jim ran a story about a community coming together to support a local variation of the "No Farms, No Food" movement that sought to publicize the problems confronting American farms. That thread was interrupted by the hiatus in newspaper comic strip work caused by COVID-19. The Tribune Syndicate suspended cartoons, began publishing re-runs. By the time they resumed publication work, Jim had decided to switch to a story line about the Pye brothers. That "No Farms, No Food" story was essentially about organization, interest groups, and a community galvanized to protect local equities—in short, the very stuff of politics. Jim sculpted those moments when *Gasoline Alley* and aspects of the political world intersected in a manner that allowed him to stick closely to his rules. He did not veer toward blatant electioneering or debate over real world policies and policies.[77] The dimension of politics that showed up in the strip when it leaned toward themes that at least suggestively hinted at contemporary political challenges often reflected matters that were important to the inhabitants of *Gasoline Alley*, including recognition of the challenges faced by American veterans; the complex political impact of the Vietnam War on American society; and enduring public health issues, especially in rural areas.[78]

Gasoline Alley's *Baleen Beluga and T-Bone*

Following Dick Moores' suggestion, Jim built up a stock of situations from his own experiences and kept them on deposit in a well from which he could draw inspiration.

One day during their time in the U.S. Navy, Jim and Ned Stern were told that they had to join a parade in Newport, Rhode Island. The sponsors of the event needed two sailors. The event might have been in honor of Navy Day, celebrated on 27 October.[79] Ned and Jim were selected, and they were asked to ride on a float. Jim recalled a beautiful young woman, armed with a bouquet of flowers, was stationed between him and Ned on the float. In conversation, Jim learned she was from Bedford, Massachusetts. Ned, who was dating a lieutenant at the time—clearly against Navy rules—urged Jim to go visit her, so sometime later Jim got himself a bus ticket, donned civilian clothes, and took two buses to New Bedford. He knew the young woman worked in the library, found the building, walked in and spotted her working at a desk. "Hi, remember me? I was on a parade float with you. We talked." The young librarian acknowledged that she did recall Jim, but when he suggested taking her to dinner after she got off work, she shot back that she had plans. Deflated, Jim thanked her, and left the library. With several hours to kill before the next bus back to Newport, he strolled around town and ended up finding the New Bedford Whaling Museum on Johnny Cake Hill.

Jim recalled: "An old geezer started showing me around and telling me stories of his own whaling experiences." When that old man was just a baby, his mom and dad, both of whom worked on whalers, would take him out on the boat. They'd put him on the deck, tie a rope around his middle, fasten one end to something stationary, and the motion of the sea would lull him to sleep as he rolled back and forth the length of the rope. Fifty years later, Jim stated that the trip to New Bedford, and the encounter with the old man in the museum, gave him the idea for the *Gasoline Alley* character Baleen Beluga, who takes a job as a waitress in Corky's diner, and eventually becomes besotted with the cook, a Navy veteran who goes by the name T-Bone. Both are partial to speech tinged with nautical expressions, and both sport distinctive tattoos that mark their time at sea.[80] The Baleen Beluga and T-Bone characters were just another example of Jim relying on a "well" of experiences in his cartooning work.

Gasoline Alley's *Gertie*

Perhaps one of the longest running characters with a continuous presence in the strip was Gertie, who was hired to tend to Walt when his wife Phyllis "died" in the strip in April 2004. The character Gertie had her origins in Jim's own mother's late life challenges following a mini stroke in the late 1980s that necessitated placing her in a nursing home. Jim had promised his mother he would never resort to a nursing home, but the situation warranted it. However, after six months, it became clear to Jim that his mother needed more care and assistance than a nursing home could provide, so with the aid and support of his family doctor, Jim took his mother home.

Once that decision was made, Jim needed to hire someone to provide daily care and assistance for his mother.

Jim's postman, Joe Blakney, was just one of those nice people who always stopped for a chat as time allowed. Blakney knew Jim was looking for a nurse to help care for his mother, and one day he told Jim that his sister, Gertie, a semi-retired nurse, was looking for work. Jim remembered:

> So, Gertie came over for an interview and as soon as she knocked on the door it was clear that she was the greatest. A sweetheart from the word "go." She was just a little darling. Polite, with a good sense of humor. She kept Momma laughing all the time. The doctor wrote a prescription for Momma that said: "Keep on laughing."

Gertie took care of Jim's mother for about three years. She pitched in and did a lot of chores such as laundry and ironing that were above and beyond the terms of her employment. Jim was, of course, eternally grateful. He recalled:

> Gertie and Momma, they'd sit around and talk. When Gertie first started, she wore a nurse's outfit, and I said I don't think you ought to do that. Just wear whatever you feel like wearing. The nurse uniform made it like a nurse-patient relationship instead of just friends. So, she wore "civilian" clothes and Momma felt relaxed.

Jim's mother passed away in 1991, and Gertie came to the funeral. "She was going to sit in the back of the church. I said wait a minute, you need to sit up front with the family. You are family."

At the outset of the comic strip, the character Skeezix was a baby when he was left on the steps of Uncle Walt's house. Walt could not look after Skeezix. Jim said:

> He didn't know how to care for a little baby, so Walt interviewed dozens of ladies who did that sort of thing and every single one failed. He didn't like them and Skeezix didn't either.

The one who won out finally was Rachel, an African American. In those days, cartoonists portrayed minorities in stereotypical ways, in drawings and story lines that would be unacceptable today. Jim stated:

> Rachel was loving, sweet, and continued to look after the Wallet family until Skeezix went off to military school for a short while. I think that's about the time she faded out of the picture, but she would come back when Skeezix got married and to attend family get-togethers.

During Jim's stewardship of *Gasoline Alley*, Walt's wife Phyllis—Auntie Blossom, as she was called, because her maiden name was Phyllis Blossom—was a well-loved figure in the strip, a sensible force, and the center of gravity for a lot of the *Gasoline Alley* community. Jim decided that she would pass away, and leave Walt, himself advanced in years, alone and sad, somewhat at a loss on how to live, clearly a troubling situation for Walt's family.[81] In Jim's words:

> Walt went into semi-depression. He was getting forgetful, so Skeezix had to find somebody to look after Walt at home; he didn't want to put him in a nursing facility. So, the same kind of thing: Skeezix had to go through interviewing all these nut cakes, and the one that won out was Gertie, an African American. I used some of the pictures I had taken of Gertie to develop my way of drawing her. She wore a little raincoat, a little rain hat. She was really demure, just a sweetheart. And so she won out and has been there ever since. She's been in the strip for over 20 years.

Jim was careful, early on, to part company with the old ways cartoon characters were drawn, the clearly stereotyped language that was put in the mouths of such characters, and the unequivocally demeaning situations they found themselves in:

> The thing that I have never done was to make fun of any races, minorities, or anything; religious clergy—you know how they do in the movies, it's always the pastor of a church who is a dumbo. I do the reverse. I have them educated and smart, and the punchline is always not at the clergy. I always had Gertie speaking correct English, as she did in real life.

This approach to character development was a critical article of faith in the way Jim went about infusing *Gasoline Alley* citizens with the traits and habits, language and social skills necessary to get along in the community Jim built in this strip. He traced that sense to early lessons from his parents, sometimes taught in very dramatic, conceivably old school ways. When he was a little boy, living in Charlotte, North Carolina, kids would often use language to describe or refer to minorities, words that were inflammatory. One day, Jim's mother overheard him using one of those words:

> Oh, boy, did my mother get mad. She sent me to get a switch off of the bush in the front yard. Those things had a bite to them. So, I picked out a tiny one. She said, you've got to go back and get a real one, and that was even more insulting and so I picked out one and oh, boy, did I get my legs switched. And she said, now you wait until your daddy gets home. And, oh, boy, did he blow up. He took his belt and chased me around the house. I learned right off: "Una Faccia, Una Razza." "One face, one race"—the "human race." My daddy used to say, "look at that black kid, or Asian kid. They've got two eyes just like you. They've got a mouth and ears, just like you. And they have one nose just like you," and he'd tweak my nose—that's probably how it got to be

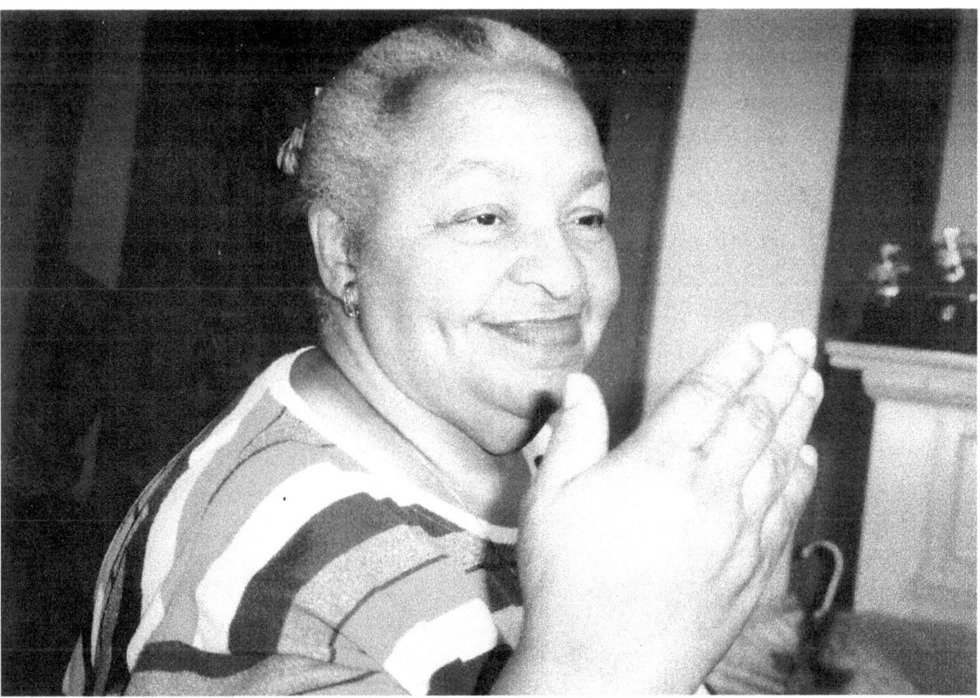

Gertie, 1985. Gertie passed away in August 2019. Her family gave Jim permission to continue using their mother in the comic strip.

so big. All that drove home the lesson: Be more open and tolerant. People are people are people. There are good people, and there are bad people, but they are still people. No matter their color.[82]

In real life, Gertie passed away in August 2019. Before she died, Jim went to visit her in the hospital.

Her family was all gathered around her and, boy, did they say wonderful prayers. They all held hands. They had me included in the family which I thought was really an honor. She passed away a few weeks later. I asked permission of the family to continue having the character Gertie in the comic. They liked the idea because in their minds Gertie was still a presence in their lives.[83]

The Gasoline Alley *"Archive"*

Jim began working on his own as the illustrator/writer for the strip *Gasoline Alley* in 1986. Over a 34-year period from 1986 to 2020, that added up to 12,410 *Gasoline Alley* cartoons, give or take a few threads for periods during which the strip would be replaced by "re-runs" from the archives of post–1986 *Gasoline Alleys* in situations when snowstorms or other natural disasters—and perhaps the occasional man-made disaster—would necessitate suspending operations.

Jim kept the originals of most of those strips. He also kept copies of each strip from the day he started working on *Gasoline Alley*, though they were not particularly good copies given the state of duplication technology in the mid–1980s. For a long time, out of an abundance of caution, Jim deposited a second copy with his uncle, Bob Parati, though after Uncle Bob moved to different homes several times, and either lost or discarded the Gasoline Alley files, Jim lost track of that duplicate set and at some point ceased providing Uncle Bob with a copy for safe keeping.[84]

Jim sent another batch of those strips to his cousin Doug Deal for safekeeping, but when Deal sold his home and moved, he placed those binders containing Jim's strips in a yard sale and they were scattered to the four winds along with other household objects.[85] As of late 2020, Jim possessed the only copy of the entire run of Gasoline alley from the beginning of his tenure as writer/illustrator for the strip.[86] The copies in Jim's own holdings are filed in large binders, in chronological order, unindexed—though in late 2020 he began organizing some of them into "themes," such as the strips having to do with music in which the Mole Hill Highlanders appear, and the strips in which Chef Meowrice has a role.[87]

Conclusion

In Jim's view, had he not secured the apprenticeship with Dick Moores, he probably would not have been able to build a career in cartooning. The relationships between strip owners, the syndicate, and newspapers were complex, and the way into the industry was through an established network, a fraternity, that guarded its front door carefully. As a consequence, in the late 1970s, it would have been hard for anyone to break into the business without the right connections.

That whole premise obscures a question on the kind of cartoon Jim might have originated the late 1970s or early 1980s had he not secured the *Gasoline Alley* apprenticeship. By the late 1970s Jim was already a talented artist with an eye for detail, a bold way of drawing scenes, and a careful way of capturing character, faces, postures. If he could have invented a strip in the late 1970s, what would Jim have produced? What characters would have been at the center of his stories? What stories would he have told?

Jim speculated that had he the chance to originate his own strip, it might have been something that would have revolved around characters that resembled Rufus and Joel, simple country folk living in the sticks, getting by on the strength of their wits and cleverness, their energy and devotion to family, friends and community. That, Jim mused, would have allowed him to integrate more of the Mole Hill Highlander–type threads that have appeared in *Gasoline Alley* from time to time beginning in the early 2000s. That kind of comic strip would have enabled him to include more direct references to the southern mountain culture, Appalachian old-time music, elder fiddlers and dancers that he met and traded tunes with during the course of his own trajectory in string band music in the 1970s and 1980s. All that would have enabled him to breathe life into citizens motivated by the values and spirit that struck him as good, sound foundations for a path in life, and would have given him the chance to depict a community that recognized the importance of friends and family, culture, and history.[88]

Jim's efforts to turn the *Gasoline Alley* strip into his own cartoon had him consciously trying to do things Moores would not have done—at least in part as the result of his mentor's own way of urging that Jim seek to draw better, write better, and think more creatively than his teacher. Jim was acutely aware that the cartoonist's approach to comic strip art and story could actually end up turning the writing and drawing work into something "stagnant." In that event, the cartoonist "loses his ear"—fails to discern when the strip is not reflecting what one hears, much less sees, around him as society changes, as tastes transform, and as what people are looking for in their favorite strips ends up shifting.[89] Everything in the industry, Jim stated, continues to change as artists and writers themselves age. "As you get older, sometimes it gets better, but sometimes it gets worse. Story lines change, ideas come slower, the time required to think up an idea and execute it lengthens. At the same time, the cartoons are being changed by the manner in which the market has acted on print newspapers, and the way cartoons are adapting to the online newspaper world."[90] *Gasoline Alley* in the early days was six to eight columns wide. When newspapers began shrinking the column inches allotted to comics, that reduced the space for lettering, and that impacted the nature of stories being told in strips that were not "one gag" comics. On his watch, Jim has seen *Gasoline Alley* reduced in size twice since the mid–1980s. As a consequence, his art has become bolder, he has adapted his way of rendering backgrounds to make things "pop" in the given space, and he looks for ways to improve his composition work. He has become more strategic in thinking about where to position characters in each frame, how to depict their postures, and he has become more attuned to where he wants to direct the reader's eye. After so many decades of working the strip, he can lay things out in his head quickly—which reminded Jim of Dick Moores' habit of sitting back after he had reached a level of satisfaction with a well-drawn frame or a well-told story and saying: "Look at this. Man, I can't believe I did that."[91]

Six

Music, and the Banjo, in *Gasoline Alley*

The Intersection of Music and Comic Strip

As the cartoonist responsible for *Gasoline Alley* since 1986, Jim has peppered his comic strip with references to old-time and bluegrass music:

- John Hartford, a friend, appeared in a long storyline in 1991.
- The Mole Hill Highlanders, one of Jim's bands, appears in the strip for the first time in 2016.
- Tommy Malboeuf, the old fiddler known as Red Tommy, shows up in the strip in the early 2000s.
- The names of distinguished old-time fiddle tunes make cameo appearances—as in an 8 December 2015 reference to "Mississippi Sawyer."
- Joel Sweeney (1810–1860), who popularized playing the banjo, is mentioned in a June 2005 story.
- The comic strip character Churchy from the strip *Pogo* shows up playing banjo at the Old Comics Retirement Home.
- Chicken Hot Rod, a band Jim recorded on his label, *Old Oblivion,* gets some prominent recognition.
- The *Gasoline Alley* character Derle—modeled on Darrell Gray—shows up as a local helicopter pilot known for his tattoos, "Bluegrass Rules" on the left arm, and "Death Before Taxes" on the right bicep.

Essentially, from 1986 on, Jim inserted music, and musicians, into the strip, some in walk-on roles, and some as characters with a continuing presence in story lines. He also seemed to "animate" string band instruments, especially the banjos that inhabited his comic strip.[1] It was not always smooth sailing for such music-themed strips on Jim's watch. For example, there were, Jim suggested, some editors—perhaps in earlier years of his tenure as writer/illustrator for *Gasoline Alley*—who were not enamored of Jim's placement of references to the old fiddlers' conventions in *Gasoline Alley*, often in the form of an advertisement for the festival stuck on a tree or telephone pole in the background of a cartoon that appeared during the part of the year when the old-time music and bluegrass festivals were scheduled. Jim commented:

> When I would put a poster on the side of a building, a poster that had nothing to do with the story—it would make reference to the Union Grove Fiddlers' Convention or Galax or some

127

local conventions, and I'd put the date on it. One of the editors said, "You can't be doing that. That's free advertising." I finally quit doing it.[2]

The Banjo in Gasoline Alley

A survey of *Gasoline Alley* from 2002 to 2020—the cartoon strips available online at GoComic.com—suggests that the banjo, in Jim's hands, was at times window dressing, prop, decoration, and at times a major living breathing character, imbued with personality and the capacity to think, communicate, emote, and perhaps even exert influence.[3]

For example, the banjo found a place in a heavenly choir in Jim's Sunday 22 December 2002 Christmas spread, the usual "Christmas greetings" single-frame drawing that he has done in anticipation of Christmas for many years.[4] Jim pointed out that the harmonica-playing band of angels in the upper right hand corner was an homage to Johnny Puleo's Harmonica Gang—including a visual reference to Johnny being kicked out of range on the stage which was a part of Puleo's stage shtick in "real life."[5] The heavenly choir, including angelic banjo players, appears in numerous *Gasoline Alley* strips. In the 21 April 2019 strip, offering "Easter Greetings," Rufus is conducting the band in a rendition of "Hail to the Chief," in a manner that makes clear the identity of "The Chief."

In that strip, the banjo occupies a central space in the front row of the angelic band, sandwiched between guitar and fiddle. The instrument is in the hands of a musician with a far more serious look on his face than the other musicians, and perhaps the only one who is poised to dance. The wings on the bass player, the mandolinist, guitar player and fiddler appear far more prominently than those on the figure of the banjo player, perhaps telegraphing a message on the character of five-string banjo players. It also appeared to be the case that while the other members of the Heavenly Band are barefooted, the banjo player was wearing boots (or at least his right foot appeared to be encased in a boot), a potentially meaningful symbolic contrast to his fellow band members. Jim did not necessarily buy into that interpretation of his drawing, but he did explain his thinking about having the Heavenly Band configured this way:

> I just wanted to have some fun. The Heavenly Band, they probably did not have a banjo and a fiddle. That is, how I depicted that Heavenly ensemble is a little different than what you'd see in the stained-glass windows of the cathedrals in Europe. One of the years I had a Dobro in there, and I think I said, "There will be no Dobros in Heaven." Just a little humor.[6]

Since about 2010, Jim tended to depict banjos in their modern form, often with resonators, and a vast white space showing the banjo's head—a reference to modern plastic alternatives to hide heads. He drew banjo players armed with banjos supported by a strap wrapped around the banjo player's right shoulder, just the way Earl Scruggs would have done it. Jim seemed to pair the banjo with the fiddle, and his band scenes often featured the Mole Hill Highlanders interacting with imaginary citizens of *Gasoline Alley* as in the instance of the 7 November 2004 tribute—of sorts—to Kentucky bluegrass.[7] The banjo player in that strip is clutching the instrument

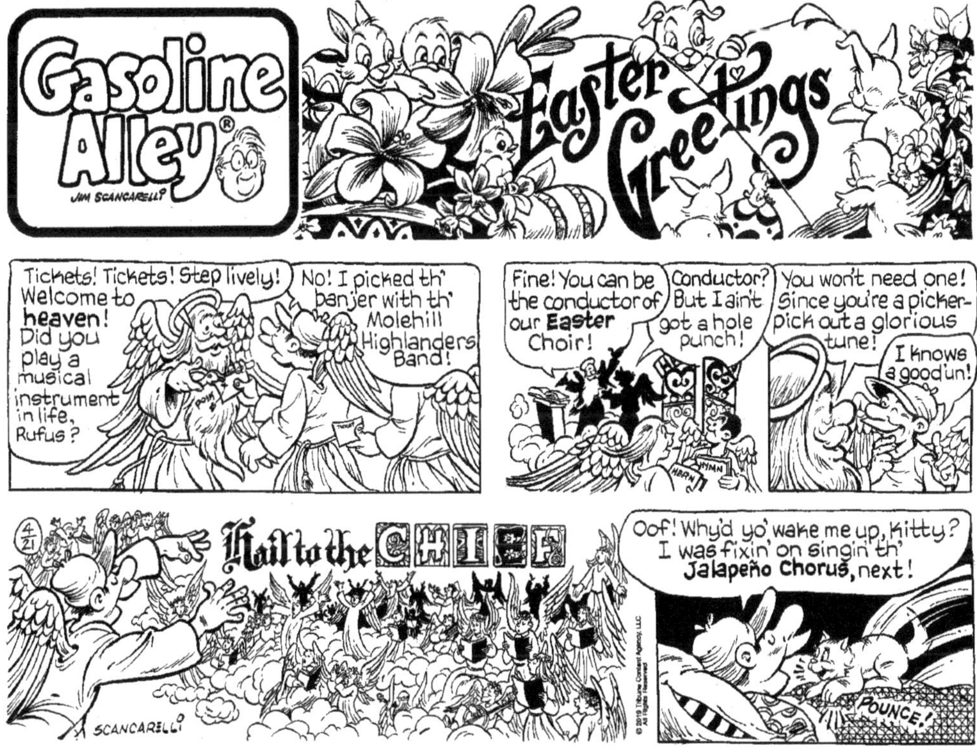

Gasoline Alley, 21 April 2019, a copy made from original production art files in Jim's personal archive for that strip, reprinted courtesy the Tribune Content Agency, LLC, and Jim Scancarelli.

with his left hand in a C chord position. There is always an attentiveness to detail in Jim's drawings that lends a realistic aspect to his depiction of the banjo and the banjo player who is often shown with the handsome face, a strong hairline, and a mouth poised for singing in a manner that signifies a dual role for the band member armed with the five-string banjo as both instrumentalist and singer, perhaps lead singer. Jim commented on the way he depicted the banjo:

> I wasn't tracing a real banjo or anything. I just wanted to get them into the scene. I draw them first, get the composition of the panel, and then I'll tighten it down. I can't see the pencil through the light box and ink it. So, I have to go over the thing with a fine point marker, so that's the second time drawing it, and the third time was inking it. By then I've done it three times and you lose a little. The spark is in the pencil. That's where it really shines. And then tightening it up, it looks really good.[8]

The 7 November 2004 strip does speak to Jim's practice of recycling good, reliable jokes with a long and distinguished history.[9] When the band in this strip strikes up the tune "Blue Moon of Kentucky," a woman in the audience breaks out in tears and the gentleman seated next to her asks, politely, what might be wrong, and wonders, out loud, whether the tearful woman might be from Kentucky, reasoning that her tears suggest that she is homesick. The woman interrupts her sobs to reply that she's not homesick. She is crying because she is a musician. Jim observed:

> That's an old joke. We used to play a tune when I was with Tommy Malboeuf and the Sanitary Cafe band, "Westphalia Waltz." Westphalia is a place in Texas. I've used that gag a couple of times and transposed some of the stuff we did with the Sanitary Cafe band over to the cartoon. The Mole Hill Highlanders say: "We're going to play the Westphalia Waltz," and a lady starts crying, and a band member says, "Oh, you must be from Westphalia," and she says, no, I'm a musician. It's an old joke. That's the good thing about an old joke. Most of the audience will never have heard of it. Except for the old-timers.[10]

Jim used that joke again, in a slightly different form, on 22 January 2017. The strip has the Mole Hill Highlanders—with Rufus on banjo, Joel on bass—taking the stage in the company of fiddler Clyde Williams and Chuck Dunlop on guitar. The strip is packed with string band jokes. Rufus tells the audience "Mainly we play fo' charity!" and Clyde Williams echoes that point, noting "Yeah! We certainly need it, too!" The band gets ready to launch into the tune "Westfalia Waltz." Rufus appears in the third frame with Clyde and tells the audience that Clyde's fiddling can make a cow "take back her milk." In the next frame, Rufus asks Clyde to tell him the chords to the tune "when we get to them." They strike up the tune in the third from the last frame, and in the next frame, the sixth in this seven frame Sunday strip, as the band "thumps" along on the "Westfalia Waltz," a woman in the front row is asked by a male figure seated to her right, "Why are you crying?" She answers, emphatically, exclaiming "They're playing the 'Westfalia Waltz'!" And when he queries whether she is from Westfalia, she answers "No! I'm a musician." It is not clear whether any of Jim's real life bands were ever actually able to elicit that kind of reaction from an audience member, bringing a concert-goer to tears, and thus it is not clear that any of his bands were ever in a position at a concert where a "real musician" might have been able to deploy such a great punchline, though the Mole Hill Highlanders managed to work that joke into their act from time to time.[11]

Interestingly, in the 7 November 2004 strip that builds the joke around "Blue Moon of Kentucky," the banjo peghead breaks the frame of the cartoon in the lower right-hand corner and protrudes across into the next frame that focuses on the band's audience. It is aimed menacingly at the audience member seated next to the woman in the audience who breaks down in tears hearing what the band projects as "music." An alternate way of looking at the frame is that it closely associates the instrument with the cartoonist: the banjo's peghead in this strip juts across the panel's right frame, directly above Jim's signature. The 22 January 2017 strip that revolves around "The Westfalia Waltz" does not have the banjo peghead intruding into the next panel, but the "weaponization" of the banjo, and the fiddle bow, is featured in the 4 January 2015 strip in which the Miceketeer fiddler is knocking the banjo picker in the nose, causing the fiddler's hat to fly off his mouse head in the third frame. Jim featured this bit of humor in this particular Miceketeer strip because it resonated with an old band experience of his[12]:

> We were in the Kilocycle Kowboy Band. Whitley played the banjo. I played the fiddle. They would gather around the microphone tight and start singing. Joe Cline played guitar. One time I had to play a break, and they were still gathered around the mike, and I jammed the fiddle bow up Whitley's nostril. The crowd went wild over that. It was a sheer accident. Whitley refused to incorporate that into the act.[13]

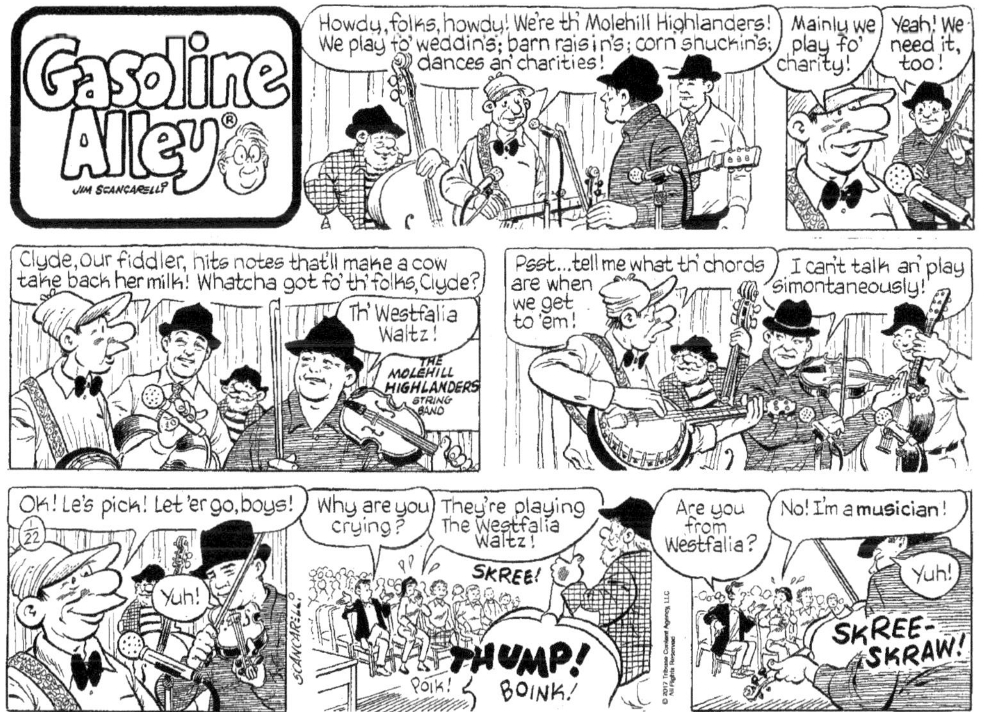

Gasoline Alley, 22 January 2017, a copy made from original production art files in Jim's personal archive for that strip, reprinted courtesy the Tribune Content Agency, LLC, with the permission of Jim Scancarelli.

This suggests that many aspects of the cartoon strip *Gasoline Alley* depict things that align closely with key moments in the history of the string band revival.

Another example of cartoons imitating life is the 17 March 2001 strip that pays respect to the iconic Gibson F-5 mandolin made by luthier Lloyd Loar in 1923 (serial number 73987).[14] The instrument was purchased by Bill Monroe in a Florida barber shop in the early 1940s. He performed and recorded with that mandolin for his entire career. In the 17 March 2001 *Gasoline Alley* strip, that mandolin had been stolen from the touring bus of Bill Monroe's band, The Bluegrass Boys, by the notorious Joe Pye, who "gifted" it to Amanda Lynn. In the first frame, Walt—holding the mandolin—and Clovia are marveling at the instrument, and wondering whether Pye had made "restitution," suggesting that he might not be as low down a character as they had made him out to be. In the last three frames, Joe Pye's reply to a son's question of whether he had purchased the mandolin at great expense is that the instrument came to Joe Pye as a real bargain, "a steal."

Banjo Content and Banjo-Based Humor in Gasoline Alley

The bulk of the music-themed *Gasoline Alley* strips that have banjo content appear after 2010. Though modern, big ticket bluegrass type banjos seemed to

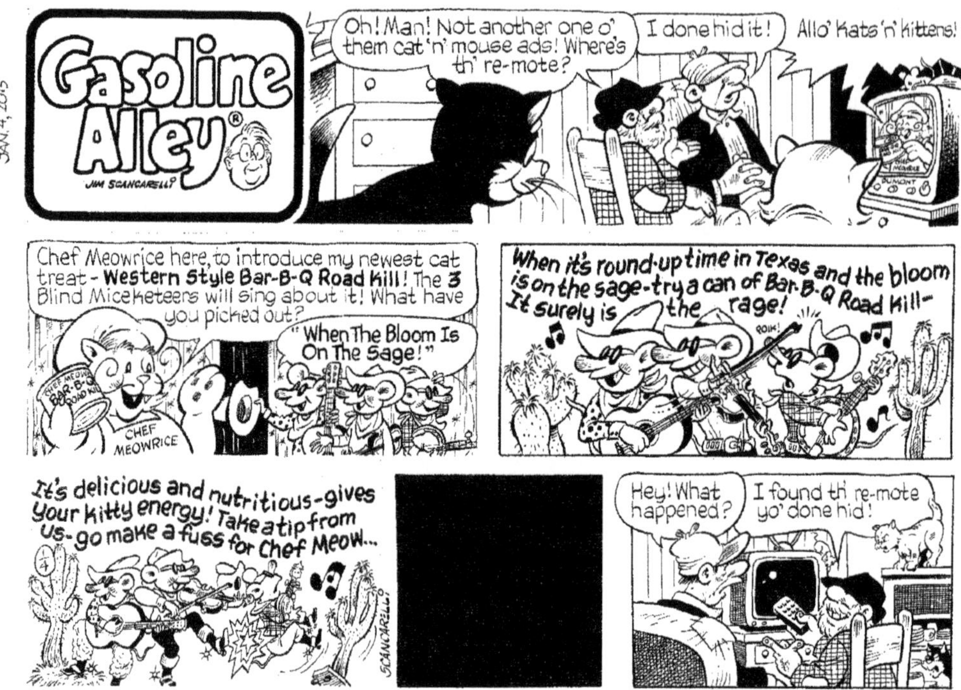

Gasoline Alley, 17 March 2001, a copy made from original production art files in Jim's personal archive for that strip, reprinted courtesy the Tribune Content Agency, LLC, with the permission of Jim Scancarelli.

dominate Jim's strips where music was the central theme, he did represent the banjo in open back form, and in more primitive stages of its development in ways that referenced minstrel banjos. One prominent frame in a 20 March 2011 strip that focused on the Old Comics Retirement Home—specifically, the arrival of Brenda Starr, and the ogling and fawning of all the old male characters as she signed her name at the registration counter—shows Churchill "Churchy" LaFemme from the comic strip *Pogo* armed with a banjo that might be an *homage* to old-time five-string banjos.[15] There does not appear to be one single, credible explanation of why the instrument is draped in sausages, shown quite visibly and clearly threading their way across Churchy's right arm, and lying conspicuously across the peghead, dangling down in a manner that is clearly distracting the canine figure that is armed with a fiddle and a bow. It is possible that the hound's attraction to the links of meat dangling from the banjo neck shows that the banjo player is the lead in that duo. However, sometimes a sausage is just a sausage.

There is one more reference to that banjo-fiddle duo in this strip. In the first frame, where Mutt and Jeff are attempting to convince Walt Wallet to come to the Retirement Home quickly because "all heck" is breaking out, Churchy from the strip *Pogo* and his dog fiddler friend are perched on the roofline, presumably playing away as pandemonium spreads around them.[16] It is not clear whether the sausages still figure in the relationship between the musicians in that two-man (or two-comic figure) band.

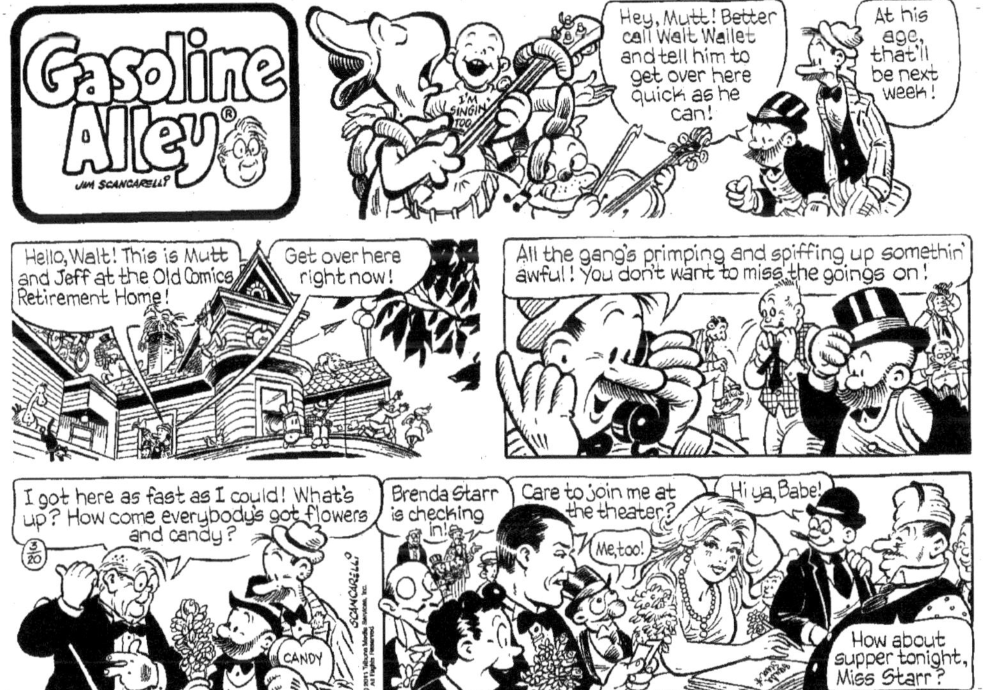

Gasoline Alley, **20 March 2011, from original production art files in Jim's personal archive, reprinted courtesy the Tribune Content Agency, LLC, with the permission of Jim Scancarelli.**

Jim makes plenty of room for banjo jokes in the strips that appeared in the five years from 2015 to 2020. In the first of a series of three strips on 23, 24 and 25 November 2015, Jim places a banjo in the hand of a schoolboy in the Thanksgiving play and gets a rousing response from the audience for an old joke that, actually, is humor more at the expense of the turkey than the banjo. The joke starts with the question, "What do you get when you cross a turkey with a banjo?" The first crack at an answer—"a five-string drumstick"—is rejected in favor of the response that you get a turkey that can pluck itself.[17]

In the 21 April 2019 Easter-focused strip, *Gasoline Alley*'s Rufus is in heaven, being "checked in" by St. Peter who asks Rufus what he did on earth. Rufus replied that he played the banjo, and was told by St. Peter, authoritatively: that doesn't count because it's a banjo. Importantly, in this strip, the old standard—"Did you play a musical instrument?" "No, I picked banjo"—is made even more specific in Rufus' response: "I picked banjer with th' Mole Hill Highlanders Band." In the third frame, Rufus responds to his angel escort's invitation to pick a tune for the Heavenly Band by saying "I knows a good'un," thus invoking the tune "Sally Goodin," a song the Mole Hill Highlanders did not appear to have recorded.[18] Jim observed:

> The angels needed somebody to direct the Heavenly Band. They didn't know what tune to use. He said, "I know a good'un." I didn't even think about that reference to the tune "Sally Goodin."

That Jim did not think this particular phrase in question was in fact a reference to the tune "Sally Goodin" does not necessarily rule out the possibility that at the moment

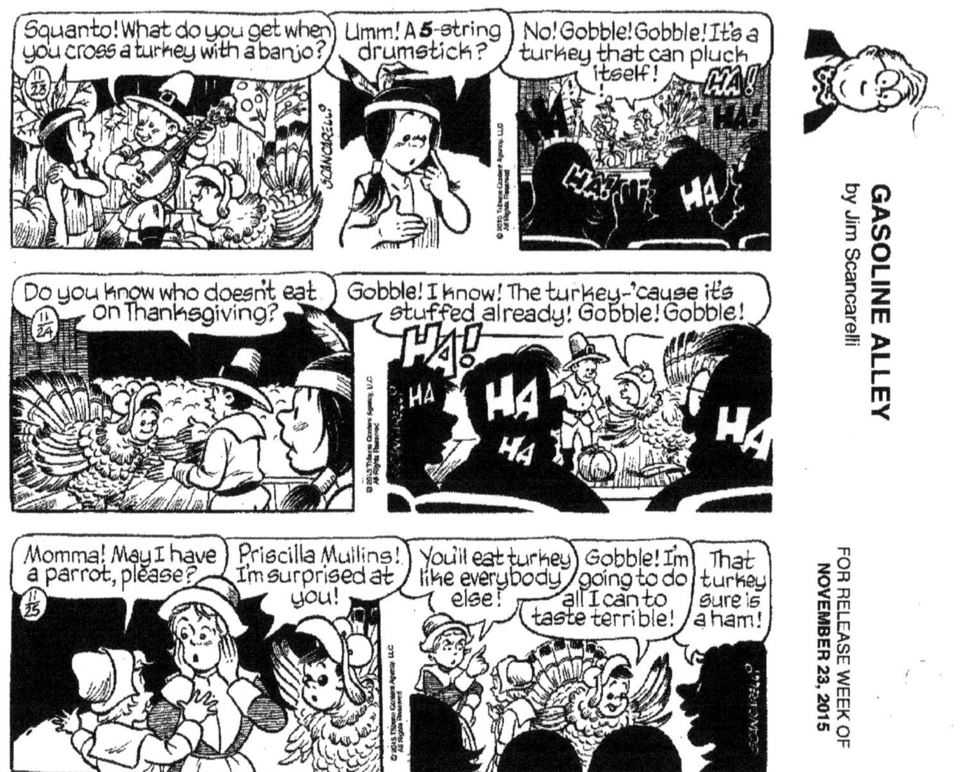

Gasoline Alley, 23–25 November 2015, from original production art files in Jim's personal archive, reprinted courtesy the Tribune Content Agency, LLC, with the permission of Jim Scancarelli.

he was creating the strip, the line did indeed strike him as a tune-specific reference. Nevertheless, his response to a question that addressed this matter resembled John Lennon's statement that he had no idea "Lucy in the Sky with Diamonds" referenced LSD, until his son came home from school one day with a note from a teacher about a drawing done in art class that struck the teacher as a treacherous, dangerous reference to the drug. Lennon immediately went to his record rack to see whether any other of the Beatles' song titles reflected inadvertent abbreviations formed from the initial letters of words in the tune titles—a story that might be apocryphal, but nevertheless serves the purpose of connecting *Gasoline Alley* to rock and roll history, if only in a very tenuous way.

In the next to the last frame of this 21 April 2019 Sunday strip, it is clear that Rufus is priming the band to play "Hail to the Chief." Jim explained:

> That was my way of sneaking in a little religion without hitting you over the head. See, they told us a long time ago that you couldn't offend anybody. You can't say God, Jesus, or Heaven. I'd always been taught to capitalize Heaven, and you don't do that with hell because the denizens down there don't deserve it. I think you can say God now. You can't say Jesus. I try to circumvent some of that stuff and just have fun with it.[19]

What is critical here is that on Easter, Jim used the tune "Hail to the Chief" as a very specific reference. Jim placed Rufus as the conductor, a decision that Saint Peter

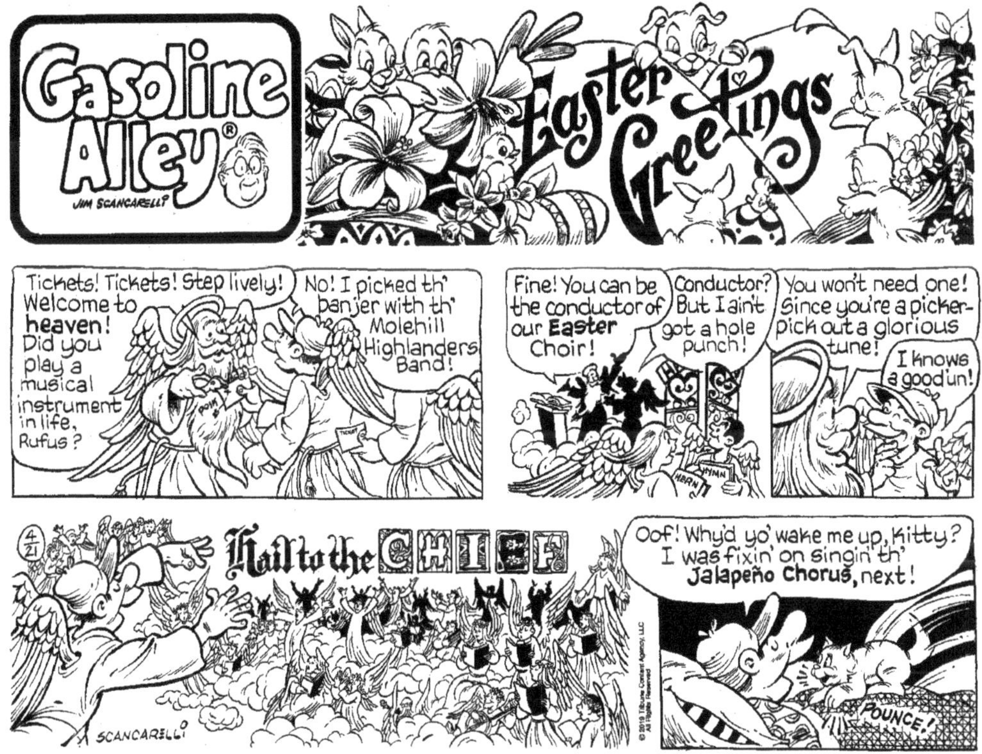

Gasoline Alley, **21 April 2019, from original production art files in Jim's personal archive, reprinted courtesy the Tribune Content Agency, LLC, with the permission of Jim Scancarelli.**

appeared to make at the Pearly Gate on the basis of Rufus' status as a banjo player.[20] That strip, in effect, confers a level of moral authority on banjo players, making this a critical moment in banjo history.

The Miceketeers String Band

On 2 November 2014, Jim introduced "The Three Blind Miceketeers," a band that was part of Chef Meowrice's ad campaign to push his newest cat treats—including such delectable delicacies as Western Style Bar-B-Que Road Kill.[21] Jim pointed out that the mice are French and are named Manny, Moe, and Jacques, and that the names should sound familiar, reminding readers of the Pep Boys and their association with a national car repair chain.[22] The masthead for the comic in this example had as its background not the customary tasteful red field for the name of the comic strip, but instead was set against a backdrop featuring the Italian flag. The Italian flag struck Jim as a good idea for that strip in which one of the Miceketeers is shown singing "Finiculi, Finicula." Jim pointed out that in this particular strip, the mice were wearing green, red, and white coats—the colors of the flag of Italy.[23]

Jim has done over 20 Chef Meowrice commercials in *Gasoline Alley*. In 2020 he compiled copies of the production art for all of those strips in a looseleaf binder and had begun doing the same for the strips that featured the Mole Hill Highlanders, building a set of reference resources "so I don't repeat the same jokes or storylines." Jim was particularly fond of the Chef Meowrice strips and the possibilities for humor that those characters presented. He recognized that the mice might not be everyone's cup of tea: "I like that sort of thing. My Uncle Bob didn't like them. Frank at the copy shop doesn't like it. He thinks it's stupid, and he says: You mean they pay you to do that?" The mice were at least loosely modeled on Ignats the Mouse from the comic strip *Krazy Kat*, and the idea of the Miceketeers was meant to respectfully reference Walt Disney's Mouseketeers.[24]

The real question, though, focuses on the origins of the idea for the character Chef Meowrice, and the birth of the band The Three Blind Miceketeers. Jim stated:

> Back in the 1940s and 1950s, Jack Benny had a thing where they would run a Lucky Strike commercial and they did it within the confines of the program. Don Wilson was the announcer and he would barge into Jack's house and say: "I've got the Sportsmen Quartet here. We've just practiced a new routine for the commercial." Jack Benny would say: "Well, I don't have time." And Don Wilson would answer: "It won't take a minute" and he would force Jack Benny to sit down and listen. The Sportsmen Quartet start singing a song that was popular, but they changed the words around to make it into a Lucky Strike commercial, which I thought was hilarious—and so did Jack Benny's audience. Every week they would do this. This gave me the idea for this French cat, Chef Meowrice. At the outset, I had him talking with a heavy French accent in the strip so I had to tone it down—not so much because the editors instructed me to, but because the readers couldn't understand it. He was always kissing the hands of the female cats. He'd say: "Where are you going after the show?" The idea about the Sportsmen Quartet came in and I thought that would be fun. The blind mice, well, they couldn't see and were always bumping into each other, bumping into the panel borders. Facing the wrong way. If they were playing a Scottish tune, they'd be playing the bagpipes. Or a Spanish tune and they'd be dressed like bullfighters. The punchline would be delivered by Rufus and Joel. Rufus loves the Chef Meowrice commercials and so does his cat—and so do all the mice in his house. They all sit around watching the commercials on TV. Joel says, of the Spanish bullfighters, "That's a bunch of El Toro." I got away with that one.[25]

In the 4 January 2015 strip, the Miceketeer band members are constantly blundering into one another while singing lyrics aimed at attracting the most skeptical cats to the food products or luring devoted cat owners to buying these culinary inventions. The trio of mice musicians are usually armed with a guitar, a fiddle and a banjo, and appear in garb suitable to the tunes they are playing. The 4 January 2015 strip has them in cowboy gear, but that varied inventively from strip to strip that featured the trio. Most of those Miceketeers themes were played out in the longer Sunday pages, but occasionally, the Three Miceketeers showed up in the shorter two or three panel weekday runs of *Gasoline Alley*, as was the case in the 4 May 2015 strip that had them dressed in smart top hats and … tails.[26] The 2 August 2015 strip, pushing the new drink called "Shrew Brew," has the trio outfitted in black jackets and red bowties while Chef Meowrice advertises this new summertime drink that goes well with Mice-A-Roni, marketed in two recipes, one with and the other without tails[27]: The blind mouse armed with a five-string banjo sometimes appears in the middle of the trio and is sometimes positioned on the band's right or left flank. The banjo player is not always the one who is clobbered by the business end of his partner's instrument, or booted out of the scene either by accident or design, suggesting that Jim did not intend the banjo-playing mouse to be the butt of jokes all the time (though the 4 January 2015 strip shows the banjo player smacked in the nose by the fiddler's bow, and then kicked on his mouse butt by the fiddler's cowboy boot).

The lyrics the band sang in these Three Blind Miceketeer themed-strips were always catchy, and frequently led to some pungent cat-food reference, as in the 5 April 2020 *Gasoline Alley* comic.[28] While there might be a reasonable basis for the argument that these references to unique foods and recipes intended to have a certain appeal to cats are actually an attempt to speak to the poignantly poor meals available at old-time music festivals, Jim thought otherwise. Jim explained that he could "get away with" references to the old songs whose lyrics have been hijacked for the cat food-focused strips because whatever readership he might have built up during his years of writing and illustrating these stories might actually know the original tune, even though his younger readers, and his younger editors, might not. Jim tried to get the lyrics to "read straight," to fit right into the melody of an old tune, like a poem, such as the lyric used in the 4 January 2015 strip, derived from the song "When the Bloom Is on the Sage."[29]

> When the bloom is on the sage
> When it's round-up time in Texas and the bloom
> is on the sage, try a can of Bar-B-Q Road Kill
> It surely is the rage
>
> It's delicious and nutritious—gives
> your kitty energy! Take a tip from
> us—go make a fuss for Chef Meow....[30]

Jim was clearly trying to think what kind of cat food would attract cats. He noted that "the bizarre thing" about these strips was having mice advertising cat food. What the Chef and the mouse musicians were trying to do, Jim explained, was divert cats from their appetite for mice, so the catchy lyric in this instance went as follows: "As every feline knows taste is a plus, they'll eat it up, instead of us. Eat what's in the can, not us." Jim continued:

> I was just trying to think of kooky things. Chef Meowrice would come up with a giant "Can-Can" sale, advertised by Can-Can dancers. Buy one can, get one can free. Can-can. Get it? Ha ha. Mice cream sandwiches with a mouse inside the sandwich. Bird souffle. Chickey Cat-chatore.[31]

In the end though, sometimes a soufflé is just a soufflé.

The Banjo as Pawn Star Thread

In July 2016, Jim inked a run of nine strips that referenced a pawn shop, and featured a banjo—and sometimes a fiddle, too—as window dressing, prominently displayed for sale.

The first cartoon in this story, that appeared on 1 July, had Skeezix heading off to find an antique store where he could have an old coin appraised.[32] "Deal's Pawn Emporium" is his first stop—the name of the store is a reference to his cousin Doug Deal. Sitting squarely in the middle of the store's picture windows are a banjo and a

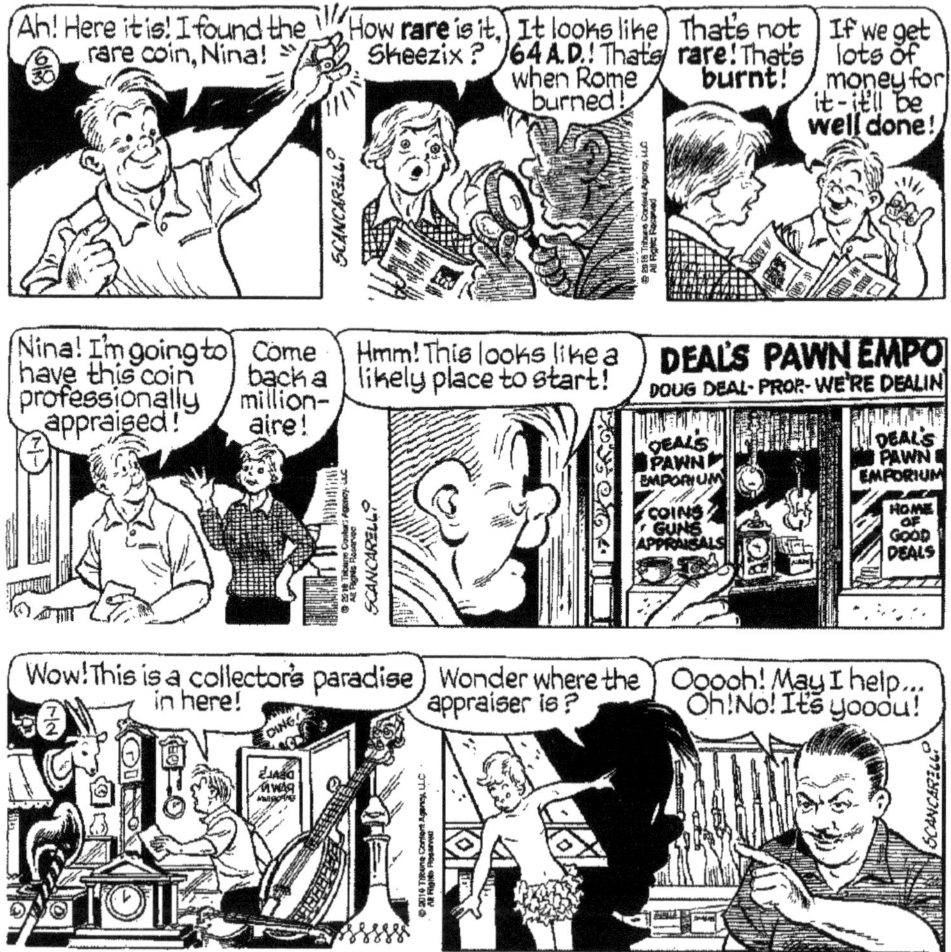

Gasoline Alley, 1 July 2016, from original production art files in Jim's personal archive, reprinted courtesy the Tribune Content Agency, LLC, with the permission of Jim Scancarelli.

fiddle, displayed in gray tones just above a clock and some other household items intended to attract passers-by. The gray tones accentuate a sad aspect to this drawing of abandoned musical instruments, underscored by the way the f-holes and the bridge on the fiddle that seem to combine in a manner resembling a morose face. If one squints, it is possible to discern a chagrined face on the old five string, hanging helplessly in the store's front window. This strip introduced a familiar character as the pawn shop appraiser, someone who has appeared in Skeezix's life before in other commercial encounters and left a distinct impression as a snake oil salesman—a reference to the Frank Nelson character from the Jack Benny show.[33]

Another banjo appears once Skeezix walks into the store, in the foreground, in enough detail to suggest Jim was trying to telegraph the message that it was a deluxe model—fancy architecture on the rim, heel cap, long fingerboard protruding over the head in the style of one of the banjos that John Hartford favored. Lying horizontally on the table, near the banjo, was a fiddle—suggesting that those two instruments were inseparable. Jim drew these objects with keen attention to architectural detail. For the banjo and fiddle in this story, that in effect imbued those musical instruments with a certain amount of character.

The scene shifts to the interior of the pawn shop in the 6 July 2016 strip in which the two main (human) characters interact across the counter, surrounded by a set of golf clubs, an accordion and an electric guitar bearing the peghead brand "Bumper"—in gray tones—attracting our attention. Jim remarked:

> Bumper. I put that in because of "Fender" guitars. Nobody ever makes that connection. Bumper. Fender.[34]

The banjo and fiddle re-appear in the 9 July 2016 comic strip as part of the second of three frames, in silhouette, but this time with the fiddle hanging where the banjo was positioned in the first strip in this thread, and the banjo occupying the lower position in the window. In the interaction between Skeezix and the pawn shop appraiser over the coin, the appraiser excuses himself and leaves the shop—with the rare coin in his hand. Skeezix says to himself, "I should leave, too, but I can't," a thought that could quite reasonably be ascribed to the banjo and the fiddle, too.[35]

Interestingly, in the 11 July 2016 *Gasoline Alley*, in the first frame of a three-frame strip, Skeezix is talking out loud to himself in a store apparently empty of other humans, denouncing the nerve of the pawn shop guy to leave with the coin. This time, the banjo and the fiddle are looking into the interior of the store from their show window perch, suggesting a level of interest in and attention to Skeezix's predicament. In a later strip, Slim, downcast because he has apparently been the cause of the disappearance of a beer stein that is probably a family heirloom, passes the pawn shop and spies the stein in the front window next to the fiddle. Though the banjo does not figure in this strip, the image of the lower bout of an acoustic guitar hanging on the wall does, and a harmonica and a wristwatch sit in the showroom window adjacent to a beer stein.[36] The 14 July 2016 strip has the fiddle, alone, in the display window, with its back to the street.[37] The fifth of seven frames shows a banjo sitting on a shelf over Skeezix's left shoulder. It looks suspiciously like the one drawn in admirable detail by Jim several days prior to this Sunday strip. In the last panel in this storyline, on 22 July 2016, the fiddle appears in the first frame, facing the interior of the store.[38] The appraiser and Skeezix are dickering over a fancy walking stick that ends up being at the center of a story for several more days. The saga of the banjo and the fiddle ends with this 22 July strip.

The fiddle and the banjo were given life and mobility in this storyline, in effect showing up as "characters" in the strip. Jim's rendering of the fiddle and the banjo did much to "humanize" those instruments, though Jim responded to that theory in a manner suggesting that this might not have been his intent:

> I was just trying to show what a pawn place looked like, and being that banjos and fiddles are a favorite of mine, I just threw them in there. The drawings are probably not accurate as far as fret count and length of neck is concerned.[39]

How Real Life Intrudes on Comic Strips

In late March 2020, Jim commenced work on a thread dealing with issues confronting the local farm collective, and the implications for the food economy. On 15 March 2020, the Mole Hill Highlander fiddler Clyde Williams appears in a Sunday strip that revolved around the fiddler's fictitious brush with infamy in a music school after gently removing a "genuine, authenticrated, Stradamagorium violin" from the premises.[40] The Mole Hill Highlanders reappear, with Rufus manning the five-string banjo, in two strips on successive days—17 and 18 April 2020—in which the band is seen performing for the gathering of *Gasoline Alley* citizens intent on saving local farms.[41]

Those strips came at the beginning of a complex series of shifts and changes occasioned by COVID-19 once that public health crisis mandated the cessation of business as usual throughout the United States. The print shop shut down, and the state of North Carolina enforced the suspension of all "non-essential" business and commerce.[42] The Syndicate's management instructed Jim to cease normal operations out of concern for his health. Strip re-runs filled the gap between the storyline about farms (in which Boog and his father Rover were featured as the main characters) and the thread involving the Pye Boys that commenced on 6 July 2020. The COVID-19 lockdowns put a halt to sending the strips to the Syndicate once the print shop closed down, so Jim had to invent a new story to follow the "no farms no food" story, one that did not seem too abrupt of a change:

> Boog and his Daddy were coming back from the farm meeting and so on their way home they bumped into the Pye boys. I had to erase all that in my head, come up with something else, and then one of the characters would say something, and I'd say, man, that's good, and so they kind of write it themselves. I know that sounds crazy, but I'll get up to the blank piece of paper, and I'll think, what am I going to do? My Uncle Bob was good to bounce stuff off of, but he's no longer with us. My cousin Doug, boy, he was good. You could bounce something off of him and right away he'd come up with good thoughts for a storyline, but he's no longer with us. Doug used to call himself my "story insultant." There's a buddy of mine, he's an architect, Ben Barry. He has a comedic mind. We won't hold it against him that he's an architect. Sometimes I will bounce something off him, and he'd say, why don't you do this, and I'd say, there's a good idea. He's then opened up the door to the blank wall. I also had another friend, Mark Cohen, a real estate salesman, who was a member of the National Cartoonists' Society, and he fed ideas to many cartoonists including Charles Schultz, Hank Ketchum, Morrie Turner, and me. My friend Mark, he was a cartoon himself. He sent me ideas for Sunday strips, and a lot of them referenced older cartoons which he loved. Anyway, I really got frustrated formulating the story that ended up being interrupted by the cessation of business owing to COVID-19. I had no idea what the dates were on the story because the Syndicate was doing reruns. I had no idea if we were going to continue to do reruns or not. The virus was the wild card. So, they decided to run the story of Joe Pye after seven weeks.[43]

In early July 2020, Jim had planned out a story that would run beginning in August, featuring Joe Pye and his ne'er-do-well sons—a storyline that at least incidentally involved musical instruments. That arc had Joe Pye and his boys scheming to gain access to a church, in the hopes that they would be able to make off with the musical instruments stored in a closet, which they would then sell or pawn and abscond with the proceeds.[44] Jim explained the story that began with the 6 July 2020 strip[45]:

> Joe Pye and the Pye Boys, those guys are ne'er do wells. And as I said before, a Joe Pye is a noxious weed that grows down south. A lot of the old comic strips by other cartoonists had a bad bunch of characters and they kept coming back—Washtub had them. The Scragg Brothers were in Lil Abner, a wild bunch of horrible guys who were always one or two steps ahead of the law. That's kind of the way the Pye boys are. I get them where they are incarcerated, and then they break out. They meet up with Joe Pye's ex-wife—who he left but had not divorced—but that was so many years ago he didn't recognize her, and she didn't recognize him. They then find out they are still married. So anyway, she tries to get them to go to church. The Pye boys and their father are still trying to keep a low profile because they think the law is after them. She gets them back into her church. The choir room has all these instruments. They had a banjo, fiddle, guitar, tambourine. Now, Clyde Williams, the Mole Hill Highlanders fiddler, his mother would play along with us in the living room and she had maracas. You know, they look like turkey legs and you put beans in them and you shake them. She would say, Clyde, play the tune "Liberty," and she would shake those maracas louder than we were playing. I have Joe Pye playing tambourine because I couldn't for the life of me think of what the word was, let alone how to spell maracas. So, I had him playing a tambourine, an instrument that I thought could show up in a church.[46]

COVID-19 necessitated (1) suspending one storyline that involved Boog and his family coming together with the community to learn about the economic challenges facing farmers and (2) figuring out how to bridge the gap with re-runs that switched to a story about Joe Pye and his sons. The story featuring the romp with the Pye boys that ended on Halloween, coasting to a complete finish on 3 November, was intended to pick up after the series of strips that involved saving local farms was suspended when the Syndicate flicked the switch to reruns in the face of the COVID-19 quarantine. The story involving the Pye Boys commenced on 6 July 2020.[47] This is what happened between late March and early July 2020:

- On 27 March 2020, Jim commenced work on a story dealing with issues confronting the local farm collective, and the implications for the food economy.[48]
- In the 1 April 2020 single-panel strip, Boog and his father Rover are driving the family pickup across a covered bridge on their way to the meeting place, Harold's Welding Shop, where the community discussion was scheduled to take place.[49]
- That storyline tied in with a series of strips beginning on 28 April 2020 that were focused on how Boog's school was starting an agri-business class.[50]
- On 29 April, Charlotte, young Boog's lady friend, starts looking for a guest speaker to address those farming issues in their school.[51]
- That story develops through 18 May 2020, at which time the Syndicate switched to re-runs featuring Walt and Gertie, a thread that begins by focusing on Gertie's efforts to get Walt to exercise and her attempt to figure out how to manage his medications—so he would remember to take the prescriptions.[52]
- On 29 May 2020, the strip shifts to a re-run involving animals that escaped from a circus. The circus animals rampaged—in a friendly sort of way—in front of Walt's porch, so that he sees lions and tigers and elephants, and Gertie

begins to worry about what she supposes are prescription drug-induced hallucinations.[53]

That storyline continued through early July, and on 6 July the strip switched back to a line of pickup trucks departing the community meeting at Harold's welding shop, crossing a stream via another covered bridge.[54] In the cab of their pickup truck, Boog says to his father that there is someone walking ahead of their vehicle who might want a lift.[55] All we see, at the right side of the single-panel strip, are the legs and torso of a gentleman in full stride, cane in his left hand, walking on the right side of the dirt road. That figure is in fact Joe Pye.[56] Jim took the story featuring the Pye Boys up to Halloween:

> There was my exit for the boys. They go into this haunted house and they are going to hide out. It's a haunted house for the trick or treaters. And they are hearing all these spooky sounds. They get scared and burst out of the place. So, that's the last we'll see of them for a while. It's a poor exit, but it's an exit, and then I'll think of some other story, and that's the difficult part. What to do next.[57]

Musical instruments and musicians—the equipment for a church band, maracas and tambourines, the Mole Hill Highlanders—helped introduce an element of coherence to this complex arc of stories necessitated by COVID-19—a case of real life intruding on comic strip life.

The Banjo as Carpentry Grade Lumber

There are two more strips worth highlighting. One is a Sunday strip from 26 June 2005 in which Slim recounts a dream of a tree that a woodsman was preparing to cut down with his ax.[58] The tree implores the ax wielding lumberjack to spare it, and to allow it to "live on" by making the tree into an instrument. "Something to do with the music field!/ My last breath now to you I yield!" The tree's last words just before it was turned into carpentry grade lumber:

Agreed, said the logger, and did me in!
A fiddle I wasn't,
to my chagrin
I'm a shipping crate
now and in a huff!
My last request
wasn't specific enough!

That strip captures Jim's sly humor. The fiddle shows up, lying supine in the next to the last frame. In the last frame, a guitar crate bears a facial expression suggesting a frown formed by the grain of the wood on the right side of that box. Anyone who has cut perfectly good lumber with the goal of making banjo necks or pots, bridges or tailpieces, might feel the angst involved in this poetic *Gasoline Alley* Sunday strip.[59]

The second *Gasoline Alley* strip worth mentioning because of the connection to string band instruments runs on 19, 20 and 21 November 2018. During those three days, the residents of the old comics retirement home are shown trying to figure out how to honor the 100th anniversary of two strips, *Mutt and Jeff* and *Gasoline Alley*.[60]

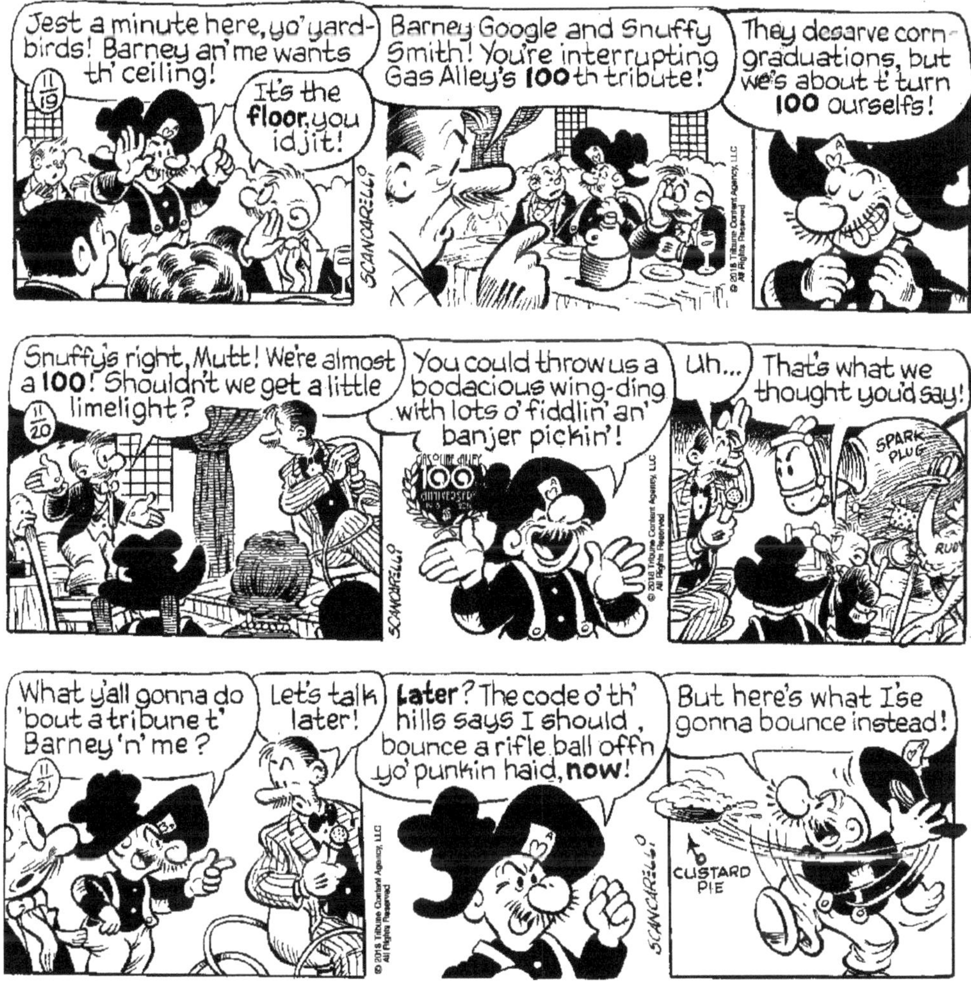

Gasoline Alley, 6 July 2016, from original production art files in Jim's personal archive, reprinted courtesy the Tribune Content Agency, LLC, with the permission of Jim Scancarelli.

The story featured various recognizable characters from other cartoons who gathered in the old comics retirement home and wondered how to highlight that achievement. In the 20 November 2020 strip, in the middle frame, Snuffy Smith suggests featuring string band music in a party honoring his strip as it approached 100 years in syndication. The message there, as Jim makes it clear, is that the banjo and fiddle combo is still the best use of instruments to produce good, old traditional music. Or as Snuffy Smith himself suggests, that pairing of strings provides the basis for the most "bodacious wing-ding" of a musical event.[61]

Conclusion

During his tenure as writer/illustrator, Jim introduced stories and characters from his life into *Gasoline Alley* with increasing frequency—including themes referencing old-time music and bluegrass, stories involving notable musicians, and jokes that have highlighted the points at which music and humor intersect.[62] On Jim's watch, *Gasoline Alley* recognized eternal truths in the course of referencing music-focused themes. In one etymologically-focused strip on 16 September 2012, Rufus attempts to explore the origins of the word "optimism," and Joel succinctly telegraphs the depth of his understanding of the word, noting that optimism is the "attitude a bagpipe player takes when he looks fo' a room t'rent."[63] *Gasoline Alley* has been sprinkled with ample references to the string band music tradition in the form of the Heavenly Band, the Mole Hill Highlanders, and Chicken Hot Rod. Banjo and fiddle players of note—including John Hartford, Clyde Williams and Tommy Malboeuf—showed up with increased consistency, in longer threads, with greater regularity in the early 2000s. "Red Tommy"—Tommy Malboeuf—is mentioned for the first time on 18 March 2003.[64] The "Ragin' Cajun," Doug Kershaw, showed up in a storyline in June 2003.[65] The Mole Hill Highlanders first appearance in the strip was on 20 March 2016.[66]

Imaginary musicians who had roles in the *Gasoline Alley* strip included mandolin player Amanda Lynn, Joe Pye and the Traveling Truebadours, and Chef Meowrice and the Three Blind Mice musicians (who became fixtures *Gasoline Alley* beginning for the first time in a Sunday strip on 3 February 2008). Those characters sometimes played music on the same stage with *Gasoline Alley* citizens Rufus and Joel, who themselves joined the Mole Hill Highlanders, Jim's "real life" band, from time to time.[67] Jim suggested:

> Banjos and fiddles will always show up in scenarios that involve the Mole Hill Highlanders, but who knows what ideas will surface in the future. I never thought of banjos and fiddles as being characters … but now, that seed is planted. Dick Moores and Frank King would never have gone along with what I've been doing. Well, maybe Frank would come closer because he had a lot of fantasy in the Sunday pages. I kind of follow in that train of thought. What I'm doing doesn't look like either of them anymore, but I kept the characters in character. My interests are fiddling and banjoing, and trains, and it's easier for me to do more with those subjects than it would be doing something with a subject about which I just don't know anything.[68]

In keeping with that practice of featuring aspects of his interests and hobbies in the strip, during the last quarter of 2020, Jim was working on *Gasoline Alley* strips for the first quarter of 2021. A strip he devised for 17 January 2021 revolved around Rufus' announcement to the Mole Hill Highlanders—the cartoon version of that musical agglomeration in which Rufus holds the banjo player's slot—that "Lew Stern" is writing a book about the band! Rufus' revelation is that the book is entitled *Dracula Meets the Mole Hill Highlanders*. Joel, who plays bass for the imaginary incarnation of this actual old band, asks whether the book might become a best seller. Rufus replies in a manner suggesting that remaindered copies of the publication will reside in the recently refinished basement in the home of Chuck Dunlop, who was the guitar player in both the real and the cartoon version of the band—and that, thus, the book will be a "best cellar." In several artfully drawn frames in this Sunday strip, images of Clyde Williams armed with a fiddle are prominent in the forefront of the frames in which the band appears—befitting his status as the "elder" fiddler. The strip also offers glimpses of Chuck Dunlop and his six-string guitar, and a bespectacled Mark

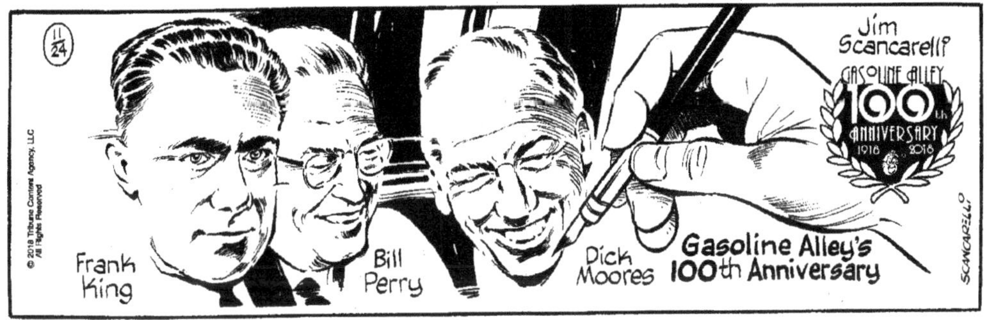

Gasoline Alley, 24 November 2018, from original production art files in Jim's personal archive, reprinted courtesy the Tribune Content Agency, LLC, with the permission of Jim Scancarelli. Jim's 100th anniversary strip honoring his predecessors.

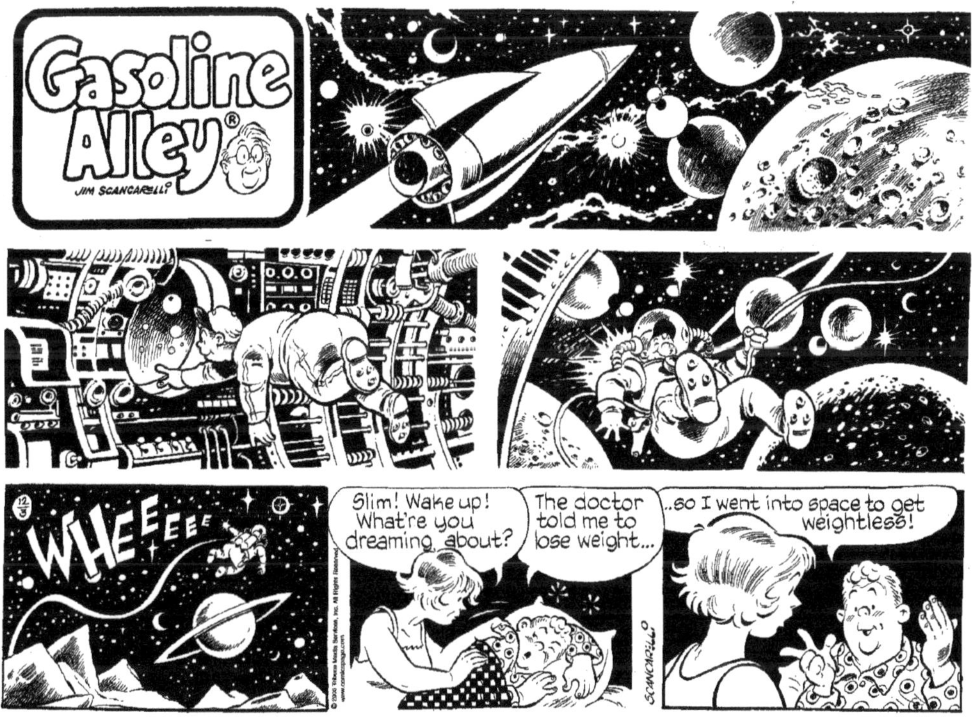

Gasoline Alley, 3 December 2006, from original production art files in Jim's personal archive, reprinted courtesy the Tribune Content Agency, LLC, with the permission of Jim Scancarelli. Jim drew this Sunday strip to honor the artwork of Wally Wood and Jack Davis of *Mad Magazine*, two of his "top cartoonist inspirations."

Wingate, the band's second fiddler. The late Jim Whitley's place in the band as the bass player is filled by Joel, and Jim Scancarelli, the banjo player for the "actual" band, retreats behind the scenes to his role as writer/illustrator for *Gasoline Alley*, allowing Rufus to assume the vaunted status as the Mole Hill Highlander bearer of the banjo.[69]

When one looks closely at the entire corpus of his *Gasoline Alley* work, what stands out is the extent to which the banjo, the fiddle, and string bands themselves have become characters in Jim's comic strip for these many years. Importantly, when a banjo itself figures in the mix, when a five-string is at the center of a *Gasoline Alley* theme—whether it be a single panel one-gag Sunday cartoon, or a story that runs for several days or more—the citizens inhabiting the areas in and around *Gasoline Alley* seem content recognizing that sometimes a banjo is just a banjo.[70]

Conclusion:
The Sweep of His Life Story

Jim had a good, long run as a fiddler and a banjo player from the 1960s to the early years of the 21st century. He played in several local bands in Charlotte, North Carolina, including the Mole Hill Highlanders, the Kilocycle Kowboys, and Sanitary Cafe—as well as a slew of short-lived bands that played locally through the early 2000s. Jim contributed to the fiddle festival culture beginning in the mid–1960s, recording the band contests and impromptu jam sessions at Old Time Union Grove Fiddlers' Convention for Pierce Van Hoy. He participated in Van Hoy's effort to revise

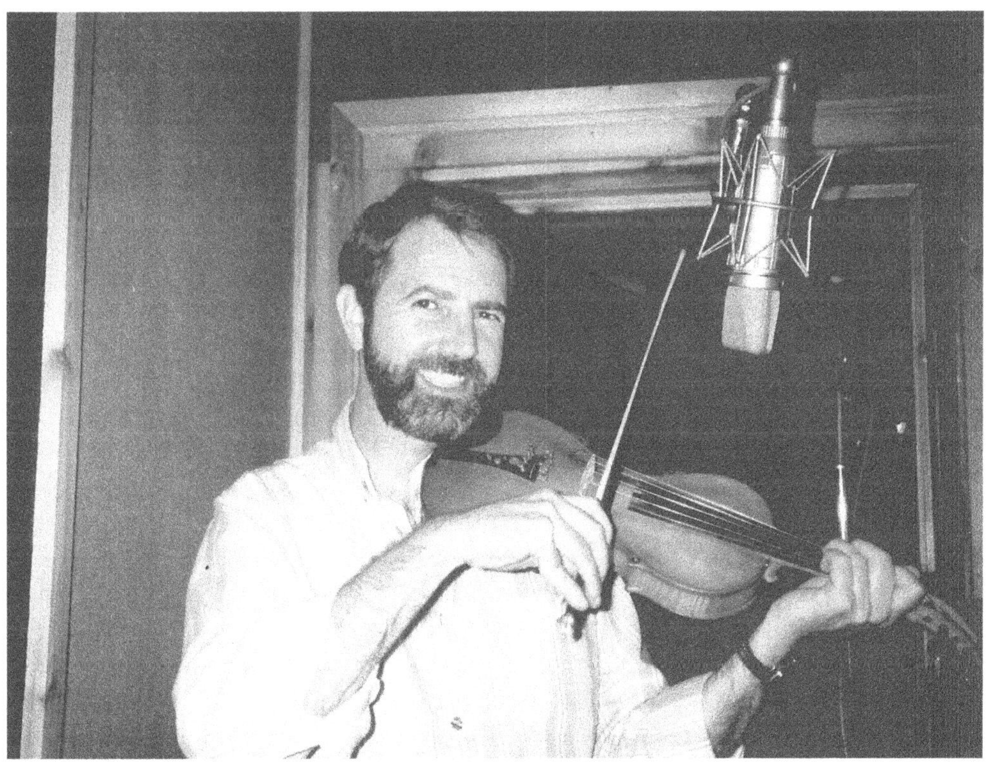

Jim Scancarelli at the microphone recording Steve Kilby's first album called _Sunday Night_ recorded at Bobby Patterson's studio, Heritage Records, outside of Galax, Virginia, and released in 1992.

Union Grove's contest rules in 1970 in a manner aimed at leveling the playing field between old-time music and contemporary bluegrass, foreclosing the possibility that more modern music and electrified instruments would steal the show. Jim did his fair share of field recordings of elder banjo and fiddle players in and around his hometown of Charlotte, North Carolina, contributing those recordings to the Library of Congress' American Folklife Collection. He honed his own fiddling around accomplished fiddle players like Clyde Williams, Tommy Malboeuf, Kenny Baker, and Vassar Clements.

Beginning in the late 1960s, Jim spent just over a decade as a freelance artist, working for advertising agencies, magazines, and publishing houses before he tried his hand at drawing and writing cartoons. He became Dick Moores' assistant in 1979, and in 1986 became the fourth writer and artist for the syndicated comic strip *Gasoline Alley*. He turned a youthful passion for newspaper comics, and a precocious talent for drawing, into a lifelong love affair with a classical art form, and ushered *Gasoline Alley* past its 100th year in print.

Jim's interests in art, in drawing and cartoons, and his banjo and fiddle playing co-existed in time and space and were entwined in unique ways. He drew on his musical friendships to populate *Gasoline Alley* with string band musicians, and he drew cartoons that celebrated traditional music and honored performers of note. Old-Time and bluegrass musicians knew him as a fiddle and banjo player who drew cartoons. Cartoonist colleagues referred to Jim as a writer/artist who played fiddle and banjo.

Piles of Other Interests

Jim's early interest in comic strip art developed into a collecting interest focused on graphic artwork, original cartoon drawings, and signed panels. Early cowboy movies and television shows, and even earlier radio broadcasts of shows that featured stories of the American West, led to a long infatuation with artifacts of television shows such as "Gunsmoke." Jim was also drawn to model building early on, an interest that in large part reflected his enduring affection for steam engines and old, historic railway towns. His grandfather, Otto Parati, a Southern Railway Company engineer, nurtured Jim's abiding interest in steam engines and railroad history. Jim's years in radio and television work gave rise to a deep love for the stories and the characters developed for early radio shows, and a long-lasting taste for the dramatic format of radio shows. That carried over into adulthood when he acted on the urge to collect radio transcription disks that reflected his enduring fascination with old recording technologies—and it added the tinge of showmanship to some of his performances with the Mole Hill Highlanders.[1]

Model Building: Jim was a model railroader and model builder, a hobby interest encouraged by both his grandfather and father. Jim's creativity in that area motivated him to start work on a project when he was 14 years old creating an elaborate model of Cliffside, a Carolina mill town. He put his imagination to work during the years he spent developing a series of unattached "dioramas"—fabricating the buildings, train

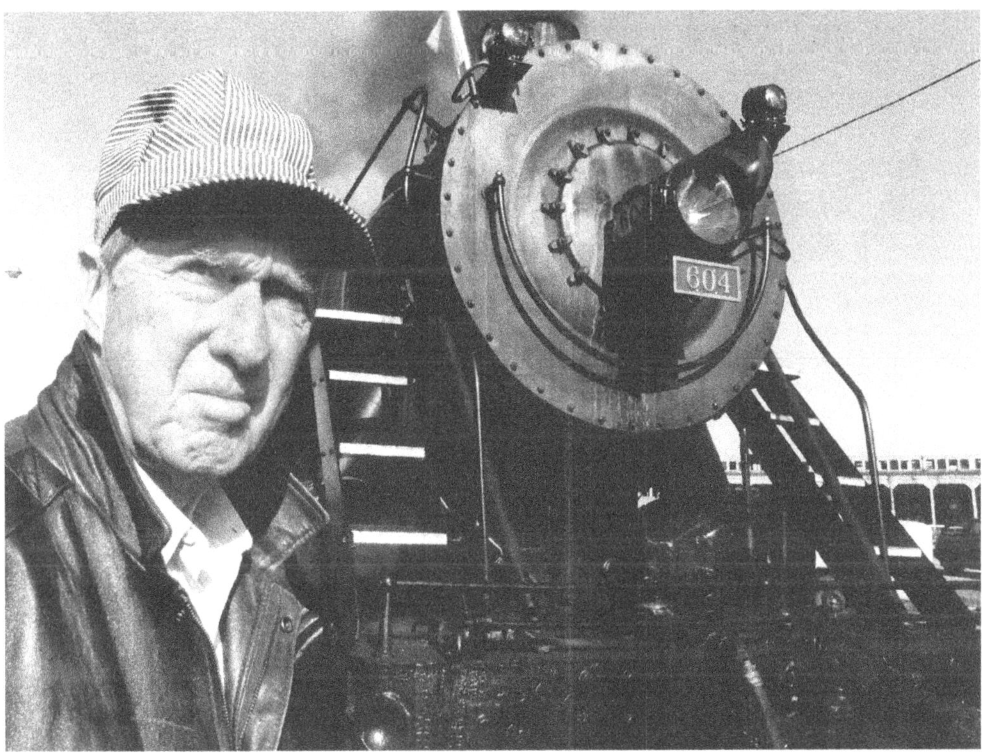

Lee Kolbe at Spencer Shops, Salisbury, North Carolina, 1980s. Jim stated: "Lee was a grand illustrator, painter, model railroader. He prepared museum quality railroad models. I met him when I was 13 years old. He and my Uncle Bob worked together at Stylecraft Packaging Service."

components and terrain objects from parts of hobby kits, and creating the human figures from an amalgam of body parts from tiny dolls and toy soldiers.[2] Model building was a "great escape," Jim said, a way of finding relief from daily routine, school—and later, work obligations and deadlines.[3] He worked on that project, off and on, in between other life obligations—homework, chores, service in the Navy, day jobs—from roughly 1955 to 1986, when the responsibilities of drawing and writing the *Gasoline Alley* comic strip edged out other interests, and necessitated putting aside any further work on what Jim calls his "Lilliputian wartime 1944 southern mill town patterned after the real Cliffside."[4]

Lee Kolbe, who ran an art studio with Jim's Uncle Bob Parati, was a master model builder. In 1999, Kolbe was asked by a local museum in Charlotte to build a replica of how the city might have looked in 1715. Kolbe and his son Scott focused on building houses, and Jim joined in with the responsibility for fabricating authentic-looking trees and shrubs. Kolbe, Jim mused, was an exceptionally creative force who could turn a blob of plastic into a revolutionary war era soldier on a horse. Jim learned a lot from that association with Kolbe.

Collecting: Jim was an inveterate accumulator. His collecting interests were less attuned to the dollars and cents advantages of buying and selling artifacts of yesteryear than they were to the thrill of being able to hold, read and re-read, and marvel

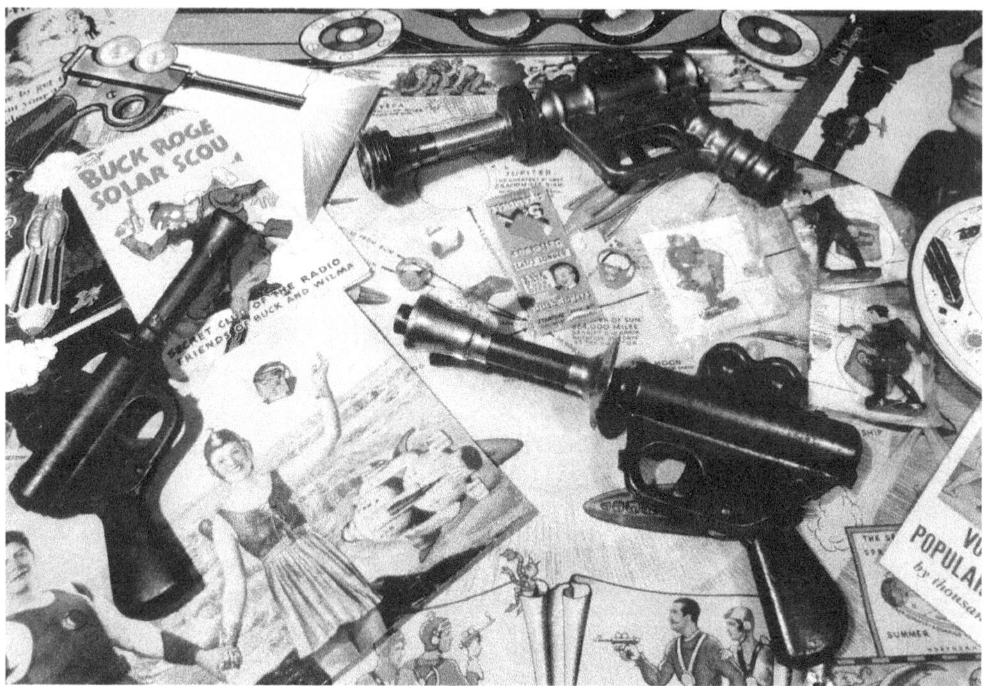

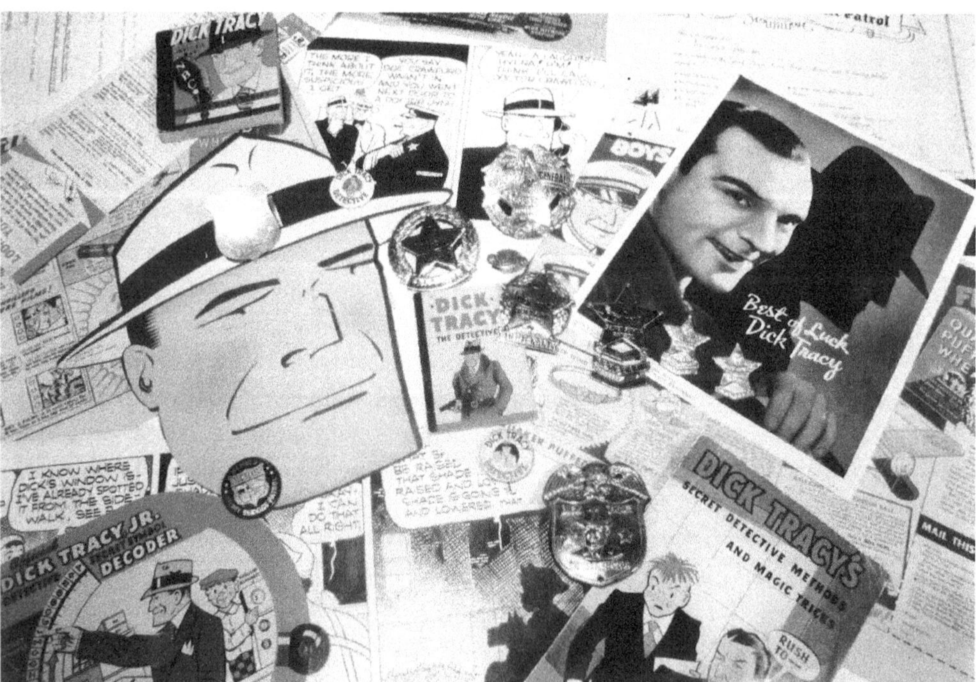

Top and above: **A fraction of Jim Scancarelli's collection: Sci-Fi related items, and Dick Tracy related premiums.**

at these reminders of days gone by. He amassed a collection of buttons, pins and other memorabilia, in addition to the comics and premiums associated with the Lone Ranger, Jack Armstrong, Amos and Andy, Dick Tracy, and many other cartoon and comic strip heroes, and radio and television characters.[5]

Steam Engine Collectibles: Jim built a considerable collection of photographs and post cards depicting steam engines and railway systems in his part of the country. He credits his grandfather with his sense of the way moments of significant technological, social, political and economic change crept up on America and wrought transformations that had ripple effects on all aspects of life. For Jim, the steam engines were an especially important example of this. Beyond collecting images and art depicting railroads, Jim drew illustrations for railroad-focused books and publications.[6]

Radio Transcription Disks: Jim collected radio transcriptions disks, the big 16-inch disks that radio stations employed in the 1940s. One side could contain 15 minutes of recorded material before disks with extended playing grooves became available. Jim was devoted to old radio shows—Amos and Andy, Jack Benny, the Lone Ranger, among many others. When he worked at WBT he found a significant cache of old 16-inch transcription disks in the basement of the transmitter tower, some of them made of glass, that were in use during the Second World War. Jim worked out an arrangement to clean up the basement and inventory the disks. He made tape recordings of many of those radio programs. Once his appetite had been whetted by what he found at WBT, he continued to look for these transcription disks at antique stores and flea markets.[7]

Hoppy Cards: Another collecting interest—connected in theme and motivation to his infatuation with old cowboy movies, old cowboy singers, and western television shows—is Jim's accumulation of remembrances of "Hopalong Cassidy," the central character in a series of short stories and novels penned by Clarence Mulford in the early 1900s. Those stories became the basis for a television series in the early 1950s that starred William Boyd and Hopalong's horse, Topper.[8] In the early 1950s, when Jim was in second grade, Hopalong Cassidy was all the rage.[9]

Radio Premiums: Jim remembered the premiums offered on the boxes of dry cereals such as Cheerios—though his favorite breakfast cereal was Shredded Wheat. Cereal boxes advertised trinkets and give-away toys for ten cents and a box top mailed to a corporate address—"brass rings that turned your fingers green," as Jim recalled, with fondness. He built up an impressive collection of radio giveaways and other premiums, and comic books. In his adult life, he had a bit more discretionary income that enabled him to acquire more than what the ten cents offer by dry cereal companies got him in his youth. That dime represented a major investment of meager allowance money in the fifties. So, when in the 1970s he told his mom that he had spent $40 on a Tom Mix Number One comic, she told her son that he had no regard for money. Much later, the fact that copies of that ten-cent comic book were fetching $1,000 in the early years of the 21st century validated Jim's $40 investment.[10]

* * *

Jim's lifelong collecting interests, and his immersion in model building earlier in his life, reflected his sense of how time had diminished community, and how attentiveness to history and older ways of life could provide balance in a world that no longer offered an equilibrium between the comforting aspect of old ways and the eternal rush toward modernity. That commitment to community was also reflected in

Gasoline Alley, which, in his hands, became a sprawling village based on the endearing relationships between strip characters, fueled by the loyalty of devoted readers who stuck with the strip for many long years. All this resonated with the way he seemed to create the basis for community through musical friendships, tight knit bluegrass bands, links to like-minded folks intent on preserving the history of the annual Union Grove fiddlers' convention[11] He was drawn to old string band music that was "forceful" and possessed "great drive" while retaining "tonal sensitivity," and he learned to appreciate the balance of carefully thought out style, and stage exuberance from old fiddlers who showed him the way to play loud, clean lines pushed forward by clever chording. In the 1970s, Jim felt comfortable in the embrace of a band that sought to capture the "spirit and style" of the music that its fiddling leader first heard on the Grand Ole Opry in the 1930s played by string bands like Dr. Humphrey Bate and his Possum Hunters.[12] The enduring friendships of musicians fueled his passion for old, traditional fiddling and string band music.

A Brief Brush with Movie Acting

Radio shows, music, old broadcasting and recording technologies—and movies—became a thread in Jim's life story. And that led, perhaps inexorably, to Jim's brief brush with Hollywood "fame" in two movies in the early 1980s.

The first, *Stroker Ace*, starred Burt Reynolds as a NASCAR driver. The 1983 movie, directed by Hal Needham, was an unmitigated flop. Jim remembered being in one scene with Loni Anderson, who played a Sunday school teacher in the movie. Her character (at least initially) spurned all of Stoker's advances. In the script, in one scene, Jim was standing next to Anderson. That scene was cut, though a crowd scene in the movie, in which Jim participated as an extra, made it into the final cut—for a fraction of a second.

The second movie, *Reuben Reuben*, was a 1983 comedy-drama directed by Robert Ellis Miller and starring Tom Conti and Kelly McGillis. The film was about a creatively blocked Scottish poet with few if any redeeming qualities. The film is based on the life of the Welsh poet Dylan Thomas. Jim recalled the famous director being "big stuff." "When he walked onto the set, what he said, you did." He sported a scarf around his neck that gave him the appearance of the archetypical World War II combat pilot. Jim was in a party scene in the movie. In one part of that scene he was standing next to the lead actor and talking to the female lead. In the next scene, Jim is seated on the sofa behind the female actor to whom the lead male was talking—suggesting an editing error. *Reuben, Reuben* was nominated for Academy Awards for Best Actor in a Leading Role (Tom Conti) and Best Writing for a Screenplay Based on Material from Another Medium. It did little for Jim's career.[13]

Jim got the gig as an extra on those two movies through the Fincannon Brothers, Mark and Craig, who together constituted a motion picture casting company established in Charlotte, North Carolina, in 1980. "I always wanted to be in *Gunsmoke*," Jim said, but the company did not have any ties into that television show, so he managed to lock down a slot as an extra in the Burt Reynolds' movie that was first called "Stand on It," but was released as *Stroker Ace*. Jim's recollection is that he did not get paid for *Stroker Ace*, though he earned $45.00 for two days of work on *Reuben Reuben*. He distinctly remembered the "caste system" on movie sets: stars ate first, followed by the crew, and the leftovers from what was available in the catered meals went to the extras. "The first day I missed out on eating, but the second day I got some food." He also remembered that it was the first time he saw someone on the crew armed with a "portable phone," though it was massive compared to what became available just a decade or two later.[14]

The Spirit of Old Things

Growing up during the Second World War, Jim admired the industry and imagination unleashed by the national-level commitment to win the war, and the post-war spirit of enterprise, the surge of innovation fueled by the first stages of the Cold War. As a young boy, he saw the last throes of the steam engine as railroads geared up for the transformation from steam to diesel engines—a transformation made much more personal by his grandfather, a civil engineer who worked hard on train safety issues during his career with the Southern Railway. From his grandfather, Jim learned that modernization brings change that is good, but also makes a dent in earlier ways and practices that were intricately involved in shaping lives, communities, nations.

Jim went on to develop an abiding respect for transitional moments that leave in their wake old innovations that were surpassed after making their mark on society.

During his years in uniform in the New England region, and during his life in Charlotte—North Carolina's railway hub—Jim never missed an opportunity to visit static displays of steam engines relevant to local history on the east coast, museums that heralded the story of steam locomotives, and local opportunities to witness operational steam engines that were passing through the Charlotte area on runs meant to herald these historic artifacts. He sought out opportunities to photograph steam locomotives on their way to local fairs and commemorations of the way science and commerce harnessed power to revolutionize transportation in an age of innovation.

When he worked at WBT, Jim came to appreciate the aesthetics and the stories behind the old style unidirectional vocal microphones—the kind that prompted singers like Frank Sinatra to insist on using the Telefunken U47 in the fifties and sixties. Jim had an appreciation for the older microphones that became the centerpiece of the onstage ballet that bluegrass band members practiced during the days of Bill Monroe, when banjo players, guitarists, mandolin players and fiddlers would weave in and out of the huddle of band's members to get to the microphone for their break, almost always executing that maneuver without casualties.

During his field recording work for the Union Grove fiddlers' convention in the late 1960s through the mid–1970s, and his own involvement with his label "Old Oblivion," he mastered the techniques of recording on what then passed for portable tape recorders. He used a variety of machines to copy and process the sound, and to splice the reel-to-reel tapes so they could be used by companies that pressed the records. He adapted to changing technologies that led to a rapid succession of tapes and machines that replaced the devices with which he became familiar during his radio and television days.

Jim never quite resisted change, but he did ruminate on the way wonderful old things—fiddle tunes, steam engines, old style cartooning, ancient recording technologies—would just wither away in the face of new styles and ways of doing things, modern inventions and technological innovation. It was just a fact of life, something his grandfather talked about, often tearfully, while recalling the fading echo of steam engines, the elegance of railway cars and the stylish aspect of transportation on the Southern Railway system. Undoubtedly, Jim liked older things—the special creative touch of veteran cartoonists, the tempered way elder fiddlers went about playing archaic tunes, the stately elegance combined with the massive dimensions and significant power of old locomotives. He probably liked stories about older things almost as much as he liked the older things themselves.

He has never let a computer into his life. He has never entered the internet zone. He does not now—and never will—have email. During the last quarter of 2020 he found that his antique flip phone had a limited messaging capacity. He used that means of communicating sparingly, preferring "old fashioned" letters and favoring long phone calls above other ways of communicating when face-to-face alternatives were not an available option. However, when that flip phone gave up the ghost—when the provider ceased servicing that model—he bit the bullet and got himself an iPhone, but not without a good deal of gnashing of teeth. He continued to use 20-year-old brass pen nibs with capillary channels for his illustration work. He addressed envelops in a flowing, distinguished handwriting, and always used U.S. Postage stamps that commemorated some aspect of railroad history.

Jim once observed that his old friend James "Chick" Martin was an "old-time North Carolina farmer," but clarified his view, adding that Martin was "old-time perhaps not due to age." Martin's age aside, Jim asserted that his banjo-playing friend was "old" as the result of a "personality and countenance" that reflected "an up-bringing once typical in the south." Jim continued:

> Chick is tall and lanky, and the years of hard work are mirrored in his face and have left him somewhat stoop shouldered. He has a keen rapport with the past and recognizes the swift changes that occur in daily life often suppress the time honored and hallowed things of an era gone by. Chick does not dwell in the past but has set about preserving things around him.

All that described the qualities and character that drew Jim to Chick Martin, and to others like the fiddlers Clyde Williams and Tommy Malboeuf, and Dick Moores, and his teacher Mr. Moure; as well as his beloved grandfather, Otto Parati. And all that reflected important aspects of Jim himself.

The Elwood P. Dowd Drum and Bugle Corps

Jim created and participated in all manner of opportunities for people to come into contact in the context of communities of music, associations of like-minded collectors, comic book conventions celebrating classic strips and their illustrators.

The Elwood P. Dowd Drum and Bugle Corps, though, might have been the most unique community of all. The group's name was clearly meant to invoke the memory and meaning of the 1950 comedy-drama, starring James Stewart and Josephine Hill, that revolved around the life of a man, Elwood P. Dowd, whose best friend was an invisible rabbit in excess of six feet tall named Harvey.

The nucleus of the Drum and Bugle Corps emerged in Charlotte around Harry Joyner and Bob Carroll, who tended to meet their friends casually, often accidentally, on trips to the local pharmacy where they would get into heated arguments on politics and current events of the day. Jim was invited to the Bugle Corps' second meeting, where it became clear that attendance committed one to a lifetime membership, though the club itself charged no dues and had none of the paraphernalia of an organized entity.[15] At some point, the group began inviting "guests," specialists who could hold forth on niche topics including:

- Kevin E. Moran, a scientist, engineer and thinker who had worked for a bunch of aeronautic companies developing guided missile systems and for computer companies, for Kodak, and for electronic businesses. In retirement, he turned his expertise and his abiding curiosity to the subject of the Shroud of Turin. Moran was involved in "hands on" analysis and laboratory research on the actual cloth. He is credited with more that 25 presentations to the Drum and Bugle Corps[16];
- Phil Morris, who started out with a traveling magic show that morphed into a performance focused on ghost stories. Morris created his "Dr. Evil" character in the late 1950s—and much later reached a settlement with the film producers of the Austin Powers movies over his trademark claim.[17] In the early 1960s, he was a circus ringmaster who crafted gorilla suits in his basement. In 1965, Morris began building what became the base of operations for his worldwide costume distributorship.[18]
- Eileen Fulton, who was born in Asheville, North Carolina, in September 1933, and played the character Lisa for almost 50 years on the CBS soap opera *As the World Turns.*[19]
- Floyd "Chunk" Simmons, Charlotte's first Olympian who won two bronze medals in the decathlon, one in 1948 in London and the second in 1952 in Helsinki. In 1958, he portrayed the character Commander Bill Harbison in the film *South Pacific.*[20]
- Brooks Lindsey, who played the role of "Joey the Clown" on WSOC, the rival television station to WBT in Charlotte, and Al Munn, who worked at WSOC and later owned WIST radio.[21]

Fifty years after the Drum and Bugle Corps emerged as a way for "a bunch of old geezers" to socialize regularly, Jim thought of it as a place where people who dreamed up ideas could go to share their stories, where a concentration of creative talent could get together regularly and think enduring thoughts.[22] To Jim, the Drum and Bugle Corps provided a gathering place for people who could see the "pooka," as Jimmy Stewart did in the film that lent its name to this Charlotte association of like-minded, happily argumentative friends.[23]

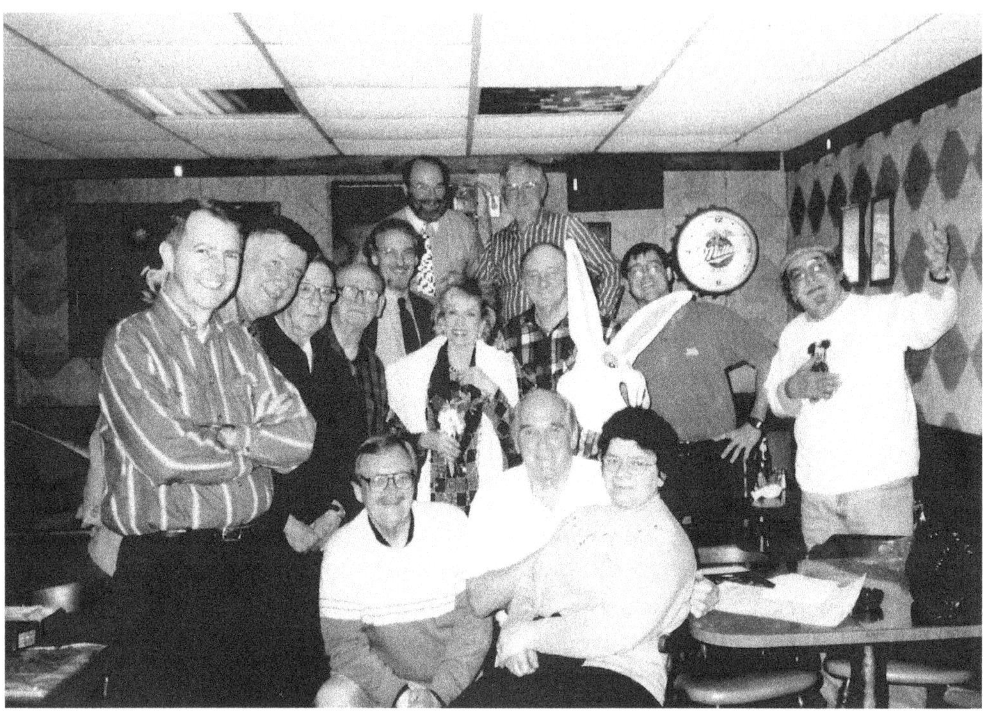

The Elwood P. Dowd Drum and Bugle Corps, named in honor of the six-foot tall rabbit Harvey in Jimmy Stewart's famed movie. Photograph by Bob Carroll.

Good, Old Jokes, Some Clear Life Rules

From Jim's perspective, a good joke is one that evokes a hearty laugh, but a joke is still a good one if it provokes groans of despair in reaction to corny content or dated material. He was not above relying on the "low hanging fruit" approach to getting a laugh in *Gasoline Alley*. With Rufus, Joel, Walt and other *Gasoline Alley* citizens, he felt himself in good company, and plodded on in his cartooning, and in everyday conversations, celebrating the tried-and-true old T.V. favorites, mothballed humor from radio days, artifacts of old newspaper cartoons and comic books, elements of the visual humor on which publications such as *Mad Magazine* thrived.

Jim liked to take the easygoing approach to life. He sought to take the gentlemanly way in discourse, remained generally unperturbed by circumstances, unfazed by surprises. He was emotional about old friends and departed family members. He cherished old memories and surrounded himself with all manner of artifacts of his youth, things that connected him to family and friends. All that showed up in his cartoon work, and in his everyday life.

He took the path of a God-fearing, church-going man, but he did not wear his religion on his sleeve. He was adamantly against drink, against drugs, and never quite understood how those kinds of things could grab hold of a person and tear their lives apart, how people could succumb to a temptation that was just ruinous. In the 1970s, he saw musician friends destroyed by giving in to those and other temptations. He remembered creative forces whose lives were cut short, and the loss of those talented souls still nagged at him fifty years later. He did not appear to urge abstinence on others, but made clear that he did not drink, and did not smoke, and did not do drugs. That, in his explanation, was how he escaped alive from high school, the Navy, the string band revival and the old-time fiddlers' conventions in the 1970s, a lifetime of band performances, the radio and television industry, freelance art, and the cartooning world. Toward the end of 2020, Jim reflected on how sudden health challenges that sidelined him in 2017 prompted him to spend more time thinking about the wonder of life—the frailty of this gift, as he called it. Just celebrating the "chance" to wake up and live another day, Jim made clear, is reason enough to be thankful.[24]

Jim offered his services as a writer/illustrator to many good causes. He designed book covers and undertook illustration work for diverse special projects. He promoted the "Physician's Assistant Concept" in *Gasoline Alley*, an idea according to which former military medics and corpsmen were trained to assist physicians in their civilian practices, a plan that began to gain traction in the 1970s.[25] He supported the National World War II Memorial Campaign in the early 2000s with a *Gasoline Alley* story line that resulted in donations to that cause worth several thousand dollars, and priceless publicity for that campaign.[26] He has honored American farmers, and brought attention to the continued erosion of small farms in the U.S. He has featured the efforts of rural communities to protect their environment, the food chain, and forested areas in his cartoons. Jim has used *Gasoline Alley* to promote the importance of supporting small businesses, and to dramatize the pressures of that political interests and market forces exert against such valued community assets.[27]

Impressed by History, Heroes

Jim regarded it as a singular privilege when he had the chance to meet real heroes, troops who went to war and sacrificed for the country, soldiers and seamen who demonstrated indomitable spirit and commitment to mission.[28]

Over the years, in Charlotte, North Carolina, he ran into U.S. pilots who flew planes during World War II. Some had gone to Canada when they were not yet 18 where they could get the training and have the chance to fly before they would have been eligible to enlist in the U.S. and fly planes in the war.

Jim met a number of survivors of Stalag Luft 3, a Luftwaffe-run prisoner of war camp where captured Western Allied air force personnel were incarcerated. The camp was established in March 1942 in the German province of Lower Silesia near the town of Sagan, 160 kilometers southeast of Berlin.

A friend of Jim's, a movie buff, William C. Cline—the author of *In the Nick of Time: Motion Picture Sound Serials*—introduced Jim to Bob Crot, one of the first Americans to figure out he could go to Canada and become a pilot in the Royal Canadian Air Force, something he could not accomplish in the U.S. given age and stringent requirements governing access to flight training. Crot was sent to Britain and trained as a Spitfire pilot. He was shot down, captured by the Germans, and sent to Stalag Luft 3 where he honed a capacity for leaving the camp undetected. During those brief departures from the prison, he scrounged the kind of documents and intelligence the American POWs in Stalag Luft 3 needed to complete their plans for escape, and then snuck back into the camp to provide the gathered information to the POWs planning the escape.[29]

Jim met Kenneth Daniel Williams, who trained as a bombardier, was later sent to crew training on the B-17 heavy bomber, and was then assigned to the 351st Bomb Group, 508th Squadron. Williams had his aircraft shot out from under him over Germany in 1943. Williams was captured—and attained notoriety for wearing a flight jacket emblazoned with a painted "Murder, Incorporated" logo that made him famous in the German newspapers of the time.[30] Jim also befriended Alan Newcomb, a pilot shot down in 1947 who wrote an account of his "stay at the German Rest Camp for Tired Allied Airmen at Beautiful Barth-on-the-Baltic," entitled *Vacation With Pay* (Destiny Publishers, 1947).[31] Jim made the acquaintance of the Rev. Eugene Lewis Daniel, Jr., who was captured by the Germans and sent to several camps during his wartime incarceration, including Stalag Luft 3.[32]

Jim read all he could get his hands on about their wartime stories and their capture and time as Prisoners of War; as he approached his own August 2020 birthday, he was immersed in a book by William Ash, *Under the Wire*, co-authored with Brendan Foley, about Ash's time as an American Spitfire pilot, and his exploits as a "legendary POW escape artist at Stalag Luft III." These were not national leaders, corporate giants, great artists or scientific minds, but common folk called to serve who rose to the occasion. He was preoccupied with the thought that once these heroes died, their stories would no longer be heard. He had the urge to help contribute to acts that would memorialize their lives. Some of the precious memoirs these men had penned for their immediate families, and collections of photographs and reflections, had already disappeared. He lamented the fact that, in the blink of an eye, aspects of historical memory were gone.[33] He never missed the opportunity to honor the sacrifices these heroes made during their time in uniform.[34]

The Music in Jim

Jim had a profound appreciation for a fine banjo, a carefully made fiddle—and enjoyed dwelling on the history of old instruments, the way their archaic past clung to them even while they were making new music.[35] Though he did not turn up his nose at original music and more modern compositions, his heart was with the old tunes, the elder fiddlers, ancient recordings, music that was vintage, stuff plucked from Smithsonian Folkways recordings, tunes learned from old fiddlers who showed up at old-time music festivals and played broken, brittle old tunes with their own internal structure, a logic that defied music theory, and a provenance often lost in the mist of history.

He never sang much, though he probably pitched in from time to time to croon backup in the various bands with which he made music. Of course, he lent his voice to various radio shows while he was at WBT, including "The Yellowjacket," a farce that referenced Adam West's television show, *Batman*. The WBT radio show could be looked at as a homage to dramatic—and often comedic—radio shows dating from

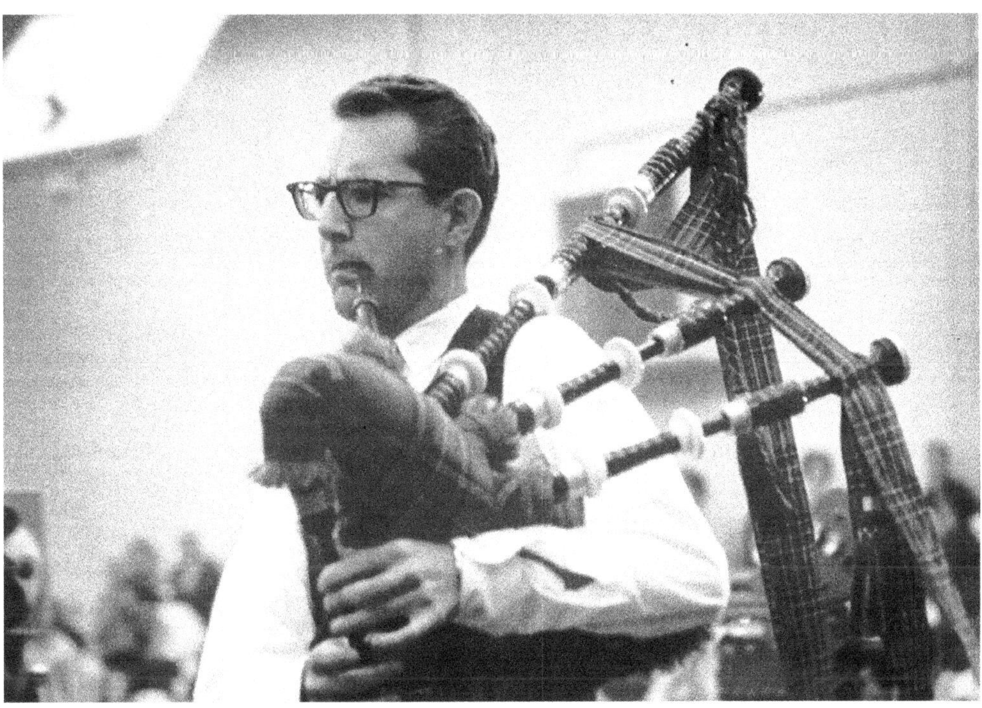

Jim Scancarelli playing bagpipes. No date.

the 1940s that Jim enjoyed as a youth. Jim's voice in the service of such productions as "The Yellowjacket" was melodious, with a clear tinge of the old south, a pronounced North Carolinian lilt.

Though he essentially stopped playing in string bands in the 1990s and put down his fiddle and banjo in the first decade of 2000s, he continued to celebrate the music of the string band revival, the tunes he played and the tunes he heard and learned at old-time and bluegrass festivals in the sixties, seventies and eighties. He shares copies of the Mole Hill Highlanders and Sanitary Cafe band music that he had recorded on his Old Oblivion label. He tells stories of the old-time fiddling prowess of Clyde

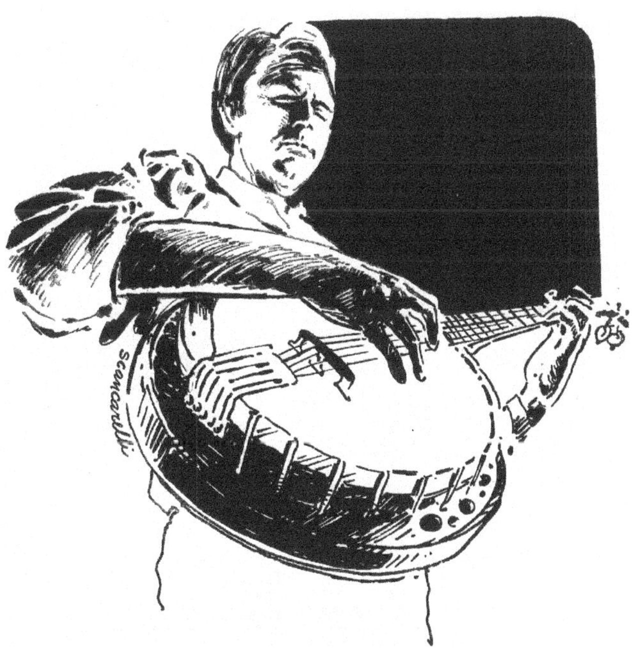

Self-portrait by Jim Scancarelli. 1984.

Williams and Tommy Malboeuf. He celebrates the music of John Hartford, Earl Scruggs, Bill Monroe, and he recalls with deep fondness musician friends like Jim Greene, Jack Reddick, Darrell Gray, Mark Wingate, Chuck Dunlop, and others. Through the second decade of the 2000s, he still talked about the musical prowess of band partners—Chuck Dunlop, Mark Wingate, Jim Whitley. Jim memorialized many of these musicians in *Gasoline Alley* strips in long-running stories, themes that had them rubbing shoulders with

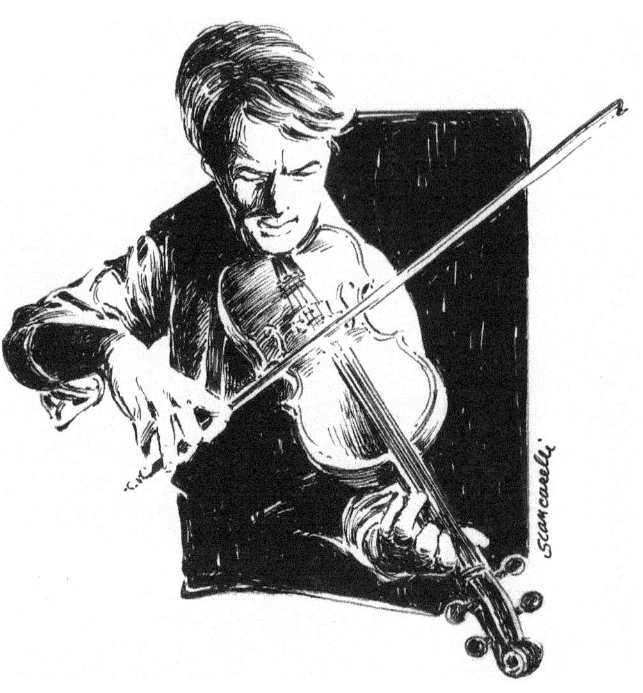

Self-portrait by Jim Scancarelli. 1984.

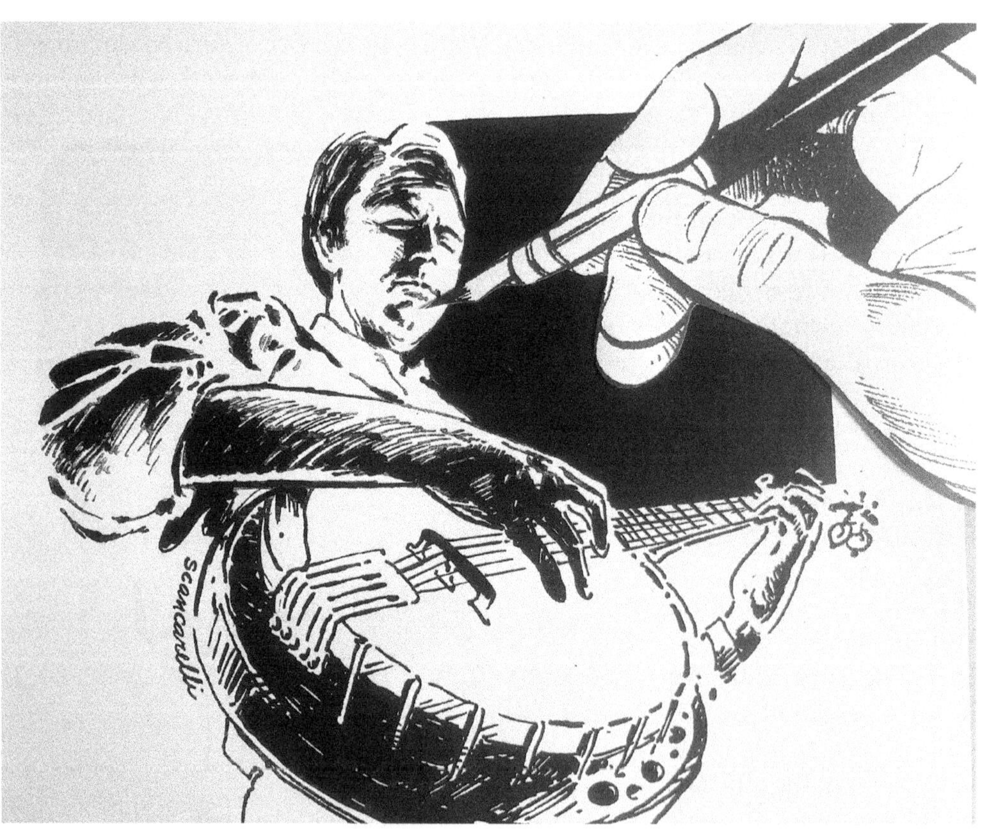

Gasoline Alley citizens, including the musically inclined Rufus (sometimes armed with a banjo) and Joel (occasionally behind a bass fiddle).

As he approached his 81st birthday—August 2022—his telephone voice continued to modulate with the same frequencies that can be heard in the audio reproductions of "The Yellowjacket" in which Jim created the voice character of Mr. Mockingbird, Warden Borden Gordon, and Aunt Sally.[36] He speaks slowly and clearly, connects sentences with the wondrous device of phrases that convey an enthusiasm with the subject at hand, and a preference for essentially simple, informal, and straightforward grammatical constructions that invite conversation, that seek to elicit wild guesses so as to keep a good story going. He can become philosophical about life, and even teary eyed in reminiscing with old friends and family members about "the old days," but he retains an enthusiasm about everything he has done, everyone he has met, and would gladly do it all again—with the possible exception of his stint in the Navy. In a metaphor that Jim preferred, life is a "beautiful train ride." Friends, family, co-workers, neighbors, and loved ones board the train and disembark continuously, taking off on their own journeys, often unexpectedly. "We do not know at which station we ourselves will step down" from the train. "Live in the best way, love, forgive, offer the best of who we are."[37] That way, what you leave behind is not just an empty seat.[38]

Opposite, bottom: **Self portrait of Jim drawing his own self portrait—a hand drawing of a hand drawing, so to speak.... July 2021.**

Appendix 1:
Discography and Videography
Jim Scancarelli
(Arranged Chronologically)

This discography/videography contains information about recordings that captured Jim Scancarelli's fiddle and banjo playing. The list includes commercial recordings; studio tapes of radio or television performances with bands; field recordings; informal jam session tapes made by Jim or others capturing band music; jam session or other informal musical gatherings playing alone or in a group of musicians that did not constitute a band; as well as recordings that do not quite fall into any of those categories.

Mole Hill Highlanders Airtime on WFMX Radio

In 1970, Odell Wood had a radio show at WFMX in Statesville, North Carolina, a popular country station.[1] Wood let the Mole Hill Highlanders band members hang around the studio and dig through his records of early bluegrass musicians. One day, the band asked whether they could have a half hour on his show to get their music out over the airwaves. Wood said that it didn't matter to him whether he was talking or spinning a record, he got paid the same, so the band cut some reel-to-reel tapes at Chuck Dunlop's house, and eventually assembled those recordings on an audio tape for the radio station. The Mole Hill Highlanders music was broadcast on 13 shows on WFMX, between 1 May 1970 and 21 July 1970, before station management took note of the arrangement and decided that the band should pay for the airtime. Eventually, the station's managers offered the band what Jim called "the preacher's discount" to keep the program going, but the band members could not afford the radio station's price tag for airtime. That, Jim said, marked the end of their run on WFMX. In recent years, Chuck Dunlop digitized all 13 shows thus establishing the basis for a future black market in pirated Mole Hill Highlander recorded music.

Mole Hill Highlanders Band Airtime on WRAL-TV

In 1936, following an open audition at WBT in Charlotte, Homer Drye joined the Briarhoppers, and became "Homer A. Briarhopper." Sometime during 1940–1941, he left WBT to go to WPTF in Raleigh, North Carolina, where he founded the band called Homer A. Briarhoppers' Dixie Dudes. In 1954, Homer was named "Mr. Disc Jockey USA." By the early 1970s, he had a show called "Daybreak with Homer Briarhopper" on WRAL-TV.[2] Drye hosted the Mole Hill Highlanders on his television show sometime in the fall of 1970 or possibly the spring of 1971.[3] Chuck Dunlop, Jim Scancarelli, Mark Wingate, Darrell Gray, and Jim Whitley—that is, all the band members minus the fiddler, Clyde Williams—drove to Raleigh from Charlotte for the early morning show. Jim Scancarelli recalled the band played two or three tunes at the station.

Videos of a Festival in the Early 1970s

Sometime in the early 1970s, Jim and Dot Jackson, a writer and local columnist for *The Charlotte Observer*, put their heads together and came up with an idea for a local fiddlers' convention. They found a venue just outside of Charlotte in the Andrew Jackson Museum, in the Waxhaw area on the border between North and South Carolina. Both North Carolina and South Carolina have staked claims as Andrew Jackson's birthplace. Jim recalled that the turnout was decidedly poor. The audience for the musicians who did come to perform—including Arthur Leake Caudle and Marcus Hamilton, the cartoonist who played folk guitar—was noticeably sparse. The festival organizers awarded Caudle "first prize" out of respect, and on account of the fact that not enough people came to provide the basis for a good contest. Through at least 2020, Jim retained a master copy of the 10.5-inch reel-to-reel tape that captured the proceedings of that festival; Jim may have taped the festival music on smaller tapes and then, later, transferred them to the larger master tape.[4]

Mole Hill Highlander Half-Hour TV Show, WTVI, 1970

The Mole Hill Highlanders did a one-half hour television show at WTVI in Charlotte, North Carolina, in 1970 that was captured on video tape by the Public Broadcasting Service member television station licensed to Charlotte.[5] The plan for the show involved having the band members arrayed on a stage, as though they were performing music at a cafe. The station rolled out round tables, positioned the tables to create that setting, and directed the camera crew to position their machinery and then take seats at the tables as though they were the audience. Clyde Williams arrived late and—as Jim remembered—looked like a wreck. He had been doing some welding work, and came directly from that project, his hair frizzled up and his pants burned with a bunch of tiny holes from the welding rig. He did not want to do the show, and certainly had no inclination to take a position on the stage, so Sam Rowe—who had at some prior point recorded the band in Chuck Dunlop's backyard—told Clyde he could stand on stage out of camera range. Mark Wingate served as Master of Ceremonies for the performance. When Wingate in his capacity as MC would make a reference to Williams—for example, when the fiddler would be called upon to kick off a tune—Clyde's fiddling could be heard, but he was not visible alongside the other band members. An audio tape of that show survived in the holdings of Jim,

Mark Wingate, and/or Chuck Dunlop, but as of January 2021 had not surfaced in any of those personal archives.

Mole Hill Highlanders on the Union Grove "Talking Machine Records"

The Mole Hill Highlanders, including Jim Scancarelli, were recorded playing "Possum Hunter's Stepdance" on the album "Hub of the Universe" (SS-4) and "Chinese Breakdown" (SS-5), both of which were produced as LPs under the Union Grove Talking Machine Records label.[6] Chuck Dunlop noted that after the original Mole Hill Highlanders broke up in 1971, Clyde continued to perform under that band name.[7] The original Mole Highlanders appeared only on SS-4 and SS-5. Clyde Williams and the Mole Hill Highlanders were recorded playing the tune "Huckleberry Pond" on an album called "Union Grove Old Time Fiddlers' 49th Convention" (SS-7).[8] The Mole Hill Highlanders were recorded playing "Lady of the Lake" on an album called "Fiddle and Banjo" on the Union Grove Talking Machine Records label (SS-10).[9]

Mole Hill Highlander releases on the "Old Oblivion" Label

Old Oblivion's second release, "The Mole Hill Highlanders: Old Time String Band Music," (Old Oblivion OO-2), came out in May 1970, recorded by Sam Rowe, and produced and designed by Jim; the cassette tape was digitally re-mastered at Audioworks in Charlotte, North Carolina, by Mike Robinson. The recording features Clyde Williams on fiddle, Jim on banjo, Mark Wingate on harmony fiddle, Chuck Dunlop on guitar, and Jim Whitley on bass. Whitley played jaw harp on the cut of "Molly Hare." Jim wrote the liner notes that described the small Piedmont North Carolina community called Mole Hill, where Clyde Williams lived on Old Plank Road, just beyond the water plant on NC-16.[10] The band gathered there in October 1969 and played music around a big oil stove in the living room in the presence of an audience that consisted of Clyde's mother, his two sisters and their children, a hound, and several cats.

The third recording released on the Old Oblivion label was "The Mole Hill Highlanders: Old Time String Band Music, Volume 2" (Old Oblivion OO-3), with music by the same lineup. Jim wrote in the liner notes that in the spring of 1970, the band stopped in Statesville, North Carolina, at radio station WFMX where Odell Wood, the brother of banjo player A.L. Wood, broadcast a daily radio show of country and bluegrass music. The analog tapes were re-mastered to digital form in 1993.

Number five released on the "Old Oblivion" label was "Bluegrass Sanitary Cafe," featuring Jim and Tommy Malboeuf. Don Wright played banjo on the recording, and Steve Kilby played guitar, mandolin, and mandola. Bill Williams played bass, and Pat Cocklin provided vocals. Tony Anaya played guitar and Angelica Anya played cabasa on one cut. The sound effects were recorded at the Philadelphia Deli in Charlotte, North Carolina; cassette tapes were prepared from those original recordings in December 1991 by Mike Robinson at Audioworks, in Charlotte, North Carolina.

The seventh recording, "Twin Fiddles," (OO-7) featured the music of Jim Scancarelli (lead fiddle), Tom Malboeuf (harmony fiddle), and Jim Greene (guitar). The three met at Greene's home in Charlotte for a jam session in June 1996. "After a couple of tunes," Jim wrote in the brief liner notes for that recording, "Jim Greene reached over and turned the cassette player on and recorded the music for our enjoyment later. All tunes were done in one take and whatever clinkers and imperfections were left in as we kept the tape rolling." Tommy's dog Tip can be heard tapping his tail against the microphone stand.

Other Cuts on Commercial Recordings

Jim Scancarelli played banjo on one cut of an album called "Mountain Music at Its Best: Old Time Tunes Recorded at the 38th Annual Old Fiddlers' Convention at Galax, Virginia." Jim teamed with Gus Meade (fiddle) and several other musicians on the side B tune, "Robinson County." They called their band the Rye Straw Chitickers. The album came out on the label W.H. Butner, Tobbaccoville, North Carolina, in 1974.[11]

Jim Scancarelli fiddled the tune "Frosty the Snowman" on a cassette recording, "Christmas Presence" recorded by Wayne Seymour and Fred Reynolds. Seymour, a multi-instrumentalist whose interest in traditional music dated back to his days in high school in the 1960s, teamed up with Reynolds in the early 1980s. The two musicians recorded two Christmas cassettes on Doug Rorrer's Flyin' Cloud label. Seymour asked Jim to fiddle on the cut of "Frosty the Snowman" on the second cassette, "Christmas Presence." Jim did it in one take. Seymour and Reynolds used a classically oriented fiddler on the other cuts. Later they had the two cassettes combined into a CD, omitting Jim's fiddling on "Frosty" because they ran into copyright problems.

Jim performed the three tunes—"Leather Britches," "Ouk Pik Waltz," and "The 8th of January"—on fiddle, with guitar accompaniment by Wayne Seymour, and banjo accompaniment by J. Eanes, for a Flyin' Cloud Records disc (FB-0007) that was called "Virginia Carolina Sampler." The recording work was done at the Flying Cloud Studio in Madison, North Carolina, in January 1986 and April 1988, and the recording was released in 1988.[12]

Jim played fiddle on the recording "11/26/54," a 1988 recording featuring Steve Kilby released as Heritage HRC 074.[13]

In 1989, Jim Scancarelli played fiddle on four cuts of an album, "Doctor River," featuring the music of Bruce Piephoff (vocals, acoustic guitar, harmonica), Scott Manning (lead guitar, steel guitar dobro), Arnie Solomon (mandolin), Kathy Rorrer (background vocals) and Doug Rorrer (bass, lead guitar). Flyin' Cloud issued the recording (FC-001) on their country music list. Jim played "Glennwood" (cut 15), "Better for my Eyes than Carrots" (cut 16), "Hambone" (cut 17), and "Doctor River" (cut 18). The LP "Doctor River" was reissued as part of a CD package in 2001, combined with another Piephoff recording, "Razor's Edge."[14]

Jim played fiddle on a recording of guitarist Steve Kilby's tunes called *Sunday Night* (Heritage HRC-C-099, released 1992). The 14 featured tunes were all written by Kilby. Musicians included Donnie Scott (dobro), Bill Williams (bass), David Johnson (fiddle and viola), Butch Barker (bowed bass), and Jim who played fiddle on "Grissel Tail" and "Kilby's Branch." Jim provided fiddle accompaniment on two cuts: "Grissel Tail" (cut 20) and "Kilby's Branch" (cut 21).[15]

The WPAQ "Merry Go Round"

Jim played on WPAQ in Mount Airy, North Carolina, in 1990 or early 1991 with a band that included Steve Kilby (guitar), Debbie Larson (bass), Ramona Church (banjo), and Johnny Williams (mandolin). The station was known for their old-time and bluegrass music program, "The Merry Go-Round," a live radio broadcast from the historic Earle Theatre in Mount Airy, a program that originated in 1948 under the auspices of Ralph Epperson.[16]

The Central Piedmont Community College
Recording Sessions, 2004

The Kilocycle Kowboys played two sessions, two hours each, at Central Piedmont Community College (CPCC) in Charlotte, North Carolina, in 2004. Jim recalled the sessions as a training opportunity for a student engineer at the community college. Jim Whitley worked at the college; he and Joe Cline set up the two sessions. The teacher required acoustic instruments to give the students experience with something other than electrified live music. At the time, the small community college recording studio was equipped with up-to-date technology.[17] Jim played fiddle on one of the two-hour sessions. Glen Alexander did the fiddling on the second session. Joe Cline noted that bass player Darrell Gray was not present for the first session. Gray dubbed the bass part for the first two songs at the beginning of the second recording session, and then recorded the other two tunes "live."[18] Apart from that first session at the community college in 2004, the Kilocycle Kowboys did not record any other music while Jim Scancarelli manned the fiddle for the band. Cline retained hand-written notes on the disk of the CPCC sessions.[19]

Miscellaneous Jam and Performance Recordings

In the last quarter of 2020, Danny Bowers, a North Carolinian bluegrass musician, provided several CDs containing Jim Scancarelli's fiddling recorded in 1986, 2007 and 2010:

- Jim Greene (guitar), Jack Haley (banjo), Judy Sherrill and Jim Scancarelli (fiddle). Recorded at Balls Creek Fiddlers' Convention, North Carolina, on 27 January 1986, and Jim Greene's house on 1 February 1986. Jim recalled that recording as a "montage" of musical "stuff" that included Irish tunes and square dance music. He also recalled that the band cobbled together for the Ball's Creek festival could not find a place to practice in the school facility utilized for such purposes. All the rooms in the building were occupied by other bands busily practicing for the contest. So, Jim and friends set up and ran through their repertoire in a men's bathroom with Judy playing bass.
- Solo Fiddle, Jim Scancarelli. 16 September 2007. Jim remembered one tune in particular that he played on this self-made recording, "Tune for Tip," written in honor of Tommy Malboeuf's beloved hound, Tip. Jim "made up" the tune and played it at contradances in the early 2000s.

- Red Tommy and Jim Scancarelli (and Joanne Hall). Recorded 7 October 2007, 14 October 2007, 20 October 2007, and 28 October 2007. Jim recalled that Joanne Hall took the low part on her fiddle, Tommy Malboeuf took the high part, and Jim stayed on the melody line.
- Timmy Martin and Jim Scancarelli at Galax, Virginia, 15 August 2010. Recorded at WPAQ. In Jim's memory, this was the last real big time jam session in which he participated, and the last Galax he attended. The musicians, including Jim, were all sitting around Leon Marlowe's festival campsite in a semi-circle. A WPAQ attendee happened on their jam and thought it worth listening to, so he taped it. Jack Haley played banjo, Timmy Martin and Jim brought their fiddles to the mix.[20]

YouTube Videos

In 2010, Jim Scancarelli occasionally played at a weekly Monday evening contradance held in Charlotte, North Carolina. Two videos on YouTube, both posted in March 2010, are attributed to a band named "Poultry in Motion" that included Jon Singleton (fiddle), Jim Scancarelli (fiddle), Phil Lessor (banjo), Joe Cline (guitar), and Ruth Kee Wherry (bass). One video captured the band playing "Jack of Diamonds" at a contradance that featured Dean Snipes as the caller.[21] The second video featured the band playing two fiddle tunes: "Crockett's Honeymoon" and "Dixie Hoedown."[22] Jim thought it might have just been a gaggle of musicians who got together to play these contradance events and found themselves operating under the handle "Poultry in Motion." Jim also remembered that, at the time, he knew the tune "Crockett's Honeymoon," as well as "Dixie Hoedown," but thought that "Jack of Diamonds" was one he probably did not know—though he recalled that not knowing how to fiddle a tune never stopped him from figuring out the basic chord structure and providing some sort of contribution to the ensemble's work.[23]

Appendix 2:
Gasoline Alley Strips
Referenced in Chapter Six

All the *Gasoline Alley* strips referenced in Chapter Six can be found on the Gocomics.com website at following links:

The banjo in a heavenly choir (22 December 2002): https://www.gocomics.com/gasolinealley/2002/12/22

The banjo in a tribute—of sorts—to Kentucky bluegrass (7 November 2004): https://www.gocomics.com/gasolinealley/2004/11/07

The strip in which the Miceketeer fiddler is knocking the banjo picker in the nose with his bow (4 January 2015): https://www.gocomics.com/gasolinealley/2015/01/04

A strip that has Churchy from the comic strip *Pogo* playing banjo at a party in full swing at the Old Comics Retirement Home (20 March 2011): https://www.gocomics.com/gasolinealley/2011/03/20

Banjo in the Thanksgiving Day strip (23 November 2015): https://www.gocomics.com/gasolinealley/2015/11/23

Banjo in the Easter-focused strip (21 April 2019): https://www.gocomics.com/gasolinealley/2019/04/21

The strip in which Jim introduced "The Three Blind Miceketeers" (2 November 2014): https://www.gocomics.com/gasolinealley/2014/11/02

The strip that had the Miceketeers dressed in smart top hats and tails (4 May 2015): https://www.gocomics.com/gasolinealley/2015/05/04

The strip, featuring the Miceteteers, in which Chef Meowrice promotes his new canned foods recipes. (2 August 2015): https://www.gocomics.com/gasolinealley/2014/11/02

A Miceketeer themed-strip typifying the pungent cat-food references of those cartoons. (5 April 2020): https://www.gocomics.com/gasolinealley/2020/04/05

The Banjo as Pawn Star Thread, beginning on 1 July 2016, nine strips that referenced a pawn shop, and featured a banjo—and sometimes a fiddle—as window dressing, including these seven strips: https://www.gocomics.com/gasolinealley/2016/07/01;

https://www.gocomics.com/gasolinealley/2016/07/06; https://www.gocomics.com/gasolinealley/2016/07/09; https://www.gocomics.com/gasolinealley/2016/07/11; https://www.gocomics.com/gasolinealley/2016/07/14; https://www.gocomics.com/gasolinealley/2016/07/17; https://www.gocomics.com/gasolinealley/2016/07/22

A Sunday strip in which Slim recounts a dream of a tree that a woodsman was ready to cut down with his ax (26 June 2005): https://www.gocomics.com/gasolinealley/2005/06/26

A strip in which key *Gasoline Alley* characters and friends from the Retired Comics Home acknowledge the 100th birthday of the *Mutt and Jeff* cartoon (20 November 2018): https://www.gocomics.com/gasolinealley/2018/11/20

Interviewees

Ben Barry earned a Bachelor of Architecture degree from the University of Tennessee (Knoxville) in 1972. Following an internship in Finland, he returned to settle in Charlotte, North Carolina, where he worked for 30 years as an architect and held positions in a number of small commercial ventures along the way. He has designed office buildings in the historic district of Waxhaw, and has done work in the renovation, construction, and architectural drawing aspects of the business. He also has experience in residential home design and construction management. Since 2000, he served as the Director of the B.I.G. Ride, a non-profit cross-country bicycle tour organized to raise awareness of brain injuries and fund brain injury programs founded by his late wife, Lee Anne Barry. He is also on the board of directors for Hinds Feet Farm, a post-traumatic brain injury program in Huntersville, North Carolina. He wrote the book *Moment by Moment on the B.I.G. Ride* with Lee Anne, who experienced brain injury as a young girl and died in a tragic accident in 2007. He is a member of the Elwood P. Dowd Drum and Bugle Corps in Charlotte, North Carolina.

Bob Carlin was born in New York City in 1953. He played bass with the Millstone Valley Boys in the early 1970s and with the Delaware Water Gap from 1974 to 1980. In 1980 he played banjo with the band Dance All Night. In the late 1980s, he played with Bruce Molsky, and with Joe Thompson in the Joe Thompson Band. Beginning in the mid–1990s, Carlin toured with John Hartford throughout the United States, Canada, and Japan. For over fifty years he has documented American musical traditions as a fieldworker, writer, record and radio producer, lecturer, and performer. Carlin has received four Grammy nominations for his many recordings as artist, producer, and engineer for labels including Rounder and Smithsonian Folkways. He has performed, recorded, and taught minstrel stroke style, Piedmont finger picking, and clawhammer banjo in the style and tradition of southwestern Virginia and northwestern North Carolina down picking, and has performed American folk music for audiences in Europe, Canada, Japan and Australia. He has also explored the African roots of the banjo with the Malian musician Cheick Hamala Diabate. He is the author of over one hundred articles for periodicals such as *Guitar Aficionado, The Fretboard Journal, Bluegrass Unlimited and Acoustic Guitar*, as well as numerous album notes and museum exhibition catalogues. He is the author of *The Birth of the Banjo: Joel Walker Sweeney and Early Minstrelsy,* and *String Bands in the North Carolina Piedmont*. In 2016, Backbeat Books, an imprint of the Hal Leonard Corporation, published Carlin's pictorial, *Banjo: An Illustrated History*.

Joe S. Cline was born in Concord, North Carolina. He served in the U.S. Coast Guard from 1966 to 1970. In January 1969, Cline was deployed to the Vietnam theatre of operation aboard the USCGC Sebago, one of five high-endurance cutters that patrolled the South Vietnamese coastline, mainly in the Gulf of Siam, forming Coast Guard Squadron One, reporting to the USCG headquarters in Saigon. After his duty with the Coast Guard, Cline attended Gaston College in Dallas, North Carolina, and was graduated in 1973. The Kilocycle Kowboys formed as a band in 1972. In their time, the band opened for Riders in the Sky and backed Lulu Belle and Scotty Wiseman on numerous occasions. Cline logged 37 years with the Kilocycle Kowboys. After banjo player Jim Whitley passed away in 2008, Cline, Darrell Gray, and Glen Alexander (fiddle) "did two or three jobs with other banjo pickers, but without Jim W., it just didn't feel the same." In 1982, Cline stage managed the first Charlotte Folk Music Festival at Latta Plantation Park near Huntersville, North Carolina. He ran the festival through 1991. Cline played guitar, mandolin, tenor banjo, and sang for the Celtic band called Magpye, a Charlotte ensemble, from 1988 to 2000. He was a member of several other local bands including Country Matters, The Red Ball Ranch Hands, and the Dirt Creek Band. He served as radio station host and programmer for WNCW-Spindale in North Carolina from 1995 to 2008. In 2017, Cline played for nine months with the Briarhoppers, a band with a lineage that went back to the 1930s as a WBT radio band.

Clinton Corbett is an artist, designer and educator from North Carolina, currently serving as an adjunct instructor in Central Piedmont Community College's Advertising and Graphic Design Department. She earned a *certificate de stage* in painting at the International Summer Academy in Nice, France, and pursued postgraduate studies at the *Ecole Nationale Supérieure des Arts Appliqués et des Métiers d'Art* (ENSAAMA) in Paris in 1979 and 1980. From 2000 to 2004, she worked as a Senior Editor for Sudler and Hennessey in New York. From 2004 to 2008, she served as an Art Director at Sudler. During 2003–2020, she attended continuing education classes, intermittently, at the School of Visual Arts in New York, focusing on graphic design, and studied painting, drawing, and printing at the Art Students League in New York City. Corbett has designed promotional materials for Untitled Theater Company #61 in New York for 11 years, during which time she worked on the design aspects of five books of plays written by Vaclav Havel.

Chuck Dunlop's life has both an academic trajectory to it, and a musical one. He earned an A.B. degree from Stanford University in 1965, where he studied English literature and philosophy, a Master of Arts in Philosophy from Duke University in 1969, and a Ph.D. from Duke in 1973. After a succession of instructorships at Duke University and the University of North Carolina at Charlotte, Dunlop began teaching philosophy at the University of Michigan's Flint campus in the early 1970s. He was promoted to Associate Professor in 1977. He spent the 1980–1981 school year as a Visiting Associate Professor at the University of Cincinnati. He returned to Flint and was promoted to the rank of Full Professor in 1985. In 1987, he earned a Master of Science degree in Computer Science at Wright State University and taught there as a Visiting

Assistant Professor of Computer Science from 1987 to 1988. He spent the next year as a Visiting Lecturer in Philosophy at the University of Waikato in New Zealand. He returned to Flint in 1990, and retired in 2008, with the title of David M. French Professor Emeritus, and Professor Emeritus of Philosophy. As for the musical aspect of his life, beginning in the late 1960s, in North Carolina, Dunlop sought out musical partners with an interest in playing bluegrass. He met Mark Wingate, a talented multi-instrumentalist, and through Mark encountered the fiddler Clyde Williams who lived outside of Charlotte in an area known as Mole Hill. With Jim Scancarelli they formed The Mole Hill Highlanders. In Flint, Michigan, in the early 1970s, Dunlop and several musical associates formed a band called the Dixie Hoedowners. In 1989, in Hamilton, New Zealand, he played in a band called the Mystery Creek Bluegrass Company. In the late 1990s, in Ann Arbor, Michigan, he played with several bands including one called the Traver Creek Ramblers. In the early 2000s, he played with a group that went by the name Southern Flavor. He sought out like-minded string band music enthusiasts wherever he lived, immersed himself in a network of local musicians, and allied himself with bands in far flung places.

Eric Ellis, from Wilkes County, North Carolina, a banjo player for over three decades, has played bluegrass with Bobby Hicks, Jim Buchanan, Tony Rice, Jimmy Gaudreau, Mike Auldridge, Wes Golding, Wayne Benson, and Clay Jones. Eric remembered opening for Jim and Jesse McReynolds in November 1978 in Statesville, North Carolina, following the Love Valley Four, J.D. Benfield's band—Benfield was, at the time, a manager on WFMX-FM in Statesville. He also remembered playing some music with Jim Scancarelli in the 1980s, and jamming a bit, informally, when Jim was with the Kilocycle Kowboys.

Marcus Hamilton was born in Lexington, North Carolina. He studied commercial art in college and had a long career as an illustrator for magazines, including *The Saturday Evening Post* and *U.S. News and World Report* before Hank Ketcham, the creator and illustrator of the *Dennis the Menace*, selected Hamilton to work on the daily comic strip. Ketchum retired in 1995, and Hamilton has been doing the daily panels since then. Hamilton was awarded the cartooning industry's highest honors for "Best Newspaper Cartoon Panel of the Year" at the 59th Annual National Cartoonists Society Reuben Awards ceremony in Scottsdale, Arizona, in May 2005.

Tom Hanchett is a community historian in Charlotte, North Carolina. He served as Staff Historian with the Levine Museum of the New South for 16 years, where he curated a permanent exhibit, "Cotton Fields to Skyscrapers," among other exhibitions. He is the author of *Sorting Out the New South City: Race, Class and Urban Development in Charlotte, 1875–1975* (University of North Carolina Press, 1998) and is working on a history of affordable housing in Charlotte. He is also a fiddle player who knew Jim from the numerous smaller ("obscure") fiddle festivals that were popular in North Carolina in the early 1970s and was closely familiar with Jim's archival work with WBTV promotional photograph files.

Robert C. Harvey is a cartoonist and comics chronicler who has cartooned in all the medium's forms—comic strips, gag cartoons, and comic books as well as editorial cartoons. After graduating from the University of Colorado in 1959, Harvey served in the U.S. Navy. He taught English in Wyandotte High School in Kansas City, Kansas, in the late 1960s. For over 25 years he was the convention manager of the National Council of Teachers of English. He is the author of *The Art of the Funnies* (1994), an aesthetic history of newspaper comic strips, and its sequel, *The Art of the Comic Book* (1996), in addition to *Accidental Ambassador Gordo: The Comic Strip Art of Gus Arriola* (2000), and *Milton Caniff Conversations* (2002), a collection of two dozen interviews conducted with Caniff over the years of his career, starting in 1937 and ending in the 1980s. Harvey's book, *Meanwhile…. A Biography of Milton Caniff, Creator of Terry and the Pirates and Steve Canyon*, was published by Fantagraphics in June 2007. In 2014 he published *Insider Histories of Cartooning: Rediscovering Forgotten Famous Comics and their Creators*. Harvey is a member of the National Cartoonists Society and the Association of American Editorial Cartoonists.

Tom Isenhour from Salisbury, North Carolina, played mandolin with the Garland Shuping Band, the original High Country Boys, and Wild Country. Isenhour started playing rhythm guitar to back his brother Bob on the banjo in the early 1960s. Tom was drawn to the string band music at the summertime fiddlers' conventions in Virginia and North Carolina. He began attending those in the mid–1960s. Union Grove and Galax were the two big ticket gatherings; Tom also attended the smaller gatherings that kicked off the fiddlers' convention season in March and stretched through to August. Besides being an accomplished band musician with a long track record as a stage performer, Isenhour has a reputation as an inveterate collector of bluegrass memorabilia—records, photographs, posters, the songbooks bands sold at festivals, sheet music, and some notable statuary of Monroe, Flatt and Scruggs, Hawkshaw Hawkins and others. His personal bluegrass museum in his home in Salisbury was featured in the pages of *Bluegrass Unlimited* in October 2016.

Martha Kiker is a stringed instrument player with long connections to the traditional and folk music scene in Charlotte, North Carolina, and a close association with the Charlotte Folklore Society. In the late 1980s and early 1990s, Kiker participated in forming the Annabelles, a band focused on traditional music that consisted of Vera Gamble, Dot Stiles, and Carole Outwater. All the members of the band played autoharp. The Annabelles soon began including mountain dulcimer, clawhammer banjo, guitar and bass in their music. Kiker was involved in working out musical arrangements for the band. She played banjo in a band called Twisted Laurel in the 1990s. Jim joined that band late in its lifespan, in the early 2000s, and played alongside Martha, Ruth Wherry (bass), and Jim Greene (guitar) when the band provided the music for contra dances in Charlotte.

James Stephen Kilby was born into a musical family in North Wilkesboro, North Carolina. His grandfather, Cranor Kilby, was an old-time fiddler and banjoist, and his father, Clifford Kilby, was a guitarist and tenor singer who played with the Carolina Playboys, and with L.W. Lambert and the Carolina Neighbors. Kilby began playing the guitar at age twelve. In the late 1960s, he played guitar with the Green Valley Boys, a group that included guitarist Harvey Baity, banjoist Morris Beshears, and bass fiddler James Kerley. A later incarnation of that band called Bluegrass Times featured Kilby and Baity on guitars, Eric Ellis on banjo, Don Phillips on fiddle and James Kerley on bass. In 1975 Kilby joined Hoyt Herbert and the Strings of Five. That bluegrass band recorded the album "Just Pickin'" in 1978. In the early 1980s, Kilby played with

Blue Ridge Grass, the Sullivan Brothers and the Clarence Greene–John Hartley Band. From November 1985 to late 1991 he picked the guitar in Garland Shuping's band, Wild Country. Kilby won the North Carolina state championship at Cool Springs School and first place at the 1970 and 1980 Galax Old Fiddlers' Conventions. He was also the "best all-around performer" at Galax in 1980. In the late 1990s Steve played in the Wilkes County–based bluegrass band Kingsberry Run, with mandolin player John Akin, banjoist Ramona Taylor, fiddler Nathan Leath and bassist Bill Williams. Kilby also worked as a weekend recording engineer with Heritage Records in Galax, Virginia. Jim Scancarelli played fiddle on an album that Kilby recorded for Heritage Records in 1988 (Heritage HRC-074).

Bob Liljestrand is the owner of Bob's Photo in Wallingford, Kentucky. He has written several books about historic railway systems that feature his photographs of rolling stock fleets, freight equipment, and other aspects of regional short lines. He produced ALCO Reference Number 1 (The Railroad Press, 1998) featuring photographs of brand-new locomotives as they emerged from the American Locomotive company's shops in Schenectady, New York, including early steam engines and diesels produced in the last days of that company. In *New England's 1930's Steam Action: Worchester* (The Railroad Press, 2000), he wrote about and compiled his photographs of the Boston and Albany mainline. He co-authored *Freight Equipment of the New York Central and Railway Milk Cars* with Dave Sweetland (The Railroad Press, 2001). Two volumes, *The New Haven Railroad's Boston Division* (2001), and *The New Haven Railroad's Electrified Zone* (2001)—co-authored with Robert Abramson—document that railway system. In 2002, he teamed with David Sweetland on four books: *Passenger Cars of the New Haven Railroad*; *Equipment of the Delaware and Hudson Railroad: Passenger Cars*; *NYC Electric Locomotives and MU Cars*; and *Boston, Revere Beech and Lynn Railroad*. He has published over 50 books of photographs and history on railway systems, and maintains a business, Bob's Photos, specializing in photographs of steam and diesel engines and other artifacts of U.S. railways based on over 1,000 albums of photographs. Jim Scancarelli has long been an avid customer of Bob's Photos, and a friend for decades sharing a continuing interest in the history of locomotives.

Rick Norwood manages and edits *Comics Review* (*www.comicsrevue.com*), bi-monthly small press comic book that reprints classic comic strips, including Milton Caniff (*Steve Canyon*), Dick Moores (*Gasoline Alley*), Burne Hogarth (Drago), and many others. His publishing company, Manuscript Press, has also published books by Hal Foster (*Prince Valiant*), John Blaine (*Rick Brant*), and science fiction by R.A. Lafferty and Hal Clement. Norwood attended the Massachusetts Institute of Technology, where he was one of four writer-editors of the early underground comic *God Comics*. In 1979, Norwood received a Ph.D. in mathematics from the University of Southwestern Louisiana. He was a member of the Institute for Advanced Study in Princeton, New Jersey, in 1980–81 and is currently a professor of mathematics at East Tennessee State University in Johnson City, Tennessee. Norwood has contributed to publications in algebraic topology. He has written a book on logical thinking titled *How to Think*. He was the film/TV reviewer for *SF Site*, a webzine, and he provided commentary for Filmation Associates' DVDs—*Flash Gordon, Prince Valiant* and *Defenders of the Earth*. His science fiction stories have appeared in *Twilight Zone Magazine, Black Gate, Analog Science Fiction* and *The Magazine of Fantasy & Science Fiction*.

John Rose, an American newspaper comics artist and editorial cartoonist, graduated from James Madison University in 1986 with a Bachelor of Fine Arts degree in Art and Art History. He has worked on the comic strip *Barney Google and Snuffy Smith* since 1998, first as an inking assistant to Fred Lasswell and then as the strip's cartoonist beginning in 2001. He is the third artist to have officially drawn the series for King Features Syndicate since its creation. Rose began as an editorial cartoonist for the Byrd Newspapers of Virginia in 1988. In 1991 he created the weekly activity page—"Kids' Home Newspaper"—for Creators Syndicate. Rose worked for the Byrd weekly *The Warren Sentinel* until 1993 when he was hired as an art director and cartoonist for the Byrd daily, *The Daily News-Record* in Harrisonburg, Virginia. Three book collections of Rose's work on *Barney Google and Snuffy Smith* have been published: *The Bodacious Best of Snuffy Smith* (2013), *Balls of Fire! More Snuffy Smith Comics* (2016) and *Snuffy Smith in His Sunday Best* (2018). In 2015 Rose won the Lum and Abner Memorial Award by the National Lum and Abner Society, for his contributions to rural comedy. He won the "Best in Show—Art" award for daily newspapers at the Virginia Press Association Awards Banquet in 2018. He was recognized with a First Place award from the Tennessee Press Association in 2018 for "Best Use of Humor in an Ad" for a series of public service ads about wildfire prevention he created for the *Knoxville News Sentinel* featuring Snuffy Smith. *Barney Google and Snuffy Smith* celebrated its 100th anniversary in June 2019. Since the early 2000s, Rose has had key characters from *Gasoline Alley* appear in walk-on roles in his strip, and Barney Google and Snuffy Smith have appeared in *Gasoline Alley* stories from time to time, especially in sequences revolving around activities at the Old Comics Retirement Home.

Mark V. Sanderford earned a Bachelor of Arts degree in music composition from the University of Illinois. He moved to Galax, Virginia, and taught elementary school, and later attended Appalachian State University where he earned a master's degree in biology. He completed a Ph.D. in biology at Wake Forest University in Winston-Salem, North Carolina. In the late 1990s, Sanderford worked in the Division of Arts and Sciences, Danville Community College, Danville, Virginia. He was involved in research projects on the mechanical and acoustic signals emitted by moths that showed temporal patterns, information that led to studies of the hypothesis that such stimulus repetition might convey data about animal behavior. He co-authored a study of courtship sounds of the polka-dot wasp moth and was part of a team that studied and reported on mating acoustic signals and tympanic organ response in certain types of moths. The work he did with various colleagues over these years was intended to shed light on behavior, ecology and evolution. In the late 1960s, he began taking photographs of old-time and bluegrass musicians at the old-time music festival at Mooresville, North Carolina. He took most of his many photos at the Old Fiddlers' Convention in Galax, Virginia. Sanderford learned the basics of fiddling from Mark Wingate, a member of the Mole Hill Highlanders. A left-handed fiddler himself, Sanderford went on to play fiddle with Enoch

Rutherford's Gold Hill Band, the Virginia-Carolina Buddies, and Dave Sturgill's Band.

Walt Saunders played guitar, and occasionally bass fiddle, for a variety of local Virginia bands "that nobody has ever heard of," some of which never really had a proper band name. In the 1960s, he played in the bluegrass band called the Bailey Brothers, working with Charlie Bailey whose musical life began in the mid–1930s in Tennessee. Saunders drove the bus and undertook other support roles—"roadie" work—for the Johnson Mountain Boys in the 1980s and the early 1990s. He joined the staff of *Bluegrass Unlimited* in July 1967. In 1969 Marion Kuykendall began writing the "Notes & Queries" column for the magazine. Her last column appeared in December 1974. As the readership grew, unanswered questions began to pile up. In late 1984 Saunders was approached about taking over the column. His first column appeared in the February 1985 issue and continues today. According to the managing editor of *Bluegrass Unlimited*, Ms. Linda Shaw, in July 2016 Saunders calculated that he had had answered over 3,000 queries. Saunders worked closely with people like Dick Freeland of Rebel Records. He recalled the days when Ray Davis worked on station WBMD in Baltimore, Maryland, in the early 1960s, broadcasting from Johnny's Used Cars. He recalled when Davis' Wango Records label recorded the Stanley Brothers under the name "John's Gospel Quartet" and "John's Country Quartet." His memory reached back even further to the days when Davis was on XERF, Del Rio, Texas, one of the Mexican border stations, and to Red Shipley's 40 year run as a DJ and MC in and around northern Virginia and Washington, D.C. Saunders has an encyclopedic mind for information on song provenance, song writers, and musicians dating back to the pre-history of bluegrass—a mind he deployed in the interest of bluegrass history as a *Bluegrass Unlimited* writer.

Wayne Seymour first met Jim Scancarelli sometime in the early 1960s. Seymour, a multi-instrumentalist whose interest in traditional music dated back to his days in high school in the 1960s, teamed up with Reynolds in the early 1980s. They recorded two Christmas cassettes with Doug Rorrer on his Flyin' Cloud label. Jim played fiddle on "Frosty the Snowman" on the second cassette, "Christmas Presence."

Bob Smakula, a West Virginia fiddler and banjo player who has played old-time music since the 1970s, is the owner of Smakula Instruments in Elkins, West Virginia, and has been making and repairing old-time instruments for more than 47 years. Smakula Fretted Instruments near Elkins in Randolph County, West Virginia, has been a going concern since 1989. His small independent business specializes in the restoration and sales of fine musical instruments including banjos, guitars, mandolins, and members of the violin family. He has counted among his clients Bill Kirchen, Ry Cooder, Noam Pikilney, Tracy Schwarz, and the late Mike Seeger. Before that, he worked with his father at Goose Acres, in Cleveland, Ohio, beginning in the mid–1970s. His interests in old-time banjo and fiddle music were kindled when his family traveled to the West Virginia State Folk Festival in Glenville, West Virginia, where he got to hear the music of Melvin Wine, Ira Mullins, Glen Smith, Peter Hoover, Dave Milesky, and the Red Clay Ramblers. Since 1999, he has consistently placed in the top five in the Appalachian String Band Festival banjo contests. He has written about stringed instrument repair and restoration for *Old Time Herald*.

Jody Stecher is an American singer and musician who plays bluegrass and old-time music on banjo, mandolin, fiddle and guitar. He was born in Brooklyn, New York, in 1946. He got his first banjo at the age of 12 and immersed himself in music in the days when there was nothing in the way of a clear line separating old-time music and bluegrass. In the 1960s, he played as a member of the New York Ramblers with Winnie Winston and David Grisman. Stecher has recorded and performed music for sixty years with bands including Perfect Strangers, The Peter Rowan Bluegrass Band, and has performed and recorded solo and with his wife Kate Brislin.

Ned Stern went to Wakefield High School in Arlington, Virginia, where he and Jim Scancarelli worked on the school newspaper staff in the mid-fifties. After he completed a degree in Fine Arts from the American University in Washington, D.C., Ned joined the U.S. Navy and served first on a destroyer, with the rank of Sonarman Third Class, and then in the Public Information Office at Naval Station Newport (NAVSTA Newport), a base located in the city of Newport, Rhode Island, where he and Jim deployed their artistic talents on behalf of the U.S. Navy. After his time in uniform, Ned taught drawing at the University of Michigan and the University of Cincinnati. He has worked in his field for the Smithsonian Institution, the U.S. Navy, and International Telephone and Telegraph (ITT) among other institutions and corporations. He maintains a studio at the Pendleton Art Center in Cincinnati, Ohio. His work has been shown in numerous local galleries and private museums and corporate collections.

Tom Walsh met Jim Scancarelli in 1969 at a fiddlers' convention in Elkin, North Carolina. The two of them had just started out on the fiddle and managed to earn what Walsh described as "encouragement" medals in the contests around the area. Walsh formed the Mallard Creek String Band in the early 1970s, possibly on the basis of relationships formed at the fiddlers' conventions. In 1974, the band's cut of "Whiskey Before Breakfast" was captured on an album, "Fiddler's Grove Old Time Fiddler's and Bluegrass Festival" (Volume 5, released under the label Galaxie III Studios). The Mallard Creek String Band was the first band in which Joe Cline and Jim Scancarelli played together.

Ruth Kee Wherry played bass, guitar and sang in her father's family band in the forties and fifties. Her father, John D. Kee, played fiddle with J.E. Mainer and His Rambling Mountaineers, and with The Tar Heel Cornshuckers. In 2001 the Kee Family and Ruth Kee Wherry received the Charlotte Folk Society Heritage Award for their role in Charlotte's live country music radio during those decades. Ruth played bass for the Flat Possum Hoppers that played around Charlotte, North Carolina, in the first decade of the 2000s. She was joined by Mark Helms (mandolin), John Cone (guitar), Tom Estes (banjo), and Tom Hanchett (fiddle). Ruth and Martha Kiker, a clawhammer player, were in a band called Twisted Laurel in the early 2000s; Jim Scancarelli joined them on the fiddle. The band played for local contradances. In the first months of 2016, Ruth told Wayne Erbsen that she was still trying to learn to play the fiddle that she inherited from her father.

Bob "Quail" White met Jim Scancarelli at a fiddlers' convention in Elkin, North Carolina, in the mid–1960s. White was immersed in the Chapel Hill old-time and bluegrass music scene dating to the days of the "Big White House" on Ashe Avenue in the mid–1960s where all the bluegrass musicians lived and picked over in Raleigh, North Carolina. White became the bass player in the New Deal String Band. Al McCanless was the fiddler and one of the founding members of that band along with Buck Peacock, Leroy Savage, Gene Knight and Frank Greathouse. Bob White, called Quail by close friends and almost everyone else, was an Appalachian State University professor who studied and taught in China during the 1980s and 1990s. In the early 1980s, he traveled to China as part of the Appalachian State University–*Dong Bei Gong Xue Yuan* academic exchange program. That program was among the first US–China university exchanges established in 1980. White and his wife lived, taught, and conducted research in Shenyang in 1983 and 1984 in a year-long faculty exchange. He focused his research interests on the symbolism of the Chinese revolution. In 1985, he completed an undergraduate degree in international studies and in 1987 he entered the Duke University graduate program in the Department of History where he focused on Chinese history. He studied propaganda output of the Chinese Communists from the 1920s to the beginning of World War II and the period of the Chinese civil war, and through the first decades following the establishment of the People's Republic of China. He was particularly interested in the Third Revolutionary Civil War period in the Northeast in the years between 1945 and 1949. He received a Jacob Javits Fellowship, completed course work and language exams in 1989 and completed an M.A. thesis on the symbolic import of the philatelic output of the Liberated Areas during the Chinese Revolution. White returned to China in 1990 to do research work. He began teaching Chinese and Asian History part-time at Appalachian State in 1992, and in 1995 assumed a position as Executive Director of ASU's International Education Office. He worked in that office, and led student trips to China, until he retired in 2011. Quail still plays some music in old-time and bluegrass circles in his part of North Carolina.

Jeanette Williams was born in North Carolina and raised in Virginia in a family of eight children where musical interests ranged from rock to gospel, Broadway musical tunes, and classic country music. In her twenties she sang country music, and in 1989 she joined a band called Clearwater and began singing bluegrass. She married Clearwater band member Johnny Williams in 1991. In 1994, she released her debut solo album, "Dreams Do Come True," under the Flyin' Cloud Records label. In the mid–1990s, the Clearwater band was renamed Jeanette Williams and Clearwater. She recorded a second album with her husband Johnny in 1996, called simply "Johnny and Jeanette Williams." A string of recordings and a host of awards marked her musical career in the 1990s and early 2000s. In 2014, her first single was released. In 2019, Midwest Records released "Johnny and Jeanette Williams—Thirty Years Later." She met Jim Scancarelli in 1990, when he joined Clearwater on stage as fiddler. He played with Clearwater at a succession of local fiddlers' conventions in the early 1990s.

Mark Wingate learned to play banjo and fiddle in Charlotte, North Carolina, with neighborhood friends Jim Whitley and Darrell Gray. Wingate joined with Clyde Williams, Jim Scancarelli, and Chuck Dunlop to form the Mole Hill Highlanders—Scancarelli invented the name. Williams, then in his late forties, was the band leader, the "elder fiddler." In 1971, shortly after the Mole Hill Highlanders came to the end of their run, Mark Wingate, Jim Whitley, Darrell Gray, and Thom Case formed a band called Chicken Hot Rod in Winston-Salem. That band played colleges all over the eastern states in 1971 and 1972. In 1972, Sally Davis, Erica Hunter, and Louisa Branscomb formed Bluegrass Liberation. Lynn Gray joined them later. Wingate married Sally Davis in 1973. Their daughter Sarah Siskind's songwriting prompted them to move to Nashville in 1996, where they played for dances, participated in the local bluegrass and acoustic music scene, and organized instrument demonstrations at the Country Music Hall of Fame. Sally joined with four other women to form the bluegrass group Tennessee Heartstrings. Wingate played in the acoustic trio Kindling Stone, mixing original music with songs from the shape note and Shaker traditions. The couple relocated to Brevard, North Carolina, in 2015, where they participated in the local old-time jams and played for the occasional square dance; and Wingate played with the Blue Ridge Bakery Boys. Wingate has a long and continuing interest in early fiddling, including some tunes from James Buckley's 1855 fiddle book.

Chapter Notes

Acknowledgments

1. Sometime in August 2020, Frank Kalian told Jim that the book about him needed to have some sex in it. I promised Jim I would include Frank's advice in the "Acknowledgments," and Jim would then be able to refer to this footnote as the book's "sex content."

Introduction

1. Author's notes, interview with Jim Scancarelli (telephone), 21 August 2020, 5:19 p.m.–6:29 p.m.

2. Scancarelli, "The Old Cross Roads," *Bluegrass Unlimited*, January 2000, p. 5.

3. Scancarelli, "The Head of the Class," *Bluegrass Unlimited*, April 2011, pp. 40–42.

4. Jim Scancarelli, "The Mole Hill Highlanders," *Bluegrass Unlimited*, October 2004, pp. 34–37.

5. https://newspapercomicstripsblog.wordpress.com/2016/04/02/red-ryder/.

6. https://www.gocomics.com/gasolinealley/2006/04/30; https://www.gocomics.com/gasolinealley/2015/07/19; and https://www.gocomics.com/gasolinealley/2017/09/26.

7. In an odd codicil to this story, sometime in early January 2021, Verizon appears to have reversed its decision, and resumed support for the flip-phone model that had served Jim's purposes for such a long time. By that time, Jim had immersed himself in magic ways of the iPhone and he elected to stick with the best that the 21st century had to offer.

Chapter One

1. Author's notes, interview with Jim Scancarelli (telephone), 7 August 2020, 3:00 p.m.–4:55 p.m.

2. Frances' father was Otto Hugh Parati (1883–1956) and her mother was Josephine Latta Parati (1883–1973). She had two sisters, Helen Cobb Parati, who died in infancy, and Mary Elizabeth Parati (1915–2007), who married Julian Lee Deal, a descendent of Robert E. Lee. They had two children, Linda Hartwell (born 1942) and Douglas Lofton Deal (1951–2018). Frances had a brother, Robert, who was Jim's mentor in art, music, collecting and, as Jim recalled, "a role model for being a

good person." 9 November 2020 (4:59 p.m.) Text Message from Jim Scancarelli to Lew Stern; Author's notes, interview with Jim Scancarelli (telephone), 9 November 2020, 11:00 a.m.–11:30 a.m.

3. Jim pointed out that he was born in Gotham Hospital in the Bronx, a facility that no longer exists, but his brief stay there meant that Jim and Batman shared a home, perhaps another portentous indication of his future in the cartooning industry. Wartime postal correspondence between America and Italy was subjected to censorship. The telegram sent by Jim's parents announcing Jim's birth to his father's family in Sicily was altered by censors, and in Palermo the Scancarelli family believed that Peter and his wife had given birth to a baby girl. Author's notes, interview with Jim Scancarelli (telephone), 7 August 2020, 3:00 p.m.–4:55 p.m.

4. Author's notes, interview with Jim Scancarelli (telephone), 18 August 2020, 4:00 p.m.–6:02 p.m.

5. "Granddaddy was from Rome, and the Romans did not think much of the Sicilians. He always thought the Sicilians crawled out from under a rock." Author's notes, interview with Jim Scancarelli (telephone), 21 May 2020, 3:10 p.m.–5:53 p.m. Jim visited Italy in 1968. His father's brother Guido was intent on taking Jim around to see important landmarks and significant historical sites. Guido balked at taking Jim to see where his father was born and other places near the little village Castelbuono. Years later, in Jim's adulthood, he met a man while walking around the track at a local YMCA in Charlotte, North Carolina. That gentleman was on his way to Italy, and Jim talked about his family home in Sicily. When the friend returned from his trip, he contacted Jim to share photos he had taken when he went in search of the Scancarelli natal village, and while the friend never found the house in which Peter Scancarelli lived as a young man, he did take photos in the vicinity, and managed to capture Jim's Aunt Lucia's house on film. He also took a photo of a well to which Jim's father and his brother Guido walked when they were kids charged with the chore of filling up jugs of water for the household. Author's notes, interview with Jim Scancarelli (telephone), 7 August 2020, 3:00 p.m.–4:55 p.m.

6. Jim noted that later in her life, Mary Josephine changed her last name, Latta, to Dean; she just did not like her name, Jim recalled, and preferred

the name Dean. Author's notes, interview with Jim Scancarelli (telephone), 7 August 2020, 3:00 p.m.–4:55 p.m.

7. Benjamin Franklin Cobb was born in January 1826 in Wayne County, North Carolina to Enoch Cobb and Mary Sasser. Cobb attended Jefferson Medical College in Philadelphia, Pennsylvania, from 1846 to 1847, wrote a thesis on the subject of placenta praevia, and achieved a medical degree in 1847. In 1850, he married Winnifred Catherine Loftin (1834–1906) and set up a medical practice in Duplin County, North Carolina. In March 1862, he was certified as having successfully passed the Confederate Army Board of Medical Examination. One month later Cobb was ordered to report to Goldsboro, North Carolina, where he was assigned as a medical officer under Major General T.H. Holmes, who commanded the Department of North Carolina. Cobb worked alongside seven surgeons and four assistant surgeons who established a hospital (S.O. 80/5, Department of North Carolina). At the end of April 1862, Cobb was appointed as a surgeon in the Provisional Army of the Confederate States; his commission was back dated to March 1862. From May to July 1862, he held that position until ordered to relieve the surgeon who headed S.O. 266 in the district of Cape Fear. In September of that year, his commission and rank as surgeon was confirmed by the Senate of the Confederacy, and one month later Cobb was sent to Fort St. Philip. He served with the 40th North Carolina Heavy Artillery until November 1862 when he tendered his resignation, a formal request he withdrew in December 1862. He served in that capacity until July 1863 when he was appointed surgeon at Fort St. Philip which, in July 1863, was renamed Fort Anderson. Cobb held a succession of assignments in garrisons in Smithville, Brunswick County, and Magnolia, North Carolina, between December 1864 and February 1865 when he was relieved from duty and ordered to report to the 3rd Military District command. He was paroled by the Provost Marshal of the U.S. Army in Goldsboro, North Carolina, and returned to Duplin County, where he practiced medicine through 1874, when he was named Vice President of the Medical Society in Wilmington, North Carolina. He opened a practice in Catawba County, North Carolina, in June 1880, moved to Richmond, Virginia, in 1887, and was licensed to practice medicine in Virginia in that year. He died in his home in Richmond, Virginia, in August 1888. His widow, Winnifred, continued to live in Richmond through at least 1891. She passed away in 1906. The couple had a total of nine children. https://www.findagrave.com/memorial/146652585/benjamin-franklin-cobb and https://www.findagrave.com/memorial/146654459/winifred-catherine-cobb. Based on F.T. Hambrecht and J.L. Koste, *Biographical Register of Physicians Who Served the Confederacy in a Medical Capacity*, May 2015, unpublished database.

8. Author's notes, interview with Jim Scancarelli (telephone), 20 May 2020, 4:13 p.m.–6:38 p.m.

9. Sometime in the 1970s, Jim and his friend Jim Culp planned a trip to Europe, so Jim hired his cousin to help with housework while Jim was traveling. While Jim was gone, his cousin Chris set about tidying up. When Jim returned, he spotted a stick protruding from a trash bin and, curious, he grabbed ahold of it, and retrieved what turned out to be an old fiddle bow. The frog was missing, and it was not in terribly good shape, but it was noticeably old, so Jim did a little poking around and learned that his grandmother had saved Benjamin Cobb's fiddle bow, and it ended up being tucked away in a corner of the house that Jim's cousin sought to clean up while Jim was in Europe. Jim rescued it from the trash bin, and had it repaired, but it was too light in weight and consequently it chattered across his strings when he tried to use it, but it still struck him as a worthwhile keepsake, and he retained it. Author's notes, interview with Jim Scancarelli (telephone), 8 January 2021, 3:00 p.m.–3:55 p.m.

10. Jim used his mother's attempt to chart out the family's history, and the basic genealogical information his mother had captured, to develop a basic sense of the family's background: "My grandmother's husband Otto Parati. Otto is a Germanic name, not a real Italian name! But his mother was from Germany. How about that! We found that out later. Parati in Italian means a wall covering, wallpaper or paint: *Carta da parati*." Author's notes, interview with Jim Scancarelli (telephone), 7 August 2020, 3:00 p.m.–4:55 p.m.

11. Otto Hugh Parati was born in Italy on 2 July 1883 to Arthur and Helen Parati. He came to the U.S. as an immigrant in 1901. He was a Civil Engineer with the Southern Railway in Greensboro, North Carolina in 1910, and by 1918 was working for that company in Charlotte. He was married to Josephine Latta. He had three children: Frances J., Mary Elizabeth, and Robert Parati; one child died very young. Otto Parati died at the age of 72 in February 1956 in Charlotte, North Carolina. https://www.findagrave.com/memorial/100306322/otto-hugh-parati.

12. Jim said: "Granddaddy had a set of special drafting French curves used to plan the placement of curvature on railroad tracks. I have that set and every now and then, I'll pull one of the curves out and rule something in on the comic strip in Granddaddy's memory." Author's notes, interview with Jim Scancarelli (telephone), 20 May 2020, 4:13 p.m.–6:38 p.m.

13. In 1916, Edmund L. Goodman opened a haberdashery at 5 West 46th Street in Manhattan. The store, which quickly became known as an "English-styled clothier," earned a reputation as an exclusive men's store. That year, Goodman purchased the Euclid Building and commissioned the architect Beverly King to create an "English atmosphere for his tweeds and ties." The store opened at the 568 Fifth Avenue address at the end of 1924. Goodman passed away in 1952. Finchley's continued to do business until the 1970s. By 1978, Finchley had joined with Weber & Heilbroner, a lower Manhattan men's clothing company that began doing business in 1909. The firm was known as

Weber & Heilbroner and Finchley. The Finchley building was marked for demolition in April 2017. http://daytoninmanhattan.blogspot.com/2012/11/finchleys-castle-nos-564–568–5th-avenue.html and "For a Haberdasher's Castle in Midtown, a Final Tip of the Hat," *New York Times*, 20 April 2017, https://www.nytimes.com/2017/04/20/nyregion/finchleys-castle-fifth-avenue-manhattan.html.

14. Author's notes, interview with Jim Scancarelli (telephone), 3 May 2017, 1:00–2:00 p.m.

15. "He was very proud and happy! You should have seen him when he went to vote for the first time!" 9 November 2020 (4:59 p.m.) Text Message from Jim Scancarelli to Lew Stern; Author's notes, interview with Jim Scancarelli (telephone), 9 November 2020, 11:00 a.m.–11:30 a.m.

16. For example, Jim had the character Uncle Walt reminisce in a Sunday panel in the mid–1980s about the wartime blackouts, the civil defense wardens who sought out homes that failed to turn the lights off and use blackout curtains. Author's notes, interview with Jim Scancarelli (telephone), 7 August 2020, 3:00 p.m.–4:55 p.m.

17. Author's notes, interview with Jim Scancarelli (telephone), 8 August 2020, 4:55 p.m.–5:53 p.m.

18. Author's notes, interview with Jim Scancarelli (telephone), 8 August 2020, 4:55 p.m.–5:53 p.m.

19. Author's notes, interview with Jim Scancarelli (telephone), 7 August 2020, 3:00 p.m.–4:55 p.m.

20. Author's notes, interview with Jim Scancarelli (telephone), 20 May 2020, 4:13 p.m.–6:38 p.m.

21. He remembered tears welling up in his eyes, "just like Granddaddy." Author's notes, interview with Jim Scancarelli (telephone), 20 May 2020, 4:13 p.m.–6:38 p.m.

22. For a history of the Sisters of the Holy Cross in Washington, D.C., see https://www.academyoftheholycross.org/about-us/mission-heritage-beliefs/history.

23. The Cathedral of St. Matthew the Apostle is located between St. Matthew's Court, NW, and Rhode Island Avenue, in Washington, D.C. Jim's family's apartment was located just east of the cathedral, or not far from the corner of 14th Street and N Street.

24. Author's notes, interview with Jim Scancarelli (telephone), 20 May 2020, 4:13 p.m.–6:38 p.m.

25. Author's notes, interview with Jim Scancarelli (telephone), 20 May 2020, 4:13 p.m.–6:38 p.m.

26. Author's notes, interview with Jim Scancarelli (telephone), 20 May 2020, 4:13 p.m.–6:38 p.m.

27. Author's notes, interview with Jim Scancarelli (telephone), 7 August 2020, 3:00 p.m.–4:55 p.m.

28. https://www.oldmodelkits.com/.

29. Author's notes, interview with Jim Scancarelli (telephone), 7 August 2020, 3:00 p.m.–4:55 p.m.

30. 9 November 2020 (4:59 p.m.) Text Message from Jim Scancarelli to Lew Stern; Author's notes, interview with Jim Scancarelli (telephone), 9 November 2020, 11:00 a.m.–11:30 a.m.

31. Five and a half decades later, Jim lamented: "But now all of that knowledge is irrelevant because of new technologies and techniques. Typing is different, photography is different, everything is now digital, but the basics are there, it's just a different idiom. Another era came in and wiped things out." Author's notes, interview with Jim Scancarelli (telephone), 20 May 2020, 4:13 p.m.–6:38 p.m.

32. Author's notes, interview with Jim Scancarelli (telephone), 23 June 2020, 3:16 p.m.–5:48 p.m.

33. Jim clearly meant to reference Humphrey Bogart in the role of Captain Queeg in "Caine Mutiny," rolling and clicking a pair of steel ball bearings in his hand and fumbling them at moments of stress. Author's notes, interview with Jim Scancarelli (telephone), 20 May 2020, 4:13 p.m.–6:38 p.m.

34. The U.S. Army Air Corps was the aerial warfare service of the U.S. Army between 1926 and 1941.

35. One year, in a Wakefield High School variety show staged by students, Mr. Gibson took the role of a stagehand. Unshaven, wearing jeans, carrying a lunch pail, he sat on a corner of the stage and ate his lunch when the show began. As the play progressed, the spotlight would catch him, still eating. He never uttered any lines. He just sat and ate, and was periodically captured in the spotlight, until the end of the play when he wordlessly packed up his lunch pail, and—as a good stagehand—began breaking down the scenery, taking part of the set away with him as the play ended. Jim thought that was perhaps the highlight of the production, and one of the funniest things he had ever seen. Author's notes, interview with Jim Scancarelli (telephone), 9 August 2020, 3:10 p.m.–5:25 p.m.

36. 9 November 2020 (4:59 p.m.) Text Message from Jim Scancarelli to Lew Stern; Author's notes, interview with Jim Scancarelli (telephone), 9 November 2020, 11:00 a.m.–11:30 a.m.

37. Author's notes, interview with Jim Scancarelli (telephone), 8 August 2020, 4:55 p.m.–5:53 p.m.

38. Author's notes, interview with Jim Scancarelli (telephone), 8 August 2020, 4:55 p.m.–5:53 p.m.; Letter to Jim Scancarelli from Conchita Mitchell, 1966 President, Wakefield Alumni, upon his selection for induction into the Wakefield High School Hall of Fame. 10 April 2017; Jim's letter accepting the honor, June 2017; Wakefield High School Hall of Fame certificate, Inductee Number 55, June 2017.

39. Jeremy Amick, "'Kiddie Cruise'—Local Veteran Shares Story of Service in U.S. Navy During the Late 1950s," *War History Online*, 28 February 2018, https://www.warhistoryonline.com/guest-bloggers/kiddie-cruise-local-veteran-shares-story-service-u-s-navy-late-1950s.html; Lon Dawson., *Cradle Cruise: A Navy Bluejacket Remembers Life Aboard the USS Trever During World War II* (Chicago: Wind Rose Books, 2009).

40. Author's notes, interview with Jim Scancarelli (telephone), 9 August 2020, 3:10 p.m.–5:25 p.m. Jim's high school friend Ned Stern was assigned to Naval Station Newport (NAVSTA Newport) at the same time Jim was. Ned told me: "As with Jim, I also remember the Chief Petty Officer who recruited me was so nice; well until the swearing in when he said loudly "stand up straight sailor, you're in the Navy

now." Things went downhill from there. At the time, there were no Hollywood movies depicting basic training, so no one knew what to expect at boot camp. 23 August 2020 (12:03 p.m.) email from Ned Stern to Lew Stern; 22 August 2020, interview with Ned Stern (telephone), 10:00 a.m.–10:57 a.m.

41. Author's notes, interview with Jim Scancarelli (telephone), 9 August 2020, 3:10 p.m.–5:25 p.m.

42. "While I was awaiting assignment to a destroyer it was not a desk job that awaited me but a deck force job. After being assigned to the *Arcadia* print shop and then to the photo lab, I made 3rd class photographers mate and was transferred to the admiral's staff in the PIO office as artist and photographer." 18 January 2020 (10:22 a.m.) Text Message from Jim Scancarelli to Lew Stern.

43. COMCRUDESLANT was headquartered at Naval Station Newport, Rhode Island, until the early 1970s, when it was transferred to Norfolk. By that time, Jim's enlistment had come to an end and he was a civilian again. https://en.wikipedia.org/wiki/Commander,_Naval_Surface_Forces_Atlantic and https://www.cnic.navy.mil/regions/cnrma/installations/ns_newport.html.

44. "USS *Arcadia* was one of four Klondike-class destroyer tenders built at the tail end of World War II for the United States Navy, and the third U.S. Naval vessel to bear that name. Destroyer tenders were typically named after U.S. National Parks." https://en.wikipedia.org/wiki/USS_Arcadia_(AD-23).

45. Author's notes, interview with Jim Scancarelli (telephone), 20 May 2020, 4:13 p.m.–6:38 p.m.

46. Author's notes, interview with Jim Scancarelli (telephone), 9 August 2020, 3:10 p.m.–5:25 p.m. Jim remembered doing cruises aboard the Arcadia to Puerto Rico, Florida, and Brooklyn, New York. He also remembered serving as the editor of the ship's newspaper while on board the *Arcadia*. He wrote "snappy articles" about shipboard life and drew cartoons for that publication. He recalled enlisting several of his more creative shipmates to be his "investigative reporters." Jim said: "It was amazing what dirt they would dig up," though the newspaper's staff exercised extreme care regarding the stories they published, especially if officers were involved. 29 November 2020 (10:36 p.m.) Text Message from Jim Scancarelli to Lew Stern. One of Jim's many stories worth re-telling: "While aboard the *Arcadia* we docked in Florida just in time for baseball spring training. Our captain arranged a game between the Pittsburgh Pirates and our motley crew. I shot photos of the mass slaughter for the ship's newspaper but the Pirates graciously gave us a run or two. Don Osborne was the Pirates coach and I shot a great portrait of him that should have graced a Topps Gum Card collection." 29 November 2020 (10:20 a.m.) Text Message from Jim Scancarelli to Lew Stern.

47. Author's notes, interview with Jim Scancarelli (telephone), 20 May 2020, 4:13 p.m.–6:38 p.m.

48. Ned Stern completed a degree in Fine Art from the American University in Washington, D.C. He taught drawing at the University of Michigan and the University of Cincinnati and has worked in his field for the Smithsonian Institution, the U.S. Navy, and International Telephone and Telegraph (ITT) among other institutions and corporations. He maintains a studio at the Pendleton Art Center in Cincinnati, Ohio, and his work has been shown in numerous local galleries and private museums and corporate collections. http://www.nedstern.com/index.html.

49. Jim used the term "cumshaw" to refer to this aspect of Navy life. The term was used in his day to speak to a circumstance in which sailors obtained something outside of official channels or without payment, usually by trading or bartering. In the 21st century, younger sailors may use the term "drug deal" instead of cumshaw. See Orveline Valle, "19 Terms Every US Navy Sailor Will Understand," *Business Insider*, 5 January 2015, https://www.businessinsider.com/19-terms-every-us-navy-sailor-will-understand-2015–1.

50. Jim also managed to stretch USN rules regarding leave and travel to take advantage of various opportunities outside of Rhode Island to ride on or just see static displays of old steam engines, another one of his life-long interests. Author's notes, interview with Jim Scancarelli (telephone), 9 August 2020, 3:10 p.m.–5:25 p.m.

51. Amy Worthington Hauslohner, "Fiddlin' Around with the Funnies," *Bluegrass Unlimited*, August 1989, pp. 42–43; Author's notes, interview with Jim Scancarelli (telephone), 21 May 2020, 3:10 p.m.–5:53 p.m. Jim recalled: "Dick Hogle, one of the Admiral's artists in the Public Information Office, played jazz drums and was frequently hired by various clubs in Newport to back many of the big-name jazz greats who came to town, like Dizzy Gillespie, Thelonious Monk, and hosts of others I never had heard of. Ned Stern and I would attend many of the shows, and though I wasn't into that idiom of music, it was fun. Hogle went on to be an explosive engineer and became a technical director in the motion picture industry. Anytime a building was demolished or bombs went off in a film, they were executed by Dick Hogle!" 9 November 2020 (4:59 p.m.) Text Message from Jim Scancarelli to Lew Stern; Author's notes, interview with Jim Scancarelli (telephone), 9 November 2020, 11:00 a.m.–11:30 a.m.

52. 9 November 2020 (4:59 p.m.) Text Message from Jim Scancarelli to Lew Stern; Author's notes, interview with Jim Scancarelli (telephone), 9 November 2020, 11:00 a.m.–11:30 a.m.

53. Author's notes, interview with Jim Scancarelli (telephone), 20 May 2020, 4:13 p.m.–6:38 p.m.

54. "It gave [me] a good outlook on how this country was formed, and how easily things could go down the tubes." Author's notes, interview with Jim Scancarelli (telephone), 9 August 2020, 3:10 p.m.–5:25 p.m.

Chapter Two

1. 11 August 2020 (11:06) Text Message from Jim Scancarelli to Lew Stern; Author's notes, interview

with Jim Scancarelli (telephone), 11 August 2020, 3:00 p.m.–4:01 p.m. Sometime in late 1963, as Bob Parati's *Yellow Pages* account began to contract in the face of newer, quicker technological ways of generating those small ads, Fred Clark gave Jim his first paying job illustrating a full-page newspaper advertisement for *The Carolina Israelite*, a newspaper published in Charlotte from 1944 to 1968 by Harry Golden. Jim's job was to draw the renowned writer Harry Golden, a Jewish humorist, and the author of a 1961 book about Carl Sandburg, as well as an image of Sandburg, the poet and biographer of Abraham Lincoln. Jim had a vague recollection that the advertisement was for Golden's book on Sandburg. In yet another of those moments of symmetry in Jim's life, in the 1970s Clark gave the opportunity to design a movie poster for a national moving picture distributor to Mitch Kolbe, the son of Lee Kolbe who had worked with Bob Parati in their graphic arts studio. Lee Kolbe had helped Jim learn the ropes in that studio in the early 1950s. Author's notes, interview with Jim Scancarelli (telephone), 8 January 2020, 3:00 p.m.–3:55 p.m.

2. Author's notes, interview with Jim Scancarelli (telephone), 11 August 2020, 3:00 p.m.–4:01 p.m.

3. "Quite a come down from the Yellow Pages checks." 9 November 2020 (4:59 p.m.) Text Message from Jim Scancarelli to Lew Stern.

4. https://en.wikipedia.org/wiki/Jim_Scancarelli.

5. Author's notes, interview with Jim Scancarelli (telephone), 11 August 2020, 3:00 p.m.–4:01 p.m.

6. http://btmemories.com/sounds/programs_of_yesterday.html. Also see Kenneth M. Johnson, *The Johnson Family Singers: We Sang for Our Supper* (Jackson: University Press of Mississippi, 1997)

7. "I missed my four-year pin. They had a miniature old TV camera for a lapel pin. I never did get one." Author's notes, interview with Jim Scancarelli (telephone), 21 May 2020, 3:10 p.m.–5:53 p.m. That seemed to be the avid collector in Jim lamenting a missed chance to put his hands on an artifact of that experience.

8. Jim and his friend Marcus Hamilton worked at WBTV when televisions were switching from black and white to color, and art departments had to be alert to the way color slides for various shows—such as the weather report—would show up on black and white televisions, which were still owned by many Americans. Author's notes, interview with Marcus Hamilton (telephone), 2 September 2020, 10:28 a.m.–11:13 a.m.

9. Author's notes, interview with Jim Scancarelli (telephone), 21 May 2020, 3:10 p.m. 5:53 p.m.; 9 November 2020 (4:59 p.m.) Text Message from Jim Scancarelli to Lew Stern; Author's notes, interview with Jim Scancarelli (telephone), 9 November 2020, 11:00 a.m.–11:30 a.m.

10. Author's notes, interview with Jim Scancarelli (telephone), 21 May 2020, 3:10 p.m.–5:53 p.m.; Amy Worthington Hauslohner, "Jim Scancarelli: Fiddling Around with the Funnies," *Bluegrass Unlimited*, August 1989, p. 43.

11. According to the WBT website, *BT Memories*, in the late 1940s and early 1950s before TV took off like a rocket, WBT broadcast Arthur Smith's "Corner Store," a 15-minute daily transcribed show. In later shows, Tommy Faile and Don Reno joined the group. Jim recovered four complete shows from transcription discs, the first dated 28 September 1948; the remaining three were from 1952. http://btmemories.com/sounds/programs_of_yesterday.html.

12. The fifteen-minute show featured country music with an electric guitar lead by Arthur Smith and his band, The Crackerjacks, and skits and gospel music. https://www.otrcat.com/p/arthur-smiths-corner-store; https://www.oldtimeradiodownloads.com/variety/arthur-smiths-corner-store.

13. Author's notes, interview with Jim Scancarelli (telephone), 21 May 2020, 3:10 p.m.–5:53 p.m.

14. Bob Carlin, *String Bands in the North Carolina Piedmont* (Jefferson, North Carolina: McFarland, 2004), pp. 179–180.

15. In 1971, shortly after the Mole Hill Highlanders came to the end of their run, Mark Wingate, Jim Whitley, Darrell Gray, and Thom Case formed a band called Chicken Hot Rod in Winston-Salem. Joe Cline recalled that Jim Whitley played banjo and sang tenor vocals. Grey, "The Ditch Wizard," played bass and sang baritone and bass vocals. "Lizard" Thom Case, "The Kink of Country Music," played guitar and sang the lead vocals. Mark Wingate played fiddle and sang baritone. Cline wrote that Jim Whitley, Darrell Gray, and Mark Wingate grew up in Charlotte's Thomasboro neighborhood, and had played together in a band called Queen City Ramblers, named after the car company. The Chicken Hot Rod band auditioned in New York at a coffee house in 1971—perhaps the Bottom Line. For several years, they played a circuit of college coffeehouses. Author's notes, interview with Jim Scancarelli (telephone), 21 May 2020, 3:10 p.m.–5:53 p.m. Jim did the artwork for the Chicken Hot Rod band. He remembered that they called Don Reno to ask for permission to use the name, and that Don charged them $25 for that honor. Mark Wingate recalled that the agreed-upon amount was $250. In his words: "We—Chicken Hot Rod—sent half, the remainder to be sent upon receipt of some letter of permission from Reno. Nothing was ever received, we never sent the rest, and we never heard any more from Reno or his people. We actually met him after that, but it was hard to tell if he even remembered the 'deal' at all." 14 December 2020 (6:57 p.m.) email from Mark Wingate to Lew Stern. Also see https://www.facebook.com/KilocycleKowboys/posts/1368272923271967 and Author's notes, interview with Jim Scancarelli (telephone), 21 May 2020, 3:10 p.m.–5:53 p.m. Joe Cline very kindly pointed out the "historic" website that called "The Kilocycle Kowboys: Choice Hillbilly Music" that had somehow burrowed into the internet and was salvaged on web.archive.org. The website was probably last active between 2004 and 2007, but remains accessible at this link: https://web.archive.org/web/20070311154406/http://www.kilocyclekowboys.com/index.htm.

16. Jim said, of Boggan: "He was a wonderful person. Out of all the radio, TV or newspaper, magazine interviews I've done, I would put him at the top. He let you talk. He asked the most intelligent questions. He never interfered when you were talking." Author's notes, interview with Jim Scancarelli (telephone), 10 July 2020, 2:00 p.m.–4:08 p.m.

17. 9 November 2020 (4:59 p.m.) Text Message from Jim Scancarelli to Lew Stern; Author's notes, interview with Jim Scancarelli (telephone), 9 November 2020, 11:00 a.m.–11:30 a.m. That was, unfortunately for Jim, not the first such experience for him in the realm of live broadcasting: "Another time on another radio show at WBT, an all-night country music show that all the truckers loved, the host let me have an hour of program time. I was doing a bluegrass segment. So, he was the MC; it was still his show, and I was the guest playing bluegrass tapes and records, and these truckers started calling in and complaining: 'What is all this? Go back to the regular program.' They didn't care for the bluegrass, and after about the third show I think that was about it. I had to quit." Author's notes, interview with Jim Scancarelli (telephone), 10 July 2020, 2:00 p.m.–4:08 p.m.

18. Author's notes, interview with Jim Scancarelli (telephone), 10 July 2020, 2:00 p.m.–4:08 p.m.

19. The "Back Story" from the Yellowjacket sound vault: "He was mild-mannered Rex Mundane, a brickmaker by day, crime fighter by night. When the State Attorney General flashed the dreaded Yellowjacket signal on the back of the Mundane garage, Rex and his devoted spouse, Shirley, would don their leotards, crank up the Beige Beauty, their '37 Nash (with the luggage carrier on the back), and race out to confront the current peril threatening the denizens of Centerville. Other characters in this real-life drama were Calvin, Rex's semi-bright sidekick, Warden Borden Gordon of State Prison, and the many evildoers without whom there would have been no show: Mr. Demeanor, Lenny Lomax, Dr. Albatross, Mr. Shoehorn, Dr. Intern and the not-so-diminutive Mr. Big." http://btmemories.com/sounds/yellowjacket.html.

20. Author's notes, interview with Jim Scancarelli (telephone), 23 June 2020, 3:16 p.m.–5:48 p.m.

21. "Chickenman" was an American radio series created by Dick Orkin that spoofs comic book heroes, inspired by the mid–1960s *Batman* TV series. The series was created in 1966 on Chicago radio station WCFL and was then syndicated widely. In the series, "Benton Harbor," a shoe salesman at a large downtown Midland City department store, spends his weekends "striking terrific terror into the hearts of criminals everywhere as that fantastic fowl, Chickenman." In reality, he just hangs around the Police Commissioner's office and irritates the Commissioner's secretary, Miss Helfinger. Each episode began with a four-note trumpet sound echoed with Benton Harbor's "Buck-buck-buck-buuuuuck" chicken call, followed by a rousing cry of "Chicken-mannnn!" and voices shouting, "He's everywhere! He's everywhere!"

https://en.wikipedia.org/wiki/Chickenman_(radio_series)#:~:text=Chickenman%20was%20an%20American%20radio, Radio%20during%20the%20Vietnam%20War.

22. Author's notes, interview with Jim Scancarelli (telephone), 10 July 2020, 2:00 p.m.–4:08 p.m.

23. "Charles Crutchfield, President of WBT, said 'Don't get another job. I'll get to the bottom of this and re-hire you.' I'm still waiting for that call." 9 November 2020 (4:59 p.m.) Text Message from Jim Scancarelli to Lew Stern; Author's notes, interview with Jim Scancarelli (telephone), 9 November 2020, 11:00 a.m.–11:30 a.m.

24. "In addition to his art direction, Scancarelli wrote radio comedy, illustrated kids' magazines including *Child Life, Children's Digest, Jack and Jill,* and *Humpty Dumpty.* He also operated a studio creating art materials for slide presentations for more than 10 years." See "Pumping Life into Gasoline Alley," *Carolina Portfolios,* pp. 18, 47.

25. Author's notes, interview with Jim Scancarelli (telephone), 20 July 2020, 5:30–6:30 p.m. and 9 November 2020 (4:59 p.m.) Text Message from Jim Scancarelli to Lew Stern; Author's notes, interview with Jim Scancarelli (telephone), 9 November 2020, 11:00 a.m.–11:30 a.m.

26. Marcus Hamilton credits Jim with making the connection to Hank Ketcham. Hamilton was watching a television interview that featured the originator of "Dennis the Menace," and heard Ketcham state, perhaps somewhat wistfully, that he hoped to find someone to take over the daily strips so he could do some traveling, enjoy some leisure. Hamilton called Jim, wondering whether he had a good phone number for Ketcham. Coincidentally, Jim had met Ketcham at a National Cartoonists Society convention. Jim had taken a photograph of Ketcham, and promised to send a copy to the cartoonist, so Jim came away from the event with Ketcham's phone number. Hamilton explained: "If it hadn't been for Jim Scancarelli, I probably wouldn't have called Hank Ketcham," and the opportunity that emerged to take over the work on the "Dennis the Menace" dailies would not have emerged. Author's notes, interview with Jim Scancarelli (telephone), 10 July 2020, 2:00 p.m.–4:08 p.m.

27. Some of the illustration work Jim did continued through 1980 and 1981, by which time Jim was working as Dick Moores' assistant on *Gasoline Alley.* Very quickly, though Jim realized he would have to devote far more time to his work with Moores and ceased taking on freelance work. Author's notes, interview with Jim Scancarelli (telephone), 11 August 2020, 3:00 p.m.–4:01 p.m.

28. An April 1980 "Cousin Cooter" strip in *Turtle: A Magazine for Preschool Kids* had Cooter's friend Flapper, a big old bird, complaining of not being able to fly anymore. Cooter makes clear that his bird friend is overweight and devises a daily exercise routine for Flapper that involves 50 sit-ups a day. When Flapper suggests that Cooter join him in this workout, Cooter states unequivocally that turtles do not bend in the middle, staking out the

basis for his exemption from the rigorous exercises recommended for Flapper. "Cousin Cooter: Sit Up and Fly Right," *Turtle*, April 1980.

29. Alex Dueben, "'If You Worry About It, It'll Never Come': Interview with Jim Scancarelli," *The Comics Journal*, 18 March 2019, http://www.tcj.com/if-you-worry-about-it-itll-never-come-an-interview-with-jim-scancarelli/ and https://www.lambiek.net/artists/s/scancarelli_jim.htm.

Chapter Three

1. https://maxhunter.missouristate.edu/songinformation.aspx?ID=246.

2. http://www.hillbilly-music.com/dj/story/index.php?id=16651 and https://countrymusichalloffame.org/artist/connie-b-gay/.

3. The Magnus Harmonica Corporation, originally the International Plastic Harmonica Corporation, was founded in 1944 in New Jersey by Danish immigrant Finn Magnus (1905–1976). Jim's harmonica was probably made by the International Plastic Harmonica Corp. in Newark, New Jersey, after 1945. It was, quite likely, a Magnus model, with 10 single holes and 20 reeds, and a gray plastic comb with blue plastic cover plates adhered to top and bottom. https://americanhistory.si.edu/collections/search/object/nmah_1306529; https://www.patmissin.com/gallery/gallery07.html. Jim remembered: "The Magnus stayed in tune. I had a 12-hole Hohner diatonic harmonica before my grandmother bought me the chromatic one. It was the best thing. I loved it. The chromatics, for some reason—either me blowing hard or maybe the reeds were weak—never did stay in tune for very long. You'd always have to buy another one." Author's notes, interview with Jim Scancarelli (telephone). 31 May 2020, 3:15 p.m.–5:47 p.m.

4. Jerry Murad's Harmonicats played together from 1947 to 2009. The original group consisted of Murad (chromatic and lead harmonica), Bob Hadamik (bass harmonica), Pete Pedersen (chromatic harmonica), and Al Fiore (chord harmonica). Between the early 1950s and the late 1960s, they cut two dozen albums. https://en.wikipedia.org/wiki/Jerry_Murad%27s_Harmonicats.

5. Author's notes, interview with Jim Scancarelli (telephone), 31 May 2020, 3:15 p.m.–5:47 p.m.

6. Author's notes, interview with Jim Scancarelli (telephone), 7 August 2020, 3:00 p.m.–4:55 p.m. Ned Stern, Jim's old chum from high school, later a buddy in the U.S. Navy, recalled Jim's prowess on the harmonica. 22 August 2020, interview with Ned Stern (telephone), 10:00 a.m.–10:57 a.m.

7. 9 November 2020 (4:59 p.m.) Text Message from Jim Scancarelli to Lew Stern; Author's notes, interview with Jim Scancarelli (telephone), 9 November 2020, 11:00 a.m.–11:30 a.m.

8. Amy Worthington Hauslohner, "Jim Scancarelli: Fiddling Around with the Funnies," *Bluegrass Unlimited*, August 1989, p. 43.

9. 9 November 2020 (4:59 p.m.) Text Message from Jim Scancarelli to Lew Stern; Author's notes, interview with Jim Scancarelli (telephone), 9 November 2020, 11:00 a.m.–11:30 a.m.

10. Amy Worthington Hauslohner, "Jim Scancarelli: Fiddling Around with the Funnies," *Bluegrass Unlimited*, August 1989, p. 43.

11. Author's notes, interview with Jim Scancarelli (telephone). 3 May 2017, 1:00 p.m.–2:00 p.m.

12. Jim recalled one of his sessions with Vassar sometime in the late 1980s: "Vassar came to Charlotte. I had the flu. I was in my sick bed and I got a phone call about 0130–0200 from Darrell Gray, one of the original Chicken Hot Rod band members. He called and said you need to get over here. There is a monster jam session and Vassar is over here. I got out of bed, got dressed, drove a couple of blocks over to this house that belonged to a banjo player—though he wasn't home at the time. But Tony Rice and his brother Wyatt were there. I was better than I was when we were at that Wolf Trap jam but I ain't no Vassar Clements, that's for sure. I was sick. And the next day I had to go to the Sand Hills Opry down in South Carolina to play a show. [...] Everyone around here knows the Opry is [a reference to] Sand Hills, not the Nashville Opry. So, Vassar said, 'What? You're going to go to the Opry?' So, good old Vassar, we played some stuff. He showed me some tricks on how to do some backward double stops, hitting two strings at one time and making a chord. Worked every time. Well, for him it worked every time. For me, not so much." Author's notes, interview with Jim Scancarelli (telephone). 21 May 2020, 3:10 p.m.–5:53 p.m. and Author's notes, 23 August 2020 interview with Jim Scancarelli (telephone), 3:19 p.m.–4:59 p.m.

13. Author's notes, interview with Jim Scancarelli (telephone). 3 May 2017, 1:00–2:00 p.m. and 19 August 2020 (11:27 p.m.) Text Message from Jim Scancarelli to Lew Stern. Nance taught classical guitar in Charlotte, North Carolina, in the early 1970s. With Mary Ann Godla co-authored *Music Through Guitar* (General Words and Music, 1972); *The Up-To-Date Method for Classical Guitar* (Carlstadt, New Jersey: Lewis Music Publishing, 1971 and 1973); *Mariachi Mexicano* (Kjos Music Company, 1973); and *Gospel Guitar* (Kjos Music Company, 1974), among other books.

14. Scott Zimmerman was the senior luthier at Fender Research and Development from 1980 to 1984. He started at Fender in early 1977 when they were still making the Artist and Concertone models and saw the last two carved and engraved Concertones being made. The earliest Fender banjos were sub-contracted out but only for a short period, perhaps in the early 1970s. By the late 1970s, banjo production was accomplished "in house" by Fender. The necks were made in the Fender factory. All the pearl inlay cutting work was accomplished in the factory. The resonators were subcontracted out, as was the work of fitting the rims to tone rings. In those days, the Fender archtop and flathead rings were made of heavy bronze; that alone probably contributed to making those Fenders competitive with Gibson banjos. Chuck Erickson was consulted by Fender on the

design of the Concertone model. David Schenkman noted that Erickson brought a Gibson RB-6 with him to Fender to discuss the design for the Concertone. The company leadership liked the banjo enough to decide to use a slightly modified fiddle peghead and the exact RB-6 head inlay on the Concertone. Schenkman suggested that Erickson's influence accounts for the thin Fender neck; Erickson used to make very sleek and fast necks for his banjos. Zimmerman recalled that around 2003 Fender contemplated resuming the production of banjos. They had Zimmerman build a prototype with inlay designs similar to the Concertone. The prototype was nickel plated. Not long after that, Fender decided not to pursue the project. Zimmerman got to keep the banjo, and gave it to David Schenkman to sell, which he did, though sometime in 2017 or so, the person who purchased the prototype sent it back to Schenkman. As of January 2021, that banjo was for sale on Schenkman's website. https://turtlehillbanjo.com/2001-fender-prototype and 9 May 2017 (2:25 p.m.) email from Dave Schenkman to Lew Stern; 3 January 2021 (7:30 a.m.) email from Dave Schenkman to Lew Stern.

15. Author's notes, 23 August 2020 interview with Jim Scancarelli (telephone), 3:19 p.m.–4:59 p.m.

16. Author's notes, interview with Jim Scancarelli (telephone). 8 August 2020, 10:44 a.m.–11:15 p.m.

17. Author's notes, interview with Jim Scancarelli (telephone). 21 May 2020, 3:10 p.m.–5:53 p.m.

18. Jim remembered trying to figure out how to get power out of the fiddle bow. The trick was that to get "the sweep," the wrist has to stay loose. "I was more stiff-armed. Tommy Malboeuf had more of a loose wrist, but he scrubbed the bow," he moved it across the strings in shorter strokes than Baker. Together, he said, he and Tommy Malboeuf ended up improving one another's fiddle playing. Jim learned to visualize Baker's fiddle bow work. Baker, Jim said, moved his bow as though there was an invisible post in front of the bridge, a log that guided his bow onto one path, and it appeared to Jim that Baker sawed back and forth across with the length of his bow, guided by that imaginary post that kept him perfectly fixed in one position, moving his bow consistently along one path across the strings. Author's notes, interview with Jim Scancarelli (telephone), 3 September 2020, 4:45 p.m.–5:30 p.m.

19. Author's notes, interview with Jim Scancarelli (telephone), 3 September 2020, 4:45 p.m.–5:30 p.m.

20. Jim thought that Kenny Baker was always generous in the positive comments and encouragement he offered younger fiddlers. "Kenny played a tune, and Tommy Malboeuf and I learned it. I made up a third part [to that two-part tune], playing it as an even lower part. I played it for Kenny. 'By golly,' Baker said to Jim, 'I wish I'd thought of that.'" 24 August 2020, interview with Jim Scancarelli (telephone), 4:00 p.m.–6:08 p.m.

21. The phrase "Hogan's goat," as in "As smelly as Hogan's goat," seems to be commonly traced to an expression that had its origins in the mid–1800s, referencing a European goat farmer who owned a particularly disgusting goat: "Legend has it that Hoek Hogan, a European farmer, was responsible for an incomprehensibly hideous creation. The year was 1855. Apparently, farmer Hogan had bred a goat so smelly and ugly that people remember it today, honoring the poor creature with the phrase Hogan's goat, which they use to refer to something that has been screwed up beyond all recognition. 'Don't touch my car's engine! You don't know what you're doing, and you will screw it up like Hogan's goat.'" *Erickson's Living Tribune*, 10 October 2013, https://www.ericksonliving.com/tribune/articles/2013/10/whered-phrase-come-59. Even if that is "urban legend," or a self-replicating definition of the etymological origins of the phrase with no basis in linguistic fact, there is still a compelling connection with Jim's own career as a cartoonist: In one online speculation, the phrase referencing that odious "Hogan's goat" derived from R.F. Outcault's cartoon, "Hogan's Alley," a strip that began in 1895 and by the next year came to be called "The Yellow Kid." https://www.reddit.com/r/etymology/comments/2i2j03/drunker_than_hogans_goat/.

22. Jim remembered how Clyde Williams taught him how to wield a fiddle bow. Jim did not know how to read music and felt that he was barely fluent enough in old-time and bluegrass to take the stage with fiddle and banjo in hand. Williams' whole "teaching without teaching" approach was, to Jim, a way of communicating skill sets and information without establishing a hierarchy in a relationship, perhaps keeping with the loose and friendly leadership model of the band itself in which the members looked to Williams as the leader but brought their own music and ideas to the mix. 24 August 2020, interview with Jim Scancarelli (telephone), 4:00 p.m.–6:08 p.m.

23. 24 August 2020, interview with Jim Scancarelli (telephone), 4:00 p.m.–6:08 p.m.

24. In late 2020, Jim voiced a certain amount of impatience with what he learned about contemporary methods for picking up basic fiddle playing. He thought the contemporary teaching techniques prolonged the agony of the beginner's first steps. He acknowledged that there was a good deal of "Just Do It" involved in how he, and perhaps some of his fiddling colleagues, learned fiddling in the late 1960s and early 1970s. The notion that a sense of bowing, a rhythmic dynamic, the musical momentum of old-time fiddling could be communicated by intensive listening instead of trial and error was, to Jim, a bit befuddling. He seemed to favor an approach to learning fiddle that was reminiscent of what some recall of the U.S. Navy's approach to teaching newly enlisted recruits to swim, which—at least metaphorically, though to an extent actually—involved tossing the enlistee into the deep end of the pool and hoping for the best. Author's notes, interview with Jim Scancarelli (telephone), 9 August 2020, 3:10 p.m.–5:25 p.m.

25. Author's notes, interview with Jim Scancarelli (telephone), 3 September 2020, 4:45 p.m.–5:30 p.m.

26. http://www.anythingmusical.com/john-sipe-violins.html; https://bluegrasstoday.com/john-sipe-passes/ and https://fiddlerman.com/forum/the-violin/jonathan-sipe-violins-charlotte-nc/.

27. Jim Scancarelli, "Head of the Class," *Bluegrass Unlimited*, April 2011, p. 40.

28. Author's notes, interview with Jim Scancarelli (telephone), 20 October 2020, 3:05 p.m.–5:12 p.m.; 21 October 2020 (8:28 p.m.) email from Chuck Dunlop to Lew Stern.

29. Author's notes, interview with Jim Scancarelli (telephone), 18 August 2020, 4:00 p.m.–6:02 p.m.

30. http://wbtbriarhoppers.blogspot.com/2012/04/tom-briarhopper-and-fiddlin-jim.html.

31. http://wbtbriarhoppers.blogspot.com/2011/07/fiddlin-hank-warren.html.

32. Tom Warlick wrote: "As a young fiddler, he formed Warren's Four Aces, and then was a member of the Blue Ridge Mountaineers and the Tennessee Ramblers." Warren recorded with the Tennessee Ramblers, and appeared with that band in the 1936 file, *Ride Ranger Ride*, with Gene Autry. See Warlick, *The WBT Briarhoppers*, p. 35. Also see Bob Carlin, *String Bands in the North Carolina Piedmont* (Jefferson, North Carolina: McFarland. 2004), 177–181. Warren was in *The Girl of the Golden West*, a Metro-Goldwyn-Mayer movie produced in 1938, and *Ride Ranger Ride*, the film in which he played multiple roles as well as joining the Tennessee Ramblers; band members played the role of Texas Ranger musicians for the movie. https://en.wikipedia.org/wiki/Ride_Ranger_Ride.

33. Author's notes, interview with Jim Scancarelli (telephone), 3 September 2020, 4:45 p.m.–5:30 p.m.

34. http://wbtbriarhoppers.blogspot.com/2012/04/tom-briarhopper-and-fiddlin-jim.html. Also see Thomas and Lucy Warlick, *The WBT Briarhoppers: Eight Decades of a Bluegrass Band Made for Radio* (Jefferson, North Carolina: McFarland, 2008), 33–35.

35. Author's notes, interview with Jim Scancarelli (telephone), 10 July 2020, 2:00 p.m.–4:08 p.m. and Warlick, *The WBT Briarhoppers,* pp. 151–152.

36. "They did a lot of recordings. They did a fantastic version of 'Kentucky.' They used three mandolins on that number. Hank played one on that cut. I never heard anything like that. They were a good Christian bunch of guys—they didn't smoke, drink, and that was a good plus." Author's notes, interview with Jim Scancarelli (telephone), 10 July 2020, 2:00 p.m.–4:08 p.m.

37. See C.P. Heaton, "The 5 String Banjo in North Carolina," *Banjo Newsletter*, March 1976 (Volume 3, Number 5), pp. 4–9, and *Tommy Thompson: New Timey String Band Musician* (Jefferson, North Carolina: McFarland, 2019), p. 53.

38. Author's notes, interview with Jim Scancarelli (telephone). 27 June 2020, 3:10 p.m.–5:13 p.m.

39. Mark Wingate noted that his wife, Sally Wingate, won a banjo prize there one year and drank moonshine with Tommy Jarrell. "And they pronounce Francisco with the emphasis on the first syllable." 14 December 2020 (6:57 p.m.) email from Mark Wingate to Lew Stern.

40. Author's notes, interview with Jim Scancarelli (telephone). 27 June 2020, 3:10 p.m.–5:13 p.m. Galax was cancelled in 2020 in the face of the public health threat presented by COVID-19. The only other time the event was cancelled was during World War II.

41. "Library of Congress duplication project, 1970; original recordings on five 7-inch sound tape reels at 7 1/2 ips and two 5-inch reels at 3 3/4 ips recorded by Jim Scancarelli from 1964–1969. Original recordings of Uncle Frank Rayborn made in Charlotte, North Carolina in 1964; Bascomb Lamar Lunsford was recorded at home in South Turkey Creek, North Carolina, in February 1966; Norman Edmonds, Jimmy Edmonds, Mack Samples, and James Scancarelli recorded June 14, 1969 and August 10, 1969 in Woodlawn, Virginia; James "Chick" Martin recorded August 16, 1969 at home in Rabbit's Crossing, near Siler City, North Carolina; Wade Ward recorded on May 25, 1969 at home in Independence, Virginia; Arthur Leake Caudle was recorded in Lancaster, South Carolina, at the home of Mack Samples on May 10, 1969; Wilson Douglas was recorded at the West Virginia State Folk Festival at Glenville, West Virginia, on June 21, 1969." https://catalog.loc.gov/vwebv/search?searchCode=LCCN&searchArg=2009655376&searchType=1&permalink=y; Jim Scancarelli Duplication Project, LWO-5965, 11 pages of notes on the musicians and their recordings, provided courtesy of Todd Harvey, Collections Specialist, Reference, American Folklife Center, Library of Congress.

42. Mark Wingate remembered seeing Frank Rayborn playing banjo on the north side of the second block of West Trade Street on the sidewalk outside the spiked iron fence that surrounded the big church there. 14 December 2020 (6:57 p.m.) email from Mark Wingate to Lew Stern.

43. Jim recalled: "Frank Rayborn said he could pick the banjo like Earl Scruggs when he took his shoes off … but he was embarrassed to do it in public." 18 September 2020 (1:30 p.m.) Text Message from Jim Scancarelli to Lew Stern. Author's notes, interview with Jim Scancarelli (telephone), 8 August 2020, 10:44 a.m.–11:15 p.m. C.E. Ward told Jim that Uncle Frank's name was Raybon. Jim recalled that Ward may have dated Uncle Frank's niece. 14 September 2020 (6:15 p.m.) IM from Jim Scancarelli to Lew Stern. Another variant of his name was Raeborn, captured that way on the citation from the North Carolina Folklore Society honoring Jim with the Brown-Hudson award. "Jim Scancarelli—Musician and Preservationist," *North Carolina Folklore Journal*, 49.1 2002, pp. 119–121. Charlie Webb recounted that in January 1955 he spotted "Uncle Frank Raborn" playing banjo in downtown Charlotte. Webb wrote: "I ran across the street to a drug store and bought a Brownie camera just to take these photos; I never used the camera again. To hold the neck, he had fashioned a special rest attached to his chair and had replaced the first 5 frets with a piece of tin. He picked two ways: normally with his good hand, or by hammering on with his right hand.

He played the notes by the dual action of moving his right leg (the rim resting normally on his right thigh) and by pushing the neck against the rest with his left shoulder. Then he switched hands and played with his good hand by hammering on. Think about that! Right hand used to pick with a 'normal' string orientation. Then switch to a different finger action and a different string orientation. He did a creditable job both ways, in spite of the cold, and in spite of his handicap. He had a good lick with his normal right hand. I couldn't stick around to hear him play more; my bus was about to pull out for Asheville." "One-armed Banjo Player," *Banjo Hangout*, 14 January 2012 (Archived). https://www.banjohangout. org/archive/225510.

44. Author's notes, interview with Jim Scancarelli (telephone), 18 August 2020, 4:00 p.m.–6:02 p.m.

45. "Ball lightning is an unexplained phenomenon described as luminescent, spherical objects that vary from pea-sized to several meters in diameter. Though usually associated with thunderstorms, the phenomenon is said to last considerably longer than the split-second flash of a lightning bolt." https://en.wikipedia.org/wiki/Ball_lightning. Jim recalled: "Tommy Malboeuf and I were playing outside in Statesville, North Carolina, just outside of a schoolhouse once. They were on a picnic table. A storm blew in." Jim recalled the cement pad on which the table sat being soaked, and recalled thinking to himself, that's not a particularly good situation in a storm, especially for someone holding a fiddle fitted with steel strings. The storm coughed up ball lightning, and that was a scary moment because "if you get hit by that lightning, you don't get to go to the next fiddler's convention." Author's notes, interview with Jim Scancarelli (telephone), 18 August 2020, 4:00 p.m.–6:02 p.m.

46. Mark Wingate pointed out that there is a Rabbits Crossing in Chatham County. "My guess is that it is where Siler City's Glendon Road crosses Bonlee Road, and there is some history of Chatham County being known for its high-quality rabbits." 14 December 2020 (6:57 p.m.) email from Mark Wingate to Lew Stern and https://www.ourstate.com/north-carolina-history-chatham-county-rabbit/.

47. Author's notes, interview with Jim Scancarelli (telephone), 27 June 2020. 3:10 p.m.–5:13 p.m.; Author's notes, interview with Jim Scancarelli (telephone), 28 June 2020 4:06 p.m.–5:07 p.m. Jim especially remembered a "possum dance" Martin would perform onstage, getting down on his back, arching himself up on his hands and feet, and propelling himself in that posture across the stage.

48. Author's notes, interview with Jim Scancarelli (telephone), 18 August 2020. 4:00 p.m.–6:02 p.m. Chick Martin lived near Tommy Edwards who, in 1972, cofounded The Bluegrass Experience, a North Carolinian band that has existed for about 47 years. In 1972, the group won the World's Championship Bluegrass Band title at the Union Grove Fiddler's Convention. For nine years, the group played weekly at the Cat's Cradle in Carrboro, North Carolina. In 2011 he produced a CD, *North Carolina History, Mystery, Lore and More*.

49. Mack Samples was a teacher in South Carolina who Jim bumped into at a fiddlers' convention, and almost every Sunday for some long while, Jim would get invited to eat lunch at Sample's home in Lancaster, an hour or so from Charlotte, North Carolina. In 1968, Samples took Jim to Glenville, West Virginia, for the festival held annually at the state teacher's college. Mack's family came from Charleston, West Virginia, and he introduced Jim to a good number of West Virginian musicians. "I got to meet old West Virginia pickers. You talk about old, archaic music. The timing, the meter of the tunes they played were just so 'broken.' They'd hold one line longer than another. My mind couldn't perceive it, but it was good music." Jim remembered sharing his views about "modern" bluegrass, and "newgrass" with Samples, and being told, firmly, "Music is music. Doesn't matter what it is. Music is what counts. Don't pigeonhole it." "Boy, I learned that from him," Jim said, fifty years later, still retaining the gist of that lesson. 24 August 2020, interview with Jim Scancarelli (telephone), 4:00 p.m.–6:08 p.m.

50. Author's notes, interview with Jim Scancarelli (telephone), 18 August 2020. 4:00 p.m.–6:02 p.m.

51. Author's notes, interview with Jim Scancarelli (telephone), 21 August 2020, 5:19 p.m.–6:29 p.m. and Author's notes, interview with Jim Scancarelli (telephone), 18 August 2020, 4:00 p.m.–6:02 p.m.

52. Jim reminisced: "After Uncle Wade's wife died, he had a girlfriend for several years. He died in her arms. I got invited to play in the band at the funeral for Uncle Wade. They played 'Kingdom's Coming,' and I didn't know it. Jimmy Edmonds went over it real quick for me. I figured out the chords, but probably just made a lot of noise." Author's notes, interview with Jim Scancarelli (telephone), 21 August 2020, 5:19 p.m.–6:29 p.m.

53. Jim Scancarelli Duplication Project, LWO-5965, 11 pages of notes on the musicians and their recordings, provided courtesy of Todd Harvey, Collections Specialist, Reference, American Folklife Center, Library of Congress.

54. Author's notes, interview with Jim Scancarelli (telephone), 21 August 2020, 5:19 p.m.–6:29 p.m.

55. https://www.slippery-hill.com/content/hubert-caldwell. In Jim's account, Hubert Caldwell could tell some truly bizarre stories and decidedly odd jokes. Caldwell told one about an old fellow who went to town to get some lager beer. Crossing a field on his return, with a mug of lager in his hand, a bull butted him from behind and sent him sprawling, spilling the beer. The bull stood his ground, snorting, pawing the earth, lowering his head, tensing his neck, rising up in a threatening posture. "I'll forgive you," the old fellow said, "since you are bowing and apologizing." He also told tales about going to the opium dens of Chicago, or as he pronounced it, "Chi-Cargo." Charles Kuralt, the CBS newsman, once worked for WBT, though he left before Jim arrived. Jim encountered Kuralt at the Galax festival one year, after the newsman's time at the Charlotte radio and television station. Kuralt was working on

a feature called "On the Road." Kuralt asked Jim to scout for him, to find musicians worth an interview. Jim directed Kuralt to Caldwell. They started taping, Jim remembered, and Kuralt asked the fiddler where he grew up. "Chi-cargo," Caldwell answered in his customary George C. Scott grumble. Jim said: "Kuralt stopped the tape. He was looking for authentic, photogenic subjects. He could not find anyone more photogenic than Hubert Caldwell, but Hubert's brogue failed to impress Kuralt." 24 August 2020, interview with Jim Scancarelli (telephone), 4:00 p.m.–6:08 p.m.

56. Author's notes, interview with Jim Scancarelli (telephone), 23 August 2020, 3:19 p.m.–4:59 p.m. Tom Paley wrote liner notes about Janet Kerr for the 1970 album "Blue Ridge Mountain Field Trip."

57. Author's notes, interview with Jim Scancarelli (telephone), 21 August 2020, 5:19 p.m.–6:29 p.m.

58. Author's notes, interview with Jim Scancarelli (telephone), 21 May 2020 3:10 p.m.–5:53 p.m.

59. Jim stated: "Clark Kessinger was the first I heard putting in the third part and I thought it was cool." 9 November 2020 (4:59 p.m.) Text Message from Jim Scancarelli to Lew Stern; Author's notes, interview with Jim Scancarelli (telephone), 9 November 2020, 11:00 a.m.–11:30 a.m. In terms of the mystery of tunes never having been captured on tape, Jim's attempt to tape in a way that would conserve reel-to-reel tape resources—by unplugging one channel, flipping the reels around, and taping on another track to get four different tracks—was something that, at least from time to time, ended up erasing some earlier tracks, contributing to the mystery of tunes that were recorded, but did not survive attempts to husband recording resources in this way. 24 August 2020, interview with Jim Scancarelli (telephone), 4:00 p.m.–6:08 p.m.; https://tunearch.org/wiki/Annotation:Goin%27_Up_Town.

60. Stern, *Tommy Thompson: New Timey String Band Musician* (Jefferson, North Carolina: McFarland, 2019), Chapter Two. In the sixties, at the school where Union Grove was held, contestants had to play three times: "You would play onstage in the auditorium. That was a very sedate atmosphere. You would just get polite applause. Then you'd move and go to the gymnasium and play there, and that was a little bit more raucous, with a larger audience. Then you'd go play the third venue, a circus tent, and wow, that was—you let your hair down on that one. It was a big thrill to go there and play." Author's notes, interview with Jim Scancarelli (telephone), 3 May 2017, 1:00 p.m.–2:00 p.m.; Pat J. Ahrens, *Union Grove: The First Fifty Years,* published by Pat J. Ahrens, 1975, pp. 150–159, 160–234; Jim Maxwell, "'Lonesome George' and Kessinger Please Crowd, Huge Throng Lured by 47th Festival," *Statesville Record and Landmark*, 12 April 1971.

61. Author's notes, interview with Jim Scancarelli (telephone). 3 May 2017, 1:00 p.m.–2:00 p.m. In 1967, Scancarelli became involved in the annual effort to turn out a recording following each Union Grove festival. Pat J. Ahrens, *Union Grove: The First Fifty Years,* Published by Pat J. Ahrens, 1975, pp.

150–159. Chuck Dunlop recalled: "It was about this time that the convention was moved from the school grounds to the farm, since the latter offered much more space, and the festival had grown significantly in size. The Union Grove convention occurred during many universities' spring break, and once college students got wind of it, hordes of them began to show up, many of them only to party. The last year I was there, the North Carolina state police force was prominent in Union Grove, and judges reportedly were seated behind card tables in the pasture to confront kids who had been busted on the premises for drug possession." 6 November 2020 (2:35 p.m.) email from Chuck Dunlop to Lew Stern.

62. Author's notes, interview with Jim Scancarelli (telephone), 23 June 2020, 3:16 p.m.–5:48 p.m.

63. Author's notes, interview with Jim Scancarelli (telephone), 23 June 2020, 3:16 p.m.–5:48 p.m.

64. Author's notes, interview with Jim Scancarelli (telephone), 3 May 2017, 1:00 p.m.–2:00 p.m.

65. Pat J. Ahrens, *Union Grove: The First Fifty Years,* Published by Pat J. Ahrens, 1975, pp. 160–234. George Pegram won the "World's Champion" prize in the "Single Performer Division" in 1971. Tommy Thompson, who performed with the New Academic String Band, won the World's Champion title for banjo in the Old-Time Category.

66. 13 August 2020 (11:54 a.m.) Facebook Message from Al McCanless to Lew Stern.

67. According to Jim Maxwell's reporting in *The Statesville Record and Landmark* of 12 April 1971, this was the lineup of contest winners for the 47th year: "Named world champion bluegrass band was A.L. Wood and the Smoky Ridge Boys, who hail from Statesville. First runner-up was L.W. Lambert and the Border Mountain Boys from Union Grove, second runner-up was the Bluegrass Buddies with Jimmy Haley from Westfield, and third runner-up was the Bluegrass Experience with Tom Edwards from Siler City. In the old-time band division, Ernest East and the Pine Ridge Boys of Mount Airy were the world champion performers. First runner-up was the Clark Kessinger String Band from St. Albans, West Virginia., second runner-up was Delmer Starling and the Original Carolina Buddies from East Bend, and third runner up was the Camp Creek Boys from Galax, Virginia. The world champion fiddler was Clark Kessinger of St. Albans, West Virginia; first runner-up was Clyde Williams of the Mole Hill Highlanders of Charlotte; and second runner-up was Neil Rossi of the Spark Gap Wonder Boys from Cambridge, Mass. Taking the banjo championship was Tommy Thompson of the New Academic String Band of Chapel Hill; first runner-up was Reed Martin of Bethesda, Maryland; and second runner-up was Kyle Creed of the Camp Creek Boys from Galax, Virginia. The champion guitarist was Tom Edwards of Siler City; first runner-up was Gene Meade [of Virginia]; and second runner-up was Tommy Conner of Copper Hill, Virginia. Winning the world championship for mandolin was Maynard Kizer of Cleveland, Virginia; and second runner-up was Roy McMillan

of Pfafftown. George Pegram was named world champion singles performer, and Evelyn Farmer of Fries, Va., playing the guitar, was selected as first runner-up. Michael Auman, was second runner-up singles performer and Ted Gauthier of Mobile, Alabama, a mandolinist, was third runner-up in this category." See Jim Maxwell, "'Lonesome George' and Kessinger Please Crowd, Huge Throng Lured by 47th Festival," *Statesville Record and Landmark*, 12 April 1971. http://newspaperarchive.com/us/north-carolina/statesville/statesville-record-and-landmark/1971/04–12/page-4. The liner notes for the Union Grove Talking Machine Record (SS-5) stated that Clyde Williams won the first old-time fiddle prize at Union Grove in 1971.

68. 19 November 2020 (1:23 p.m.) email from Chuck Dunlop to Lew Stern; Author's notes, interview with Jim Scancarelli (telephone), 19 November 2020, 3:50 p.m.–4:55 p.m.; Author's notes, interview with Mark Wingate (telephone), 19 November 2020, 11:30 a.m.–12:10 p.m.; Author's notes, interview with Jim Scancarelli (telephone), 19 November 2020, 3:50 p.m.–4:55 p.m.

69. Of his friend Jim Whitley, Jim said: "Whitley had a powerful memory, and a super personality. He could take the stage by storm. You could feel the energy. Nothing fazed him. He had a way of twisting things so in the end hecklers in an audience would come around. He could play any instrument, and he could keep any show going. He'd tell funny stories when a band member broke a string. When he died, that took the air out of it." Author's notes, interview with Jim Scancarelli (telephone), 21 August 2020, 5:19 p.m.–6:29 p.m. Joe Cline echoed that sentiment about Whitley. After he died, the Kilocycle Kowboys played together for one or two more gigs, but, Cline remembered, it was just not the same and the band came to the end of its run. Author's notes, interview with Joe Cline (telephone), 18 August 2020, 9:00 a.m.–10:02 a.m.

70. Liner Notes, Union Grove Talking Machine Records, SS-5.

71. Jim came in fourth place clawhammer banjo contest at Galax in 1975. Howard Wallace of Cincinnati, Ohio, took first place. Bruce Corveth of Piney Creek, North Carolina, and Rick Goad of Spring Valley, Ohio, landed in the second and third spots in the contest, just above Jim. Fifth place went to Harold Hausenfluck of Richmond, Virginia. http://www.oldfiddlersconvention.com/1975win.htm.

72. Author's notes, interview with Jim Scancarelli (telephone), 3 May 2017, 1:00 p.m.–2:00 p.m.

73. "I did write some stuff and it was a little program, called 'Easter Time is Music Time.' Sales [of that booklet] were slow or non-existent. We used to get the albums all the time to sell—Van Hoy never did push them. He might have hired some teenage gals from the school [to sell some] but they didn't push them much. Nobody knew about them. So, there's about as many of them left over as there was when we got them." Author's notes, interview with Jim Scancarelli (telephone), 3 May 2017, 1:00 p.m.–2:00 p.m. In 1965, WBT expressed interest in doing an hour radio show featuring the Union Grove fiddlers' convention. Jim helped with some of the tape-recording work. The station assembled a very credible show that pleased Jim. A digitized version of that program exists "somewhere" in Jim's private holdings. 24 August 2020, interview with Jim Scancarelli (telephone), 4:00 p.m.–6:08 p.m.

74. https://www.discogs.com/artist/5260771-Mole-Hill-Highlanders; Author's notes, interview with Jim Scancarelli (telephone), 3 May 2017, 1:00 p.m.–2:00 p.m.

75. Author's notes, interview with Jim Scancarelli (telephone), 3 May 2017, 1:00 p.m.–2:00 p.m.

76. Mark Wingate recalled that collection of tapes and remembered: " There was a fascinating cut of a Black fiddler, named Harvey Gaither, who played an archaic version of 'Sally Goodin' that has renewed meaning in the era of the Carolina Chocolate Drops and Jake Blount." 14 December 2020 (6:57 p.m.) email from Mark Wingate to Lew Stern; 26 December 2020 (1:09 p.m.) email from Mark Wingate to Lew Stern; Bob Carlin, *String Bands in the North Carolina Piedmont* (Jefferson, North Carolina: McFarland, 2004), p. 39.

77. Jim referred to "The Union Grove Archive" in a tongue in cheek way, intended to reference a box of old tapes from long ago Union Grove festivals that Libby Van Hoy found in her home. Pierce Van Hoy brought the boxes to Jim's studio in the Radio Center Building on South Boulevard in Charlotte in the early 1970s, and Jim used them to develop the LP compilation in honor of the 50th Union Grove fiddlers' convention. Author's notes, interview with Jim Scancarelli (telephone), 27 August 2020, 4:00 p.m.–6:12 p.m.

78. Jim recalled that George Pegram was once hired by the Southern Railway Company—the company that employed Jim's beloved grandfather, Otto Parati. Pegram's job was to walk from car to car playing the banjo. 24 August 2020, interview with Jim Scancarelli (telephone), 4:00 p.m.–6:08 p.m. Bob Carlin said that George Pegram had a job with the Southern Railway Company entertaining at their meetings and conventions. 27 August 2020 (9:59 a.m.) email from Bob Carlin to Lew Stern, and Mark Walker and Oberia Walker, interview. Also see Musical Change in the Western Piedmont project. University of North Carolina at Chapel Hill, Southern Folklife Collection, SFC Audio Cassette FS-20050/604. https://finding-aids.lib.unc.edu/20050/. Jim remembered that Red Parham was a "wonderful harmonica player." Author's notes, interview with Jim Scancarelli (telephone), 8 September 2020, 3:00 p.m.–4:34 p.m.

79. Harper Van Hoy, whose father had established the convention, recalled that Hargrove had won third place in banjo in 1965, and after being reminded that Hargrove's specialty was media law, Harper Van Hoy asked for Hargrove's help in drawing up a contract for an American University filmmaker who had expressed an interest in making a film. Harper Van Hoy wanted to ensure that the film would be used for educational purposes, and not

for any commercial endeavors that might impact the Van Hoy family's interests and utilize the Union Grove name in a manner over which he and the convention would have no control, so Wade Smith focused on the work of the magistrate in processing those arrested for infractions around the convention grounds involving drinking and illegal drugs, and Wade Hargrove drafted a contract for the filmmaker that his wife typed on the spot. Stern, *Tommy Thompson: New Timey String Band Musician* (Jefferson, North Carolina: McFarland, 2019), 55–56.

80. Author's notes, interview with Jim Scancarelli (telephone), 20 May 2020, 4:13 p.m.–6:38 p.m.

81. In 2002, the North Carolina Folklore Society honored Jim with its annual Brown-Hudson Award. In the accompanying citation, Tom Hanchett highlighted Jim's field recording work. See "Jim Scancarelli—Musician and Preservationist," *North Carolina Folklore Journal*, 49.1, 2002, pp. 119–121.

Chapter Four

1. 10 October 2020 (5:17 p.m.) email from Mark Wingate to Lew Stern. Wingate was born in 1948. "I was a young teen at the time the Beverly Hillbillies came out, so I heard Earl play the theme and I really liked the sound of that. I think that was my main inspiration to want to try and learn to play it. I told my parents that I was interested in playing the banjo, so for Christmas I got what they thought was a banjo, but it was really a uke, a plastic banjo uke. That was my first stringed instrument. Before that I bought a harmonica at the dime store and played around, but I didn't really pursue it." Wingate eventually fixed the banjo uke up with a fifth string and was motivated to learn chords. "I started getting interested in the hymn books at church, trying to figure out how that notation led to music. Got ahold of the Pete Seeger book, and at the same time got ahold of *Sing Out!* magazine. At this same time the whole folk thing—Kingston Trio, and Peter, Paul, and Mary, that whole Hootenanny phase—was happening. I was already playing guitar and banjo a little bit in high school. I listened to the Grand Ole Opry on the chance that I would hear a bluegrass group. And I also found Wheeling Jamboree on radio station WWVA that featured bluegrass. I got interested in the folk music on one side, and—like everybody else—heard the popular radio music of the day. I was working at a grocery store and a customer was reaching for his change to pay for his groceries, and he had some fingerpicks in his hand mixed with his change. That turned out to be a policeman, Slim Burgess, who played the five-string banjo. He played with a neighbor of mine, Pete and Carol Grigg. I was able to visit their house. They let me come and be a fly on the wall while their band was rehearsing. When they took a break, I would try to play a little bit. They were kind of my musical parents—my family really wasn't musical." Wingate and his friends "would go and scour the record shops and read the liner notes of all the albums. It was like going to the library. We'd learn about all

these groups, try to piece together what this music was really all about—kind of like Plato's cave, we were reading very partial and biased information and we'd try and imagine what was really out there in three dimensions." A library in Charlotte had a copy of the Harry Smith anthology: "I was able to borrow that and that introduced me to the old 78s—music from the twenties and thirties. About that same time, I had decided maybe I could find bluegrass records that weren't available as LPs, so I started going to Salvation Army and bookstores, places where they had those 78s." He started collecting 78s, and that introduced him to Django Reinhardt, blues, and black gospel. "My tastes became eclectic and expansive, and that has been where I've been ever since." Around that time, Wingate began playing as a bluegrass band with three neighborhood friends; that became the band Chicken Hot Rod: "Our first name was the Great Speckled Band, which we thought was a clever play on Great Speckled Bird, but then Ian and Sylvia formed a country rock group called Great Speckled Bird, so we figured we needed to find a different name, and we came up with Chicken Hot Rod." Author's notes, interview with Mark Wingate (telephone), 23 September 2020, 11:37 a.m.–12:03 p.m.

2. 17 September 2020 (12:03 p.m.) email from Chuck Dunlop to Lew Stern.

3. In the summer of 1968, Wingate played in a jug band called Mr. Cola's Cooterfoot Wine Bottle Band that recorded one 45 featuring "Rocky Top" and "I'm a Woman" (Quintet Recording Company, Winston-Salem, North Carolina QD-3016-A). 10 October 2020 (5:17 p.m.) email from Mark Wingate to Lew Stern. Jim recalled Mark Wingate's musicality: "He'd come over to my art studio, and I'd play an old bluegrass or a fiddle tune record. He'd would listen, go home, and then call me, play it over the phone—and he had it down, completely." Jim remembered that about 1965, he met Mark at a local contest. "C.E. Ward and I drove up and Mark was in his car fiddlin' away and pulling his bow short so it wouldn't hit the roof liner." Author's notes, interview with Jim Scancarelli (telephone), 22 April 2020, 6:50 p.m.–8:00 p.m.; Author's notes, interview with Jim Scancarelli (telephone), 31 May 2020, 3:15 p.m.–5:47 p.m.; 9 November 2020 (4:59 p.m.) Text Message from Jim Scancarelli to Lew Stern; Author's notes, interview with Jim Scancarelli (telephone), 9 November 2020, 11:00 a.m.–11:30 a.m.

4. Jim thought it was about 1968 when he and the musicians who would become the Mole Hill Highlanders went over to Clyde William's house. "We met in September 1967 or 1968—at Freedom Park. We all sat out and played. That was probably the seminal meeting. They were just jamming. I went and got my banjo because I lived just around the corner. […] After the festival in the park, Mark called me and said we were going to meet over at Clyde Williams' and I said, 'yeah.'" Author's notes, interview with Jim Scancarelli (telephone), 24 September 2020 (5:57 p.m.–6:03 p.m.).

5. Author's notes, interview with Mark Wingate

(telephone), 23 September 2020, 11:37 a.m.–12:03 p.m. The band gathered at Williams' home in October 1969 and played music around a big oil stove in the living room in the presence of an audience that consisted of Clyde's mother, his two sisters and their children, and a hound and several cats. In the Liner Notes for Old Oblivion 00-1, Jim wrote: "There was a 3-D sort of picture of Jesus on the wall whose eyes would follow you regardless of your position in the room. 'Play "Liberty," Clyde,' the momma hollered and would beat out a rhythm on Mexican maracas as we played. The evening wore on, the music got hot and so did the room. The ladies would call for a break and served pineapple upside down cake they had baked and iced cold Cheerwine (a Southern cola). "Rest period's over," Clyde would command, and the music continued 'til after midnight. It was not uncommon to play one tune for over a half an hour all the while bringing it to a boil. Clyde wildly improvised the melody and caught up in the spirit of the thing would bellow a loud, 'Yuh' of approval and hit hotter licks with his bow (some never repeated again)." Chuck Dunlop recalled: "The Mole Hill Highlanders played at numerous small fiddlers' conventions, winning ribbons at many of them—ribbons that provided virtually the only decorations on Clyde's living room wall. The other decoration was a 3-D model of Jesus' head." 6 November 2020 (2:35 p.m.) email from Chuck Dunlop to Lew Stern.

6. Author's notes, interview with Chuck Dunlop (telephone), 16 September 2020, 11:00 a.m.–11:39 a.m. and 16 September 2020 (10:36 p.m.) email from Chuck Dunlop to Lew Stern. Wingate recalled: "Now, Clyde got ahold of a tape recorder and made some reel-to-reel tapes of himself playing the fiddle—can't remember if he was trying to do multi track or not. I still have these reel-to-reel tapes. [On the tape] he's talking to his niece Angie, and he says: 'OK, Angie we're going to play the new fiddle.' I think he tried to make a fiddle. So, he's playing onto the tape recorder on the new fiddle." Author's notes, interview with Mark Wingate (telephone), 23 September 2020, 11:37 a.m.–12:03 p.m.

7. Author's notes, interview with Jim Scancarelli (telephone), 20 May 2020, 4:13 p.m.–6:38 p.m.

8. Charles Wolfe wrote: "On November 9, 1925, George D. Hay arrived in Nashville. Hay's vocation was a relatively new one; he was a radio announcer. Just over two years before, Hay had been a popular journalist for the Memphis *Commercial Appeal*, where he wrote a humorous column revolving around dialogue between a white judge and numerous black defendants. The title of the column was 'Howdy, Judge,' and it gave Hay the nickname of 'the solemn old Judge'—even though he was a young man of twenty-eight. When the Commercial Appeal started radio station WMC in 1923, Hay was 'drafted' and made announcer. He was so successful that within a year he had been hired by one of the country's most powerful stations, WLS in Chicago. [...] Here Hay had continued his success, announcing his act in a deep stylized voice and blowing an imitation steamboat whistle he carried." Charles K.

Wolfe, *Tennessee Strings: The Story of Country Music in Tennessee* (Knoxville: University of Tennessee Press, 1977), pp. 54–55.

9. Author's notes, interview with Jim Scancarelli (telephone), 16 September 2020, 5:40 p.m.–6:08 p.m.; 17 September 2020 (9:38 p.m.) Text Message from Jim Scancarelli to Lew Stern; Author's notes, interview with Chuck Dunlop (telephone), 16 September 2020, 11:00 a.m.–11:39 a.m.; 16 September 2020 (10:36 p.m.) email from Chuck Dunlop to Lew Stern.

10. Chuck Dunlop, "When Strings Become Bridges," *Bluegrass Unlimited* (Forthcoming, 2021).

11. Author's notes, interview with Chuck Dunlop (telephone), 16 September 2020, 11:00 a.m.–11:39 a.m.; 16 September 2020 (10:36 p.m.) email from Chuck Dunlop to Lew Stern. In his collection of Mole Hill Highlander memorabilia, Jim has two such horns that Clyde Williams had cobbled together.

12. 19 November 2020 (1:23 p.m.) email from Chuck Dunlop to Lew Stern.

13. Author's notes, interview with Jim Scancarelli (telephone), 19 November 2020, 3:50 p.m.–4:55 p.m.

14. Author's notes, interview with Jim Scancarelli (telephone), 19 November 2020, 3:50 p.m.–4:55 p.m.

15. Wingate noted: "The Stanley Brothers had a local radio show and Rex would come in from working in the field to listen. According to his obituary, he was born in 1936 so he would have been 12 or 13 at that time, in 1949." 10 October 2020 (5:17 p.m.) email from Mark Wingate to Lew Stern; The Stanley Brothers relocated to Winston-Salem, North Carolina, in November 1950, and played on WTOB. They travelled to Nashville, Tennessee, to do their second recording session with Columbia Records, after which they returned to Winston-Salem and remained at WTOB until early January 1950. See Gary B. Reid, *The Music of the Stanley Brothers* (Chicago: University of Illinois Press, 2015). pp. 26–28; https://www.tributearchive.com/obituaries/2749843/Rex-Thomas-Hodges.

16. Author's notes, interview with Mark Wingate (telephone), 24 September 2020, 11:00 a.m.–11:58 a.m.

17. Author's notes, interview with Mark Wingate (telephone), 24 September 2020, 11:00 a.m.–11:58 a.m. Wingate remarked that "Blues in My Mind" was written by Fred Rose and Roy Acuff recorded it in 1945. 10 October 2020 (5:17 p.m.) email from Mark Wingate to Lew Stern.

18. Wingate recalled five tunes Haymore may have learned "from his own tradition": "Duck's Eyeball," "Buck Creek Gals," "Silly Bill," "Greasy String," and "June Apple." Haymore referred to the tune "June Apple" as "Waterbound." 10 October 2020 (5:17 p.m.) email from Mark Wingate to Lew Stern.

19. Red Haymore recorded "Long Road to Travel" on the 48th Union Grove Fiddlers' Convention (SS-6) LP. See: https://www.ibiblio.org/hillwilliam/BGdiscography/?v=fullrecord&albumid=7010. He played "Buck Creek Gals" as the 9th cut on the Union Grove LP (SS-4), "Hub of

the Universe (1971). See s://www.discogs.com/it/Various-Hub-of-the-Universe/release/9050588. Blanton Owen's field recordings (1963–1971) capture some of Haymore music. See https://finding-aids.lib.unc.edu/20027/.

20. "Haymore would say 'You're going to have to meet Frank Freeman, and Ham.' Then he'd tell stories about Freeman's eccentricities and how Haymore would want to get him to play banjo at a fiddlers' convention. Freeman didn't drive so you'd have to pick him up, but you'd go to his house and he'd never be ready. He was a recluse and an agoraphobic. He lived in a house with his mother and legend has it that the house was stacked up with newspapers and milk containers/jugs, so there were just little trails through the house through the stacks. Freeman was known in the area of Winston Salem as an exceptional musician, but it was almost impossible to play with him in any organized way because of his eccentricities." Author's notes, interview with Mark Wingate (telephone), 28 September 2020, 10:00 a.m.–12:00 p.m.

21. Author's notes, interview with Mark Wingate (telephone), 24 September 2020, 11:00 a.m.–11:58 a.m.

22. Ham was younger than Clyde Williams. He listened to all manner of radio stations. Interestingly, Clyde Williams never gave any indication that he admired the music of fiddling Arthur Smith. Wingate noted that Ham played in a band on the radio, Smokey Graves' band: "He played for dances in the catchment area of that radio station. More than Haymore, Johnny Ham was aware of and listened to other fiddlers. I don't know that he gravitated to the fancy fiddlers. Or those more technically accomplished than the Grand Ole Opry fiddlers. He did favor tunes that were not played for entertainment—tunes with tradition, handed down tunes." "Something about that time was very exciting." Author's notes, interview with Mark Wingate (telephone), 24 September 2020, 11:00 a.m.–11:58 a.m. Wingate said: "He talked often about his time playing with Smokey Graves. I think that was as close as he got to being a professional musician. He also mentioned Tommy Floyd, a DJ and maybe a musician. Johnny also aspired to work as a radio DJ and announcer, I'm pretty sure. He mentioned receiving compliments on his 'radio voice.'" 10 October 2020 (5:17 p.m.) email from Mark Wingate to Lew Stern.

23. Author's notes, interview with Mark Wingate (telephone), 28 September 2020, 10:00 a.m.–12:00 p.m. Looking back, Wingate wondered if this "heritage" framing was something Williams came to later: "Something similar was going on with the early 20th century collectors and advocates for Anglo-Saxon heritage." 14 December 2020 (6:57 p.m.) email from Mark Wingate to Lew Stern.

24. Mark Wingate stated: "There was a local fiddler Clyde played with sometimes. [...] He didn't say that the other guy wasn't a good fiddler, but that he only played simple tunes, like 'Greenback Dollar.' I interpreted that to mean that he thought of the

dance tunes he learned from the Opry fiddlers were more complex and worthy of attention, whereas 'Greenback Dollar,' etc., were just melodies to songs. Somehow, they just didn't contain as much musical information or complexity." 28 September 2020 (1:29 p.m.) email from Mark Wingate to Lew Stern.

25. Author's notes, interview with Mark Wingate (telephone), 28 September 2020, 10:00 a.m.–12:00 p.m. Other Mole Hill Highlanders band members also had the sense that Williams was aware of what his life looked like, how his home registered with visitors, and what this might have said about him to band members and other friends. For example, Chuck Dunlop observed: "Clyde's house and furnishings were extremely modest, with a bare wood floor and little on the walls (except for prize ribbons and a Jesus whose eyes appeared to follow anyone who looked at him). Our initial Mole Hill Highlander gatherings were always held at Clyde's house, but at some point, in the spring I think, we met at my place—perhaps because we were doing a recording session and my place was a good venue for that. I lived in a modern 2-unit condo in the woods outside of Charlotte, and my furnishings included a large, plush white carpet in the living room. The next time I went over to Clyde's, there was a new (but rather flimsy) rug spread out in the living room where we always played our music. I felt bad about that, assuming that Clyde had seen my carpet, and decided that he needed to provide an upgraded environment to emulate mine. Over time, however, due in part to the dancing that his sister's children often did while we played our music, Clyde's rug began to disintegrate, and within a few months, all that was left was a one-foot border around the periphery of the room, whose wooden floor was again very visible. Nobody ever remarked on that, and the remaining fragment of Clyde's rug remained in place for as long as I visited him." 24 November 2020 (11:25 a.m.) email from Chuck Dunlop to Lew Stern.

26. Wingate explained that Williams wanted to sound like the Possum Hunters, and that it was the banjo player in that band who—in Wingate's view—was responsible for putting this leap beat into a tune. Author's notes, interview with Mark Wingate (telephone), 28 September 2020, 10:00 a.m.–12:00 p.m. and 10 October 2020 (5:17 p.m.) email from Mark Wingate to Lew Stern.

27. In those days, Dunlop played a 1947 D18 Martin guitar that he had purchased for around $300. That guitar was stolen from Dunlop in 1972. On 14 July 2019, Jim included references to that instrument in a *Gasoline Alley* strip, complete with its serial number, to help locate that guitar. Dunlop recovered his guitar in 2021 after it had been sold in an eBay auction, thanks to the cooperative auction winner. 12 August 2021 (9:04 p.m.) email from Chuck Dunlop to Lew Stern.

28. "What Clyde wanted was a sound with a heavy beat. I never could emulate what was in Clyde's memory. He had this idea of just how the Possum Hunters did it. Well, when I found some old records of the Possum Hunters, and played them,

we didn't sound anything like the Possum Hunters. The banjo player played with a flatpick. What Clyde remembered was the rhythm. It was a heavy beat, and that's what he was trying to get me to do, to transfer me from the clawhammer style. I had no idea of what he was driving at, and I couldn't read his mind." The end result, though, in Jim's view was a real "slick" band sound. Author's notes, interview with Jim Scancarelli (telephone), 31 May 2020, 3:15 p.m.–5:47 p.m.; Author's notes, interview with Jim Scancarelli (telephone), 22 April 2020, 6:50 p.m.–8:00 p.m.

29. Author's notes, interview with Jim Scancarelli (telephone), 3 May 2017, 1:00 p.m.–2:00 p.m.

30. 13 November 2020 (12:44 a.m.) email from Charles Dunlop to Lew Stern.

31. 13 November 2020 (10:24 a.m.) email from Charles Dunlop to Lew Stern. Mark Wingate observed: "Jim played banjo with Clyde Williams the way banjo players played with fiddlers in bands before the folk revival, when things became 'codified.' The banjo in old-time music in those days was seen as a necessary support for the fiddle. So, Jim was playing banjo exactly in that tradition. His instincts were good; he had good musical sense. His banjo playing was very right brain versus left brain: he just played exactly the right thing." Author's notes, interview with Mark Wingate (telephone), 19 November 2020, 11:30 a.m.–12:10 p.m.

32. Author's notes, interview with Mark Wingate (telephone), 28 September 2020, 10:00 a.m.–12:00 p.m. Jim's sense was that Clyde Williams wanted him to play the banjo in a way that was far more percussive than melodic. Occasionally, Williams would grab Jim's banjo and start playing it with a flat pick, Possum Hunter style. Decades later, Jim would lament that he could never play the five string the way Williams wanted it played. Author's notes, interview with Jim Scancarelli (telephone), 3 May 2017, 1:00–2:00 p.m. and Author's notes, 23 August 2020 interview with Jim Scancarelli (telephone), 3:19 p.m.–4:59 p.m.

33. 9 November 2020 (4:59 p.m.) Text Message from Jim Scancarelli to Lew Stern; Author's notes, interview with Jim Scancarelli (telephone), 9 November 2020, 11:00 a.m.–11:30 a.m.

34. Koken, *Fire on the Mountain: An American Odyssey* (Kennett Square, Pennsylvania: Mudthumper Music, 2017), passim.

35. Chuck Dunlop recalled: "On one such occasion, Clyde's sister noticed that the fingers on my left hand were bleeding. She called that to Clyde's attention; he nodded, smiled, and kept right on fiddling. And I didn't stop either." 6 November 2020 (2:35 p.m.) email from Chuck Dunlop to Lew Stern.

36. Author's notes, interview with Mark Wingate (telephone), 28 September 2020, 10:00 a.m.–12:00 p.m.

37. To a certain extent, Wingate mused, playing with the fiddler Tommy Malboeuf was described in that way by people who played with him. Author's notes, interview with Mark Wingate (telephone), 28 September 2020, 10:00 a.m.–12:00 p.m.

38. After his time with the Mole Hill Highlanders, Williams became very well known within the Charlotte milieu, and attracted local newspaper coverage as well as the attention of the Charlotte Folk Music Society.

39. 14 December 2020 (6:57 p.m.) email from Mark Wingate to Lew Stern and Author's notes, interview with Mark Wingate (telephone), 23 September 2020, 11:37 a.m.–12:03 p.m.

40. Author's notes, interview with Jim Scancarelli (telephone), 27 August 2020, 4:00 p.m.–6:12 p.m. and 6 November 2020 (2:35 p.m.) email from Chuck Dunlop to Lew Stern.

41. Dunlop recalled that the Mole Hill Highlanders did the "Mississippi Sawyer" stunt on stage at least once, to the gaping amazement and amusement of the audience. 17 December 2020 (2:45 p.m.) email from Chuck Dunlop to Lew Stern.

42. 12 November 2020 (1:20 p.m.) email from Mark Wingate to Lew Stern.

43. 13 November 2020 (10:24 a.m.) email from Charles Dunlop to Lew Stern.

44. https://en.wikipedia.org/wiki/WVBZ. The Statesville, North Carolina, station was managed by J.D. Benfield for many years; he also served, at the same time, as director and announcer. It was, Benfield reminisced in 2006, one of the only stations on which listeners could hear bluegrass during the week. Benfield's wife Sue also worked at the radio station. Odell Wood, R.C. Harris, and Hoyt Herbert, among other musicians, were also station employees. Benfield had a little singing group called "Love Valley Four." Statesville, in the 1970s, was a good place for bluegrass music. Forty or fifty years later, banjo pickers remembered Hoyt Herbert's Sunday evening bluegrass radio show, and Jim and Jesse playing in Statesville in 1978. J.D. Benfield's Love Valley Four opened for the McReynolds brothers at that concert. They were followed by the band Wells Fargo; Eric Ellis played banjo. https://www.banjohangout.org/archive/161873. Jim recalled that besides running the radio station, J.D. Benfield also had a yard waste and trash pickup service. Author's notes, interview with Jim Scancarelli (telephone), 31 May 2020, 3:15 p.m.–5:47 p.m.

45. Author's notes interview with Jim Scancarelli (telephone), 20 May 2020, 4:13 p.m.–6:38 p.m.

46. Author's notes interview with Jim Scancarelli (telephone), 20 May 2020, 4:13 p.m.–6:38 p.m. Chuck Dunlop stated: "Our shows always included a couple of Mole Hill Highlander numbers but did not consist solely of that material. We included everything from old cylinder recordings to bluegrass." 6 November 2020 (2:35 p.m.) email from Chuck Dunlop to Lew Stern.

47. In the late 1960s, Dunlop lived outside of Charlotte, on Poplar Tent Church Road, just a few miles from the home of J.E. Mainer. The Mole Hill Highlanders band members once paid J.E. a visit. Mainer told them about discovering a Stainer fiddle lying in pieces by the railroad tracks near his house. Mainer gathered up the parts, glued them back together, and ended up with a fine instrument.

Dunlop remembered being invited to the 100th birthday party of Wade Mainer, J.E. Mainer's brother, in 2007. Wade Mainer lived in Flint, Michigan, for many years. Dunlop played banjo with a band at the party. Burton Melvin "Mel" Ray Hammon (1925–2017), a fiddler who had known Wade for many years, was the fiddler for that band. 16 September 2020 (10:36 p.m.) email from Chuck Dunlop to Lew Stern. That band might have been Old South, a band formed by Hammon in 1980 with his wife Marjorie, his son Ron, and brother George. Old South was inducted into the Michigan Bluegrass Hall of Fame in 1999. Dunlop remembered Ron Hammon, Mel's son, and Mel Hammon's wife Marge being present on the stage for that event. He also recalled that Wade Mainer and his wife Julia played a set. 17 September 2020 (12:03 p.m.) email from Chuck Dunlop to Lew Stern. And see https://obits.mlive.com/obituaries/flint/obituary. aspx?n=melvin-hammon&pid=183975241&fhid= 10724.

48. Author's notes interview with Jim Scancarelli (telephone), 20 May 2020, 4:13 p.m.–6:38 p.m. Dunlop confirmed Jim's story about the Mole Hill Highlanders stint in the early 1970s hosting a weekly thirty-minute radio show from WFMX in Statesville. Band members told J. E. about the show, and he promised to tune in. The station management wanted proof of the popularity of the Mole Hill Highlanders, so on the air the band implored the radio audience to send in cards and letters. Within a few days, the band received a dozen or more testimonials which, upon close examination, were all revealed to have been written by J. E. Mainer. Author's notes, interview with Chuck Dunlop (telephone), 16 September 2020, 11:00 a.m.–11:39 a.m. and 16 September 2020 (10:36 p.m.) email from Chuck Dunlop to Lew Stern.

49. Show number 1: 1 May 1970. Show number 2: 8 May 1970. Show number 3: 12 May 1970. Show number 4: 19 May 1970. Show number 5: 26 May 1970. Show number 6: 2 June 1970. Show number 7: 9 June 1970. Show number 8: 16 June 1970. Show number 9: 23 June 1970. Show number 10: 30 June 1970. Show number 11: 7 July 1970. Show number 12: 14 July 1970. Show number 13: 21 July 1970. I am indebted to Chuck Dunlop for sending me a complete set of these shows on CDs.

50. Author's notes interview with Jim Scancarelli (telephone), 20 May 2020, 4:13 p.m.–6:38 p.m.; Author's notes, interview with Jim Scancarelli (telephone), 15 September 2020, 3:45 p.m.–5:07 p.m.

51. The Kilocycle Kowboys band played some unique venues. Jim remembered: "We were booked by a talent agency and we ran up and down North and South Carolina, wherever the agency had booked jobs for us. We would go down to Charleston sometimes and go over toward the northeastern part of North Carolina where we'd play on a golf course. Down to Myrtle beach, realtors would try to sell condos. They'd set up on golf courses, and we'd get booked in there to play music while they were trying to sell condos. Didn't pay much but it was fun." Author's notes, interview with Jim Scancarelli (telephone), 31 May 2020, 3:15 p.m.–5:47 p.m.

52. Author's notes, interview with Joe Cline (telephone), 18 August 2020, 9:00 a.m.–10:02 a.m.

53. Wingate remembered that Whitley was a high energy personality: "He was never admired for his banjo playing except for the energy of it. He never achieved that level where other people say, 'How did he do that? I must learn to do that.' He was the leaf on the tree—didn't start any tradition of his own. He was an entertainer. Mainly people were amazed by his energy and his ability to be spontaneously entertaining. He was a good tenor singer and [...] a wonderful MC. Probably he deserves at least 60 percent of the credit for Chicken Hot Rod band's successes. He was kind of driven." Author's notes, interview with Mark Wingate (telephone), 24 September 2020, 11:00 a.m.–11:58 a.m.

54. A late 1980s account of Joe Cline's involvement with another band, Chicken Hot Rod, formed in Winston Salem around 1969, states: "'One day,' says Joe, 'this poor, raggle-tailed college drop-out named Jim Whitley came into Reliable Music to slobber over the banjos. The rest is history; it's all downhill from there.' After their initial acquaintance, Jim Whitley and Joe used to go to downtown Charlotte's authentic coffeehouse, Johnny Swinger's Round-Up (also called The Attic and The Twelfth Fret), where many local musicians would jam together in the late 1960s. In the early '70s Jim Whitley took off with his high-school buddies [Mark Wingate, fiddle, and Darrell Gray, who played bass] and another friend from college ["Lizard" Thom Case] to form Chicken Hot Rod and play music full-time [...] Chicken lasted three years, then Jim Whitley moved back to Charlotte. Whitley and Cline started playing together regularly because of fiddler Jim Scancarelli. "Scancarelli called me up one day," relates Joe, "and said he'd gotten a request to play a gig, if he had a band. Scancarelli told them he had a band, and it was called The Kilocycle Kowboys. He just made it up on the spot. He was hired so he needed to round up some Kowboys. Jim Whitley and I were the Kowboys he rounded up. We could have gotten a fourth but was easy to see that the amount of money we would get would be better divided by three than by four. Therefore, we've mostly been a three-piece band." Sometimes as Kilocycle Kowboys, sometimes just as themselves with a fiddler, Joe and Jim have been playing together now for about sixteen years, with fiddlers like Scancarelli, Bob Ennis, Mark Wingate, or Howard Eury." Jill Johnson, "The Saga of Whitley and Cline," *Charlotte Folk Music Society Newsletter*, May 1988, https://www.facebook. com/KilocycleKowboys/posts/the-saga-of-whitley-and-clinefrom-the-mounthy-newsletter-of-the-charlotte-folk-m/829813010451297/. Jim Scancarelli produced the only album recorded by the Chicken Hot Rod band on his "Old Oblivion" label. In his remembrance of Chicken Hot Rod, Cline wrote that the album "was recorded live in the studio direct to two-track tape. Mostly original

songs from Thom; one song from Darrell [Gray]; a bluegrass standard or two, in original arrangements and the aforementioned Early Morning Radio Show, with a special appearance by Brother Norman Tabernacle and his choir (Big Jim, doing the best impression of Rev. Mull you've ever heard.) Art Menius, in *Bluegrass Unlimited* a year or so ago, called it "the funniest bluegrass album ever made." Unfortunately, it does not do justice to the bluegrass ability of the band. They stayed on the coffee-house circuit for about two years, before poverty took its toll [....]" The other three members of the band returned to Charlotte. Cline replaced Thom for a number of dates, Jim Scancarelli replaced Mark and the name changed to the Kilocycle Kowboys. Posted in bit.listserv.bglass-l. 3:00 a.m., 3 July 1997. https://groups.google.com/forum/print/msg/bit.listserv.bgrass-l/qDDnMjpvV_M/24TWap3oOyM J?ctz=5472772_72_76_104100_72_446760. Mark Wingate recalled that the band played some jobs in New York State, North Carolina, South Carolina, Kentucky, Tennessee, Virginia, Iowa, Minnesota, South Dakota, and Louisiana. 14 December 2020 (6:57 p.m.) email from Mark Wingate to Lew Stern.

55. Author's notes, interview with Joe Cline (telephone), 18 August 2020, 9:00 a.m.–10:02 a.m.

56. Posted in bit.listserv.bglass-l. 3:00 a.m., 3 July 1997. https://groups.google.com/forum/print/msg/bit.listserv.bgrass-l/qDDnMjpvV_M/24TWap3oOy MJ?ctz=5472772_72_76_104100_72_446760. Mark Wingate added: "The band would be hired at some function as the evening entertainment. Usually people would be eating and the band would 'stroll' from table to table, banter with the folks a bit—Whitley was the master of this—then play a few tunes, then move on to another table. This could work at a country club dining room or at a more informal cook-out or barbecue. Tablecloths and china or paper plates and Dixie cups." 14 December 2020 (6:57 p.m.) email from Mark Wingate to Lew Stern.

57. Author's notes, interview with Joe Cline (telephone), 18 August 2020, 9:00 a.m.–10:02 a.m.

58. Jim mused that this was good practice for the COVID-19 lockdowns. 27 October 2020 (1:55 p.m.) Text Message from Jim Scancarelli to Lew Stern.

59. Author's notes, interview with Jim Scancarelli (telephone), 20 October 2020, 3:05 p.m.–5:12 p.m.

60. https://groups.google.com/forum/#!topic/bit.listserv.bgrass-l/qDDnMjpvV_M; 18 August 2020 (10:07 a.m.) email from Joe Cline to Lew Stern.

61. 6 November 2020 (2:35 p.m.) email from Chuck Dunlop to Lew Stern.

62. Jim recalled that a "demo" made by Thom Case in Nashville, Tennessee, featuring songs he wrote was assigned an Old Oblivion number (OO-6), but the project never came to fruition, and Jim never received a copy of what Case had intended to turn into a cassette. Interestingly, at some point, Tommy Malboeuf utilized the Old Oblivion label, and issued a home-made recording as 00–6. The product was called "Tommy Malboeuf: Orange Blossom Special." That recording featured the fiddling of Tommy Malboeuf who was joined by Hannah Vogel (guest fiddle), J.P. Van Hoy (bass, guitar, keyboard), Clay Lunsford (guitar, banjo), Mary Umbarger (autoharp), Gay Tatman (flute, penny whistle) and Stephanie Spranta (vocals). J.P. Vanhoy engineered the recording, and Tommy's son, Danny, designed the cover. Jim allowed the possibility that he had simply told Tommy Malboeuf to go ahead with his project, and to use the OO-6 number and Old Oblivion label but had forgotten the sequence of events that led to the release of the "Orange Blossom Special" cassette. Author's notes, interview with Jim Scancarelli (telephone), 19 November 2020, 3:50 p.m.–4:55 p.m.

63. 6 November 2020 (2:35 p.m.) email from Chuck Dunlop to Lew Stern.

64. "Tommy Malboeuf, the wonderful fiddle player, and he and I used to get together. He taught me a lot of fiddle. We'd sit for days and days and days just going over stuff. He was called 'Red Tommy'—or 'RT'—because he had red hair. As he got older, he began to call himself Gray Tommy. Malboeuf. It's French and means bad beef." Author's notes, interview with Jim Scancarelli (telephone), 9 August 2020, 3:10 p.m.–5:25 p.m.

65. Author's notes, interview with Jim Scancarelli (telephone), 3 May 2017, 1:00–2:00 p.m.

66. Mark Wingate said: "There was such a café in Winston-Salem that had the 45 of Get Down on Your Knees and Pray, by Bill Monroe. Jim Whitley and I would make the occasional pilgrimage to listen to it a time or two. We probably made quite the sight to the regulars as we reverently leaned down to the speakers to hear better. Maybe we even kneeled." 14 December 2020 (6:57 p.m.) email from Mark Wingate to Lew Stern.

67. 24 August 2020, interview with Jim Scancarelli (telephone), 4:00 p.m.–6:08 p.m.

68. Information accompanying a YouTube presentation of this album on "Take's Bluegrass Album Channel" indicates that the LP "Bluegrass on the Mountain" was recorded in January 1969 at Butner Recording Studios in Rural Hall, North Carolina, and that Cullen Galyean wrote most of the songs. Most of the cuts were recorded in one take after running over them in the studio. The master was released as an "independent" label" by Gert Haedler in Germany, under the name "Homestead." The album photo was taken behind Lanier's Meat Processing Company in Tyro, North Carolina, which was in those days provided a venue for music. The band recorded this album so they would have a souvenir to sell during the tourist season schedule of gigs in Cherokee, North Carolina. See: https://www.youtube.com/watch?v=RIAyzn8Kux4. Also see https://www.discogs.com/The-Border-Mountain-Boys-Bluegrass-On-The-Mountain/release/13134140 and Richard Thompson, "L.W. Lambert Passes," *Bluegrass Today*, 30 January 2014, https://bluegrasstoday.com/l-w-lambert-passes/.

69. https://bluegrasscountrysoul.com/bluegrass-country-soul-festival-musicians/. A single 35 mm print of footage from that 1971 festival was the subject of a project to restore the video "Bluegrass

Country Soul." The original footage was gifted to the Bluegrass Music Hall of Fame and Museum in Owensboro, Kentucky, in November 2019. https://files.constantcontact.com/fc6eeae4701/187584d1-c4a9–44f0-a71f-0b44c2547487.pdf and https://myemail.constantcontact.com/Now-is-the-Time-to-Save-Bluegrass-Country-Soul.html?soid=1130896484047&aid=UBR8WB74NPc.

70. Marty McGee, *Traditional Musicians of the Central Blue Ridge: Old Time, Early Country, Folk and Bluegrass Label Recording Artists, with Discographies* (Jefferson, North Carolina: McFarland, 2000), p. 109.

71. Jim Scancarelli noted that Tommy Malboeuf's biological father was named Hendricks. "Tommy thought it might be spelled Hendrix. The father played guitar and that's how Tommy got the music talent or gene." 21 September 2020 (10:49 p.m.) Text Message from Jim Scancarelli to Lew Stern. Malboeuf taught fiddling in North Carolina perhaps from the late 1980s or early 1990s through at least the early 2000s; one student recalled that his business card read: "Fiddle Lessons? Sure! Call Tommy Malboeuf." Sometime in the late 1990s, Jim made a video of Tommy Malboeuf playing 18 fiddle tunes. The video was intended for his students—and may have been an item he sold along with several cassette tapes that he Malboeuf had made commercially. Malboeuf's son David generously shared a copy of a DVD version of the video that survived in his personal library. Malboeuf appears to have allowed students to record his fiddling, so there would seem to be a cache of cassettes of his fiddling work in attics or basements somewhere. See https://www.youtube.com/watch?v=Bel4a9cpymo. Malboeuf's son Danny ("Kolaboy" on YouTube, https://www.youtube.com/user/kolaboy/featured) has a video (audio only) on his YouTube playlist of his father's original composition, "Andrea's Waltz." https://www.youtube.com/watch?v=Bel4a9cpymo. In the comment section on this YouTube channel, Patrick Malboeuf calls his father "The Ritchie Blackmore of fiddle," a reference to the English guitarist and songwriter who founded the band Deep Purple in 1968 and was known for his "jam-style hard rock music that mixed guitar riffs and organ sounds" (https://en.wikipedia.org/wiki/Ritchie_Blackmore). The musician D.M. Franklin Kane is David Malboeuf, brother to Danny and Patrick, both of whom are guitarists and composers. Kane is a singer, a bassist, and guitarist from Statesville, North Carolina, who has composed and recorded with his band, The Crown Ambassadors. See Jennie Thompson, "Indie Hipster Gives Songs a Reason to Exist," *News and Record* (Greensboro, North Carolina), 21 September 2007. Updated 25 January 2015. https://greensboro.com/life/go_triad/indie-hipster-gives-songs-a-reason-to-exist/article_737e50cd-5ecb-5c25–819c-f513e90b4d25.html.

72. https://www.discogs.com/Big-Country-Bluegrass-Up-In-The-High-Country/release/12028054.

73. Author's notes, interview with Jim Scancarelli (telephone), 20 May 2020 4:13 p.m.–6:38 p.m.

74. When Tommy's mother sold the house on the lake, he moved to an apartment behind a Methodist church. Jim recalled some terrific jam sessions at that place. He also remembered the Bluegrass Mouse. "There was a little mouse hole in the wall where we were jamming, and while we were playing a mouse jumped out. I went to get my camera, and the mouse retreated to its hole. But the creature came out again, stood up on its hind legs, and lingered. I set my camera on telephoto, hit the remote button and got a picture of that mouse. Still have it." 24 August 2020, interview with Jim Scancarelli (telephone), 4:00 p.m.–6:08 p.m.

75. Jim's cousin Doug Deal married a woman whose mother was related to Tommy Malboeuf"s stepmother. Author's notes, interview with Jim Scancarelli (telephone), 21 August 2020, 5:19 p.m.–6:29 p.m. Malboeuf had a fox terrier, a little black and white hound with a white-tipped tail and white socks, who he named "Tip." "He was the most loving dog I'd ever seen," Jim recalled: "You could put him in the palm of your hand when he was a pup." He grew up loving fiddle music. Tommy could tell Tip: "Jim's coming," and the dog would wait by the door until Jim's car appeared. "Then he'd run to the car and I'd have to open the door and give him a lift back to the house. He'd snuggle up inside Jim Greene's guitar case while we were playing music, or just sidle up to me, put his paws on my feet—maybe to keep me from tapping away. At the end of a visit, I'd say goodbye, get into my car, and about a mile down the road I'd discover that Tip had snuck into my car. I'd have to turn around and drive him back home." Tip got hit by a car one morning, crossing a highway on the way back home from visiting a girlfriend. Tommy was heartbroken. He had raised that hound, walked with him to the grocery store and treated him to some liver or chicken which he'd take home and cook up for Tip. He nursed him after he got in a wrestling match with a bobcat that chewed Tip up. Fifty years later, Jim still recalled the depth of Malboeuf's devotion to his little hound. Author's notes, interview with Jim Scancarelli (telephone), 21 August 2020, 5:19 p.m.–6:29 p.m.; 13 November 2020 (8:32 p.m.) Text Message from Jim Scancarelli to Lew Stern.

76. 24 August 2020, interview with Jim Scancarelli (telephone), 4:00 p.m.–6:08 p.m.

77. 24 August 2020, interview with Jim Scancarelli (telephone), 4:00 p.m.–6:08 p.m.

78. 2 November 2020 (11:50 p.m.) Text Message from Jim Scancarelli to Lew Stern. Jim and Tommy may not have played any of the versions of that composition that emerged from their efforts to get at the tune at any of their usual venues for fiddling. If they taped the results of their collaboration, those recordings did not materialize in Jim's personal archive through late 2020. Author's notes, interview with Jim Scancarelli (telephone), 2 November 2020 (11:26 a.m.–12:00 p.m.) Iva Davies, Christopher Gordon and Richard Tognetti wrote the score for the movie version of "La Musica," which can be heard at https://www.youtube.com/watch?v=DXRA5E0YdK4.

79. Jim remembered that Mike Robinson, who recorded and mixed the CD in December 1991, had machinery capable of achieving musical "nuances," and "old ances as well," reflecting the way Jim elevated old groaners to exalted status as classical joke lines in *Gasoline Alley*. He mixed the recording on a small speaker, instead of speakers the size of moving trucks, reasoning that most people only have players with small speakers, so he needed to shoot for something that would be manageable on their listening devices. Author's notes, interview with Jim Scancarelli (telephone), 20 October 2020, 3:05 p.m.–5:12 p.m.

80. Author's notes, interview with Jim Scancarelli (telephone), 20 October 2020, 3:05 p.m.–5:12 p.m. Tommy Malboeuf often said the bluegrass bands he heard in the late 1980s at festivals began to move bluegrass from what Bill Monroe hoped to achieve to a newer bluegrass: "They play the pretty out of it." Tommy thought what he heard in the 1990s was "running scales," not music; "Bluegrass died when Monroe did." What Tommy liked about the old music was the evocative, emotionally raw quality of simple tunes and songs that came from mill workers, farmers, entertaining themselves. Author's notes, interview with Jim Scancarelli (telephone), 20 October 2020, 3:05 p.m.–5:12 p.m.

81. Author's notes, interview with Jim Scancarelli (telephone), 19 November 2020, 3:50 p.m.–4:55 p.m.

82. https://en.wikipedia.org/wiki/Sheb_Wooley.

83. https://en.wikipedia.org/wiki/Tommy_Sands_(American_singer); Author's notes, interview with Jim Scancarelli (telephone), 20 May 2020 4:13 p.m.–6:38 p.m.

84. Author's notes, interview with Jim Scancarelli (telephone), 20 May 2020, 4:13 p.m.–6:38 p.m.; Tim Clodfelter, "Western Film Fair Coming Back to Winston-Salem for One Last Ride," *Greensboro News and Record*, 20 June 2017. https://www.greensboro.com/entertainment/film_tv/western-film-fair-coming-back-to-winston-salem-for-one-last-ride/article_5a9e5bd6–5052–5b2e-aed1-ea5b10babb62.html.

85. "Guthrie T. Meade, May 17, 1932—February 8, 1991." Hillbilly Music: Source and Symbol. ("Biographical Note," Guthrie T. Meade Collection (#20246), Southern Folklife Collection, University of North Carolina at Chapel Hill.) https://exhibits.lib.unc.edu/exhibits/show/hillbilly_music/biographies/meade.

86. Bethany Fuller, "Fiddler's Grove Festival Keeps Focus on Family Atmosphere," *Statesville Record and Landmark*, 29 March 2011, https://statesville.com/news/fiddlers-grove-festival-keeps-focus-on-family-atmosphere/article_c74a87b7-bb51–5afa-a10b-eec6e1d16b26.html.

87. https://www.discogs.com/Various-Fiddlers-Grove-Ole-Time-Fiddlers-Bluegrass-Festival-1974-Vol-5-/release/14510769.

88. 18 August 2020 (10:07 a.m.) email from Joe Cline to Lew Stern; Author's notes, interview with Chuck Dunlop (telephone), 16 September 2020, 11:00 a.m.–11:39 a.m.

89. https://en.wikipedia.org/wiki/Clark_Kessinger.

90. Author's notes, interview with Jim Scancarelli (telephone), 21 July 2020, 3:45 p.m.–4:57 p.m.

91. Jim recalled: "If we played 'Mississippi Sawyer,' Gene would not be playing melody, but his chord patterns just dragged the music out of me. In essence, he was playing the tune, but just not canned licks." 9 November 2020 (4:59 p.m.) Text Message from Jim Scancarelli to Lew Stern; Author's notes, interview with Jim Scancarelli (telephone), 9 November 2020, 11:00 a.m.–11:30 a.m. As one review proclaimed: "Gene Meade (Eden) set the mold for backing up fiddlers with his driving, spectacular guitar styles. A recently released DVD of Gene's appearance at the 1964 Newport Folk Festival has hundreds of young guitarists trying to emulate his style." *Rockingham County Musicians,* Museum and Archives of Rockingham County, 28 October 2019. https://themarconline.org/archived/rockingham-county-musicians "Playing with a guitarist who has a strong drive and the confidence to take control can make that a whole lot easier. Prime example in my opinion is Uncle Dennis Hall from Galax, Virginia. Dennis learned from Clark Kessinger's guitarist, Gene Meade. He has a strong drive, smooth, balanced tone, and runs that provide extra drive (and even a little kick wherever it might be needed)." In "What Fiddlers Like in Old-time Backup Guitar—In Their Own Words," *Oldtime Central*, 26 November 2019, https://oldtime-central.com/what-fiddlers-like-in-oldtime-backup-guitar-in-their-own-words/.

92. Author's notes, interview with Jim Scancarelli (telephone), 19 August 2020, 10:44 a.m.–11:15 a.m. Jim remembered a Dirt Creek Band gig in a bar during which a patron threw a beer bottle at the band; Jim believes to this day, forty years later, that the projectile was meant for him. "Something whizzed past my ear, and I heard a crash. We were on a small stage with our backs toward the plate glass window in the front of the establishment, and that shattered. Had the bottle connected with my head, you wouldn't be doing this book today." Author's notes, interview with Jim Scancarelli (telephone), 21 August 2020, 5:19 p.m.–6:29 p.m. and Author's notes, interview with Jim Scancarelli (telephone), 8 September 2020, 3:00 p.m.–4:34 p.m.

93. 24 August 2020, interview with Jim Scancarelli (telephone), 4:00 p.m.–6:08 p.m. The banjo player, Tommy Joy, suggested that it was a pick-up band that was together very briefly, and may have used the name "Pine Ridge Boys," though that memory might not be sturdy enough to swear to.

94. Tommy Joy built banjos and banjo necks in the Charlotte, North Carolina, area through at least mid–2016. https://www.banjohangout.org/archive/319975 and https://www.banjohangout.org/archive/126791.

95. Eugene Chadbourne, "Mountain Ramblers: Artist Biography," https://www.allmusic.com/artist/mountain-ramblers-mn0000408384.

96. Author's notes, interview with Jim Scancarelli

(telephone), 19 August 2020, 10:44 a.m.–11:15 a.m. Joe Cline recalled that the band leader was Jim Sharpe, and that Sharpe did the booking work for that band. Thus, it was probably Sharpe who booked the band into what was known as the New Dixie Saloon. 23 November 2020 (8:48 a.m.) email from Joe Cline to Lew Stern.

97. 29 November 2020 (2:38 p.m.) Text Message from Jim Scancarelli to Lew Stern.

98. Author's notes, interview with Jim Scancarelli (telephone), 23 June 2020, 3:16 p.m.–5:48 p.m.

99. In 1993, Debbie Larsen was in the Gold Hill Band with Enoch Rutherford, Wiley Mayo, Dale Morris and Dave Lawson. Martha Spencer and Erika Godfrey, "Remembering Enoch Rutherford," *Mountain Music Magazine*, 18 June 2018, https://mountainmusicmagazine.weebly.com/mountain-music-legacies/remembering-enoch-rutherford.

100. https://www.facebook.com/photo.php?fbid=4839920590007&set=a.1638992088795&type=3&theater.

101. Author's notes, interview with Jim Scancarelli (telephone), 19 August 2020, 10:44 a.m.–11:15 a.m. See https://jeanettewilliams.com/ and Murphy Hicks Henry, *Pretty Good for a Girl: Women in Bluegrass* (Chicago: University of Illinois Press, 2013), p. 333.

102. Jim said: "Holy Mackerel, you could play one of those tunes for 20 minutes. Wears you out. That's how I got my wrist all out of shape. Author's notes, interview with Jim Scancarelli (telephone), 20 May 2020, 4:13 p.m.–6:38 p.m. At a 24 August 2020 one-hour picking session on Facebook, Joe Cline and Glen Alexander agreed: "The best thing about contra dances is that nobody listens to the music. And we can get to learn the tune in the first ten minutes of playing it for a dance." https://www.facebook.com/TheViolinShoppe.

103. Author's notes, interview with Jim Scancarelli (telephone), 18 August 2020, 4:00 p.m.–6:02 p.m.

104. Author's notes, interview with Jim Scancarelli (telephone), 21 August 2020, 5:19 p.m.–6:29 p.m.

105. https://nativeground.com/a-word-about-the-free-bluegrass-fiddle-tabs/.

106. https://www.youtube.com/watch?v=a2qM2JRoGQ0.

107. https://www.youtube.com/watch?v=qONNDALk-Bg&t=166s.

108. https://www.youtube.com/watch?v=qONNDALk-Bg.

109. "Notes and Queries," *Bluegrass Unlimited*, November 1988, p. 17, and Author's notes, interview with Jim Scancarelli (telephone), 31 August 2020, 3:39 p.m.–4:30 p.m. The terms of art used to refer to a particular local or regional way of playing traditional banjo or fiddle tunes—the use of the term "style" versus "sound"—have been part of long discussion of the extent to which Round Peak represents something distinct from Galax type old-time music, whether music of that sort played in Galax differs from Surry County traditions, when these geographic terms became associated with a particular sound or style. Ruchala made the case that "these techniques were associated with the playing of Kyle Creed, who lived at the time near Galax, Virginia. Given the importance of the Galax Old Fiddlers' Convention and the influence of Creed, who lived near Galax in the 1970s, it is perhaps understandable that these quirks of North Carolina banjo picking came to be known (if briefly) by the Galax, Virginia name." James Randolph Ruchala, *Making Round Peak Music: History, Revitalization and Community*, a dissertation submitted to the Department of Music, for the degree of Doctor of Philosophy, Brown University, May 2011, pp. 412–413. Jim's use of the term "Galax Sound" seemed to be keyed to the goal of distinguishing between old-time music and early bluegrass music in an area broader than Galax or Round Peak. Since much of his exposure to those different styles took place at festivals, it is reasonable to say that he was talking about a piece of North Carolina that encompassed his "area of operation" in and around Charlotte, extending to the areas where fiddlers' conventions that Jim attended in the 1970s in and around Ball's Creek, Northmoor, Star, Mooresville, Albemarle and elsewhere. Author's notes, interview with Jim Scancarelli (telephone), 3 May 2017, 1:00–2:00 p.m. However, his use of that term "Galax sound" probably had less to do with the way the regions and localities thought of their specific musical traditions, and more to do with the kinds of fiddling—and banjo playing—he heard at Galax, and associated with fiddlers who he met at the Galax festival, meaning it was probably a far more informal use of the term than the sources Ruchala pointed to in explicating issues related to Galax and Round Peak style.

110. Jim said: "Otis played 'Fortune' like nobody's business." Author's notes, interview with Jim Scancarelli (telephone), 27 August 2020, 4:00 p.m.–6:12 p.m. See "Otis Burris and Fortune," https://www.youtube.com/watch?v=iVxy-kP0jWU. Burris was born in 1917 in western Grayson County, Virginia. The liner notes that accompanied the Field Recorders' Collective 2012 release "Parley Parsons—Old Galax Fiddling" (FRC 705, 2012) state that Burris was "of the first generation of mountain fiddlers influenced by radio and phonograph." https://fieldrecorder.org/product/parley-parsons-old-galax-fiddling/. He was captured on four cuts on a County Records 1966 release "Virginia Breakdown" (County Records 705) playing with The Mountain Ramblers. https://www.discogs.com/release/8408760. See Eugene Chadbourne, "Mountain Ramblers." https://www.allmusic.com/artist/mountain-ramblers-mn0000408384. Burris was recorded playing fiddle on two tunes with the Camp Creek Boys at the Hillsville Fiddlers' Convention in Hillsville, Virginia, in 1969. They played "Arkansas Traveler" and "Fortune," and were captured in a field recording by Kilby Spencer. https://soundcloud.com/kilby-albert-spencer/sets/otis-burris-with-the-camp. Alice Gerrard recorded Burris, along with James Lindsey, Eldridge Montgomery, Wendell

Cockerham, on 8 January 1987 at Burris' home in Galax, Virginia. Southern Folklife Cassette FS-200006/8714 (digitized), https://finding-aids. lib.unc.edu/20006/. Hank Bradley said of Otis Burris' fiddling: "I had a lot of time intently observing Otis Burris, watching his bow arm and I take my bowing from Otis, as much as I could in those days. [...] He played in a very relaxed and fluid way but if he wanted an accent, he'd change bow directions. That's about the simplest way to explain it. And he could play as smooth as he wanted or he could play as rough as he wanted. Totally flexible. I've been trying to do that ever since." Jody Stecher, "The Incomparable Hank Bradley," *Fiddler Magazine*, Fall 2020, Volume 27, Number 3, p. 7.

111. "Bluegrass Discography." Steve Kilby, 11/26/54. Heritage, 1988. https://www.ibiblio.org/hill william/BGdiscography/?v=fullrecord&albumid= 3416.

112. Author's notes, interview with Jim Scancarelli (telephone), 27 August 2020, 4:00 p.m.–6:12 p.m.

113. Author's notes, interview with Jim Scancarelli (telephone), 27 August 2020, 4:00 p.m.–6:12 p.m.

114. Author's notes, interview with Jim Scancarelli (telephone), 27 August 2020, 4:00 p.m.–6:12 p.m. Reddick had a building on his farmland that he turned into a venue called "The Old Music House." Kenny Baker played fiddle with Bill Monroe from 1957 to 1959, during which time he recorded two notable instrumentals, "Panhandle Country" and "Scotland"—twin-fiddled with Bobby Hicks. In 1958, Baker went back to working in mines, but rejoined Monroe in 1962. In 1968, with his children grown up, he felt free to re-enlist with Monroe for a third time, from 1968 to 1983. See https://www.bluegrasshall.org/inductees/kenny-baker/. Sometime in 1968 or so, Kenny Baker went to spend some time at Joe Greene's home, and during that time Baker and Greene visited, and traded tunes at, Reddick's "Old Music House." Robert White saw both of them jam there after one of the shows that took place at Reddick's Old Music House. In 1968, County Records released "High Country" featuring Kenny Baker and Joe Greene (Country 714). White speculated that the Country Records LP might have emerged as an idea at the jam he witnessed at Jack Reddick's home. Author's notes, interview with Bob White (telephone), 17 September 2020, 10:30 a.m.–11:20 a.m. Robert "Quail" White remembered: "Kenny Baker left Monroe for a period of some months, and to the best of my knowledge lived with Joe Greene during that time. The two of them came to 'The Old Music House' several times during that period. I was lucky enough to be there two or three times when late night sessions took place after hours. Greene and Baker were the 'star attractions' and I sat in playing bass and guitar along with several others of the New Deal String Band /Ashe Avenue 'Conservatory of Bluegrass Music' crowd. I recall Allen McCanless, Ray Blackwell, Buck Peacock, Rodney Hutchins, Gene Knight, Durwood

Edwards, Frank Greathouse were all in attendance." 21 September 2020 (6:41 p.m.) email from Robert White to Lew Stern. Bob "Quail" White met Jim Scancarelli at a fiddlers' convention in Elkin, North Carolina, in the mid–1960s. White was immersed in the Chapel Hill old-time and bluegrass music scene dating to the days of the big white house on Ashe Ave in the mid–1960s where all the Bluegrass musicians lived and picked over in Raleigh, North Carolina. White became the bass player in the New Deal String Band. Al McCanless was the fiddler and one of the founding members of that band along with Buck Peacock, Leroy Savage, Gene Knight and Frank Greathouse.

115. Andrew Wallace, "NFFA to NCTA: The Organization Broadens Its Mission," *Folklife Center News*, Spring 2002, Volume 24, Number 2, pp. 3–10; Joseph McLellan, "A 'Bluegrass' Festival at Wolftrap," *Washington Post*, 11 July 1977. https://www. washingtonpost.com/archive/lifestyle/1977/07/11/ a-bluegrass-festival-at-wolftrap/b0b53e10–4607– 4efc-8b29–151f0b8960c0/.

116. Author's notes, interview with Jim Scancarelli (telephone), 21 May 2020 3:10 p.m.–5:53 p.m.

117. Hartford, *Steamboat in a Cornfield* (New York: Crown Publishers, Inc., 1986).

118. Author's notes, interview with Jim Scancarelli (telephone), 21 May 2020 3:10 p.m.–5:53 p.m.

119. Author's notes, interview with Jim Scancarelli (telephone), 21 July 2020, 3:45 p.m.–4:57 p.m.

120. https://classic-banjo.ning.com/xn/detail/26 67446:Comment:107893.

121. Author's notes, interview with Jim Scancarelli (telephone), 27 August 2020, 4:00 p.m.–6:12 p.m.

122. Thinking back on the performance repertoire of the Mole Hill Highlanders, Jim thought that the band may not have been playing tunes the way they were "written." The Mole Hill Highlanders "were playing the music they felt." The "sound" of the band emerged from the way the players figured out how to complement one another. Mark Wingate "seconded" Clyde Williams. Jim "filled in the holes" that emerged at transitional points in tunes and sought to give the band the energy to drive forward at the beginning of phrases, to give the tune enough kick to get it from the first part of a traditional tune to the second part. Chuck Dunlop's guitar kept the band on the right timing for a tune; in keeping with Clyde's insistence on guitar work that played down melodic runs, Dunlop stuck to chords. "We were tight," he said of the Mole Hill Highlanders. Playing with that band gave Jim "the finest times I ever had in my life." Author's notes, interview with Jim Scancarelli (telephone), 15 September 2020, 3:45 p.m.–5:07 p.m. and 16 September 2020 (10:36 p.m.) email from Chuck Dunlop to Lew Stern.

123. Author's notes, interview with Jim Scancarelli (telephone), 27 August 2020, 4:00 p.m.–6:12 p.m.

124. Jim's recollection was that Rafe Brady was the fiddler who transposed Ebeneezer from the

key of G to F. "Jack Reddick told me about it and I liked it in that gear. In G it sounds more traditional or old-timey. When in F ... it opened the tune up for some improvements and, as Jack said, some smooth gliding patterns. Almost like a new tune." Rafe Brady's album "Cherokee Rose" (Heritage Records, 1981) contains a cut of "Ebeneezer" played in F (Side B, Cut 8). 14 October 2020 (9:13 p.m.) Text Message from Jim Scancarelli to Lew Stern; https://www.discogs.com/Rafe-Brady-Cherokee-Rose/release/9676354. The County Sales website says this about Rafe Brady: "Brady was one of a handful of near legendary musicians from the rich musical area around Galax, Va. and Mr. Airy, N.C. He played with many professional bands but did little or no recording while in his prime years." https://www.countysales.com/products/24974?variant=12292077027431.

Brady was 68 years old when the Heritage label LP was recorded. Brady was accompanied on various cuts by Ron Mullenex (clawhammer banjo), Tom Mylet (clawhammer banjo), Bobby Patterson (bluegrass banjo), and Dale Morris (guitar and bass). https://www.discogs.com/Rafe-Brady-Cherokee-Rose/release/9676354. Jim's version of "Ebenezer" in the key of F—"F-eneezer"—was captured on the 11th track of the recording by Jim on "Bluegrass Sanitary Cafe" (Old Oblivion OO-5). That triggered some memories for Jim: "Jimmy Vipperman played Ebeneezer in F and was real slick with it. His daddy Johnny Vipperman used to be a sideman with Bill Monroe and often played with Johnny and Jeanette's Clearwater band. One year we played at Mountain Park contest and Johnny Vipperman won 1st guitar by just playing loud solid G runs behind us. He was a great picker and friend." 15 October 2020 Text Message (9:13 p.m.) from Jim Scancarelli to Lew Stern.

125. Author's notes, interview with Jim Scancarelli (telephone), 27 August 2020, 4:00 p.m.–6:12 p.m.

126. Jim added: "As Chick Martin said, 'It's in there, but getting it out ... meaning that 'getting it out' is another proposition altogether." 9 November 2020 (4:59 p.m.) Text Message from Jim Scancarelli to Lew Stern; Author's notes, interview with Jim Scancarelli (telephone), 9 November 2020, 11:00 a.m.–11:30 a.m.

127. Author's notes, interview with Jim Scancarelli (telephone), 27 August 2020, 4:00 p.m.–6:12 p.m.

128. In Jim's recollection, Gus Meade compiled about 20 names by which the tune "Sweet Sixteen" had come to be known, including "Buffalo Nickle," a name Jim was never really able to relate to the basic theme of the tune which had to do with a young maiden. Author's notes, interview with Jim Scancarelli (telephone), 27 August 2020, 4:00 p.m.–6:12 p.m.

129. Author's notes, interview with Jim Scancarelli (telephone), 27 August 2020, 4:00 p.m.–6:12 p.m. "You talk about pain," Jim said, and immediately that called to mind the character Peter Pain, the "mascot" created for Ben Gay, the pain-relieving salve. Peter Pain "was a lump-jawed, toad like demon with a bowler hat." He came armed with a pitchfork; Jim said at that moment in his fiddling career, it felt like one had been jabbed into Jim's fiddling hand. Author's notes, interview with Jim Scancarelli (telephone), 27 August 2020, 4:00 p.m.–6:12 p.m. See https://www.flickr.com/photos/neatocoolville/8306105398.

130. Author's notes, interview with Jim Scancarelli (telephone), 28 June 2020, 4:06 p.m.–5:07 p.m.

131. Jim would wake up in a sweat from this was a recurring theme. Author's notes, interview with Jim Scancarelli (telephone), 31 May 2020, 3:15 p.m.–5:47 p.m. Years later, Jim wondered what that might have meant, perhaps in Freudian terms. When the connection between the linguini image and his family name was pointed out, he felt he finally found a basis for understanding that dream.

132. Jim told this story: "The Mole Hill Highlanders went to Galax one year. Cold. Frost on the ground in August! Clyde Williams was not with us. Kyle Creed comes up and says, 'I've been walking around listening to all the bands. Not much music on the ground.' We played a tune for him, and he said: 'Well, still not much music on the ground.'"

133. Scancarelli, "The Old Cross Roads," *Bluegrass Unlimited*, January 2000, p. 5.

Chapter Five

1. Author's notes, interview with Jim Scancarelli (telephone), 24 August 2020, 4:00 p.m.–6:08 p.m. Jim remembered that at some point, later in his life, he answered the query about careers by suggesting he'd be interested in pursuing work as a dog masseuse. 9 November 2020 (4:59 p.m.) Text Message from Jim Scancarelli to Lew Stern; Author's notes, interview with Jim Scancarelli (telephone), 9 November 2020, 11:00 a.m.–11:30 a.m. The thread in *Gasoline Alley* in which Walt weaves a story about a life of adventure as an archeologist starts on 6 January 2014 and runs to 8 March 2014 with the heart of the story about the safari running from mid–January to early February 2014. Jim gave an original piece of *Gasoline Alley* artwork from this thread to his old friend Wiley C. Grant III during a visit that reunited the friends not long after that story was published. See https://www.gocomics.com/gasolinealley/2014/01/06 to https://www.gocomics.com/gasolinealley/2014/03/08.

2. Author's notes, interview with Jim Scancarelli (telephone), 23 June 2020, 3:16 p.m.–5:48 p.m.

3. Author's notes, interview with Jim Scancarelli (telephone), 23 June 2020, 3:16 p.m.–5:48 p.m.

4. Author's notes, interview with Jim Scancarelli (telephone), 20 May 2020, 4:13 p.m.–6:38 p.m. Jim stated: "in those days it was difficult, if not impossible, for a lady to break into a male-dominated field. That's why Dalia Messick changed her name to Dale and went on the create *Brenda Starr*. Folks thought she was a man!" Jim Scancarelli, "Premium Memories," *Dialogue*, April 1997.

5. Author's notes, interview with Jim Scancarelli (telephone), 20 May 2020, 4:13 p.m.–6:38 p.m.

6. Author's notes, interview with Jim Scancarelli (telephone), 20 May 2020, 4:13 p.m.–6:38 p.m. Jim planned his *Gasoline Alley* stories out 4 to 6 months ahead, so in late August 2020 he was contemplating the strip that would appear just ahead of Christmas that year. He envisioned a strip that had Bunky asking Santa why he laughed so much, to which Santa would reply: "Because I only work one day a year." In another frame, Bunky would proclaim: "This will be the greatest Christmas ever," to which Santa a would add: "But none will ever beat that wonderful first one." Jim also envisioned shepherds playing Sicilian bagpipes ("zampogna") in the Nativity scene, instruments that had a shape reminiscent of what would result, Jim said, if you butchered a cow, put a set of pipes on the carcass, and inflated it." That got Jim to thinking about a story his father told of the "old country," Sicily, where the practice during Christmas was that if a family placed a wooden spoon outside, in front of a door or a window, the shepherds would know to play Novena music at that home. The shepherds would either be invited to eat a meal with the family or they would receive some money for sharing their music. Years later, Jim found a recording of zampogna music, and recalled it was decidedly atonal in character. Author's notes, interview with Jim Scancarelli (telephone), 27 August 2020, 4:00 p.m.–6:12 p.m.

7. In late October 2020, after a long week of work ("slinging the ink") on the *Gasoline Alley* strips for February 2021, Jim thought about how his mother taught him drawing, writing the letters of the alphabet, and other life skills, and he remembered how his mother taught him to read: "There is a teaching method called the Montessori System. Momma used her own variation of this to teach me to read and write way before kindergarten. She made a game out of a lot of it, drawing cartoons, not unlike what they do on Sesame Street nowadays." 27 October 2020 (1:08 a.m.) Text Message from Jim Scancarelli to Lew Stern.

8. Author's notes, interview with Jim Scancarelli (telephone), 19 October 2020, 5:11 p.m.–5:30 p.m.; 21 October 2020 (2:25 p.m.) Text Message from Jim Scancarelli to Lew Stern.

9. "You had to have ten cents to buy a comic. I didn't have any money at all. One time I asked Daddy for ten cents for a comic book. He finally got it, but [...] money was tight. Ten cents was a lot of money." Author's notes, interview with Jim Scancarelli (telephone), 23 June 2020, 3:16 p.m.–5:48 p.m.

10. Author's notes, interview with Jim Scancarelli (telephone), 23 June 2020, 3:16 p.m.–5:48 p.m.

11. "I even wanted to work for Al Capp but that never happened. The way he drew, that was a big influence." Author's notes, interview with Jim Scancarelli (telephone), 23 June 2020, 3:16 p.m.–5:48 p.m.

12. "Wash Tubbs was an American daily comic strip created by Roy Crane and Leslie Turner that ran from April 14, 1924 to 1949, when it merged into Crane's related Sunday page, Captain Easy." https://en.wikipedia.org/wiki/Wash_Tubbs.

13. Jim heard that many cartoonists, at least those in his age cohort who went on to illustrate and write strips for the syndicates, probably had a long spell as sickly kids that confined them to bed rest, and they drew cartoon characters for their own entertainment. "I talked with many of the old guard cartoonists who voiced similar hypotheses." 9 November 2020 (4:59 p.m.) Text Message from Jim Scancarelli to Lew Stern; Author's notes, interview with Jim Scancarelli (telephone), 9 November 2020, 11:00 a.m.–11:30 a.m. Interestingly, not long after that health challenge, Jim and his mother moved to Charlotte, and a doctor there had a very different recommendation for Jim's care in the aftermath of his bout with illness: the doctor told Jim to get outside and play in the sunshine. By that time, though, his relationship with Dick Tracy, Amos and Andy, Little Orphan Annie, Sergeant Preston, the Green Hornet and others, was firmly cemented. Author's notes, interview with Jim Scancarelli (telephone), 20 July 2020, 5:30–6:30 p.m.

14. Author's notes, interview with Jim Scancarelli (telephone), 7 August 2020, 3:00 p.m.–4:55 p.m. and "Jim Scancarelli, Class of 1959 in Wakefield High School's Hall of Fame," *Warrior News*, Fall 2017. http://comicsdc.blogspot.com/2017/11/jim-scancarelli-class-of-1959-from.html.

15. Author's notes, interview with Jim Scancarelli (telephone), 27 June 2020, 3:10 p.m.–5:13 p.m.

16. Tribune publisher Robert McCormick sold the *Times-Herald* to the *Washington Post* in 1954. "In March 1954, the *Times-Herald* was purchased by Philip Graham, owner of the *Post*. For a time, the combined paper was officially known as *The Washington Post and Times-Herald*, but the *Post* consolidated its market position by discontinuing the rival paper. The *Times-Herald* portion of the nameplate became less and less prominent on a second line in ensuing years and was dropped entirely in 1973." https://en.wikipedia.org/wiki/Washington_Times-Herald.

17. Author's notes, interview with Jim Scancarelli (telephone), 23 June 2020, 3:16 p.m.–5:48 p.m.

18. Author's notes, interview with Jim Scancarelli (telephone), 23 June 2020, 3:16 p.m.–5:48 p.m.

19. Author's notes, interview with Jim Scancarelli (telephone), 23 June 2020, 3:16 p.m.–5:48 p.m. In 1988, Jim won the Best Story Strip award— bestowed at the 1989 gathering of the National Cartoon Society in Canada. Right after that, the Society eliminated that award, explaining that story strips had diminished in number, so the category was no longer viable. Author's notes, interview with Jim Scancarelli (telephone), 27 August 2020, 4:00 p.m.–6:12 p.m. Also see https://www.pinterest.com/pin/299207968966650350/ and Anton Emdin, "Spotted: The Jack Davis Knockout," 21 April 2011, https://www.antonemdin.com/blog/2011/04/spotted-jack-davis-knockout.

20. Sam Sweet, "A Boy with No Birthday Turns Sixty," *The Paris Review*, 3 March 2016, https://www.theparisreview.org/blog/2016/03/03/a-boy-with-no-birthday-turns-sixty/.

21. Author's notes, interview with Jim Scancarelli (telephone), 23 June 2020, 3:16 p.m.–5:48 p.m.

22. Author's notes, interview with Jim Scancarelli (telephone), 20 October 2020, 3:05 p.m.–5:12 p.m.

23. https://www.nationalcartoonists.com/in-memoriam/george-breisacher/.

24. Author's notes, interview with Jim Scancarelli (telephone), 23 June 2020, 3:16 p.m.–5:48 p.m.

25. 9 November 2020 (4:59 p.m.) Text Message from Jim Scancarelli to Lew Stern; Author's notes, interview with Jim Scancarelli (telephone), 9 November 2020, 11:00 a.m.–11:30 a.m.

26. "William Morgan DeBeck (April 15, 1890 – November 11, 1942), better known as Billy DeBeck, was an American cartoonist. He is most famous as the creator of the comic strip *Barney Google*, later retitled *Barney Google and Snuffy Smith*. The strip was especially popular in the 1920s and 1930s, and featured a number of well-known characters, including the title characters, Bunky, and Spark Plug the racehorse. Spark Plug was a merchandising phenomenon, and has been called the Snoopy of the 1920s." https://en.wikipedia.org/wiki/Billy_DeBeck.

27. From his contacts with other *Gasoline Alley* assistants, Jim discerned how to conduct himself in his relationship with the artist, and how to manage his relationships with the decision-makers who were part-owners of the strip and represented the business interests that were responsible for making decisions about comic strip placement in news media. Jim said, of the assistants: "Talking with them I learned what to do, what not to do, what to say." Author's notes, interview with Jim Scancarelli (telephone), 10 July 2020 2:00 p.m.–4:08 p.m.

28. Zschiesche went on to develop a new approach to editorial cartooning that depicted ordinary citizens commenting on their concerns. Every cartoon was set in an actual locale with the people standing in front of picturesque Victorian houses or local landmarks. His cartoon *Our Folks*, which he syndicated himself, appeared first in in 1980. Zschiesche eventually signed up 38 papers through self-syndication. See R.C. Harvey, "Growing Old in Gasoline Alley: Ninety-Four Years and Counting," *The Comics Journal*, 17 January 2013, http://www.tcj.com/growing-old-in-gasoline-alley-ninety-four-years-and-counting/.

29. "Albert Tolf (1911–1996)." Lambiek Comicopedia. https://www.lambiek.net/artists/t/tolf_albert.htm

30. Author's notes, interview with Jim Scancarelli (telephone), 10 July 2020 2:00 p.m.–4:08 p.m.

31. Author's notes, interview with Jim Scancarelli (telephone), 10 July 2020 2:00 p.m.–4:08 p.m. Marcus Hamilton's apprenticeship with Hank Ketcham differed from Jim's "training" time with Moores. Jim was at Moores' home often, since they both lived in North Carolina. Hamilton had to conduct his relationship with Ketcham, who lived in Monterey, California, via the post, in telephone conversations, and occasional visits. His entry level "orientations" during a first visit to Ketcham's studios endured as critical lessons. He recalled Ketcham stressing that for a daily that consisted of one panel, the writer/illustrator needed to capture the "complete story" in one image. That image, Ketcham taught, would emerge from working the strip as though the writer/illustrator was the director of a movie, and at the same time the photographer working the production, with the responsibility of blocking out the actions, postures, positions of the characters in the strip who for this purpose became the movie actors. "You need to move your vision all the way around [the panel] as a director would, capturing the best perspectives." "You have ten seconds of a reader's time every day," Ketcham told Hamilton. "The drawing must capture the reader's attention, and then they will read the caption." Those were critical lessons to Hamilton, but perhaps the most important take-away that Hamilton retained was Ketcham's counsel that if the cartoonist has fun doing the work, readers will pick up on that. Once it stopped being fun, readers will pick up on that, too. After about 30 years of freelance work, and 25 years on the job doing the daily *Dennis the Menace* strip, Hamilton remained amazed that he had managed to end up with a lifetime's worth of amazing opportunities. Author's notes, interview with Jim Scancarelli (telephone), 10 July 2020, 2:00 p.m.–4:08 p.m. and Author's notes, interview with Marcus Hamilton (telephone), 2 September 2020, 10:28 a.m.–11:13 a.m.

32. The artwork for *Gasoline Alley* changed over time, Jim noted: "If you look at Frank King's stuff, it is thinner line—but of course he did the drawing bigger. Those things ran like six columns wide. They were huge. So, he had a lot of freedom to do very, very thin lines and they reproduced well. Nowadays, the way things are reproduced, you can hardly even read them with a magnifying glass. That's where the fallacy comes in. Newspaper editors want the comic strips to appeal to young readers, and every kid book that you see has got very big type because young eyes can't focus on small lettering. Now, they are defeating themselves by reducing the size of the columns. I'm just wondering whether the newspaper business is going to be a thing of the past just like the steam engine, radio—years are changing. Granddaddy was right." Author's notes, interview with Jim Scancarelli (telephone), 23 June 2020, 3:16 p.m.–5:48 p.m.

33. Author's notes, interview with Jim Scancarelli (telephone), 10 July 2020 2:00 p.m.–4:08 p.m.

34. Jim noted: "I have a friend, Matt Masterson, who outside of Boston. He is *the* Dick Tracy collector. He has thousands and thousands of pieces of the original art. That's a story in itself, hunting up the original art. Matt had the chance to draw and write Dick Tracy at the point the Syndicate decided to replace Chester Gould. He knew Chester pretty well. He turned it down because, as Milton Caniff once said, being a cartoonist is like being a sequestered monk. Chained up to the drawing board. Very little free time. Matt did not want that in his life." Author's notes, interview with Jim Scancarelli (telephone), 23 June 2020, 3:16 p.m.–5:48 p.m.

35. "One time I didn't get a check and I asked Dick Moores very delicately if he had written me a check, and he said, oh, yeah. I told him I didn't get it. Several days later he called up and said that one of the dogs ate the thing. He dropped the check on the floor and the dog ate it. He had positive proof of that several days later." Author's notes, interview with Jim Scancarelli (telephone), 23 June 2020, 3:16 p.m.–5:48 p.m.

36. Jim remembered: "Every day we would walk the dogs around the pond. We'd go around the perimeter, and invariable some cows would wander in from the farm that was next door and they would go through the fence and they would—how should we delicately say this?—they would leave reminders of their presence. These Dobermans made a bee line for the cow pies. They rolled in it. They licked it. They scraped at it. Then they'd jump into the pond and get soaking wet. And guess who got to clean them up? And, boy, taking the dogs to the vet. That was a scream. Those dogs were so friendly, I got along great with them. But come the day they'd have to go to the vet, I'd have to round them up, and they knew it was veterinarian day. I don't know how they knew, but they knew, and they would not come when they were called. They wouldn't get in the car. I'd have to round them up, pick one up and physically put him in the car. Close the car door, go get another one. Open up the car door, and the first one would run out. It was like herding cattle or kitty cats or something. But we got it done." Author's notes, interview with Jim Scancarelli (telephone), 23 June 2020, 3:16 p.m.–5:48 p.m.

37. Author's notes, interview with Jim Scancarelli (telephone), 23 June 2020, 3:16 p.m.–5:48 p.m.

38. Author's notes, interview with Jim Scancarelli (telephone), 27 June 2020 3:10 p.m.–5:13 p.m.

39. Author's notes, interview with Jim Scancarelli (telephone), 27 June 2020 3:10 p.m.–5:13 p.m.

40. Author's notes, interview with Marcus Hamilton (telephone), 2 September 2020, 10:28 a.m.–11:13 a.m.

41. Author's notes, interview with Jim Scancarelli (telephone), 10 July 2020, 2:00 p.m.–4:08 p.m.

42. At some point early in Jim's tenure as the solo writer/artist for the strip, the Gillott Company ceased manufacturing them and Jim had to hunt for these instruments in flea markets. Author's Notes, interview with Jim Scancarelli (telephone), 9 October 2020, 3:24 p.m.–4:30 p.m.

43. Jim said: "Bud Fisher started *Mutt and Jeff*. He was a multi-millionaire. And he inspired a lot of other cartoonists because they wanted to be rich like Bud. I think that's what Chester Gould said: 'I want to be like Bud Fisher and make a lot of money.' And he did." Author's notes, interview with Jim Scancarelli (telephone), 23 June 2020, 3:16 p.m.–5:48 p.m.

44. Jim remembered that Ed Mack was a long-time ghost artist on *Mutt and Jeff*. "Ink-Slinger Profiles: Ed Mack," *Stripper's Guide*, 4 August 2011, http://strippersguide.blogspot.com/2011/08/ink-slinger-profiles-ed-mack.html.

45. Author's notes, interview with Jim Scancarelli (telephone), 23 June 2020, 3:16 p.m.–5:48 p.m.

46. Jim pointed out that the *Gasoline Alley* comic started on 24 August 1918, and that his own birthday was 24 August 1941, and that Dick Moores' last strip was 24 August 1980. Author's Notes, interview with Jim Scancarelli (telephone), 9 October 2020, 3:24 p.m.–4:30 p.m.

47. Author's Notes, interview with Jim Scancarelli (telephone), 9 October 2020, 3:24 p.m.–4:30 p.m.

48. That last Sunday strip that served as the vehicle for continuing the storyline carried in prior daily installments of *Gasoline Alley* had Slim taking a box of aerosol cans that he had obtained when he invested the winnings from a contest he had entered in a cottage industry that manufactured sprays that could elevate the spirits, solve a myriad of serious health challenges, and prevent squeaky shoes. When Slim enlists Rufus and Joel to help dig a hole to bury those sprays, they discover the buried U.S. Army transmitter that launches a separate story line that plays out in subsequent dailies. Author's Notes, interview with Jim Scancarelli (telephone), 9 October 2020, 3:24 p.m.–4:30 p.m.

49. Author's Notes, interview with Jim Scancarelli (telephone), 11 October 2020, 11:40 a.m.–12:01 p.m.

50. The introduction of a person of color did not necessarily sit well with some readers, who complained to the *Chicago Tribune* in writing, wondering how they could allow an interracial marital alliance between a white person and a Pacific Islander. This was the mid–1980s. "I got a letter from an irate fan saying that Teeka had black blood! I wrote back that he was right: it was India ink!" 9 November 2020 (4:59 p.m.) Text Message from Jim Scancarelli to Lew Stern; Author's notes, interview with Jim Scancarelli (telephone), 9 November 2020, 11:00 a.m.–11:30 a.m. During the course of his three and a half decades in the *Gasoline Alley* control booth, Jim has introduced an increasingly diverse set of characters in both walk on roles and as regularly featured citizens of the Alley. Additionally, Jim became acutely sensitive to what was acceptable about such matters as race. For example, in a 29 June 1987 strip that introduce a story referencing his beloved radio premium collectibles, Jim referred to "Injun-uity" cards that came packed in breakfast cereal. They each contained various wilderness survival tips. Jim included a Native American who the young *Gasoline Alley* citizen, Rover, encounters in nearby woods who shows Rover some of those outdoor skills. Reflecting on that idea over three decades later, Jim was clear that he could never get away with it these days and would not try. Author's Notes, interview with Jim Scancarelli (telephone), 9 October 2020, 3:24 p.m.–4:30 p.m.

51. See "O. Winston Link." https://en.wikipedia.org/wiki/O._Winston_Link.

52. Author's Notes, interview with Jim Scancarelli (telephone), 9 October 2020, 3:24 p.m.–4:30 p.m.

53. That *Gasoline Alley* storyline included the first use of the phrase, customarily usually uttered by Joel: "Well, Rufus, now you have gone and opened Pandemonium's box," intended as a reference to Pandora's box, but altered to fit the vocabulary that worked for Rufus and Joel. Author's Notes, interview with Jim Scancarelli (telephone), 9 October 2020, 3:24 p.m.–4:30 p.m.

54. Author's Notes, interview with Jim Scancarelli (telephone), 9 October 2020, 3:24 p.m.–4:30 p.m.

55. Author's Notes, interview with Jim Scancarelli (telephone), 9 October 2020, 3:24 p.m.–4:30 p.m.

56. Author's notes, interview with Jim Scancarelli (telephone), 23 June 2020, 3:16 p.m.–5:48 p.m.

57. Author's notes, interview with Jim Scancarelli (telephone), 10 July 2020 2:00 p.m.–4:08 p.m.

58. Kelly began his animation career in 1936 at Disney Studies. Jim noted: "Dick Moores worked for Disney, too. When I was a kid, I would see Uncle Remus and Br'er Rabbit in the funny papers on Sunday. It was continued each week. And Dick Moores was the artist, but I didn't know that. I was fascinated with the artwork. And so, after I got to meet him he was telling me he drew them. I had a book that my grandma or Momma had given me—or both—or maybe it was Santa Claus who gave me the book. It was *Br'er Rabbit Rides the Fox*. Br'er Rabbit was picking the banjo. He had harnessed the fox and was riding him like a horse. This was for little kids my age [in the mid–1940s.]" After Jim got the job as Moores' assistant, on one trip to Moores' home, he took the book and showed it to Moores. Moores drew a picture of Br'er Rabbit in the front of Jim's book and dedicated the book to him. "I thought that was so neat. Anyway, he had a whole lot of cool tales to tell about working at Disney." Author's notes, interview with Jim Scancarelli (telephone), 23 June 2020, 3:16 p.m.–5:48 p.m.

59. Jim said: "Like this story that I was getting ready to be run in early August 2020. I had no idea where this was going to go. I wanted to put the Pye boys in there. They are an unsavory bunch—Joe Pye and his three sons. They escaped from prison and they're likeable, but they are just a little too shady. They'd just as soon steal and think nothing of it. One of the lines that I used in earlier stories featuring the Pye Boys had Joe Pye saying 'What's a matter with you boys? You want to go through life working for a living?' You know what a Joe Pye is? I don't know if it is all over the country. It's in the south and up in the mountains. It's a noxious milkweed, grows big, and it's called a Joe Pye. When they drove, he had an old beat-up pickup truck. The license plate was PI = 3.14. I thought it was funny." Author's notes, interview with Jim Scancarelli (telephone), 23 June 2020, 3:16 p.m.–5:48 p.m.

60. Author's notes, interview with Jim Scancarelli (telephone), 10 July 2020, 2:00 p.m.–4:08 p.m.

61. Jim runs with these ideas to see where the situations might take his characters. He tends to like to use "old gags" repeatedly, and especially likes to put these old jokes in the mouths of Rufus and Joel. Frank, the gentleman who runs the copying business nearby Jim's home, and who scans and electronically sends Jim's strips to the printing plant, is often the last set of eyes set on Jim's original art before they head to Chicago for editing and processing. Frank, Jim reports, will often groan and mutter something about how miraculous it is that Jim manages to get paid for this stuff. Author's notes, interview with Jim Scancarelli (telephone), 20 July 2020, 5:30–6:30 p.m., and 21 July 2020 follow-up notes; Author's notes, interview with Jim Scancarelli (telephone), 23 June 2020, 3:16 p.m.–5:48 p.m.

62. Author's notes, interview with Jim Scancarelli (telephone), 16 November 2020), 6:00 p.m.–6:30 p.m., and https://www.gocomics.com/gasolinealley/2020/11/15.

63. https://www.gocomics.com/gasolinealley/2020/11/22.

64. 22 November 2020 (10:05 a.m.) Text Message from Jim Scancarelli to Lew Stern.

65. Jim corresponded with Les Leverett, the official staff photographer for the Grand Ole Opry from 1960 to 1992. At some point, probably toward the early 2000s, Jim told Leverett that he had been "appointed" the "official" photographer for *Gasoline Alley*. Leverett sent Jim a copy of his book, *Blue Moon of Kentucky: A Journey into the World of Bluegrass and Country Music as Seen Through the Camera Lens of Photo-Journalist Les Leverett* (1996). Author's notes, 23 August 2020 interview with Jim Scancarelli (telephone), 3:19 p.m.–4:59 p.m. Earlier on in the strip, Jim would mention relatives—such as his Uncle Pete—after they had passed away: "I would have Slim going past the cemetery and there would be a gravestone marker, a monument, with their names on it. I would stick friends and relatives in there. I sort of stopped doing it because it got to the point where everybody's dying and no room for the story." Author's notes, interview with Jim Scancarelli (telephone), 10 July 2020, 2:00 p.m.–4:08 p.m.

66. Jim noted that he was intrigued by an article written by Dr. Joel Salinas, who has mirror touch synesthesia. Jim, who has described his own experience of seeing colors when fiddling in various keys, said that he "named Peter Glabella after my Daddy, Peter. Glabella [was a reference to] the space between your eyes." 11 July 2020 (11:38 a.m.) Text Message from Jim Scancarelli to Lew Stern.

67. https://www.gocomics.com/gasolinealley/2011/11/30. Jim also knew Mike Seeger, Pete's half-brother. He met Mike a few times at Galax Fiddlers' Convention and talked to him on the phone numerous times. "We hit it off. I had this fascination of trying to emulate both Kenny Baker and Scotty Stoneman, and Mike had recorded Scotty. Mike sent me some reel-to-reel recordings of Scotty, who was just a fireball on the fiddle. I couldn't believe anybody could play like that—just like I couldn't believe anybody could draw like Jack Davis and Wally Wood of *Mad Magazine*. These people blew my mind." Jim mused that there had to be "some sort of correlation" between the two things, superior

fiddling and extremely great art talent, some common ground that accounted for those two very different capabilities. Jim added: "Mike Seeger had this great way of emulating the original musicians but he put himself in it, so that the old 78s he heard became his. He played the autoharp, could sing—Mother Maybell reincarnated—played fiddle, banjo, and jaws harp. I just enjoyed seeing him around at festivals." Author's notes, 10 July 2020 (2:00 p.m.–4:08 p.m.) telephone interview.

68. https://www.gocomics.com/gasolinealley/2006/07/30.

69. https://www.gocomics.com/gasolinealley/2008/05/29.

70. https://www.gocomics.com/gasolinealley/2012/07/29.

71. https://www.gocomics.com/gasolinealley/2003/06/11 to https://www.gocomics.com/gasolinealley/2003/08/12.

72. https://www.gocomics.com/gasolinealley/2017/09/12.

73. Author's notes, interview with Jim Scancarelli (telephone), 10 July 2020, 2:00 p.m.–4:08 p.m.

74. Author's notes, interview with Jim Scancarelli (telephone), 10 July 2020, 2:00 p.m.–4:08 p.m. Jim observed of C.E. Ward's way of phrasing things: "C.E. Ward used to say something was 'eat up' or 'cooter foot,' meaning it wasn't up to snuff. A cooter is a term for a turtle and that's how I came up with Cousin Cooter for *Turtle Magazine*. C.E. also said that something was 'cayarney,' meaning it was awful. This term is really derived via rural routes from the word 'carion,' dead meat. If you slur the word a bit and mispronounce it a lot, that root origin becomes apparent. If you had dirt or something on your banjo neck or banjo head, C.E. would say 'that's got caiyarn on it.'" 25 October 2020 (12:56 p.m.) Text Message to from Jim Scancarelli to Lew Stern.

75. Jim allowed that the "city" version of "beans from apple butter" was "shit from shinola," usually deployed in a sentence intended to suggest that someone cannot tell one from the other, but Jim made clear that you can't say THAT in the newspaper. Author's notes, interview with Jim Scancarelli (telephone), 10 July 2020, 2:00 p.m.–4:08 p.m. Also see Reno Bailey, "Can You Speak Cliffside?" https://remembercliffside.com/odds-ends/can-you-speak-cliffside/.

76. "I got negative mail from both political parties, each thinking their candidate was represented in the 'Alley.' Life imitating cartoons, or visa versa!" 9 November 2020 (4:59 p.m.) Text Message from Jim Scancarelli to Lew Stern; Author's notes, interview with Jim Scancarelli (telephone), 9 November 2020, 11:00 a.m.–11:30 a.m. After he took over the strip in 1986, Jim began to insert more of his own storytelling, and his own artistry, into the mix alongside of the things he did to keep the strip in touch with elements of the history of the characters and their lives, and consistent with the spirit that motivated his predecessors. At that transition point, when he took over the strip, Jim was acutely aware of the extent to which his "consumers" scrutinized *Gasoline*

Alley at critical times during its long run. Legions of avid newspaper comic strip devotees would offer their views of the strip at points when new apprentices came on board, or when newspapers altered the size and space accorded to strips requiring serious re-engineering of artwork and the space available for character dialogue. In those days, he was kept apprised of views expressed by readers in letters to the editor and communications with the Syndicate, more so than was the case in the 1990s and early 2000s when that kind of communication was conducted via email, thus leaving him in his purposely computer-less working environment dependent upon the Syndicate and friends who followed the strip online to keep him apprised of the views and comments that appeared on comic platforms about *Gasoline Alley*. 16 January 2021 (11:14 a.m.) Text Message from Jim Scancarelli to Lew Stern.

77. Interestingly, *Gasoline Alley* strips that seem to have an implicit political reference point might have a very different connotation for Jim, a very different intent with no political content at all, which is why the 2 October 2020 strip in which Joe Pye is lecturing his three boys on the importance of knowing the "right way" from the "wrong way" is intriguing. In the last frame, Pye says: "Th' wrong way is th' right way! Don't yo' see?" Reading through national news in the midst of the 2016 election campaign suggested that this particular strip might have been intended in a particularly political way, but Jim did not intend the punchline of this strip to have any political resonance. See https://www.gocomics.com/gasolinealley/2020/10/02.

78. *The Adventures of Chipper Wallet, PA-C*, Physician Assistant Historical Society, 2017.

79. Navy Day is a celebration in recognition of the naval service, generally celebrated on 27 October—President Theodore Roosevelt's birthday. The Continental Navy was established by the Continental Congress on 13 October 1775; in 1972, Chief of Naval Operations (CNO) Admiral Elmo Zumwalt authorized recognition of the Navy's birthday as 13 October. https://www.military.com/navy-birthday/the-two-navy-holidays.html.

80. Author's notes, 23 August 2020 interview with Jim Scancarelli (telephone), 3:19 p.m.–4:59 p.m. Jim's inspiration for the name of the character he dubbed "T-Bone" was a 150-pound St. Bernard dog who was the constant companion of Lucius Morris Beebe, a scion of a wealthy Massachusetts family who worked for *The Herald Tribune* in New York from 1929 to 1950, writing about city society, restaurants, fashion. He moved to Nevada in 1950, purchased Virginia City's *Territorial Enterprise* newspaper and worked there for a decade with his friend and collaborator Charles Clegg. Beebe wrote about two dozen books about the culture and characters of the West, as well as some authoritative books about early American railroads. Beebe passed away in 1966, Clegg died in 1979. There were, over time, two hounds named T-Bone who were Beebe's constant companions. See Karl Breckenridge, "Lucius Beebe, Charles Clegg and the

T-Bone Towsers," *Reno Gazette Journal.*, 22 January 2016. https://www.rgj.com/story/life/2016/01/22/breck-lucius-beebe-charles-clegg-and-t-bone-towsers/79196734/. Jim owns many of the books Beebe wrote about trains, including a signed copy of one that Beebe co-authored with Clegg, *Mixed Train Daily: A Book of Short Line Railroads* (1947). Jim remembered him as a journalist with a fine, flowing, eloquent style of writing, a man who would not hesitate to use 25 words where ten would do the job. 24 August 2020, interview with Jim Scancarelli (telephone), 4:00 p.m.–6:08 p.m.

81. The thread in *Gasoline Alley* that focused on the passing of Phyllis Blossom began on 19 April 2004 and continued through to preparations for her funeral from 27 April 2004 to 13 May 2004, at which point the thread turns to the subject of whether Uncle Walt would continue to live on his own. See from https://www.gocomics.com/gasolinealley/2004/04/19 to https://www.gocomics.com/gasolinealley/2004/05/18. Garry Trudeau's "Doonesbury" began a thread on 19 April 2004 that featured the character B.D., a U.S. Army troop deployed to Iraq, and took him from a firefight near Fallujah during which his leg was destroyed by an RPG round, through to his medevac to a field hospital—where his damaged leg was amputated below the knee—into his convalescence and his return to his family. See https://www.gocomics.com/doonesbury/2004/04/19 to https://www.gocomics.com/doonesbury/2004/05/01. Jim said: "I thought the 'passing' of Phyllis would be a major event in the comic strip world, an event that would make the press. But Doonesbury eclipsed the story. The press went wild over that storyline and didn't even mention that Phyllis 'died.'" Author's notes, interview with Jim Scancarelli (telephone), 10 July 2020, 2:00 p.m.–4:08 p.m.

82. 9 November 2020 (4:59 p.m.) Text Message from Jim Scancarelli to Lew Stern; Author's notes, interview with Jim Scancarelli (telephone), 9 November 2020, 11:00 a.m.–11:30 a.m.

83. Author's notes, interview with Jim Scancarelli (telephone), 10 July 2020, 2:00 p.m.–4:08 p.m. Jim took hundreds and hundreds of pictures of Gertie taking care of his mother. Photos of Gertie answering the phone, pretending she's washing dishes, pretending she's looking at Uncle Walt and taking his temperature—all manner of poses to provide a basis for sketching the character Gertie for the cartoon. Consequently, he had a lot of reference material to draw on in getting things such as her facial expressions just right. As recently as July 2020, Gertie's daughter Tammy Rose Guin continued to thank Jim for keeping her mother as a presence in the comic strip. 9 July 2020 Text Message from Jim Scancarelli to Lew Stern. "Tammy sends me something daily—'Happy Thursday!' 'Have a fine weekend.' 'Keep smiling.' She and her family have been praying for me. I've been praying for them. Mutual admiration society. She always said I was not a man who saw racial color. I just accepted people as people." Author's notes, interview with Jim Scancarelli (telephone), 10 July 2020, 2:00 p.m.–4:08 p.m.

84. Author's notes, interview with Jim Scancarelli (telephone), 9 August 2020, 3:10 p.m.–5:25 p.m. and Author's notes, interview with Jim Scancarelli (telephone), 26 October 2020, 3:40 p.m.–5:25 p.m.

85. Author's notes, interview with Jim Scancarelli (telephone), 26 October 2020, 3:40 p.m.–5:25 p.m.

86. Author's notes, interview with Jim Scancarelli (telephone), 26 October 2020, 3:40 p.m.–5:25 p.m. The quality of the copies varied over time, starting out on a "poor xerox," and progressing to copies made on higher quality machines later on. Many in Jim's files are yellowed with age.

87. Author's notes, interview with Jim Scancarelli (telephone), 9 August 2020, 3:10 p.m.–5:25 p.m. He also ordered stronger bookshelves to bear the weight of this collection around that time. 9 November 2020 (4:59 p.m.) Text Message from Jim Scancarelli to Lew Stern; Author's notes, interview with Jim Scancarelli (telephone), 9 November 2020, 11:00 a.m.–11:30 a.m.

88. Author's notes, interview with Jim Scancarelli (telephone), 27 June 2020, 3:10 p.m.–5:13 p.m.

89. Jim told a story that Dick Moores related about his time working with Walt Disney, a story that underscores the importance of paying attention to both big ticket transformation in, for example, technologies that reshape the way artists work on cartoons and comics, as well as the smaller details of drawing characters consistently over time. Moores worked for Disney from the early 1940s for 14 years. Sometime early in Moores' time with Disney, the office staff was working on an animated film project with a multi-plane camera. The new technology was not cooperating, and the staff was having problems with the process of getting the layers upon layers of artwork necessary to make the background appear as though it was moving in 3-D. Walt was doodling as all of this is transpiring. At some point, he looked up, looked around, and remarked: "You've all been making Pluto's nose too big," disregarding the problem at hand, but focused laser-like on the art and appearance of a lead character. Author's notes, interview with Jim Scancarelli (telephone), 27 June 2020, 3:10 p.m.–5:13 p.m.

90. Author's notes, interview with Jim Scancarelli (telephone), 20 July 2020, 5:30–6:30 p.m., and 21 July 2020 follow-up notes; Author's notes, interview with Jim Scancarelli (telephone), 23 June 2020, 3:16 p.m.–5:48 p.m. In the first two decades of the 21st century, it has become harder to sustain the place of comics in hard copy newspapers. Syndicates that own and manage long running cartoons have found themselves faced with newspapers that base their decisions on whether to keep a strip in the paper on circulation levels. Robert Harvey stated: "A good-sized daily newspaper might carry as many as 30 strips or panel cartoons. The minimum charge by a syndicate might be $15 per week per strip. So, for 25 strips, that's $375 per week; or $19,500 per year. That is big money for a newspaper teetering on the edge of bankruptcy. And remember,

$15 per week per strip is the LOWEST fee a newspaper might be paying. In many cases, the costs to newspapers are more significant. For example, the most popular strips (*Pearls Before Swine, Luann*, and *Blondie*, for example) could be charging over $100 per week." Cutting the cost to a newspaper of keeping a comic in the paper by lowering monthly costs to that publication represents the only choice available to syndicate-owned comic strips. That impacts the weekly salaries of illustrators/writers and ends up making this precarious economic calculation tougher for all parties involved. The basic mathematics of this aspect of the financial life of newspapers, and the syndicates that own the comic strips, suggests a level of complexity for the strip owners, and the strip writers/illustrators. 23 July 2020 (12:10 a.m.) email from Robert Harvey to Lew Stern. Those are all notional levels of costs and expenditures that are based on Robert Harvey's close reading of the history of cartoon strips over decades and are intended to be illustrative not arithmetically accurate.

91. Author's notes, interview with Jim Scancarelli (telephone), 27 June 2020, 3:10 p.m.–5:13 p.m.

Chapter Six

1. The ten *Gasoline Alley* strips reproduced in this chapter from original production art files in Jim's personal archive are reprinted courtesy of Tribune Content Agency, LLC, with the permission of Jim Scancarelli.

2. Author's notes, interview with Jim Scancarelli (telephone), 7 July 2020, 2:43 p.m.–4:45 p.m.

3. The Tribune Content Agency is the syndication company owned by Tribune Publishing which owns *Gasoline Alley*. GoComics.com is the largest online catalog of syndicated newspaper strips, political cartoons and webcomics. Uclick was launched in 2005 by Andrews McMeel Syndication's digital entertainment provider as a distribution portal for comic strips on mobile phones, and one year later was re-designed and expanded to include online strips and cartoons. Universal Uclick was formed in July 2009 as the result of a merger of Universal Press Syndicate and Uclick. GoComics website provides access to the *Gasoline Alley* strips from 8 April and 15 April 2001, and—continuously—from 18 April to the present. At the point when this writing project was completed in late 2020, Andrews McMeel "was not in possession" of the complete "archive" for the daily and the Sunday *Gasoline Alley* strip from the tenure of the strip's originator, Frank King (October 1918—December 1969) to Jim Scancarelli's tenure as writer/illustrator (August 1986—present) That could have been a function of the fact that the production art that contributed to the publication of *Gasoline Alley* for so many years was not systematically collected and preserved, or that aspects of ownership of the comic strip and other matters pertaining to syndication have entwined in a manner that complicated distribution via GoComics.com of *Gasoline Alley* before Jim Scancarelli's tenure. There

were undoubtedly storylines that featured music, musicians and musical instruments prior to the run of comics available on GoComic.com—including the 36-week run of a story about John Hartford in 1991. However, the bulk of the most meaningful appearances by banjo players and fiddlers, revival string bands, historical musicians and made-up musical figures and bands occur in the 2000s. For example, Ralph Stanley shows up in 2000 several times; Joel Sweeney in 2005; "Red" Tommy Malboeuf has his first walk on appearance in the early 2000s; the Mole Hill Highlanders are first featured in the strip in 2016; and the Miceketeers make their debut in November 2014. Thus, for the purposes of an examination of the prevalence and meaning of musical themes and musician characters (real and fictitious) in *Gasoline Alley* during Jim Scancarelli's tenure as writer illustrator, GoComics.com is a perfectly adequate resource.

4. https://www.gocomics.com/gasolinealley/2002/12/22.

5. 9 November 2020 (4:59 p.m.) Text Message from Jim Scancarelli to Lew Stern; Author's notes, interview with Jim Scancarelli (telephone), 9 November 2020, 11:00 a.m.–11:30 a.m.

6. Author's notes, interview with Jim Scancarelli (telephone), 7 July 2020, 2:43 p.m.–4:45 p.m.

7. https://www.gocomics.com/gasolinealley/2004/11/07.

8. Jim suggested that a lot of cartoonists think that the pencil gives them more flexibility in drawing their characters: "It's looser and the feel is there, the action of the guy running is really got the ommmph. You can just feel the tilt of the body. The leg muscles pushing. By the time you ink the thing it's lost its life. My Uncle, who was an artist—it was the most amazing thing—he would take his pencil and he'd draw this swooping line and I knew he saw it in his head. That swoop was the action. He knew where to put the arms. It wasn't like a stick figure. Then he'd refine it and it still retained that action. When he had to ink it, it just didn't have the life that the pencil work did." Author's notes, interview with Jim Scancarelli (telephone), 7 July 2020, 2:43 p.m.–4:45 p.m.

9. https://www.gocomics.com/gasolinealley/2004/11/07.

10. Author's notes, interview with Jim Scancarelli (telephone), 7 July 2020, 2:43 p.m.–4:45 p.m.

11. https://www.gocomics.com/gasolinealley/2017/01/22; Author's notes, 8 August 2020 interview with Jim Scancarelli (telephone), 4:55 p.m.–5:53 p.m.; 1 September 2020 (2:37 p.m.) email from Bob Smakula to Lew Stern.

12. https://www.gocomics.com/gasolinealley/2015/01/04.

13. Author's notes, interview with Jim Scancarelli (telephone), 7 July 2020, 2:43 p.m.–4:45 p.m.

14. See http://www.mandolincentral.com/lloyd-loar-mandolin-mon and https://www.mandolincentral.com/79641.

15. https://www.gocomics.com/gasolinealley/2011/03/20.

16. Jim said that he drew the hound eying the sausages in his 20 March 2011 strip with an eye toward making the dog resemble Beans, Little Jimmy's faithful dog companion in a strip called *Little Jimmy* that was created by Jimmy Swinnerton in 1904 as a Sunday strip. A daily strip was added in 1920 and continued through the late 1930s. The Sunday comic continue until Swinnerton's retirement in 1958. Author's notes, interview with Jim Scancarelli (telephone), 7 July 2020, 2:43 p.m.–4:45 p.m. and https://en.wikipedia.org/wiki/Little_Jimmy.

17. https://www.gocomics.com/gasolinealley/2015/11/23.

18. https://www.gocomics.com/gasolinealley/2019/04/21.

19. Author's notes, interview with Jim Scancarelli (telephone), 7 July 2020, 2:43 p.m.–4:45 p.m.

20. Jim liked the Jalapeno Chorus, a reference to the Hallelujah Chorus. He noted that some readers thought he was putting in a plug for the president, somehow reading a reference to "Hail to the Chief" in the word "Jalapeno." 9 November 2020 (4:59 p.m.) Text Message from Jim Scancarelli to Lew Stern; Author's notes, interview with Jim Scancarelli (telephone), 9 November 2020, 11:00 a.m.–11:30 a.m.

21. https://www.gocomics.com/gasolinealley/2014/11/02.

22. https://www.pepboys.com/9; Author's notes, interview with Jim Scancarelli (telephone), 9 November 2020, 11:00 a.m.–11:30 a.m.

23. Author's notes, interview with Jim Scancarelli (telephone), 7 July 2020, 2:43 p.m.–4:45 p.m.

24. Author's notes, interview with Jim Scancarelli (telephone), 7 July 2020, 2:43 p.m.–4:45 p.m.

25. Jim explained that the sleazy businessman on Jack Benny's television show was portrayed by the actor Frank Nelson: "The funny part was, in the Jack Benny show, that sleezt guy was everywhere. He was a doctor, a clerk in the department store, a dentist, the ticket taker at the train station or airport." Jim played on that running gag in several multi-day *Gasoline Alley* strips. Author's notes, interview with Jim Scancarelli (telephone), 7 July 2020, 2:43 p.m.–4:45 p.m.

26. https://www.gocomics.com/gasolinealley/2015/05/04.

27. https://www.gocomics.com/gasolinealley/2015/08/02.

28. https://www.gocomics.com/gasolinealley/2020/04/05.

29. https://www.gocomics.com/gasolinealley/2015/01/04. Of the lyric "When the Bloom is on the Sage," Jim noted: "This was the theme song played on Tom Mix's radio program, a western cowboy themed show." 9 November 2020 (4:59 p.m.) Text Message from Jim Scancarelli to Lew Stern; Author's notes, interview with Jim Scancarelli (telephone), 9 November 2020, 11:00 a.m.–11:30 a.m.

30. This particular *Gasoline Alley* goes to black at the point Joel finds the hidden television remote, and unceremoniously shuts down the Chef Meowrice commercial. 9 November 2020 (4:59 p.m.) Text Message from Jim Scancarelli to Lew Stern; Author's notes, interview with Jim Scancarelli (telephone), 9 November 2020, 11:00 a.m.–11:30 a.m.

31. Author's notes, interview with Jim Scancarelli (telephone), 7 July 2020, 2:43 p.m.–4:45 p.m.

32. https://www.gocomics.com/gasolinealley/2016/07/01.

33. Frank Nelson portrayed the rude salesman on the *Jack Benny Show*, first on radio and then on TV. He did McDonald's commercials for a time, not as the rude persona but as the man who said, "Yeeeeees." He also voiced characters based on his salesman character on "The Flintstones." He played the role of game show host Freddie Filmore on the "I Love Lucy"—as well as several other characters in that series. In the last year of "I Love Lucy," the Ricardos moved to Connecticut and Frank Nelson and Mary Jane Croft (who would later replace Vivian Vance on "The Lucy Show") were their next-door neighbors, the Ramseys. https://en.wikipedia.org/wiki/Frank_Nelson_(actor).

34. https://www.gocomics.com/gasolinealley/2016/07/06; Author's notes, interview with Jim Scancarelli (telephone), 7 July 2020, 2:43 p.m.–4:45 p.m.

35. https://www.gocomics.com/gasolinealley/2016/07/06. Jim felt that much of this sort of analysis of his strips ended up reading more "pastafazoola" into the story than he had intended to accommodate in terms of depth of meaning. That, of course, means that sometimes a fiddle and a banjo and a candle stick phone are just a fiddle and a banjo and a candle stick phone. 9 November 2020 (4:59 p.m.) Text Message from Jim Scancarelli to Lew Stern; Author's notes, interview with Jim Scancarelli (telephone), 9 November 2020, 11:00 a.m.–11:30 a.m.

36. https://www.gocomics.com/gasolinealley/2016/07/11.

37. https://www.gocomics.com/gasolinealley/2016/07/14. An unrelated Sunday strip on 17 July 2016 has Nina and Skeezix shopping in a Thrift Store. https://www.gocomics.com/gasolinealley/2016/07/17.

38. https://www.gocomics.com/gasolinealley/2016/07/22.

39. Author's notes, interview with Jim Scancarelli (telephone), 7 July 2020, 2:43 p.m.–4:45 p.m.

40. https://www.gocomics.com/gasolinealley/2020/03/15.

41. https://www.gocomics.com/gasolinealley/2020/04/17 and https://www.gocomics.com/gasolinealley/2020/04/17.

42. Author's notes, interview with Jim Scancarelli (telephone), 7 July 2020, 2:43 p.m.–4:45 p.m.

43. Author's notes, interview with Jim Scancarelli (telephone), 7 July 2020, 2:43 p.m.–4:45 p.m.

44. "The Pye Boys will all be getting the instruments out of a closet in this church. The banjo strings are all rusty. They had to tie two strings together, all the time afraid they'd get tetanus." Author's notes, interview with Jim Scancarelli (telephone), 7 July 2020, 2:43 p.m.–4:45 p.m.

45. https://www.gocomics.com/gasolinealley/2020/07/06.

46. Author's notes, interview with Jim Scancarelli (telephone), 7 July 2020, 2:43 p.m.–4:45 p.m.

47. https://www.gocomics.com/gasolinealley/2020/07/06.

48. https://www.gocomics.com/gasolinealley/2020/03/27.

49. https://www.gocomics.com/gasolinealley/2020/04/01.

50. https://www.gocomics.com/gasolinealley/2020/04/28.

51. https://www.gocomics.com/gasolinealley/2020/04/29.

52. https://www.gocomics.com/gasolinealley/2020/05/18.

53. https://www.gocomics.com/gasolinealley/2020/05/29.

54. https://www.gocomics.com/gasolinealley/2020/07/06.

55. Interestingly, the color of the pickup switched from red to black and blue between the point at which the vehicle entered the bridge and its emergence on the other end of the bridge. The shift in the color of the pickup truck points to the fact that local papers colorize the strips that appear in their newspapers, and not all of them are necessarily consistent and careful in that process. Author's notes, interview with Jim Scancarelli (telephone), 19 November 2020, 3:50 p.m.–4:55 p.m.

56. That 6 July 2020 strip consisted of a single panel. Jim pointed out that he would sometimes do a strip that consisted of a single panel with no borders or gutters. Movement in the strip would have the characters going from left to right, speaking in 3 balloons that were separated by a covered bridge or a downtown scene. Such single strips might have people in the foreground while the main characters were walking along. That single strip was "a graphic device" Jim used from time to time to delineate action, and to introduce a bit of artistic variety into the mix. 19 November 2020 (11:37 p.m.) Text Message from Jim Scancarelli to Lew Stern.

57. Author's notes, interview with Jim Scancarelli (telephone), 7 July 2020, 2:43 p.m.–4:45 p.m. Beyond the "what to do next" question, another challenge that confronts comic strip writers is how to remember which gags they had already used. Jim kept a "file," a "horrible" notebook just jammed and crammed with post-it notes, scraps of paper, pieces of napkins on which he has over the years jotted down jokes and gags and stuffed them into that book. He consults that resource, crosses out gags he's already deployed, but in Jim's view there are certain things a comic strip writer can get away with multiple times, especially if the context in which the joke is used changes over time. Here, to make his case, he invokes Jack Benny: if it is funny the first time, it will be funny the second time. 9 November 2020 (4:59 p.m.) Text Message from Jim Scancarelli to Lew Stern; Author's notes, interview with Jim Scancarelli (telephone), 9 November 2020, 11:00 a.m.–11:30 a.m.

58. https://www.gocomics.com/gasolinealley/2005/06/26.

59. Jim pointed out that this is the essence of the Brescian legend that is inscribed in Latin on his fiddle: "In life, I was a tree in the Sylvan woods and succumbed to the cruel woodman's axe. In death, I am now a sweet melody." 9 November 2020 (4:59 p.m.) Text Message from Jim Scancarelli to Lew Stern; Author's notes, interview with Jim Scancarelli (telephone), 9 November 2020, 11:00 a.m.–11:30 a.m. On Jim's fiddles, see: Jim Scancarelli, "Head of the Class," *Bluegrass Unlimited*, April 2011, pp. 40–42.

60. https://www.gocomics.com/gasolinealley/2018/11/20.

61. As R.C. Harvey noted, "Starting with the January 18, 1982 release, [George] Breisacher wrote and Scancarelli drew *Mutt and Jeff* for the next eighteen months, until the strip, finally, expired with its June 25, 1983 release." Harvey, "November 2007: Celebrating the Centennial of the Daily Newspaper Comic Strip: Mutt, Jeff and their Precursing Creator, Bud Fisher."

62. In one of those moments that crossed the streams—music and comics—Jim noted that in early August 2020, he called Bob Smakula to say hello. Bob told Jim that the musicians John and Georgia Lilly had just shown up at his home in Montrose, West Virginia, and that they were all sitting on the porch making music. They had been singing Rod Stewart's tune, "Gasoline Alley," recorded on an album bearing that name in 1970. Bob brought the phone out to the porch and announced that he had the artist/writer for *Gasoline Alley* on the porch. The musicians struck up again, and over the phone Jim proclaimed, "Hey, keep it down or I'll charge you royalties." Author's notes, interview with Jim Scancarelli (telephone), 8 August 2020, 4:55 p.m.–5:53 p.m.

63. https://www.gocomics.com/gasolinealley/2012/09/16.

64. https://www.gocomics.com/gasolinealley/2003/03/18.

65. https://www.gocomics.com/gasolinealley/2003/06/17.

66. https://www.gocomics.com/gasolinealley/2016/03/20.

67. https://www.gocomics.com/gasolinealley/2016/03/20.

68. Author's notes, interview with Jim Scancarelli (telephone), 7 July 2020, 2:43 p.m.–4:45 p.m. and 9 November 2020 (4:59 p.m.) Text Message from Jim Scancarelli to Lew Stern; Author's notes, interview with Jim Scancarelli (telephone), 9 November 2020, 11:00 a.m.–11:30 a.m.

69. https://www.gocomics.com/gasolinealley/2021/01/17.

70. Appendix 2 contains a list of the *Gasoline Alley* strips referenced in this chapter and the links at which those strips can be found on the GoComics.com website.

Conclusion

1. Author's notes, interview with Jim Scancarelli (telephone), 21 May 2020, 3:10 p.m.–5:53 p.m.

2. https://remembercliffside.com/galleries/jim-scancarellis-cliffside model/; https://remember cliffside.com/memories/news-stories-and-columns/charlotte-artist-recreates-a-classic-carolinas-town/.

3. https://remembercliffside.com/history/articles-and-stories/the-sum-of-its-parts/. Cliffside, North Carolina, in southeastern Rutherford County, was founded in 1828 by Raleigh Rutherford Haynes, who built a textile mill on the Second Broad River that was to become the basis for a textile-fueled local economy. The Seaboard Air Line Railway constructed what ended up being a three-mile stretch of track from the mid-point between Caroleen and Henrietta to Cliffside. That stretch of steam locomotive railroad line connected a series of textile mills, and were the source of fascination for Jim, then in his early teens.

4. 16 January 2021 (7:10 p.m.) Text Message from Jim Scancarelli to Lew Stern.

5. Jim Scancarelli, "Premium Memories," *Dialogue*, April 1997.

6. Railroad trains, especially steam engines, figured prominently in *Gasoline Alley* stories from time to time. For example, between 29 May and 18 September 2014, "the Gasoline Alley Southern Railway," a "freight short line," appeared in the comic for a thread that was 56 strips long. In another adventure, in late November 2019, Engine 952, "Ol' Sally," breaks down near Corky's Diner, and the cook and wait staff of that eatery can be seen trackside. https://www.gocomics.com/gasolinealley/2019/11/22?comments=visible#comments.

7. Author's notes, telephone interview with Jim Scancarelli, 20 May 2020 (4:13 p.m.–6:38 p.m.).

8. Troy Brownfield, "How Hopalong Cassidy Brought the Western to Television," *The Saturday Evening Post*, June 2019, https://www.saturdayeveningpost.com/2019/06/how-hopalong-cassidy-brought-the-western-to-television/.

9. Author's notes, 23 June 2020 (3:16 p.m.–5:48 p.m.) telephone interview. Jim recalled that Fred Kirby played the role of a cowboy for WBT, and though he was popular, "Joey the Clown"—portrayed by Al Munn on WSOC, the rival television station to WBT in Charlotte—always beat him in the ratings. However, the radio and television industry's "ratings" metric might not have always been the best indicator of "popularity." The actor who portrayed the television character Hopalong Cassidy, William Boyd, once came to Charlotte, perhaps in 1950. Young Jim was downtown to witness the parade in which Boyd participated as a guest of honor. Jim's Uncle Pete had finagled a room with a view above the street, so the unfolding tableau stuck in Jim's memory. Hopalong came along in the parade, and received a decent welcome, but when Fred Kirby appeared in the procession, the kids went wild, running into the streets, mobbing Kirby, creating pandemonium—a significant greeting for their local T.V. star. Author's notes, 23 August 2020 interview with Jim Scancarelli (telephone), 3:19 p.m.–4:59 p.m. Also see Thomas and Lucy Warlick, *The WBT Briarhoppers: Eight Decades of a Bluegrass Band Made for Radio* (Jefferson, North Carolina: McFarland, 2008), p. 120.

10. Author's notes, interview with Jim Scancarelli (telephone), 20 July 2020, 5:30–6:30 p.m. Reno Bailey and Jim contemplated collaborating on a book about radio premiums, but the project never materialized. Author's notes, interview with Jim Scancarelli (telephone), 23 June 2020, 3:16 p.m.–5:48 p.m. In 1997, Jim wrote: "The day I went into the Navy, my parents cleaned out my room—and my premiums, comics, Big Little Books, and all the things I had went into the trash can! Even my Iver Johnson bicycle. Nothing was sacred. Years later, though, I unearthed my old Tom Mix Bullet Telescope (with bird call inside), Signal Arrowhead, and Siren Ring. Somehow, they had been spared. Jim Scancarelli, "Premium Memories," *Dialogue*, April 1997.

11. Scancarelli, "The Old Cross Roads," *Bluegrass Unlimited*, January 2000, p. 5.

12. Jim Scancarelli, "The Mole Hill Highlanders," *Bluegrass Unlimited*, October 2004, pp. 34–37.

13. Author's notes, interview with Jim Scancarelii (telephone), 23 June 2020, 3:16 p.m.–5:48 p.m.

14. Author's notes, interview with Jim Scancarelli (telephone), 21 July 2020, 3:45 p.m.–4:57 p.m. Renumber from here on, add note to notes.

15. Alice Drosinis and her husband Paul ran the restaurant and welcomed the group into their deli. Once a month, before the Drum and Bugle Corps would gather, she would put out a plate with a large carrot, which someone at the table would devour, leaving the top of the carrot and the greens, a symbol of Harvey's presence at the meeting. Sara Melandro was, for a time, the "cat wrangler" for the Drum and Bugle Corps, responsible for herding the membership at their regular gatherings, keeping programs moving and schedules intact. Author's notes, interview with Jim Scancarelli (telephone), 27 August 2020, 4:00 p.m.–6:12 p.m.

16. 9 November 2020 (4:59 p.m.) Text Message from Jim Scancarelli to Lew Stern; Author's notes, interview with Jim Scancarelli (telephone), 9 November 2020, 11:00 a.m.–11:30 a.m.; Barrie M. Schwortz, "Is the Shroud of Turin a Medieval Photograph?" *The Review of Religions*, 1 April 2001, https://www.reviewofreligions.org/385/is-the-shroud-of-turin-a-medieval-photograph-a-critical-examination-of-the-theory/.

17. Bruce Henderson, "A Showman to the End, His Gorilla Suits Launched a Costume Empire," *Charlotte Observer*, 25 September 2017, https://www.charlotteobserver.com/news/local/article175326976.html.

18. Filmmaker Roger Patterson purchased a gorilla suit from Morris and altered the face that Jim Scancarelli had molded for Morris for his film on Bigfoot. Morris toured for several years giving lectures on Bigfoot and amassed a significant "Bigfoot archive." He offered to give $10,000.00 to anyone who could prove that Bigfoot was a fake. 9 November 2020 (4:59 p.m.) Text Message from Jim Scancarelli to Lew Stern; Author's notes, interview with

Jim Scancarelli (telephone), 9 November 2020, 11:00 a.m.–11:30 a.m.

19. https://en.wikipedia.org/wiki/Eileen_Fulton.

20. "'Chunk' Simmons Dies at 84; Olympian, Masters Thrower." http://masterstrack.com/chunk-simmons-d/.

21. 9 November 2020 (4:59 p.m.) Text Message from Jim Scancarelli to Lew Stern; Author's notes, interview with Jim Scancarelli (telephone), 9 November 2020, 11:00 a.m.–11:30 a.m. Munn wrote *Diary of Squandered Valor: First Convoy to Murmansk* (2012); Jim did the cover and illustrations for that book.

22. Author's notes, interview with Ben Barry (telephone), 16 October 2020, 11:01 a.m.–11:31 a.m.

23. A pooka is a "shapeshifter" that can take any form at will, and figures prominently in many Irish folk tales and Irish mythology.

24. Author's notes, interview with Jim Scancarelli (telephone), 15 September 2020, 3:45 p.m.–5:07 p.m.

25. Physician Assistant Historical Society, *The Adventures of Chipper Wallet PA-C*, 2017.

26. Letter from Colonel Dave Fabian (USA-Ret.), Director of Communications and Public Affairs, The Army Historical Foundation, to Mr. Skeezix Wallet (c/o Jim Scancarelli). 15 March 2010; 26 October 2000 letter from Senator Bob Dole to Jim Scancarelli. A 2010 drawing by Jim depicting Skeezix and his grandson saluting U.S. Army troops geared for combat, stretching from revolutionary war militia to World War I and World War II troops, who faded into lightly sketched outlines as they receded toward the left side of the drawing, was printed and gifted to all those who donated to the Army Historical Foundation. The caption has Skeezix's grandson asking, "Gramps, why are some of them fading away?"

27. *Guide and Finding Aid for James (Jim) Scancarelli Papers*, Physician Assistant Historical Society, Johns Creek, Georgia.

28. Albert R. Munn, *Diary of Squandered Valor: First Convoy to Murmansk*, Charlotte, North Carolina, 2012.

29. Jim tended to remember the singularly most poignant aspect of some of the war stories Crot told. Jim remembered Crot telling him of spending time incarcerated in small, cramped and dark, dank cells. One was a jail, the "Cooler," that had a ceiling made of wood. There was sufficient space between the slats of wood that the sun could creep in. Crot carried around a photograph he found in a newspaper of a dogwood tree in blossom. He would place that photo on the floor, in a patch of sunlight, and be transported. "It kept him sane." Author's notes, interview with Jim Scancarelli (telephone), 21 August 2020, 5:19 p.m.–6:29 p.m.; 9 November 2020 (4:59 p.m.) Text Message from Jim Scancarelli to Lew Stern; Author's notes, interview with Jim Scancarelli (telephone), 9 November 2020, 11:00 a.m.–11:30 a.m. Jim said that Crot was the basis for the character that James Garner played in the movie *The Great Escape*. The Garner character was a "composite" of the dozens of U.S. and allied scrounges held

as POWs during World War II. 7 January 2021 (2:29 p.m.) Text Message from Jim Scancarelli to Lew Stern.

30. http://www.merkki.com/murderinc.htm. Jim shared a pew in his church with Williams. "He had a bone crushing handshake." 9 November 2020 (4:59 p.m.) Text Message from Jim Scancarelli to Lew Stern; Author's notes, interview with Jim Scancarelli (telephone), 9 November 2020, 11:00 a.m.–11:30 a.m.

31. https://www.americanairmuseum.com/person/2133.

32. https://memory.loc.gov/diglib/vhp-stories/loc.natlib.afc2001001.12668/.

33. Author's notes, interview with Jim Scancarelli (telephone), 21 August 2020, 5:19 p.m.–6:29 p.m.

34. https://www.gocomics.com/gasolinealley/2020/08/23.

35. Jim Scancarelli, "Head of the Class," *Bluegrass Unlimited*, April 2011, pp. 40–42. Sometime around 2010, he contemplated writing about Fender banjos, the company that produced the one five-string banjo that he played for over forty years. He made a running start on that project, contacting Tom Morgan who directed Jim to reach out to Bill Emerson, something he never got around to doing. Author's notes, interview with Jim Scancarelli (telephone), 20 October 2020, 3:05 p.m.–5:12 p.m.

36. "The Yellowjacket." Number 2. Courtesy Jim Scancarelli. "Sound Vault: The Yellowjacket." *BT Memories: A Project by and for Fans and Former Employees of WBT and WBTV, Charlotte, North Carolina*, http://btmemories.com/sounds/yellowjacket.html The spelling, and name order, of the handle given to Warden Borden Gordon varied over time, Jim recalled, with the character sometimes being referred to as Warden Gordon Borden, and the last two letters of at least the last two names switching from "-en" to "-on" and maybe even "-an" upon occasion. Author's notes, interview with Jim Scancarelli (telephone), 30 November 2020, 11:18 a.m.–11:45 a.m.

37. Martha Kiker gave Jim a copy of the poem titled "A Beautiful Train Ride." 9 November 2020 (4:59 p.m.) Text Message from Jim Scancarelli to Lew Stern; Author's notes, interview with Jim Scancarelli (telephone), 9 November 2020, 11:00 a.m.–11:30 a.m.

38. Or, as Rufus and Joel—stalwart *Gasoline Alley* citizens—would say, life is a "bodacious wing-ding with lots of fiddlin' and banjer pickin' and if you're lucky, yo' get to ride on the back o' th' garbage truck." 9 November 2020 (4:59 p.m.) Text Message from Jim Scancarelli to Lew Stern; Author's notes, interview with Jim Scancarelli (telephone), 9 November 2020, 11:00 a.m.–11:30 a.m.

Appendix 1

1. https://en.wikipedia.org/wiki/WVBZ. The Statesville, North Carolina, station was managed by J. D. Benfield for many years; he also served, at the same time, as director and announcer. Benfield

recalled in 2006 that it was one of the only stations on which listeners could hear bluegrass during the week. Benfield's wife Sue also worked at the radio station. Odell Wood, R.C. Harris, and Hoyt Herbert, among other musicians, were also station employees. Forty years later, banjo pickers remembered Hoyt Herbert's Sunday evening bluegrass radio show, and Jim and Jesse playing in Statesville in 1978. J.D. Benfield's band, Love Valley Four, opened for the McReynolds brothers at that concert. They were followed by the band Wells Fargo; Eric Ellis played banjo. https://www.banjohangout.org/archive/161873. Jim recalled that besides running the radio station, J.D. Benfield also had a yard waste and trash pickup service. Author's notes, interview with Jim Scancarelli (telephone), 31 May 2020, 3:15 p.m.–5:47 p.m.

2. https://history.capitolbroadcasting.com/media-assets/daybreak-with-homer-briarhopper/.

3. 17 September 2020 (12:03 p.m.) email from Chuck Dunlop to Lew Stern.

4. 24 August 2020, interview with Jim Scancarelli (telephone), 4:00 p.m.–6:08 p.m.

5. https://en.wikipedia.org/wiki/WTVI.

6. https://www.discogs.com/label/859359-Union-Grove-Talking-Machine-Records.

7. 6 November 2020 (2:35 p.m.) email from Chuck Dunlop to Lew Stern.

8. https://www.ibiblio.org/hillwilliam/BGdiscography/?v=fullrecord&albumid=7372. Tommy Malboeuf also appears on this recording playing "Orange Blossom Special."

9. https://www.discogs.com/label/859359-Union-Grove-Talking-Machine-Records.

10. 20 August 2020 (3:07 p.m.) email from Joe Cline to Lew Stern.

11. https://www.discogs.com/Various-Mountain-Music-At-Its-Best-23-Old-Time-Tunes-Recorded-At-The-38th-Annual-Worlds-Oldest-And-L/release/7636597.

12. https://lccn.loc.gov/90755310.

13. https://www.ibiblio.org/hillwilliam/BGdiscography/?v=fullrecord&albumid=3416.

14. https://www.allmusic.com/album/razors-edge-mw0001266000; https://www.allmusic.com/album/anson-county-mw0001294464.

15. Marty McGee, *Traditional Musicians of the Central Blue Ridge: Old Time, Early Country, Folk and Bluegrass Label Recording Artists, with Discographies* (Jefferson, North Carolina: McFarland, 2000), p. 104.

16. https://en.wikipedia.org/wiki/WPAQ; Author's notes, interview with Jeanette Williams (telephone), 14 September 2020, 10:00 a.m.–10:24 a.m.

17. 19 August 2020 (6:15 p.m.) Text Message from Jim Scancarelli to Lew Stern.

18. 19 August 2020 (7:21 p.m.) email from Joe Cline to Lew Stern.

19. Two earlier recording sessions that featured the fiddling of Clyde Williams were undertaken at the CPCC recording studio. For a combination of reasons, the first session, produced by Tom Estes, did not yield any usable cuts. Jim and Joe Cline were invited to the second session, at which Jim Scancarelli acted as producer. Joe Cline played bass, Jim Greene picked guitar, and Estes played banjo alongside Clyde Williams on fiddle. A rough mix of that session may have survived in private hands. 22 August 2020 (10:32 a.m.) email from Joe Cline to Lew Stern.

20. Author's notes, interview with Jim Scancarelli (telephone), 29 October 2020, 5:37 p.m.–6:10 p.m.

21. https://www.youtube.com/watch?v=a2qM2JRoGQ0.

22. https://www.youtube.com/watch?v=qONNDALk-Bg&t=166s.

23. https://www.youtube.com/watch?v=qONNDALk-Bg.

Bibliography

Books

Ahrens, Pat J. *Union Grove: The First Fifty Years.* Published by Pat J. Ahrens, 1975.

Bailey, Alfred Reno. *Cliffside: Portrait of a Carolina Mill Town.* Charleston, South Carolina: Arcadia Publishing, 2005.

Blue Ridge Music Makers Guild. *Music Makers of the Blue Ridge Plateau.* Charleston, South Carolina: Arcadia Publishing, 2008.

Carlin, Bob. *String Bands in the North Carolina Piedmont.* Jefferson, North Carolina: McFarland, 2004.

Carlson, Elizabeth A. *North Carolina String Band Masters: Old-Time and Bluegrass Legends.* Charleston, South Carolina: The History Press, 2016.

Combs, Matt, Katie Harford Hogue, and Greg Reish. *John Hartford's Mammoth Collection of Fiddle Tunes.* Franklin, Tennessee: John Hartford Enterprises/StuffWorks Press, 2018.

Coston, Daniel. *North Carolina Musicians: Photographs and Conversations.* Jefferson, North Carolina: McFarland, 2013.

Fussell, Fred C., with Steve Kruger. *Blue Ridge Music Trails of North Carolina.* Chapel Hill: University of North Carolina Press, 2013.

Gayheart, Willard, and Donia S. Eley. *Willard Gayheart, Appalachian Artist.* Jefferson, North Carolina: McFarland, 2003.

Hartford, John. *Steamboat in a Cornfield.* New York: Crown Publishers, 1986.

Henry, Murphy Hicks. *Pretty Good for a Girl: Women in Bluegrass.* Chicago: University of Illinois Press, 2013.

Kingsbury, Paul, editor. *The Encyclopedia of Country Music.* New York: Oxford University Press, 1998.

Martin, Linda Lou. *The Life Story of Emory Martin: Radio's Only One Arm Banjo Player.* Edited and published by Emory Martin, 1941.

McGee. Marty. *Traditional Musicians of the Central Blue Ridge: Old Time, Early Country, Folk and Bluegrass Label Recording Artists, with Discographies.* Jefferson, North Carolina: McFarland, 2000.

Munn, Albert R. *Diary of Squandered Valor: First Convoy to Murmansk.* Charlotte, North Carolina, 2012.

Physician Assistant Historical Society. *The Adventures of Chipper Wallet PA-C.* 2017.

Ruchala, James Randolph. *Making Round Peak Music: History, Revitalization and Community,* a dissertation submitted to the Department of Music, for the degree of Doctor of Philosophy, Brown University, May 2011.

Vaughan, Andrew. *John Hartford: Pilot of a Steam Powered Aereo-Plain.* Franklin, Tennessee, 2013.

Warlick, Thomas, and Lucy Warlick. *The WBT Briarhoppers: Eight Decades of a Bluegrass Band Made for Radio.* Jefferson, North Carolina: McFarland, 2008.

Wolfe, Charles K. *Tennesse Strings: The Story of Country Music in Tennessee.* Knoxville: University of Tennessee Press, 1977.

Articles (signed)

Andrade, Roy. "Interview with Jody Stecher." *Banjo Newsletter.* August 2009. https://banjonews.com/2009–08/interview_with_jody_stecher.html.

Chadbourne, Eugene. "Mountain Ramblers." https://www.allmusic.com/artist/mountain-ramblers-mn0000408384.

Cline, Joe. "The Kilocycle Kowboys—The (Almost) Whole Story." 12 August 2017. https://www.facebook.com/KilocycleKowboys/posts/1368272923271967.

DePriest, Joe. "Venerable Briarhoppers' Career Rekindled." *The Charlotte Observer.* 22 March 2002.

Dueben, Alex "'If You Worry About It, It'll Never Come': Interview with Jim Scancarelli." *The Comics Journal.* 18 March 2019. http://www.tcj.com/if-you-worry-about-it-itll-never-come-an-interview-with-jim-scancarelli/.

Dunlop, Chuck. "When Strings Become Bridges." *Bluegrass Unlimited* (forthcoming, 2021).

Gordon, Jean. "Artist Talks About Cliffside's Connection to Gasoline Alley." *The Daily Courier.* 18 November 2012. https://remembercliffside.com/memories/news-stories-and-columns/artist-talks-about-cliffsides-connection-to-gasoline-alley/.

Harvey, R.C. "Growing Old in Gasoline Alley: Ninety-Four Years and Counting." *TCJ Archive.* 17 January 2013. www.tcj.com/growing-old-in-gasoline-alley-ninety-four-years-and-counting/.

Harvey, R.C. "A Milestone in Gasoline Alley."

Harvey, R.C. "100 Years in Gasoline Alley."

Hatley, Sandy. "A.L. Wood Honored in North Carolina." *Bluegrass Today*. 19 August 2029. https://bluegrasstoday.com/a-l-wood-honored-in-north-carolina/.

Hauslohner, Amy Worthington. "Jim Scancarelli: Fiddling Around with the Funnies." *Bluegrass Unlimited*. August 1989. pp. 41–45.

Hauslohner, Amy Worthington. "Brooklyn to Galax." *Bluegrass Unlimited*. February 1993. pp. 50–55.

Johnson, Bill. "The Saga of Whitley and Cline." *Charlotte Folk Music Society*. May 1988.

Joyner, Hermon. "Jody Stecher: Playing from the Heart." *The Mandolin Player*. 17 April 2015. http://www.themandolinplayer.net/jody-stecher.

Koken, Walt. "Tales from the Woods. Part 3: Marion." *Old Time Herald*. Volume 13. Number 3. pp. 36–38.

Lawless, John. "Wood Family Tradition Continues A.L. Wood's Legacy." *Bluegrass Today*. 12 January 2015. https://bluegrasstoday.com/wood-family-tradition-continues-a-l-woods-legacy/.

Marshall, Howard. "'King of the Folks': R. P. Christeson and his Old-Time Fiddlers Repertory." *Old Time Herald*. Volume 13. Number 3. pp. 22–35.

Menius, Art. "Tom Isenhour: From Toy Collecting to Scruggs and Monroe in Wax." *Bluegrass Unlimited*. November 2016. pp. 38–40.

Rozakis, Bob. "A Stroll Down Gasoline Alley." *Comics Bulletin*. 24 June 2002. http://comicsbulletin.com/a-stroll-down-gasoline-alley/.

Scancarelli, Jim. "Ham Beats All Meat." *Bluegrass Unlimited*. October 2000.

Scancarelli, Jim. "Hatch Print Show." *Bluegrass Unlimited*. May 2003. pp. 58–60.

Scancarelli, Jim. "Head of the Class." *Bluegrass Unlimited*. April 2011. pp. 40–42.

Scancarelli, Jim. "The Old Cross Roads (Windsor's That Is)." *Bluegrass Unlimited*. January 2000. p. 58.

Scancarelli, Jim. "Premium Memories." *Dialogue*. April 1997.

Scancarelli, Jim. "Union Grove Fiddlers' Convention." *Bluegrass Unlimited*. October 2004. pp. 34–37.

Scancarelli, Jim. "Union Grove Fiddlers' Convention." *Bluegrass Unlimited*. January 2006. pp. 46–49.

Schwartz, Ben. "An Old Comic Strip About Modern Fatherhood." *The New Yorker*. 19 June 2015. https://www.newyorker.com/books/page-turner/frank-king-old-comic-strip-about-modern-fatherhood.

Singleton, Karen. "Charlotte Folk Society Presents Heritage Award to Ruth Kee Wherry and the Kee Family." *Charlotte Folk Society Folk Calendar*. Volume 5. Issue 7. July 2001. pp. 1–2.

Stecher, Jody. "The Incomparable Hank Bradley." *Fiddler Magazine*. Fall 2020. Volume 27. Number 3. pp. 4–10.

Thompson, Richard. "L.W. Lambert Passes." *Bluegrass Today*. 30 January 2014. https://bluegrasstoday.com/l-w-lambert-passes/.

Trott, Walt. "Sheb Wooley." In Paul Kingsbury, ed. *The Encyclopedia of Country Music*. New York: Oxford University Press, 1998. pp. 598–599.

Westbrook, Bruce. "Chronicle Comics: For Nigh 100 Years, Comics Have Entertained While Mirroring Their Time." *Houston Chronicle*. 14 October 2001. https://www.chron.com/about/first-100/article/Chronicle-comics-2023912.php.

Articles (unsigned)

"Cartoon Takes Up the Cause." *Call to Duty*. 2010.

"National Cartoon Features Fictitious Davidson Student." *Mecklenburg Gazette*. 8 May 1996.

Videos (chronological order)

"Tommy Jarrell and Fred Cockerham." Film by Blanton Owen. Low Gap, Virginia. 1971. Original film elements found in the Blanton Owen Collection #20027 (https://finding-aids.lib.unc.edu/20027/), Southern Folklife Collection, The Wilson Library, University of North Carolina at Chapel Hill. https://youtu.be/Avo0M1JG6bg.

"Sitting on Top of the World at the Fiddlers' Convention." Film by Max Kalmanowicz. Produced by Sandra Sutton and Max Kalmanowicz. 1974. https://www.folkstreams.net/film-detail.php?id=309.

"Gasoline Alley." Text by Jim Scancarelli. Narration by Joe Van Riper. Technical support from Metrotape Producer Services, Inc. and Jay Howard Audio. Images courtesy of the Tribune Media Services. 1988.

"Fiddlers' Grove: A Celebration of Old Time." 1994. Produced by Susan Campbell and Donna Campbell. 1994. https://www.folkstreams.net/film-detail.php?id=262.

"The Life and Times of Joe Thompson." Film by Iris Thompson Chapman. Folkstreams. 2004. https://www.folkstreams.net/film-detail.php?id=278.

"The New Lost City Ramblers—Always Been a Rambler." The Arhoolie Foundation Presents: A film by Yasha Aginsky. 2009. https://www.youtube.com/watch?v=1roXgU96Tc0.

"A Brief History of Comic Strips with R. C. Harvey." 13 April 2019. https://www.youtube.com/watch?time_continue=945&v=WkDgiWDZsho&feature=emb_logo and http://www.rcharvey.com/video2.html.

"Listening to the Legends—Tom Warlick of the Briarhoppers." North Carolina Music Hall of Fame. Hosted by Debbie McPhatter and Veronica Cordle. 25 August 2020. https://www.youtube.com/watch?v=709II5_ra88&feature=youtu.be.

"Roger Sprung: American Banjo Museum Hall of Fame." 30 August 2020. https://youtu.be/R73uqq2Rleg.

Audio Recordings (chronological order)

"Leprechaun." Tommy Malboeuf, TM-10055. Recorded by Dewey Farmer, Kannapolis, North Carolina. No date.

Mole Hill Highlanders, WFMX, Statesville, North Carolina. Shows Number 1–13. Digitized, copied to CD by Chuck Dunlop.

"Tommy Malboeuf: Orange Blossom Special," (Old Oblivion, OO-6, 1973).

Jim Greene (guitar), Jack Haley (banjo), Judy Sherrill and Jim Scancarelli (fiddle). Recorded at Balls Creek Fiddlers' Convention, North Carolina, in 27 January 1986, and Jim Greene's house in 1 February 1986.

"Twin Fiddles," (Old Oblivion—OO-7, June 1996) featured the music of Jim Scancarelli (lead fiddle), Tom Malboeuf (harmony fiddle), and Jim Greene (guitar).

Solo Fiddle, Jim Scancarelli. 16 September 2007.

Red Tommy and Jim Scancarelli (and Joanne Hall). Recorded 7 October 2007, 14 October 2007, 20 October 2007, and 28 October 2007.

"Union Grove History." WNCW's "This Old Porch." Joe Cline (host) and Jim Scancarelli (guest). 2008.

Timmy Martin and Jim Scancarelli at Galax, Virginia, 15 August 2010. Recorded by WPAQ.

Personal Correspondence, Files, News Releases, Documents (chronological order)

Mark Wingate, notes from interview with Johnny Hamm, Winston-Salem, North Carolina. 25 August 1983.

News Release: An American Tradition, "Gas Alley," Continues Under Jim Scancarelli. Tribune Media Services. 22 April 1986.

Jim Scancarelli Biography. Tribune Media Services. December 1986.

Letter from Marge Devine, Scribe, National Cartoonists Society, to Jim Scancarelli. 11 March 1987.

Letter from Senator Mark Hatfield to Jim Scancarelli. 3 October 1988.

Letter from Rupert Moure to Jim Scancarelli. 15 October 1988. Moure was Jim's art teacher from 7th to 11th grade in Wakefield High School, Arlington, Virginia.

"Wallet Family Tree." Tribune Media Services. 1988.

American Academy of Physician Assistants, Press Release: "Gasoline Alley to Receive Public Awareness Award from American Academy of Physician Assistants. 19 April 1989.

News Release: Jim Scancarelli Wins Reubin Award for "Gasoline Alley." Tribune Media Services. 12 June 1989.

"Gasoline Alley Turns 75." Tribune Media Services. 19 October 1993.

Letter to Jim Scancarelli from Mason Adams. 4 October 1994. Adams played Wilmer Bobble on the "Gasoline Alley" radio show from 1948 to 1950, sponsored by Auto-Lite (music by the harmonica trio, The Polka Dots."

Letter from Charles M. Schultz to Jim Scancarelli, 5 May 1995.

Letter from Charles M. Schultz to Jim Scancarelli, 23 August 1995.

News Release: Legendary Comic Strip Character Grows Up and Turns 75. Tribune Media Services. 7 February 1996.

Letter to Jim Scancarelli from Les Leverett. 4 January 1997.

Letter from Hugh Downs, ABC News, to Jim Scancarelli. 28 January 1998.

Letter from Jim Scancarelli to Hugh Downs, 9 February 1998.

Letter from Hugh Downs, ABC News, to Jim Scancarelli. 13 February 1998.

Letter from Senator Bob Dole to Jim Scancarelli. 26 October 2000.

News Release: "Gasoline Alley, America's Longest-Running Serial Comic Strip, Celebrates 90th Anniversary. Tribune Media Services. 24 November 2008.

Letter from Colonel Dave Fabian (USA-Ret.), Director of Communications and Public Affairs, The Army Historical Foundation, to Mr. Skeezix Wallet (c/o Jim Scancarelli). 15 March 2010.

Letter to Jim Scancarelli announcing his induction into the Wakefield High School Hall of Fame, from Conchita Mitchell, 1966 President, Wakefield Alumni Organization, 10 April 2017.

Letter of Acceptance of induction into the Wakefield High School Hall of Fame, from Jim Scancarelli to Wakefield Alumni Organization, no date, probably 2017.

Wakefield High School, Arlington, Virginia, Hall of Fame certificate of induction, Inductee Number 55, June 2017.

Interviews Conducted by Author

Ahrens, Pat. Telephone. 11 September 2020.

Barry, Ben. Telephone. 16 October 2020.

Carlin, Bob. Telephone. 28 May 2020.

Cline, Joe. Telephone. 18 August 2020.

Corbett, Clinton. Telephone. 9 October 2020.

Dunlop, Chuck. Telephone. 16 September 2020.

Ellis, Eric. Telephone. 24 May 2020.

Hamilton, Marcus. Telephone. 2 September 2020.

Hanchett, Tom. Telephone. 8 September 2020.

Harvey, R.C. Telephone. 16 June 2020.

Hatley, Sandy. Telephone. 22 September 2020.

Isenhour, Tom. Telephone. 15 September 2020.

Kiker, Martha. Telephone. 19 September 2020.

Kilby, Steve. Telephone. 18 November 2020.

Liljestrand, Bob. Telephone. 19 October 2020.

Melandro, Sara. Telephone. 22 September 2020.

Norwood, Rick. Telephone. 17 October 2020.

Rose, John. Telephone. 18 November 2020.
Sanderford, Mark V. Telephone. 18 September 2020.
Saunders, Walt. Telephone. 30 September 2020.
Sherrill, Judy. Telephone. 30 October 2020.
Smakula, Robert. Telephone. 8 January 2020.
Stecher, Jody. Telephone. 17 September 2020.
Stern, Ned. Telephone. 22 August 2020.
Thomas, Sally. Telephone. 8 September 2020.
Walsh, Tom. Telephone. 17 September 2020.
Wherry, Ruth. Telephone. 18 September 2020.
White, Robert. Telephone. 17 September 2020.
Williams, Jeanette. Telephone. 14 September 2020.
Wingate, Mark. Telephone. 23, 24 September, 19 November 2020.

Telephone Interviews with Jim Scancarelli Conducted by Author

9 July 2019.
10 July 2019.
29 October 2019.
10 January 2020.
22 February 2020.
22 April 2020.
20 May 2020.
21 May 2020.
22 June 2020.
23 June 2020.
7 July 2020.
10 July 2020.
20 July 2020.
21 July 2020.
27 July 2020.
28 July 2020.
7 August 2020.
8 August 2020.
9 August 2020.
11 August 2020.
18 August 2020.
19. August 2020.
21 August 2020.
22 August 2020.
23 August 2020.
27 August 2020.
31 August 2020.
2 September 2020.
3 September 2020.
5 September 2020.
8 September 2020.
10 September 2020.
15 September 2020.
17 September 2020.
18 September 2020.
19 September 2020.
23 September 2020.
26 September 2020.
8 October 2020.
9 October 2020.
10 October 2020.
11 October 2020.
19 October 2020.
20 October 2020.
21 October 2020.
26 October 2020.
29 October 2020.
19 November 2020.
30 November 2020.
12 December 2020.
13 December 2020.
8 January 2021.
17 January 2021.

Index

www.ingramcontent.com/pod-product-compliance
Ingram Content Group UK Ltd.
Pitfield, Milton Keynes, MK11 3LW, UK
UKHW051853150726
7214IPUK00021B/403